Social Theory:
Central Issues in Sociology

Social Theory:
Central Issues in Sociology

John Scott

SAGE Publications

London ● Thousand Oaks ● New Delhi

SAGE Publications Ltd
1 Oliver's Yard
55 City Road
London EC1Y 1SP

SAGE Publications Inc
2455 Teller Road
Thousand Oaks, California 91320

SAGE Publications India Pvt Ltd
B-42, Panchsheel Enclave
Post Box 4109
New Delhi 110 017

British Library Cataloguing in Publication data

A catalogue record for this book is available
from the British Library

ISBN 0 7619 7087 8
    0 7619 7088 6

Library of Congress control number available

Typeset by C&M Digitals (P) Ltd., Chennai, India
Printed on paper from sustainable resources
Printed in Great Britain by The Alden Press, Great Britain

Contents

Focus Boxes

Study Guide

This book is intended as a guide to self-directed learning and a textbook to support courses in sociological theory. It aims to provide the background and context from which more detailed reading and understanding of primary texts can be undertaken. Courses in social theory frequently focus on particular theorists, and timetable pressures mean that the selection of theorists considered is of necessity limited to a handful of figures. I hope that a reading of the appropriate chapters of this book will allow the maximum to be gained from lectures and from your own reading.

Each of the main chapters contains a number of 'Focus' boxes in which the views of key figures are outlined and sources for their key ideas are given. This is the point at which independent reading will help to illuminate and to deepen the knowledge gained from reading the rest of the chapter. It is also the point at which lecture material on particular theorists can most easily be related to the book as a whole. Reading the relevant section of a chapter before a lecture on a theorist or school of thought, followed by a review of that same section, is the best possible basis for then going on to read the material suggested in the Focus box and by the lecturer.

The book is also intended as a means through which postgraduate students and practising sociologists can consolidate their own understanding of the relevance of sociological theory. We have all tended to become highly specialised in our professional practice, focusing mainly on those approaches that we see as directly relevant to our own work and, perhaps, denigrating all others. I hope that a reading of this book will help to fill the seen and unseen gaps in theoretical knowledge that many of us experience.

1

Social Theory:

Should We Forget the Founders?

Those new to sociology used to be enjoined to follow the advice of Alfred Whitehead (1926) that 'a science that hesitates to forget its founders is lost'. The assumption behind this advice was that sociology should abandon its concern for 'what Marx really said' or 'what Durkheim said about' such and such. Instead, it should – like all other sciences – study the world as it actually is: forget the founders and get on with the science.

Many of those who have reservations about the 'scientific' status of sociology have, nevertheless, taken this advice to heart and have abandoned any concern for understanding or engaging with the formative statements of the nineteenth century and the first half of the twentieth century. So widespread is the assumption that the founders should be forgotten that Whitehead's advice is rarely repeated today. This abandonment of formative theory induces an amnesia or ignorance about fundamental aspects of sociological analysis. Contemporary theorists frequently cast their work as a 'new approach' or a 'new direction' for social theory, one especially attuned to contemporary conditions. All too often, however, these new ventures have ended up as restatements, in whole or in part, of ideas already well explored by earlier writers. A better acquaintance with the founders, it might be suggested, would have prevented such frequent reinventions of the wheel.

The central claim behind this book is that, contrary to Whitehead's claim, a science that forgets its founders is lost, or is, at least, in considerable difficulties. It is time to rediscover the lasting insights of the early theorists. Those who built the foundations of sociology and established its place at the heart of the social sciences set out a comprehensive framework of ideas that defined, and continue to define, the core concerns of the subject. There were, of course, many areas of disagreement and contention among these writers, and their ideas were often presented as if they are mutually exclusive. Nevertheless, their works overlapped around a number of intersecting ideas, and their distinctive theoretical viewpoints were differences of emphasis, variations in focus, or explicit positions in an intellectual division of labour in which all contending theoretical frameworks that stood the empirical test could find a place.

As a result, sociology had available to it, by the first decades of the twentieth century, a clear and systematic conspectus of ideas that provided a working basis for empirical research and for further theoretical investigations. No practising sociologist can afford to ignore this conspectus of ideas. In fact, few did ignore it until recently, and through the middle years of the twentieth century the development of new research went hand in hand with the exploration of the founding statements. A particularly strong position on this was taken by Ronald Fletcher (1971), though he perhaps overstated the level of consensus that there had been among the nineteenth-century theorists.

The massive expansion of sociology from the 1960s brought into the discipline many people from cognate social sciences who invigorated social research with an infusion of new theoretical ideas. Many members of this new generation of sociologists, however, were less familiar with the formative sociological ideas and unintentionally followed Whitehead's advice. Those they trained were also less likely to be taught the ideas of the earlier theorists and, as they entered the profession, they reinforced the emerging emphasis on the overriding need for new theoretical approaches appropriate to contemporary conditions. Correctly recognising that the world had changed since the nineteenth century and that the founders could not be expected to provide us with accounts of these new social conditions, they incorrectly concluded that the founders had *nothing* to contribute to sociological understanding.

In fact, the conspectus of ideas remained as relevant as ever before. One very simple example can illustrate the point being made. Nineteenth-century theorists cannot be expected to provide any accounts of the cultural impact of television or the internet: television was invented only in the 1920s and regular broadcasting did not begin until after the Second World War; and the internet is a technology of the 1990s. The formative concepts of culture and the process of cultural transmission through which meanings are established and identifications built, however, can still provide the central basis on which any form of communication can be understood. The formative theoretical ideas may require modification and extension, but understanding cannot proceed without them.

A recognition of the continuing relevance of the formative period in sociology allows us to identify a far greater continuity in sociological analysis than many are prepared to recognise. Contemporary theories can often be seen as recasting older ideas, building on them and extending them to new areas of application. In the course of this, the inherited ideas – whether or not they are recognised as such – are deepened, elaborated, and enlarged. 'New directions' in social theory make sense and prove useful only if we have some appreciation of the old ideas that form the starting point for the change of direction.

Formative ideas, then, play a continuing role as the defining statements of what it is to be sociological, while contemporary theories, through their engagement with this formative knowledge, can move sociological analysis forward. Instead of a succession of novel and incommensurable perspectives, we may be able to identify areas of intellectual progress in which genuine advances in sociological understanding have been made. Such progress becomes apparent if contemporary work is placed in the context of the formative ideas.

This is not to say that all contemporary theory must be seen as either reinventing the wheel or modifying it. There are genuinely new approaches, introducing ideas that were barely considered by the founders. Such work, however, must accommodate itself to existing research based on older ideas that complement its own particular focus of attention. There are also areas of genuine controversy where contemporary theorists substantially disagree with each other and with earlier theorists. It is often remarked, for example, that contemporary sociology is beset by a division between 'structural' approaches and 'action' approaches. Sociology loses much of its excitement and explanatory purchase if such differences are minimised. An awareness of the formative sociological debates, however, shows that this division was equally important 150 years ago and that the relationship between the two is one of the major areas of continuity in social theory. What emerges from such contextualisation is a realisation that the central issue in this debate has not been the question of which of the two approaches is correct (and which, therefore, should be abandoned), but the question of where the legitimate areas of application for each of them are to be found. Social reality is complex and exhibits both structural and enacted properties.

Continuity and controversy, therefore, characterise the development of sociology, and any overview of social theory must recognise this. My aim has been to produce a book that does justice to both continuity and controversy: rediscovering and consolidating the diverse achievements of the formative theorists as the bedrock for sociological analysis and documenting the areas where formative and contemporary theorists have engaged in genuine and productive debate. I stress that different forms of social theory may often be complementary rather than merely contending.

It is important to emphasise that my advocacy of the *complementarity* of sociological approaches does not mean that I advocate their immediate and eclectic synthesis into a single theoretical framework. A genuine synthesis of available bodies of knowledge may be a desirable long-term goal (Scott 1998), but it would be premature and misguided to pursue this goal at the expense of a recognition of prevailing areas of controversy and theoretical disputation.

Indeed, such eclecticism would be unhelpful and unproductive. It would be beset by intellectual contradictions whose discussion would inhibit both empirical research and theoretical advance. Matters would be no better if such a strategy were confined to those theories that had separately withstood empirical testing – however we might envisage that taking place. It is unlikely that such a synthesis could be built and, as there are too many areas in which our sociological understanding is limited, there are too many gaps in our knowledge to make such an effort worthwhile. If a theoretical synthesis is to emerge, it will be many years from now and will result from a gradual process of theoretical accommodation and integration in particular and discrete areas.

There may, however, be further obstacles to both ideas of synthesis and complementarity. Theoretical frameworks are grounded in value differences around which particular sets of concepts are organised. It was Max Weber (1904) who recognised that objectivity in sociology is achieved in the face of the value relevance of its concepts. Liberals, Marxists, feminists, and post-colonialists, for example, identify themselves in relation to varying cultural values and it is these value differences that orient them towards particular topics of investigation and sensitise them towards particular aspects of the problems that they investigate.

In the light of this it would seem ludicrous to suggest that such divergent theoretical frameworks can be treated as complementary to each other. What can be meant by the claim that debates in social theory are marked by considerable continuity and complementarity? Weber recognised that empirically founded research, on whatever value-relevant basis it is constituted, has an equal right to be considered as a valid contribution to social scientific understanding. The works of liberals, Marxists, feminists, post-colonialists, and other value-defined positions may be treated as, in principle, complementary to each other. Only if their accounts fail the scientific test of empirical adequacy can they be rejected and denied a place in the framework of sociological understanding.

My aim in this book is to elaborate this view of continuity and controversy in social theory. The development of social theory must be recaptured and understood as an intellectual enterprise built around a division of labour in which a number of complementary themes are pursued and in which genuine areas of theoretical progress can be identified. The ideas of the founding theorists are truly formative in that they provide the foundations for all later theoretical development and they embody a recognition of elements that have a continuing relevance for sociological understandings of the contemporary world.

The themes that define sociology as a discipline are cultural formation, systemic organisation, socialisation, action, conflict, and nature, and in Chapter 2 I show how these themes emerged from the 'discovery' of the social in Enlightenment discourse. Parallel intellectual undertakings in Britain, France, and Germany were built around a recognition of the social factor and an elaboration of the intellectual means through which this could be explored. A massive growth of intellectual activity, beginning in the 1830s, established 'sociology' as a discipline alongside a range of other social sciences, and formative theorists began to elaborate their central concerns. Auguste Comte and Herbert Spencer were the globally important figures in the emergence of sociology and the elaboration of its intellectual themes.

In Chapters 3 and 4 I review the range of formative theory, showing how the basic elements in social theory were elaborated in a diverse range of theorists across Europe and the United States, as well as in parts of Asia, Latin America, and Africa. Chapter 3 considers work on the cultural formation of individuals, their socialisation into particular cultures, and their systemic organisation into structures of social relations. Chapter 4 looks at formative ideas on the action and interaction of individuals, the conflict of social groups, and the conditioning of social life by natural environmental and bodily conditions. In each chapter I try to indicate the diversity of theoretical frameworks, emphasising that the formative influences in sociology cannot be reduced to Marx, Weber, and Durkheim.

The aim of these chapters is to provide a comprehensive intellectual mapping of the sociological enterprise, allowing each significant contribution to be understood in its larger context. At various points in these chapters I have included 'Focus' boxes in which I highlight particular theorists whose work can be taken as exemplary and whose study in depth will round-out the general picture presented. Those studying theory through a small selection of theorists – typically the case in university sociology today – will be able to use this book and its Focus boxes to broaden their understanding of that work.

In Chapters 5 and 6 I turn to contemporary theory, taking the Second World War as the natural divide between formative and contemporary theory. I show how knowledge and understanding of each of the themes of sociological analysis was broadened and articulated in this period, though some areas show greater advance than others. Cultural formation, socialisation, and systemic organisation are the topics considered in Chapter 5. I show that the disciplinary differentiation of sociology from social psychology has led to a relative marginalisation of social-isation within sociology. Significant intellectual advances are apparent in the study of both cultural formation and systemic organisation. Action, conflict, and nature are the themes considered in Chapter 6, and progressive intellectual work is less marked in each of these. Investigation of the natural environment was affected by the disciplinary differentiation of human geography from sociology, though environmental influences, even in geography, were marginalised until very recently. In the area of the body, however, major advances have been made by feminist and other theorists. Approaches to action have made some advance on earlier work, thanks to the attempt to theorise interaction rather than simply individual action. Less progress is apparent in the analysis of conflict, though con-temporary work has highlighted the conditions for successful collective action. Throughout Chapters 5 and 6 I continue the use of Focus boxes so that the con-tributions of particular contemporary theorists can be placed in the larger context.

Sociology originated as the science of modern society, and the key debate in contemporary theory has been the question of whether contemporary societies are still 'modern' in character. The theoretical innovations of contemporary the-orists have been geared towards this particular empirical question. It is this that I turn to in Chapters 7 and 8. Chapter 7 asks what it means to be 'modern', and I review the generally accepted arguments about the nature of modern society and its leading social institutions. In Chapter 8 I turn to those contemporary the-orists who have suggested that modernity has transmuted into 'late' or 'radical' forms or has, perhaps, acquired a 'post-modern' character. Modern social institu-tions have been seen as significantly affected by, variously, the expansion of knowledge and information, the networking of collective agencies, and the glob-alisation of social relations. In assessing these views I demonstrate that the the-orists concerned have drawn, implicitly if not explicitly, on formative theorists as well as on other contemporary theorists.

Sociology is an exciting enterprise and nothing is more exciting than the engagement in theoretical analysis and debate. I have sought to convey some of this excitement and the ideas that have emerged from sociological debates. I pro-vide no definitive answers to the many questions raised, but I hope to have reviewed the varying answers that have been given by those who can be consid-ered to have contributed to the development of social theory. In doing so, I have not limited my attention to those who have defined themselves as 'sociologists'. I take a broadly inclusive approach to social theory as this is the only basis on which genuine advance has taken place in the past and can continue to occur in the future.

2

Genealogy of the Social

This chapter traces the origins of social theory from the Renaissance. It argues that it was then, and especially during the Enlightenment, that an idea of the 'social' factor in human life was for the first time systematically developed. It examines the early years of

- British social theory

- French social theory

- German social theory

The chapter aims to demonstrate the convergence of intellectual concerns around a number of themes that have continued to structure social theory until the present. This emerging framework is considered through a discussion of the first global sociologists:

- Auguste Comte

- Herbert Spencer

Search the internet using Google, Yahoo, or any of the other search engines and you will discover that sociology was founded by Auguste Comte in the middle of the nineteenth century.[1] This is the same answer that professional sociologists will often give to non-sociologists when asked about the founding of their discipline. The claim is that Comte discovered 'society' and recognised the need for a new 'science' to study it.

Perhaps things are not so clear-cut as this implies. It is certainly true that Comte invented the word 'sociology', combining the Latin word *socius* ('society') with the Greek word *logos* ('study'), but the systematic study of society has more complex roots than this. A more satisfactory answer might be that scientific sociology originated among the intellectual heirs of Comte who built a 'classical' tradition of sociological analysis. Typically, Émile Durkheim, Max Weber, and Karl Marx are seen as the 'founding fathers' of the discipline: they moved beyond Comte's insights to establish stronger and more secure foundations. More sophisticated formulations recognise a much larger number of formative theorists as active in the nineteenth and early twentieth centuries: Tönnies, Simmel, Spencer, Pareto, and so the list goes on.

Critics of this point of view have pointed out that the named 'founding fathers' were, of course, men – and, furthermore, white men. Conventional accounts of the history of sociology mention no women and very few men from outside the ethnic mainstream of European history as contributors to it. The initial letters of Durkheim, Weber, and Marx, it is sometimes suggested, might just as well stand for 'Dead, White, and Male'. There is a great deal of truth in this. These long-dead figures were certainly male and white, though the fact that many 'classical' sociologists were ethnic Jews makes this judgement more complex than the term 'white' implies. The male bias in lists of disciplinary founders is not a simple distortion, however. Sociological work in this period was largely, though not exclusively, produced within the universities, and these academic organisations did exclude or marginalise women. The disproportionate representation of men in lists of putative founders reflects the disproportionately low number of women who had the opportunity to contribute to the discipline. Nevertheless, an accurate history of sociology ought not to ignore the contributions of female and black thinkers and researchers.

There is, however, an even deeper problem with the narrative of the nineteenth century foundation of sociology. Whatever the significance of Durkheim, Weber, Marx, and their numerous contemporaries for the formation of a social theory, its history is both longer and more complex than these accounts suggest. The discovery of a 'social' element in human life and a study of the forms of human 'society' pre-dated Comte by many centuries.

Society should not, of course, be likened to an uninhabited island awaiting discovery by an intrepid explorer. All humans live in society and have an awareness, however dim, of their social life. Systematic reflection on this social life is, nevertheless, a relatively late and unusual occurrence in human history. A systematic study of social life becomes possible only when people recognise that their association involves the existence of a distinct object – 'society' – that is more than simply the sum of individual actions. The social element in human life has properties and powers that are different from those of individuals. It is in this sense that society had to be 'discovered' before 'sociology', as the science of society, became possible.

Both society and sociology were glimpsed by the classical Greeks, but it was in the European Enlightenment of the seventeenth and eighteenth centuries that the significant breakthrough occurred. It was then that 'society' was truly discovered and 'social' influences were recognised as distinct phenomena to be studied in their own right. By the time of Comte, his contemporaries, and his successors, these intellectual discoveries were well established. They made possible the later developments in social thought that Comte christened 'sociology'. This christening was not, then, the founding point for the contemporary discipline of sociology. It is the ideas of the Enlightenment with which we must begin in order to understand the development of social knowledge.

Renaissance and Enlightenment

Systematic theorising about human affairs first appeared in classical Greece and Rome, especially during the great flowering of philosophy and science between the fifth century BC and the third century AD. Such thinkers as Plato (lived 427–347 BC) and Aristotle (lived 384–322 BC) began to investigate the political organisation of the Greek communities and to relate this to domestic and commercial activities. Their ideas put the study of ethics, law, and politics on a par with that of physics and biology. Though social life was seen largely as the public or 'political' life of the 'polity', Plato and Aristotle raised many issues that would eventually be addressed in the form of a 'social' theory.

Many classical texts were lost with the collapse of the Roman Empire, as were the social structures that had sustained the autonomous intellectual life of the classical thinkers. Though the intellectual emptiness of the European 'Dark Ages' has often been exaggerated, scholarly activity outside the Christian Church was virtually non-existent. Not until Arab expansion into the former Roman world were some classical texts rediscovered, and Muslim scholars began to re-examine them. The greatest achievement of this renewal of intellectual activity was that of Abdulrahman bin Muhammed bin Khaldun al-Hadrami (lived 1332–1406), generally known as Ibn Khaldun, who used Aristotelian ideas to explore the conditions under which strong states could resolve social conflicts. Khaldun (1377) posited a sequence of stages of political development in which the rise and fall of states reflects ebbs and flows in their spirits of cooperation and solidarity.

The rediscovery of classical texts transformed intellectual life in Western Europe. Scholars of the fourteenth and fifteenth centuries began to see themselves as participants in a 'renaissance' or rebirth of classical thought. Adopting ideas and standards of judgement from classical Greece and Rome, the Renaissance intellectuals built a 'humanistic' outlook that undermined the theological worldview fostered in the Church and made the subjectivity of human experience the starting point for all knowledge. Reflecting and reinforcing the spirit of individualism and rationalism that was developing in the emergent bourgeoisie, their ideas broke with the communal and collective outlooks of the aristocracy and the medieval burgher guilds. The new bourgeois outlook promoted the rational, calculative attitudes of the market that informed the emerging forms of capitalist activity.[2] Although it remained closely bound to established authority and to the traditionally-grounded status of the aristocracy and the Church, the growth of this outlook encouraged the treatment of both political power and religion as objects of rational, intellectual reflection. This view of the world was expressed in the political philosophies of Nicolò Machiavelli (1505) and Jean Bodin (1576) and in the new approaches to art taken by Leonardo da Vinci (lived 1452–1519) and Michelangelo (Michelagniolo di Lodovico Buonarroti, lived 1475–1564). States and state forms were seen as open to change through individual human action and not as fixed and given for all time. Unquestioning beliefs in supernatural powers grew weaker and individual human powers of thought and deliberation came to carry greater weight in deciding political issues.

This move towards 'a completely secularized attitude to the world from which all irrationalism had been expunged'[3] encouraged the conclusion that conscious human control over the world was possible if only the laws that regulate it could be uncovered and understood. Knowledge of these laws would emancipate people from domination by natural and mysterious forces. The Lutheran Reformation of the sixteenth century further loosened the intellectual grip of the Church, but the full implications of these ideas for an understanding of the 'social' world were not drawn out until scholars in the seventeenth century, in self-conscious emulation of the 'Renaissance' thinkers, began to see themselves as agents of an 'Enlightenment' in human thought.

The European Enlightenment was both a product of and a contribution to the slow development of a modern society in Western Europe. Enlightenment scholars, like those of the Renaissance, saw themselves as heirs to the classical tradition. Advocates of the powers of 'reason', they posed a self-consciously critical challenge to traditionalism. In the name of rationality and science they rejected superstition and magic, and they opposed despotic and authoritarian political regimes. Their conception of rationality was one of formal argument, of logical and mathematical ideas that could be systematised as abstract, theoretical knowledge. Such rational concerns were to be separated sharply from other forms of human thought and experience and become the sole yardstick of valid and reliable knowledge about the world.[4] This fundamental belief in the power of formal rational thought received its charter statements in the philosophy of René Descartes (1637, 1641) and the mathematics and physics of Isaac Newton (1687), while others soon applied these principles to political and moral life. Denying that human thought could be given any absolute or certain foundations, their 'anti-foundational' approach recognised no authoritative principles, identities, or boundaries except those of reason itself. No established ideas or institutions could be taken as self-evidently legitimate or authoritative. All were to be contested in the court of reason, which would bring final liberation from the inheritance of the Dark Ages. Enlightened about their true powers and abilities, people could, through the powers of their own minds, determine their own futures.

The cultural and political programme of Enlightenment – the so-called 'project' of modernity – was to organise humanity firmly around ideas of rationality, liberty, democracy, and human rights.[5] Europe was seen as moving from the ancient through the medieval or middle ages to a new, modern age in which Enlightenment ideas would be realised. This European modernity would be radically different from all the 'traditional' social orders that preceded it.

This programme was premised on an awareness of the centrality of the social element in human life. Classical and Renaissance thought had recognised the existence of political, commercial, and domestic institutions, but it was the Enlightenment scholars who first saw these as having a distinctively 'social' character in common. Discovering the social, they constructed 'society' as a distinctive object of scientific investigation. Seeing their project as the scientifically guided reform of human institutions, the Enlightenment theorists saw the need for a specifically social science to inform these reforms. This social theory arose first in Britain and then, because of the close intellectual contacts among the Enlightenment thinkers, in France and Germany.

Britain: Individualism and Romanticism in Social Theory

Thomas Hobbes (1651) and John Locke (1690) were the first to set out comprehensive social theories of politics. Immersed in debates over civil war, regicide, and revolution, their political views sought to balance state sovereignty and individual liberty. Both began from individual actions and traced their social consequences. This prepared the way for the far more extensive writings of a group of scholars in Scotland, for whom David Hume became the leading spokesman. Hume's own social theory was developed in fragmentary form through works on general philosophy (1739–40), politics and morality (1751), and English history (1754–62). He based his theory on a psychology of the individual actor and, like Locke, held that humans have certain innate characteristics that condition and propel their acts. But this was not all. These acts are shaped and informed by ideas that, unlike desires, appetites, and drives, are not innate. Ideas come to us from outside, from other people who communicate them to us linguistically. Human nature, therefore, is not completely fixed by human biology. It is shaped through learning and education and so must be regarded as both open and flexible. The motives that inform human actions are culturally formed and vary considerably through history and from one place to another.

Hume recognised two principal motives that enter into all human actions to varying degrees. These are the self-interested or egoistic motive and the 'sympathetic' or altruistic one. Egoistic motives are oriented towards the attainment and satisfaction of individual interests and involve people in rational and pragmatic calculations of individual opportunities and advantages as they strategically pursue their interests. Egoistic motives drive economic activity, establishing common interests around shared opportunities. They also create social divisions around divergent and antagonistic interests. Sympathy, on the other hand, is nurtured in intimate family relationships and is the means through which more extended feelings of fellowship towards others can grow. Sympathy is the emotional basis on which more concrete motives or passions such as ambition, avarice, self-love, vanity, friendship, generosity, and public service are formed. It allows the formation of sentiments of solidarity that tie people into cohesive social groups and establish customs and habits that regulate individual actions.

Egoistically motivated market transactions play a major part in contemporary societies, Hume argued, but modern social arrangements cannot simply be reduced to individual purposes and goals. People are educated within particular cultural traditions that lead them into the specific habits of action that are their customs. Hume held that the laws and customs that result from the 'association' of individuals with one another embody the 'spirit' of the whole people. This spirit infuses their customs and practices and gives their way of life its social character. The ideas and feelings that the members of a population share give them their solidarity as a people. In acting habitually, according to custom, people unintentionally reproduce the very social institutions that are responsible for these habits. Hume emphasised, however, that actions generally have unforeseen and unanticipated consequences. The social patterns that result from individual actions are constrained and conditioned by existing social patterns as much as they are by individual intentions.

These ideas were further developed in Adam Smith's (1766) account of the 'hidden hand' of social constraint that he saw operating in the capitalist market. Smith's account of self interest has been very influential, but his grounding of this in sentiments of 'sympathy' (1759) is often ignored. He saw sympathy as the basis of all morality and as underpinning the capacity for moral judgement in legal and political matters. Through sympathy with others, people cultivate moral virtues of character and acquire a sense of duty or justice that can temper the pursuit of their individual interest.

Smith's ideas informed the attempts of Adam Ferguson (1767) and John Millar (1779) to construct a history of the development of modern European societies.[6] These histories were a significant advance on Hobbes and Locke, who had seen individuals, prior to their exposure to civilisation, as living in a 'state of nature'. This natural state, however, was viewed as a purely imagined condition in which all social influences are absent, and the passage from a state of nature to one of civilisation was seen in equally abstract terms. The Scottish theorists recognised that social influences operate at all stages of human life and understood that the differences between civilisation and prior states of existence had to be seen as social differences. These differences were to be documented from evidence rather than merely imagined in ways that fit a preconceived theory. The study of history had to become an evidence-driven activity, oriented towards uncovering the structured processes of change through which one type of society is trans-formed into another. Using the reports of Greek and Roman historians and of contemporary travellers and missionaries, the Scottish theorists reconstructed a picture of the 'savage' and 'barbaric' hunting and herding societies from which civilised Europe had developed. In turn, it was from the more civilised agrarian societies of the feudal and medieval periods that modern societies, with their nation states and capitalist economies, had eventually developed. The forms of civil government and private property established in pre-modern civilisations had made possible the commercial activities and class relations that flowered in modern societies. These advanced forms of 'civil society' had emerged in classi-cal Rome but had been lost, along with classical culture, with its collapse (Gibbon 1776–81; Ferguson 1783).

The mainstream of English thought set out a more individualistic account of social life. This was inspired by Jeremy Bentham (1776, 1789), whose theory of action referred back to Hobbes rather more than to Locke. Bentham's 'utilitarian' theory minimised the part played by altruistic and sympathetic motives and saw all action as oriented by the selfish pursuit of pleasure and avoidance of pain. Individuals are purely hedonistic calculators of their 'utility', seeking constantly to maximise pleasure and minimise pain. On this basis Bentham built theories of politics and law according to which social control had to bend itself to the immutably rational and hedonistic motivations of individuals.

This 'utilitarianism' found its fullest and most comprehensive expression in political economy, where David Ricardo (1817), Thomas Malthus (1820), and James Mill (1821) formulated models of commodity production and distribution in competitive markets. The utilitarian view of action was later summarised in Mill's (1829) pioneering study in psychology. The utilitarians recognised that non-rational motives of sentimentality and emotion played a part outside economic life, but they held that the relations of the capitalist market had such autonomy from other social institutions that they could be analysed *as if* individuals were purely rational. They saw the task of social policy as the elimination of any residual irrationality through the reform of social institutions. Malthus's (1798) account of population growth and its relation to food supply, for example, allowed only a minor role for custom and 'moral restraint', and he saw rational self-interest as the principal driving force in human procreation. Population policy had to recognise this and could not be based on moral exhortation.

For all their philosophical radicalism, the utilitarians and other individualist theorists in Britain took for granted a very conventional and traditional differentiation between men and women. The 'individual' of these theorists was implicitly gendered as a man, as only men were thought to be capable, by nature, of the kind of rationality required for effective participation in the public world of politics and economics. Only Mary Wollstonecraft (1792) seriously questioned this assumption.[7] Denying any natural, biological basis to the conventional differentiation of male rationality from female emotionality, she argued instead that male and female characteristics result from processes of social formation. People become what they are made to be by virtue of their education and their socialisation into a particular culture. An enlightened reform of education, Wollstonecraft argued, would allow women to acquire the rational capacities that had been denied to all but a very few of them.[8]

The emphasis on culture, solidarity, and socialisation in British social theory was taken up by a group of writers who were, in many respects, opposed to the

Enlightenment project. Taking a highly conservative view of the need to retain the more 'natural' cultural practices and social institutions of the past, these so-called Romantics pointed to the contribution that such established institutions could make to social and individual stability and highlighted the dangers inherent in the excessive application of formal rationality to human affairs. Disgusted at the terror and disruption that the French revolution had initiated in the name of rationality and liberty, Edmund Burke (1790) encouraged the retention, in England, of customary institutions that restricted and inhibited individual self-interest. This was echoed in Thomas Carlyle's (1837, 1843) history of the French Revolution and the part played in historical change by 'heroic' leadership, and in Thomas Macaulay's (1849–61) history of England. Romantic ideas were promoted principally through the literature and criticism of Samuel Coleridge, William Wordsworth, John Keats, Percy Shelley, and Lord Byron.[9] Their eulogy of nature achieved its most popular expression in the dramatic account by Mary Shelley (1818), daughter of Mary Wollstonecraft, of scientific interventions into life, death, and human nature in her novel *Frankenstein*.

France: Revolution, Science, and Social Theory

In France, the Enlightenment project arose with the decay and revolutionary overthrow of the *Ancien Régime*. Its earliest expression was among so-called physiocrats, such as François Quesnay (1758) and Jean-Baptiste Say (1803), who constructed laws of agricultural activity around the role of self-interest in the expansion of national wealth. The physiocrats recognised a tension between egoistic motives and altruistic ones, but, like the utilitarians, they saw egoistic self-interest as the principal motive in human action. Such ideas influenced the influential study of political despotism written by the revolutionary leader Honoré de Mirabeau (1772).

Broader social and cultural concerns were developed by two closely associated groups of writers searching for laws of social systems and of the ideas around which these systems are organised. Denis Diderot, with Jean d'Alembert, Paul d'Holbach, and Claude Helvétius, produced the *Encyclopédie* to consolidate and summarise these emerging ideas in a 'science of man'. The most important products of these 'Encyclopaedists' were the social and political studies of Holbach (1770) and Helvétius (1772). More distinctly cultural ideas were pursued by the 'Ideologists' – Antoine Destutt de Tracy, Pierre Cabanis, and Marie François Bichat.

Taking their inspiration from biology, they saw moral values as organised systems of ideas (Cabanis 1802).

Jean-Jacques Rousseau – born in Switzerland but spending much of his life in France – was an important influence on the revolutionaries. Like his mentor Hume and the other Scottish theorists, he assumed a natural sociability and altruism in human beings. He traced, in particular, how social conditions influence individual character and autonomy. In both traditional and modern societies, he argued, a tight political control over natural human sociability is exercised through political and constitutional norms and structures of social inequality (1755, 1762). The causal power of social factors was also theorised by Voltaire (1745) in terms of a cultural 'spirit' that shapes the morality of a nation.

The most comprehensive investigator along these lines was the Baron de Montesquieu (1748). Recognising the immense variability of institutions, customs, and practices, he concluded that there can be no fixed or given human nature. The character or personality common to the members of a population varies considerably from one population to another and reflects what Montesquieu referred to as the 'spirit' (*esprit*) generated through their association. Each individual acquires a particular spirit of character from those around them, and this determines the ways in which they live their lives. It shapes their institutions and practices and it informs their actions. This was the basis of a social theory of politics in which each political constitution – monarchy, aristocracy, despotism, and republic – was seen as characterised by a distinctive spirit. Monarchies are based on a spirit of honour, aristocracies on a spirit of moderation, despotism on a spirit of terror, and republics on a 'civic' spirit. These generalisations formalised earlier suggestions about the spiritual and political decline of Imperial Rome (1734) and the spiritual conditions sustaining traditional despotism in Persia (1721).

Montesquieu also investigated the factors responsible for variations in spirit and social institutions from one place to another. He looked to the environmental factors of climate and 'terrain' (landscape, cultivation, and resources), hoping to discover any constant relationships between the 'external milieu' (the physical environment) and the 'internal' or moral milieu of a society. His argument was that an understanding of environmental influences could allow people to be more rational in applying reason to political matters and so help them better to express the particular spirit of their society. By acting in rationally appropriate ways, social stability and order would not be threatened. Applying this argument to France, Montesquieu advocated the reestablishment of aristocracy and a consequent strengthening of the spirit of moderation, seeing this as the only way of avoiding a decline into despotism.

Under the influence of the Ideologists, French social theorists gave particular attention to the intellectual aspects of social change. Anne Robert Turgot (1750) and the Marquis de Condorcet (1794), for example, saw cultural change as an orderly, structured process of historical development in which changes in intellectual ideas bring about corresponding changes in the forms of social life. They saw a clear trajectory of social development in Europe that ran from tribal barbarism through pastoralism and agriculture to contemporary French civilisation, and they traced a corresponding intellectual 'progress' from religion and superstition to an age of reason. The Italian philosopher Giambattista Vico (1725) had also produced a study of intellectual development, but he proposed a cyclical rather than a progressive view.

In France, even more than in Britain, the Enlightenment project of individualism and rationalism clashed with 'Counter-Enlightenment' conservatives who sought to roll back the intellectual and political changes of the reformers and revolutionaries. The Comte Joseph de Maistre (1796) and the Vicomte Louis de Bonald held that the Enlightenment had undermined the traditional customs and institutions that produced social order and so made the Revolution inevitable. Inspired by Burke's (1790) reflections on the French Revolution, Bonald and Maistre saw collective and communal elements in social life exercising a powerful and necessary constraint over free individual actions. Thus, Maistre (1810) highlighted the cohesive power of religion and lamented the decline in Catholic belief and practice, while Bonald (1826) explored the part played by language in perpetuating cultural traditions. They held that institutions grow slowly and gradually, without conscious deliberation and under the conditions to which they are best suited, and so acquire the authority of long-established practice. Slow organic growth, guided by tradition, is, therefore, preferable to rational political change. Bonald (1796) held that the destruction of the organic bonds and religious solidarity of traditional societies was a direct consequence of the growth of capitalism and bureaucracy. These forces of rationality were transforming all social relations in the direction of impersonality and calculability, as epitomised by the cash nexus of the market.

Influenced by both the Enlightenment idea of intellectual progress and the conservative reaction to this, the Comte Henri de Saint-Simon advocated rationally constructed forms of collective solidarity and has sometimes been regarded as the first 'socialist'. Rationality in modern societies, he argued, is indicative of the social progress that has resulted from the application of positive scientific knowledge. The term 'positive science' – referring to precise and exact knowledge based on observation and mathematics – had been coined by Germaine de Stäel (1801), but Saint-Simon became its principal advocate. Positive science, he held, had spread from one area of study to another, and a new positive 'science of man' would complete the development of the modern sciences and allow their integration into a single, unified science that he called the 'positive philosophy' (1813). This unification was possible, he suggested, because the movements of all material, mental, and cultural phenomena are governed by a single law of 'universal gravity'. Thus, laws discovered in one domain are directly translatable into those of another.

Saint-Simon saw this positive philosophy as an essential element in the Enlightenment project of cultural and social progress. He envisaged its intellectual advocates taking positions of social leadership formerly held by the clergy and reshaping social institutions on a rational, scientific basis. Reform of the educational system would be central to this as it would produce educated citizens capable of applying the positive philosophy in all they do. Impressed by the arguments of Say and the economists, Saint-Simon (1825) thought the central leadership group would be the *industriels*, the industrial entrepreneurs and workers who apply economic knowledge in practical business matters. These proto-socialist ideas of Saint-Simon were pursued as a practical task after his death by Philippe Buchez (the founder of Christian Socialism), Saint-Amand Bazard, Barthélemy Enfantin, Pierre Leroux, and, above all, Auguste Comte.

Germany: Counter-Enlightenment and Reaction

'Germany' did not exist as a unified political entity in the eighteenth century. Political sovereignty in German-speaking Europe was fragmented among a large number of principalities, duchies, and petty states, and many ethnic Germans lived within the Austro-Hungarian Empire. The Enlightenment project in these lands had first to come to terms with the task of building a strong national state, and Enlightenment and Counter-Enlightenment movements of thought were less sharply opposed than in Britain and France. German social thought stressed education *(Bildung)* as the means whereby the characters of individual citizens are formed through their inclusion in a common culture. The task of philosophy was to elucidate the cultural values that would best contribute to the formation of individual character. A strong emphasis on the cultural unity and continuity of nations characterised almost all strands of German thought, and this was often combined with a hostility towards any purely practical intervention in the material world on the basis of technical, empirical knowledge. This found its strongest expression in the Romantic emphasis on the traditional values of the past that defined German identity and that were seen as threatened by British and French ideas of individual rationality. This led to a view that the aims of the Enlightenment could best be pursued through a conservative process of modernisation.

The most unambiguously liberal philosopher in Germany was Immanuel Kant, whose works on epistemology (1781) and ethics (1788) influenced philosophical debates across Europe. In a very important contribution to the understanding of history and geography, Kant (1784) showed that advances in human reasoning and understanding have gone well beyond what any one individual can achieve in his or her own lifetime. The overall level of intellectual attainment in a population increases over time because the achievements of one generation can be passed on to the next through the communication of ideas from one person to another. Thus, language and the culture it makes possible are the means of human progress. The most important contributions to developing this insight into a social theory were those of Johann von Herder and Georg Hegel.

Herder (1784–91) sought to understand German culture by placing it in a larger context of cultural development. He took up Montesquieu's interest in the relationship between cultural spirit and the physical environment, but used this to trace a pattern of global cultural development. Charting the variety of natural environments in which humans could be found, from the North Pole to Asia, Africa, the Tropics, and America, he mapped environmental diversity onto the historical sequence of cultures that constitutes world history. He held that the biblical narrative of human origins, properly deconstructed, provides a plausible account of human origins in the Middle East and the subsequent migrations of human populations across the globe, though current research sees human origins in Africa rather than Asia. The particular historical sequence that leads from Asian prehistory to European modernity and, therefore, to contemporary Germany was driven by the motivating power of the popular spirit or *Volksgeist* that marked each successive society. The popular spirit shapes individual actions under definite environmental conditions and in the context of specific historically constituted opportunities. This collective spirit, then, is the fundamental element in the combination of factors generating historical development.

The spirit of a people defines its collective identity, motivates the actions of its members, and allows them to adapt their society to their environment. The means through which such a spirit develops is language, a capacity specific to human beings (Herder 1770). The human mind is able to form complex mental representations only because they are constructed in linguistic form and so are communicable from one person to another. The vocabulary and grammar of a language are intrinsic to the popular spirit, and language is, at the same time, the means through which a people is able to further its cultural spirit. It was for this reason that Herder advocated that intellectuals, poets, and other writers should use the German vernacular rather than the fashionable French that was then the sign of a cultivated personality.

This idea was used in the comparative ethnography of Wilhelm von Humboldt (1795–7). He shared Herder's view that people act in terms of their particular 'national character', understood as the shared animating spirit that is outwardly expressed in their customs, religion, language, and art. He saw each culture as unique, but as varying in the level of 'self-realisation' that it allows. Humboldt claimed that Western culture had allowed Europeans to cultivate their national spirits to a far higher level than had any other population.

Hegel's earliest works in epistemology (1807) and logic (1818–31) were the bases for a political theory (1821) and an account of the historical development of modernity (1831).[10] His social theory took the concept of the popular spirit as its central idea, developing this in opposition to the way in which it had been used by Friedrich Schelling (1797). Schelling had seen all physical forces – mechanical, chemical, electrical, and vital – as forms of spirit, which he saw as the ultimate active force at work in the world. In self-conscious organisms, Schelling argued, spirit becomes, for the first time, conscious of itself and able to move towards its fuller realisation. Hegel returned to the sharper distinction that Kant had made between nature and spirit, but he took over Schelling's ideas on the progressive development of spirit over time.

Hegel made a distinction between the actual or popular spirits that animate particular societies and the abstract human spirit of freedom and creativity that is only ever partially realised in them. Popular spirit is 'objectified' or embodied in the external cultural forms – the institutions and practices – and the way of life that define a particular society. The human spirit had become a dynamic and creative force only very slowly during the course of human history. It had been stifled under the despotic regimes, institutions, and customs of the ancient Oriental world – in China, India, Persia, Assyria, Babylon, and Egypt. As a result, their popular spirits had been conservative and constraining forces. In the classical Greek and Roman worlds, however, the human spirit had been liberated in democratic and aristocratic regimes that encouraged rational, critical reflection.

The classical Greeks lived in harmonious and well-integrated societies where the human spirit informed a popular spirit that found its expression in a cohesive moral order (*Sittlichkeit*), a customary, institutionalised morality rather than the principled morality of abstract ethical systems. The German world that arose when these classical systems collapsed was the first society in which the full potential of the human spirit, as a truly universal 'world spirit', began gradually to be realised. This spirit became the spirit of the new, modern world of the Renaissance and the Enlightenment, and it provided a reasoned philosophical basis on which contemporary nation states could establish a new moral order to regulate their citizens.

Hegel saw the historical development of this world spirit as occurring through a sequence of historical stages. This spirit developed earliest in family and domestic institutions. In the most primitive societies, governed solely by custom and tradition, no social organisation went beyond this familistic community, and the world spirit remained at this level in the despotic societies of the Oriental world. The development of commerce and property in the medieval world brought separate families and households together into the larger spiritual unity of a 'civil society', forming them into a hierarchy of social 'estates' or classes. In the final, modern stage, spirit is realised in the constitutional state, regulated through public law and judicial administration. The modern state transcends the economic divisions of civil society and establishes an impartial rule of law under which all 'citizens' can exercise their liberty to the full.

While tracing this historical sequence in the Western world, and seeing the German state as the ultimate embodiment of the world spirit, Hegel also saw the various institutionalised forms of spirit as continuing to exist as distinct levels of social organisation. Family relations are at the core of any modern society, but are embedded in the economic relations of civil society, property, and the market. These are, in turn, contained within an overarching structure of state relations. Only in the public sphere of the state can people achieve the full freedom of spirit that is denied to them by the alienating conditions of private life within the family and at work.

The Social Established

By the early years of the nineteenth century, Enlightenment and Counter-Enlightenment writers in Britain, France, and Germany had transformed the understanding of human affairs. They had discovered and described a specifically 'social' sphere that could be distinguished from both physical nature and individual mentality. They had, furthermore, built a systematic and disciplined basis for its study. While they brought major differences in philosophy to this scientific work and came to divergent conclusions, it was generally recognised that an empirical study of social life and its historically changing forms would complement developments in other areas of scientific work. Leading scholars felt themselves to be engaged in a similar – and, in many respects, a common – task of intellectual understanding. They were well aware of the intellectual and political differences that divided them, but they were also aware of the boundary that separated their concerns from those of their 'unenlightened' predecessors.

Their shared point of reference was the existence of a distinct and autonomous sphere of 'social' phenomena. This social reality consists of the cultural ideas and values that prevail in a population, that infuse its customs and institutions, and so bring about regular and recurrent patterns of action. It was recognised as a system of interconnected elements that fit together to form a larger 'whole' that can be characterised by its particular 'spirit' or ethos. Many Enlightenment theorists held that social reality could be analysed in much the same way as a mechanical system. Indeed, the growth of scientific knowledge in physical mechanics had been so rapid that the idea of a 'social physics' seemed highly plausible. Opponents of this mechanistic viewpoint stressed the subjective character of ideas and values and held that such spiritual entities had to be understood in terms of their inner principles rather than merely explained by their external characteristics.

There was, furthermore, a wide agreement that while individuals are, through their actions, the creators of this social reality, they are also its products. The character or spirit of each individual was seen as the result of their formation within a social whole. Because the spirit of each society varies and is unique to itself, so individual character varies according to the spirit of the society into which a person is born and lives. Human beings are, like all animals, born with a particular biological inheritance, but they are not completely determined by this. They have the capacity for conscious and rational deliberation and, therefore, for the creation and manipulation of values and ideas. For this reason, human abilities and capacities had to be seen as resulting from the interplay of biological and social determinants.

This plasticity of human characteristics that follows from their shaping by education and the acquisition of culture meant that no simple pattern of motivation could be imputed to human action. Egoistic, self-interested motives were seen as important by all the Enlightenment theorists. Rational actions, oriented to the attainment of individually satisfying goals, are one of the principal means through which social wholes are produced and reproduced. They are also, however, the means through which individuals come into conflict with each other, driven by competitive pressures to struggle for the maximisation of their interests. Nowhere is this more important than in the economic sphere of commerce and production that had become such an important element in modern societies. While some theorists – most particularly the utilitarians – stressed this as the sole human motive, most Enlightenment theorists saw cooperation and solidarity as important features of social reality and as following from specifically altruistic motives. Individuals, they argued, are predisposed by their biology and their culture to undertake actions motivated by a sympathy and concern for others and for maintaining social cohesion and solidarity.

It was argued, even by the utilitarians and radical individualists, that social phenomena cannot be seen simply as the *intended* products of particular individuals. Institutions, customs, and practices emerge and develop as the largely unintended consequences of purposive individual actions. Only rarely do they directly express a conscious and coherent human purpose. Many theorists held that they are, for the most part, unreflectively produced and reproduced through habitual actions shaped by traditional values. Thus, social wholes have properties that may not be immediately apparent to their participants and so must be uncovered through scientific analysis and investigation. These emergent properties could be the objects of forms of holistic analysis. Social wholes were, nevertheless, seen as emerging in particular physical environments that condition the biological characteristics of individuals and constrain the possibilities of action open to them. Social reality, therefore, had to be seen as the outcome of both 'spiritual' and 'material' determinants, operating in and through the socially formed actions of individuals. Theorists differed, of course, in the weight that they accorded to these factors, but they were in agreement that neither could be ignored.

This complex of ideas was the basis on which a new view of history was constructed. Institutions, customs, and practices change, albeit slowly, and whole societies can be seen to change their structures over time. Social changes do not occur at random, but neither are they completely and transparently planned. They are shaped by the internal structure of the society itself and by the environmental conditions within which it exists. History, therefore, can be seen as a structured process of development from one type of society to another. It was on this basis that the modern world was seen as the outcome of a long series of historical transformations that could, themselves, be studied scientifically and, perhaps, be formulated in 'laws' of historical change.

These were the foundations on which later nineteenth- and twentieth-century writers were able to build the more comprehensive understandings that came to be recognised as 'sociological'. The word 'sociology', I have shown, was the invention of Comte, but the discipline of sociology and the body of sociological theory that define it were not his invention alone. Through the nineteenth century and into the first half of the twentieth century there was a massive expansion and proliferation of sociological work that enlarged the various components of the Enlightenment approach to social theory.

Social Theory Goes Global

In the period from the first quarter of the nineteenth up to the second half of the twentieth century a massive expansion of social thought took place, producing what has come to be called 'classical sociology'. Often seen more narrowly as the sociology of the years between 1880 and 1920, this is defined as 'classical' because of its comprehensive, discipline-building character. The term may be misleading,[11] but it is certainly correct to identify an extended formative period in which the ideas produced in the Enlightenment and the Counter-Enlightenment were forged into comprehensive systems of social thought that continue to inspire contemporary work.

The building of this formative theory was not confined to particular countries. Its heartland lay in the key countries of the Enlightenment – Britain, France, and Germany – but it soon achieved a global impact. The leading figures travelled abroad to international meetings and congresses, they entered into extended correspondence with each other, and their works were translated into many languages. The globalisation of social theory is no recent phenomenon.

The framework of sociological analysis built in the formative period of the nineteenth and early twentieth centuries was defined by the intersection of six conceptual themes: cultural formation, systemic organisation, socialisation, nature, interaction, and conflict.

The leading theme – cultural formation – was the view that frameworks of linguistically formed and organised ideas and meanings are central to the 'social' character of human life. It is by virtue of their possession of culture that people are formed into fully human individuals. Cultures were seen as more or less integrated wholes or 'totalities' that shape all events, actions, and processes in such a way that they can be understood only in their cultural context. The most influential theorists were those who aimed to clarify the key mechanisms through which cultural formation takes place and the nature of the customs and institutions that result.

The idea of systemic organisation focused on the interconnection of individuals into social 'systems' with distinctive and irreducible properties. Conclusions about the relations among system properties could be drawn without any need to examine in detail the individual actions that are, ultimately, responsible for them. Some theorists drew on advances made in physics for their inspiration, seeing societies as systems of forces and energies that could be analysed in terms of their equilibrium conditions.[12] The success of mechanics inevitably made it the principal contender as a model for social system behaviour, but advances in biology led many theorists to explore a different conception of the social system. These writers drew the parallel between physiological processes in organic systems and the idea of the 'social organism'. An emphasis on the 'organic' quality of social life seemed to offer the advantage that historical sequences of events could be conceptualised as the results of organised processes of change from one form of social life to another. Just as biological organisms grow and develop, so social organisms could be seen as undergoing processes of development. In its strongest form, this appeared in 'evolutionist' models that depicted whole societies undergoing progressive, unilinear transformations that involved increases in differentiation and specialisation. Specialised institutions or spheres of activity – economics, politics, religion, and kinship – were seen as resulting from processes of social differentiation that split them off to form specialised system 'parts' or 'organs' carrying out particular 'functions'.

Cultural formation and systemic organisation together defined the key discovery of the social. A third theme was socialisation, understood as the mechanisms through which individuals are culturally formed into fully 'social' beings. The Enlightenment emphasis on 'education' was broadened out into more nuanced accounts of the learning processes through which individual personality and character are formed. Socialisation or enculturation is the process through which the shared ideas and values of a group are learned by individuals and become the basis of the motives that inform their actions and ensure that these are geared to the expectations of others. Psychological approaches based on the physiology of human experience and cognition had also begun to appear during the nineteenth century, and sociological approaches complemented this with accounts of how the communication of ideas and values from person to person ensures that they become incorporated into the minds of a large number of people and so become part of the shared heritage of ideas and values. Some theorists used evolutionary ideas to explore how instincts and inherited conditions enter into socialisation. Others focused on the role of cultural factors and processes of imitation and transmission.

The fourth theme in this formative period of sociology was 'nature', whereby the natural environment and the human body were seen as conditioning the ways in which people could relate to each other. The loosest forms of naturalism simply mapped the relations between types of environment and types of society. Stronger forms, however, took environmental factors as crucial determinants of the overall development of societies, seeing the environment as an infrastructure or 'morphology' that conditions social activity and requires that they 'adapt' to it. In its most sophisticated form this rested on an explicitly Darwinian view of 'natural selection'. Naturalism also requires a consideration of the biological characteristics of human populations and their shared biological characteristics, such as instincts, emotions, and interests. For many, however, this led to the use of 'racial' categories. Such racial thinking was endemic to European culture in the nineteenth century, and sociologists accepted this prevailing point of view. In some cases – even into the twentieth century – these views involved assumptions of white European racial superiority. The discrediting of strong biological conceptions of race in recent biology has led to its virtual abandonment as a category in contemporary sociological analysis. The term 'ethnicity' is now preferred as a label for what the early writers referred to as 'race'.

The fifth theme was that of action and interaction. This involved uncovering the motives responsible for human actions and tracing the patterns formed by their intersection and interweaving. Economic theorists focused almost exclusively on rational and self-interested transactions, seeing these egoistic and calculative orientations as fundamental to modern economic institutions. The wider social theories central to sociology, however, recognised that altruistic and habitual motives were also important and that an analysis of rational action could not provide a complete picture of social activity. They looked at the mechanisms of cooperative and communal interaction involved in the establishment of traditional and customary practices. In some cases, theories of action were proposed as complete alternatives to theories of social systems. All social phenomena, it was argued, are merely the outcome of individual action and must not be reified by according them properties that belong properly only to individuals. In other cases, action and system approaches were regarded as complementary ways of looking at complex social processes: if social systems could be analysed without reference to subjective actions, then those actions could, equally, be analysed without reference to the system processes except as external conditions.

The sixth theme that ran through formative theory was conflict and, in particular, the claim that social phenomena are the products, intended or unintended, of the competitive actions and struggles of groups. Individual competition had been recognised by the earlier writers, but the nineteenth-century theorists began to place far greater emphasis on group conflict. The most general forms of conflict theory saw groups as defined by their economic position, their 'race', or some other shared attribute, and as engaged in a constant process of competition, struggle, and alliance. The systemic properties of societies were seen as ever-changing outcomes of the shifting power balance among social groups. Some built conflict into an evolutionary approach and saw social change as the outcome of a struggle for existence and the survival of the fittest within a particular natural environment. These so-called 'social Darwinists' emphasised the part played by warfare and militarism in social development.

These themes run through the works of the various social theorists and were not generally pursued as exclusive 'schools' or 'traditions' of theory. Theoretical differences existed, but only occasionally did these crystallise into sharply differentiated and all-embracing intellectual frameworks.[13] There were numerous areas of intellectual disagreement, with theorists specialising in or emphasising one particular theme to the exclusion of all others. There are numerous examples of the outright rejection of one approach by advocates of another. Such disagreements, however, took place within a common discourse. There was no monolithic consensus over intellectual issues, but there was a recognition of being involved in a common enterprise whose parameters were defined by these six themes. For many theorists there was an explicit recognition of their complementarity in the explanation of social activity.

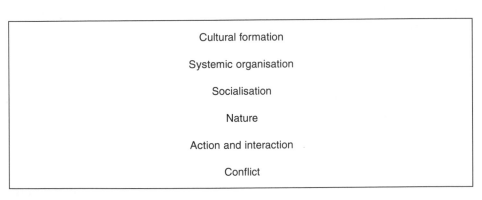

Cultural formation

Systemic organisation

Socialisation

Nature

Action and interaction

Conflict

Figure 2.1 *Themes in classical social theory*

Comte was, undoubtedly, central to this formative theory. He gave the emerging discipline a name – not wholeheartedly embraced by all who contributed to it – and he provided a framework of analysis that found followers and adherents across the world. At around the same time, the British polymath Herbert Spencer produced an equally grand synthesis of knowledge that achieved an even greater global impact. Comte and Spencer were the first global sociologists and their work dominates the whole formative period in sociological thought.

Auguste Comte and Positivism

Originally secretary to Saint-Simon, Auguste Comte shared many of his ideas about the need for a positive philosophy and about its role in rational social change. He presented his own ideas in two key works. First was a treatise on scientific method (1830–42) that was freely translated into English by Harriet Martineau (1853) and established the need for a systematic social theory. Later came his outline of 'positive politics' (1851–4). His early work sketched the outlines of a 'social physics' that would complete the development of the sciences, and it was this that he later renamed 'sociology' to distinguish it from the social physics of Adolphe Quételet.

Each science, Comte argued, has its distinctive and irreducible objects of analysis, and those of sociology are social 'organisms'. Human societies have organic properties quite distinct from those of the individual biological organisms that are their members. Human social life involves more than the mere coexistence of biological organisms found at the animal level. 'Humanity' differs from 'animality' because a 'collective being' is produced through linguistic communication. Animals have no language and so animal life involves no true 'society'. Comte's sociological method divided the study of these social organisms into social statics and social dynamics.

Social statics is described by analogy with the study of anatomical structure in biology. It concerns the coexistence and integration of interdependent elements in 'social systems' characterised by varying degrees of solidarity, harmony, and consensus. This system integration occurs, firstly, through work and property relations that relate people to the external world and through which they can meet their physical needs. However, material interdependence alone cannot generate solidarity, which Comte saw resulting from the sentiments of altruism and solidarity generated within families. Work and family relations, in turn, are regulated through the religious forms that give societies an overarching moral unity and sense of community. Coordinating the 'social organs' of work, family, and religion is the political order of the state, which sustains belief and so indirectly regulates all social activities.

States also maintain the 'class' relations through which the various social groups acquire their particular role in society. The classes are the dominant social groups within particular spheres of activity and Comte identified three such collectivities, with their principal foci in the three subsystems of industry, religion, and family. A wealthy class, based in industry, is concerned with the production and organisation of material riches, while a priestly class, based in religion, is concerned with forms of intellectual expression. A class of women, based in the family, is concerned with the key social force of morality and emotional commitment.

Social dynamics is described by analogy with the study of physiology in biology. It concerns the 'life' of the organism: the movement and circulation of its parts, and their development over time. Comte followed the Ideologists in seeing European societies developing through a sequence of intellectual stages, identifying three principal stages characterised by their particular combination of religious ideas and political forms. The initial 'theological' stage, with its sub-stages of fetishistic, polytheistic, and monotheistic belief, was associated with the development from primitive societies to the feudal societies of Europe organised through the Catholic Church. This had eventually given way to a 'metaphysical' stage centred on a critical, 'negative', and philosophical challenge to traditional theology in the name of reason. The intellectual and political changes of this period – the Renaissance and the Enlightenment – laid the basis for a third stage in which reason became a positive force in industrial expansion and social recon-struction. Comte saw his own sociology contributing to the consolidation of this 'positive' stage through a recasting of religion on a positive basis. Sociology would provide the doctrine for the new religion and sociologists would be its priests. Renewed social solidarity would be the result.

Comte's ideas on social reform through a new 'religion of humanity' inspired a massive following and were carried forward after his death in France and abroad. Pierre Lafitte promoted and elaborated the cults, sacraments, and cere-monies that Comte had seen as means of social regeneration (see Comte 1852, 1856). Similar 'positivist' groups were formed outside France, the most impor-tant being established by Benjamin Constant and Miguel Lemos in Brazil, where a Positivist Church has survived until today. Richard Congreve founded the London Positivist Society, translated three of Comte's works (Comte 1852, 1855, 1856), and trained other promoters of Comte's ideas: John Bridges (translator of Comte 1848), Edward Beesley (translator of Comte 1844), and Frederic Harrison

(1862). This group translated the *System of Positive Polity* in 1875–9 and produced a number of other works (Beesley 1868; Harrison 1877, 1918).

The more lasting intellectual legacy of Comte, however, was among those influenced by his earlier work on sociology as a positive science. Émile Littré undertook early work in medicine and lexicography, but from 1845 he produced a number of commentaries on Comte and his political project, building a 'science of morals' (Littré 1863, 1876). Similar ideas inspired the more independent work of Alfred Fouillé (discussed in the following chapter). Comte had a major influence on Russian émigrés associated with the Russian School of Advanced Social Studies in Paris. Evgeniy de Roberty (1881, 1904, 1908), for example, elaborated on Comte's idea of social life as the collective mental results of communication and the growth of scientific rationalism in furthering social development. Roberty returned to Russia in 1904 and was assassinated in 1915. Also associated with the Russian School was the more independent Maksim Kovalevsky (see the discussion in Chapter 3).

In Britain, Comte had his main influence through Harriet Martineau's (1853) condensed translation – which received Comte's approval and was itself translated into French as an accessible primer. George Lewes (1853) published a shorter summary in the same year that Martineau's book appeared, while Mill produced a more critical response (Mill 1865) that produced a response in Bridges (1866). Mill also produced an incomplete study of Saint-Simon and socialist ideas (1869). These translations and commentaries circulated widely in the United States, where Lester Ward (discussed in Chapter 3) produced his own distinctive elaboration of Comte's ideas.

Herbert Spencer and Evolutionism

Comte's sociology undoubtedly had a major influence on Herbert Spencer, who drew voraciously on contemporary scientific work and had been attracted by Comte's advocacy of a social science. Spencer, however, was no Comtean: impressed by the advances made in geology and biology, he aimed to construct a comprehensive philosophy and scientific system of his own. In doing so, he popularised the idea of 'evolution', using this concept some years before Darwin (1859) published his own work on biological evolution. Spencer's 'synthetic philosophy' appeared in serial publication over a period of thirty years and included a statement of general principles (1862) and principles of biology (1864–7), psychology (1870–2), sociology (1873–93), and ethics (1879–93). Spencer realised that he should have included a 'Principles' of physics and chemistry, but in an uncharacteristically modest statement he held that this would have made the task too large for him to complete. The whole of the synthetic philosophy was given an authorised summary by his secretary, Howard Collins (1889). Spencer also published a short statement of scientific method (1873) and presented a mass of ethnographic data in his 'descriptive sociology'. Publication of the series of volumes on 'Descriptive Sociology' continued after his death with finances provided under the terms of his will.[14]

Spencer saw all phenomena, whether planetary systems, landscapes, animate organisms, minds, or societies, as combinations of matter. The inorganic, the organic, and the super-organic were progressively more complex forms of organisation of matter. Where organic phenomena consist of physically connected matter, super-organic – social – phenomena consist of communicatively connected matter. Human organisms use language to communicate emotion and information, and stable structures of interdependence can be sustained through a flow of communicative acts. These social structures have autonomous super-organic properties, distinct from those of organic entities and irreducible to the actions of individuals (1850).

Spencer saw societies as systems that maintain an equilibrium state, much as organisms do. The actions of individuals as they pursue their goals move super-organic systems into equilibrium or disequilibrium with respect to their natural environment and the biological and psychological characteristics of their members. Disequilibrium consists of strains and tensions that pressurise individuals to act in ways that adapt their society to its environment and so re-establish equilibrium. The tendency to adaptation, therefore, is the means through which social systems change, and Spencer described this adaptive change as 'evolution'.

Social evolution occurs through processes of 'integration' and 'differentiation'. Individuals and groups are integrated or 'compounded' through increasing coalescence. Small bands of hunter-gatherers become compounded into federations and then into the 'doubly compounded' civilisations of the ancient and classical world. The most complex societies are the 'triply compounded' civilisations and nations of the contemporary world. Differentiation is a process through which societies become more stratified and their parts more specialised. Typically, a 'ruling agency' is separated out from the body of the society, initially as a form of sexual stratification. In more compounded societies, sexual divisions have been combined with economic and political differences to form complex class structures. Societies also tend to differentiate into specialised systems, each concerned with particular functions. Spencer traced the differentiation of domestic, ceremonial, political, economic, ecclesiastical, professional, and industrial activities and their super-organic connection into larger functional systems or institutions that he called 'organs'. The principal organs that he discovered in comparative work were the 'sustaining system' (concerned with productive activities), the 'regulating system' (concerned with government and inter-societal relations), and a 'distributive system' that links them.

In complex agrarian civilisations, Spencer argued, the regulatory system predominates and they tend to be 'militant': they have centralised power structures and a sharp stratification between rulers and subordinates. In the more complex modern societies, on the other hand, the sustaining system predominates and they are 'industrial' in character: individual members are recognised as 'citizens' with rights that limit the power of central government and allow them to enter into contractual relations as employers and workers. The prevailing trend of social evolution, therefore, has been from militant to industrial societies.

Spencer's work was massively influential, both in Britain and beyond, and it was he who popularised the idea of organismic systems and the associated idea of social evolution. In Britain, the work of Leonard Hobhouse (discussed in Chapter 3) drew on Spencer but added a great deal to it, while William Sumner in the United States (also discussed in Chapter 3) remained closer to Spencer's own views. Evolutionary theories were pursued in Italy by Roberto Ardigò (1879a, 1879b; see also 1870, 1893) and his followers such as Icilio Vanni (1888), Francesco Cossentini, Eugenio Rignano, and Giuseppe Ferrari (1851), none of whom added anything significant to Spencer's theory. In Spain, Francisco Giner de la Rios (1899), Gumersindo de Azcárate (1881), and Adolfo Posada (1903, 1908) utilised Spencer's ideas. Most significant of these was Posada, who combined Spencer's organicism with an account of the formation of a sense of individual self. Spencer also had an influence outside Europe. The first foreign-language book to be translated into Japanese was Spencer's *Principles of Sociology*, translated by Noritake Koutaro in 1882.

Comte and Spencer epitomise the central achievements of sociology in the formative period, but their work did not exhaust the implications of the ideas raised by the Enlightenment and Counter-Enlightenment theorists. They stimulated a much larger number of theorists who explored the complex set of themes that I have identified: cultural formation, systemic organisation, nature, conflict, interaction, and socialisation. Developing these themes, they produced numerous and frequently incompatible theories. Collectively, however, they built a broad conspectus of ideas that have continued to inform contemporary debates. Unlike Comte and Spencer, they did not all embrace the term 'sociology' or describe themselves as 'sociologists'. Some developed their theories within Departments of Economics, Political Science, Geography, History, and Anthropology, while others had no university attachments and developed their ideas as 'amateurs' or as political activists. While Departments of Sociology have continued to nurture the production of general social theory, they have never had a monopoly of its production. It is for this reason that the terms 'sociology' and 'social theory' can, with some reservations, be used interchangeably. Disciplinary labels are rarely important as indicators of fundamental conceptual divisions, and the disciplinary affiliation of a social theorist is often quite fortuitous and arbitrary. Social theory is the most general term for this kind of intellectual understanding, and sociology has been the particular, but not exclusive, disciplinary basis for this theory. In what follows I try to recognise this multidisciplinary character of social theory.

NOTES

1. All the contextual and supporting references and citations to secondary sources for Chapters 2–6 have been put into endnotes so that the main text can make clearer the chronology of the theorists discussed.

2. Weber (1904–5) explored the development of the bourgeois outlook in his account of the pre-modern and modern forms of the capitalist spirit. His argument is discussed later in this book.

3. Von Martin (1932: 21).

4. Toulmin (2001). See also Shapin (1994).

5. Habermas (1985). See also Eisenstadt (2001).

6. See Camic (1983).

7. Tomalin (1974).

8. A much earlier commentary on education by Mary Astell (1694) had proposed its reform only so that women could make a better-informed decision to embrace their distinctive role within the family.

9. Coleridge lived from 1772 to 1834, Wordsworth from 1770 to 1850, Keats from 1795 to 1821, Shelley from 1792 to 1822, and Byron from 1788 to 1824. An important and often unacknowledged influence on Wordsworth and Coleridge was Wordsworth's sister Dorothy.

10. Hegel's *Philosophy of History* was compiled from lectures delivered between 1818 and 1831 and was published posthumously in 1837.

11. Baehr (2002), but see also How (1998).

12. Mirowski (1989) has usefully discussed the impact and continuing relevance of physical ideas in economic theory.

13. The otherwise useful account of organicist, conflict, and action theories in Martindale (1961) unfortunately depicts these as coherent and unified 'schools' of thought. See also Collins (1994), which identifies systems, conflict, rational choice, and interactionist theories as distinct 'traditions' of theory.

14. See Rumney (1937). The circumstances surrounding Spencer's will are critically reviewed in Tillett (1939). See also Peel (1971) for a general overview of Spencer's life and work. Spencer gave his own account of his life in his autobiography (1904).

3

Culture, System, and Socialisation: Formative Views

Three themes from the work of the formative social theorists are considered in this chapter: cultural formation, systemic organisation, and socialisation. It is shown that a number of writers, in many countries, simultaneously explored issues of

- cultural patterns, language, and symbolic communication

- change, development, and differentiation in cultural patterns

- systemically organised social solidarity and constraint

- contradictions and equilibrium among social forces

- instinct, imitation, and habit as mechanisms of social reproduction

- the social construction and development of individual differences

The parallels and similarities between writers from different countries and working within different philosophical approaches are explored in order to show the broad similarity of orientation that had developed through sustained intellectual work and through the growth of international contacts and debate.

Cultural formation and the systemic character of social life were central to the discovery of the social. It came to be realised that the members of a population are structured into distinct groupings through the sharing of the ideas and values of their culture. Through this means they are able to form the systemic relations that constitute them as a 'society'. The members of human societies become social, and properly 'human', only because their activities are organised through the ideas that they share with each other. The shared ideas and the social relations that they underpin were typically sees as comprising social 'systems' with distinct and autonomous properties that could be made the objects of sociological investigation. Those who emphasised issues of cultural formation tended to adopt an interpretative frame of reference according to which cultural wholes had to be 'understood' by grasping the meanings of individual traits and cultural items. Those who emphasised the analysis of system properties, on the other hand, tended to adopt a causal frame of reference according to which the focus of attention must be on the interrelations of 'organs', or subsystems, and the processes through which 'equilibrium' is produced and maintained.

Some theorists of cultural formation took the acquisition of culture to be unproblematic and not in need of specific theorisation. Others recognised, however, that the 'socialisation' of individuals was itself a complex process and must also be an object of sociological investigation. Socialisation is the process through which individuals acquire the ability to communicate effectively and so to influence each other. Although analyses of culture and socialisation might seem to be obviously complementary, there were sharp divisions between ardent cultural and system theorists and extreme proponents of individual socialisation, and the two approaches were often in contention. For the most part, however, the various theorists saw themselves as participants in an intellectual division of labour and recognised that a comprehensive analysis of human activity required their cooperation.

Cultural formation and socialisation into social systems could not alone provide a full picture, and in the following chapter I will look at the analyses of nature, interaction, and conflict that provided the remaining elements of the sociological approach to human life.

Culture and Collective Mentality

The most powerful approaches to cultural analysis explored the formation of cultural systems as spiritual entities with an irreducible autonomy from the individual actions that they shape. A cultural spirit was seen as animating and motivating those who are socialised into it, and 'national' cultures and other cultural systems were seen as developing over time in progressive, degenerative, or cyclical directions. The methodological implications of this stress on cultural formation were drawn out by Wilhelm Dilthey (1883, 1910), who argued that the human or social sciences are organised around the need to 'understand' cultural wholes in order to grasp their development over time. The human sciences, he argued, were *Geisteswissenschaften*, sciences of spirit, and his 'hermeneutic' method was the means through which individual mind (subjective spirit) and collective mentality (objective spirit) could be investigated as autonomous phenomena irreducible to material facts.

Two early studies of American society by visiting Europeans pioneered the application of the idea of cultural formation in empirical work. Alexis de Tocqueville's studies of American democracy (1835–40) and the old regime in France (1856) saw laws, customs, and institutions as defined by a general structural principle, or 'spirit', that organises them. The democratic and egalitarian principles of American society, for example, were seen as responsible for its characteristically open economic and political institutions. Harriet Martineau (1837) presented a far more critical view in her sociological analysis of American society.[1] She, too, saw the customs, manners, and constitution of American society as reflecting fundamental shared beliefs in freedom and democracy: the absence of sharp class divisions, for example, reflected the egalitarianism of American culture. She discerned, however, a strong commitment to individual competitiveness and success that produced a compulsive conformity to social expectations. The society was also marked by cultural differences and social divisions. Its upper class was separated from the rest of society by its aristocratic values of exclusiveness and 'caste' solidarity; a colour line separated white Americans from 'people of colour' and repressed ordinary life in the black communities; and women were structurally disadvantaged by the dominance of male values. These inequalities of class, race, and gender, Martineau argued, represented a failure to fully realise the revolutionary spirit. Martineau's pioneering sociology also yielded a handbook of observational and interview methods (1838) and a report on her observations of religious life in Egypt, the Holy Land, and Syria (1848).

Language and Cultural Spirit

This idea of a distinctive cultural spirit had been developed most systematically in Germany through the idealism of Herder and Hegel. At its core was a recognition of the part played by language in producing and reproducing each distinctive cultural spirit. The work of Wilhelm von Humboldt on language (1836) inspired Heymann Steinthal (1851) and Moritz Lazarus (1855–7) to build a 'folk psychology' in which customs and practices were seen as expressions of an underlying 'folk spirit' or shared mentality. The implications of folk psychology were explored most fully and directly by Wilhelm Wundt (1912), in a book that summarised and recast an earlier series of five volumes. He saw language, beliefs, and customs as the collective properties of social groups and as the foundation for all mental activity. Collective mentality, he argued, consists of the reciprocal influences among individual minds that occur as a result of group membership and involvement in common activities. The ethnographies of Josef Held (1861) and Karl Volgraf (1864)[2] and work in the historical school of law and economics – Friedrich von Savigny, Wilhelm Roscher (1854), and Karl Knies (1853) – applied this idea to empirical topics. Economic and legal phenomena, for example, were seen as embodying a national, cultural spirit, and legal principles, property relations, systems of labour, and forms of money could all be traced to the specific customs and values that give them meaning. This historical approach to political and economic phenomena found an important institutional base in Gustav Schmoller (1918) and the *Verein für Sozialpolitik*. Maksim Kovalevsky (1891), working at the Russian School in Paris before returning to Russia, took a similar approach to the comparative history of economics and law, though his more theoretical work (1905, 1910) sought to avoid single-factor explanations and stressed the need to relate cultural to environmental factors.[3] A similar view was taken by Jacob Burkhardt (1860) in Switzerland and Sir Henry Maine (1861) in Britain in their investigations of the Renaissance state and the development of contract law.

Such views were articulated by theorists in many countries. In the Netherlands, Carel Gerretson (1911) set out a cultural introduction to sociology. Using Comtean ideas, Alfred Fouillé (1880, 1890, 1893, 1905) stressed the animating power of what he called *idées-forces*. These are ideas that motivate actions and define the national 'character' of a population. In a similar vein, the Bohemian theorist Tomáš Masaryk (1881) showed that national suicide rates reflect the inner spiritual character of a nation and that the high levels of suicide in Europe could be explained by the disintegration of Catholicism. His later study of Russia (1912) saw societies as dynamic systems of organisations and associations held in a state of interdependence through their cultural values.[4] Emanuel Chalupný (1916–22) summarised Masaryk's arguments in the first general text on sociology in the Czech language. Masaryk was later to become the first President of the new Czech Republic, holding office from 1918 to 1935.

Related ideas were expressed by Ziya Gökalp (real name Mehmed Ziya) in Turkey and Stefan Czarnowski in Poland. Gökalp (1924), a leader of the 'Young Turks' nationalist movement, gave particular attention to religious culture as the basis of national identity.[5] Czarnowski's account (1919) of religion and the 'national soul' stressed the significance of national 'heroes' in national identity, and he illustrated this by the cult of St Patrick in the formation of Irish national identity.[6]

Perhaps the most articulated theoretical expression of this idea of the cultural formation of nations was that of Bendetto Croce, a Marxist who converted to Hegelianism but remained on the political left (Croce 1896–1900, 1907; see also Spaventa 1909). His 'philosophy of practice' (1909, 1915) traced the 'individuali-sation' of spirit in human acts of creativity and morality. Political institutions and political action have, in addition to their economic ends, a distinctively 'ethical' dimension that alone makes action truly creative. Croce saw political elites as the principal carriers of the ethical spirit of a nation, the composition of elites and the changing balance of political forces within them reflecting a shifting balance of ideas as well as a shifting balance of material interests. He applied this argu-ment in historical studies of the Italian Baroque (1926) and nineteenth-century Europe (1932), and his ideas were expanded in a more general model by Giòvanni Gentile (1943), who placed a greater emphasis on the part played by conflict and force in politics and became an ardent supporter of the Fascist regime.

This view of an elite or aristocracy as the carriers of the spirit of a people high-lighted the need to recognise – as Martineau had done – the diversity of cultural traditions that can exist in a society. 'High' culture may be differentiated from popular culture and each may have a distinct impact on national institutions and customs. It was, perhaps, in Germany and Austria that this view received its strongest statements in the theories of Othmar Spann and Hans Freyer. Spann's (1923, 1928) 'universalism' held that any society is a distinctive whole (*Ganzheit*) or spiritual community that shapes and constrains the personalities and actions of its individual members through its system of social stratification. Individuals and groups are differentiated and ranked by their relationship to the central spiritual values and so are formed into hierarchical systems of 'social estates', each with a distinctive way of life. 'Spiritual leadership' is exercised by the aris-tocratic estate, whose way of life most clearly expresses the shared values. Spann argued that the commercial activities of modern societies have brought into exis-tence new 'social classes' that have no spiritual basis, and modern societies are marked by a clash between aristocratic principles and materialistic social classes.

Freyer, too, saw a conflict of estate and class ideas as the driving force in social change in a dynamic spiritual totality (1930, 1931; see also 1922). Like Spann, he saw aristocratic dominance as the basis of all significant cultural achievement, and he saw the industrial classes as threatening aristocratic power in the name of 'democracy'. In attacking the power of the aristocracy, these classes would also destroy its cultural achievements. Spann's advocacy of the leadership principle led him to become an ardent supporter of the Nazi regime during the 1930s, though his rejection of biological racism denied him any part in state power in Nazi Austria.[7] Freyer, too, saw Nazism as the means through which the German state could reassert hierarchy and aristocracy against the threats of liberalism and democracy.

Cultural Patterns and Customs

The most sophisticated accounts of cultural formation were those that directly explored the ways in which cultural systems are able to unify large numbers of people into relatively cohesive communities and establish the customs and traditions that define persistent ways of life. Ferdinand de Saussure explored this in lectures on language delivered between 1906 and 1911 and posthumously compiled into an influential book (1916). He saw language as the basis of a more general cultural theory that he termed 'semiology', or the theory of cultural signs. Language, like any form of communication, he held, involves two inseparable aspects, each of which can be studied only in artificial isolation from the other. There is the 'tongue' (*langue*) or linguistic system of signs and rules that define a particular language, and there is the 'speech' (*parole*) that employs these signs to convey a message in a flow of communication. Individual linguistic signs (sounded or written words) acquire their meanings from their relations to other signs within the particular linguistic system. This 'code' comprises the vocabulary, grammar, and sound patterns that define a particular tongue and that are required for any individual to speak or write and to be understood. It is the collective property of a population and is encountered and learned through the socialisation of its members. Saussure recognised that other cultural signs (such as artistic imagery and forms of clothing) were also organised into codes that define how they can be combined to convey messages. While some of these signs are conveyed linguistically, others are non-linguistic but may, nevertheless, be analysed in the same way as language.

William Sumner was the principal advocate of Spencer's sociology in the United States, working with long-time collaborator Albert Keller, who edited his final summary statement for posthumous publication (Sumner and Keller 1927–8). Sumner traced the cultural formation of what he called the 'folkways' (1906; see also 1883). He argued that the instincts with which people are born become culturally formed habits of action as a result of social learning. When similar habits and dispositions are followed across a whole society they become folkways or customary practices operating through shared norms of behaviour.

If people reflect on these norms and adopt them as more generalised principles of action, they become 'mores' defined in terms of more abstract 'moral' standards. For the most part, however, people act on the basis of custom and habit, and changes in social institutions are gradual and unplanned.

From this point of view, customs and folkways emerge from the shared principles and ideas that comprise a culture, and a related line of theory explored these principles themselves. Central to this work was Franz Boas, trained in Germany but working in the United States. Through his fieldwork experiences, Boas combined the 'geography' of Friedrich Ratzel and Adolf Bastian with Wundt's folk psychology and adopted the idea of the 'cultural area' to describe any territory with a cultural unity and boundedness that allows the autonomous development of its social life. This concept was the cultural counterpart to Bastian's environmental concept of the 'geographical province', discussed in the following chapter. The task of anthropology, Boas (1911) held, is to understand the integration of such cultural areas around their organising principles and key ideas. Individual mental characteristics result from the enculturation of individuals, which brings about a correspondence between individual and collective mentality. Boas recognised that such enculturation was rarely perfect and, consequently, that social integration was never complete, and he saw the inevitable deviance and non-conformity as the source of social change. Boas studied 'primitive' societies, his most famous studies concerning the Kwakiutl, Tsimshian, and other native Americans of British Columbia.[8] He saw social solidarity as expressed through the strong cultural pressure towards ostentatious gift giving in a 'potlatch' ceremony in which individuals maintain their status in the eyes of others by giving away large quantities of their wealth. Prohibition of the potlatch by the Canadian government in 1884 hastened social fragmentation and cultural disintegration among the Pacific Coast tribes.

Boas's theoretical ideas were developed most strongly by Robert Lowie (1917, 1920, 1927) and Alfred Kroeber (1917, 1923), and in Japan Matsumoto Junichiro produced a collective and cultural sociology that combined the ideas of Durkheim with those of Boas. The approach was extended in studies by Ruth Benedict (1934) and Margaret Mead (1928, 1930, 1935), and in the linguistic theories of Edward Sapir (1921) and Benjamin Whorf.[9] Perhaps the central theoretical point made was that cultures exhibit specific 'patterns' or styles that define the attitudes and orientations expressed in the activities of their members. In acquiring their culture, individuals learn to act in these patterned ways.

Sociologists in the United States who articulated complementary ideas included John Stuckenberg and Charles Cooley. Stuckenberg (1880) made the important point that individuals are not united into social groups as total personalities but only in those aspects of their personalities relevant to the activities of each group.

His views were similar to those developed later by Robert MacIver (1937, 1942). Stuckenberg argued that individuals are typically involved in a range of different groups, in which they participate in various 'social personalities'. It is, then, people's roles or social selves that are the units of social wholes. Stuckenberg (1898, 1903) proposed the word 'sociation' to describe this unification of people into a 'society'.[10] Social interaction is a process in which people 'sociate' – form societies and social entities – through their specialised participation in joint activities.

Stuckenberg's view of social personalities and their sociation presaged the later and more sophisticated views of Cooley (1902, 1909, 1918), for whom a society is a network of communicative interaction through which a 'social mind' of shared social meanings is formed. This social mind may be differentiated into various interwoven spheres of activity and the diversity of individual minds reflects any differentiation of the social mind. Cooley gave particular attention to the formation of 'primary groups' built around close, face-to-face relationships, which he saw as the basic units of the larger society and the means through which individuals acquire their sense of self. He described this self as a 'looking-glass self', derived from the attitudes and reactions of others as they are reflected in the mind of the individual concerned. Each individual's experience reflects the interlocking consensual reflections of others, much as an individual's physical reflection is multiplied in a hall of mirrors. Society as a whole is a product of the sociation of such reflected selves.

FOCUS: FRANZ BOAS

The most influential view of the cultural formation of social life was that of the anthropologist Franz Boas, especially in *The Mind of Modern Man* (1911). His work has influenced virtually all the leading writers in this area. The implications of his view for language and thought were developed by Edward Sapir and Benjamin Whorf as the 'Sapir–Whorf hypothesis'. You can review these key ideas by looking at Whorf's 1940 essay on 'Science and Linguistics' in his *Language, Thought and Reality* (1956), pages 207–19.

Biographical background and commentary on Boas can be found in George Stocking's *Volksgeist as Method and Ethic* (1996). A critical review of his influence on the later studies of Margaret Mead can be found in Derek Freeman's *Margaret Mead and the Heretic* (1984).

Culture and Communication

This view of societies as culturally formed individuals 'sociating' through networks of communication was also central to the work of a group of Hegelian theorists in Britain who followed the political and ethical philosophy of Thomas Green (1879) and Francis Bradley (1876, 1893) at Oxford.[11] Edward Caird, Sir Henry Jones, and Bernard Bosanquet, together with John Muirhead, John Mackenzie, and Edward Urwick, developed these ideas through their involvement in social work training in the London 'School of Sociology'. Run by the London Ethical Society, this School was incorporated into the London School of Economics (LSE) as the Department of Social Science and Administration in 1912. The initial intention of the English Hegelians was a clarification of Spencer's account of how aggregations of discrete individuals become bonded into super-organic systems (Jones 1883).[12] Social bonds require internal moral commitments that are shared by the members of a society and organise their thoughts, experiences, and actions. This 'social inheritance' or 'tradition' forms the minds of individuals, but it has a reality only *in* their minds.

The 'social mind' was recognised as a dispersed system of individual knowledge sustained through communication (Bosanquet 1899). The individual self, therefore, must be seen as a social self and as 'society individuated' (Bosanquet 1897; Jones 1910). Each individual need know only what is specifically involved in his or her actions, and an individual mind is a system of dispositions that correspond to the various social groups of which a person is a member. Social reality is an ongoing process of communication that produces, reproduces, and transforms the contents of individual minds and thereby sustains a collective system of ideas, meanings, and moral values. In later works, Bosanquet (1921) elaborated on this using ideas taken from Benedetto Croce.

Advocates of a 'New Liberalism', these 'Oxford idealists' opposed excessive individualism and sought to establish citizenship rights and a communitarian framework of social welfare. Modern states were expanding citizenship rights and giving individuals the powers to achieve the ideals that define their society and so to contribute to the 'common good' (Ritchie 1895). Their political contention was that states must ensure the minimal social conditions that would allow their members to act as effective citizens. Education – especially in sociology – is the principal means through which individuals are able to act more rationally and with true freedom (Caird 1885; Jones 1919). The practical implications of this view were taken up in teaching texts by Mackenzie (1895, 1918) and Urwick

(1912, 1927) and in the empirical work of both Urwick (1908) and Helen Bosanquet (1898, 1902, 1906).[13] The later work of Richard Tawney (1921, 1931), including his account of the role of religious culture in the rise of capitalism (1926), drew on these same ideas.

Particularly prominent in developing this approach was Leonard Hobhouse, who held the first Chair of Sociology in Britain at the LSE.[14] Studies in the philosophy of knowledge (1896), evolutionary psychology (1901), and comparative morals (1906) were followed by a four-volume 'Principles of Sociology' (1918, 1921, 1922, 1924) in which Hobhouse set out a view of the 'social mentality' as a network of communicating minds (see also Ginsberg 1929). Much of his earlier work was also summarised in an overview statement of evolutionism (Hobhouse 1913). His particular contribution was to show how a social mentality can organise networks of social relations into overlapping social structures. A 'society' comprises clusters of rules or norms organised as the 'institutions' that regulate the social relations of its members (see also Ginsberg 1933). Hobhouse's model of social systems as combinations of social relations and social rules owed much to the influential Robert MacIver, whose early essays had been compiled into an influential text (1917). MacIver worked at Aberdeen and had been External Examiner at the LSE. He completed *Community* in 1914, shortly before moving to Canada, where, soon after his arrival, he published a popular summary of his ideas (1921). Some similar views were also set out by Douglas Cole (1920).

Alfred Radcliffe-Brown also contributed to this view with ideas taken from Durkheim (discussed below), seeing societies as consisting of structures whose parts function to maintain this structure (1935, 1937; see also 1922). A social structure consists of the actual relations of interdependence among individuals living in a particular place, where this interdependence occurs because the individuals share a system of rules and sentiments that are transmitted from generation to generation. Solidarity and cohesion are maintained through ceremonial and ritual actions that reinforce the commitment of individuals to their culture. A similar view was taken by Edward Evans-Pritchard (1937, 1940) in his empirical studies of the tribal societies of the southern Sudan. Influenced by his Oxford colleague Robin Collingwood (1940), he took the idealist position that the social relations of these societies could be understood only in relation to the conceptual systems that organise them (see also Evans-Pritchard 1948).[15]

> ## FOCUS: LEONARD HOBHOUSE
>
> These themes were pursued and summarised in the wide-ranging works of Leonard Hobhouse, most particularly in his *Social Development* (1924). Hobhouse had his main influence within Britain and helped to form a distinctive approach to the development of national and global citizenship. A succinct summary of his views can be found in his 1920 essay on 'Sociology', in his posthumous collection on *Sociology and Philosophy* (1966), pages 23–57.
>
> Critical and biographical accounts of Hobhouse can be found in the collection edited by John Hobson and Maurice Ginsberg, *L.T. Hobhouse: His Life and Work* (1931). Background on the Oxford idealists, who had a great influence on Hobhouse, can be found in David Boucher's *The British Idealists* (1997).

Cultural Development and Differentiation

The focus of these explorations into the collective mentalities that ensure the cultural formation of individuals was what Comte had termed 'social statics'. The social dynamics of cultural formation were also explored, however. From this point of view, cultural systems were variously seen as exhibiting a linear movement of intellectual progress or regress, or a cyclical movement of 'rise' and 'fall'. Comte had proposed his 'law' of the three stages and Wundt's folk psychology, for example, depicted a similar evolutionary sequence of cultures running from the stage of 'primitive man' through the 'totemic age' and the 'age of heroes and Gods', to the world empires and national states that mark the development of a larger 'humanity'.

Cycles of Cultural Change

Other views of cultural change traced a pattern of degeneration rather than evolution. The most important of these was the Russian nationalist Nikolai Danilevsky (1869), who stressed the ethnic unity and uniqueness of cultural systems in world history and saw each culture as organised around a central animating spirit that drove its development according to the internal logic of its defining principles. Cultures pass through phases of growth and decay, and world history is marked by a succession of dominant cultures. Thus, the nineteenth century was a time at which western culture was in decline and eastern, Slav culture was in the ascendant. This view had a great influence on Oswald Spengler's (1918–22) view of cultural birth, growth, maturity, decay, and death. He held that all cultures have a similar life course of around 1000 years and face similar problems of degeneration as they decline towards their inevitable death. The expansion of technical and practical civilisation at the expense of moral and aesthetic culture is a typical feature of the late stage of cultural development, and Spengler saw twentieth-century Europe as having entered this final stage of its history: there was an exaggerated emphasis on technicality and practical reason, which could no longer be harnessed by the exhausted culture. Spengler's 'reactionary modernism' had a strong affinity with Nazism, and he came to see this as a means of spiritual renewal in Germany.[16] Kroeber's later work (1944) echoed the strong views of cultural integration taken by Spengler, though he did not draw the same political conclusions from them.

A variation on this view was proposed by Pitirim Sorokin, an émigré from Russia to the United States. Sorokin had been a student of Danilevsky and also studied with Roberty and Kovalevsky. Sorokin's work in Russia focused on revolution (1925) and social mobility (1927). He left Russia for the United States in the early 1920s and, having produced an encyclopaedic survey of sociological theory (1928) in which he articulated his relation to a variety of other theorists, he began a series of studies in the sociology of culture (1937–41, 1941, 1942). His 'integralism' grasped cultural wholes by identifying their internal principles of organisation and tracing their development in accordance with these principles: each culture follows a process of growth in which an inherent, underlying pattern both defines its integrity and shapes its overall development. Sorokin modified Comte's law of the three stages – distinguishing ideational, idealistic, and sensate stages – and saw these defining a series of cyclical transformations that produce the historical succession of human civilisations. The modern era in the West, he held, is simply the latest entry of culture to a sensate or 'empirical' stage.

Evolution of Traits and Institutions

An important strand in nineteenth-century thought was the attempt to explore the evolution of cultural ideas. Cyclical theories of cultural change had been largely descriptive, seeing the cycles as driven by the internal, vital logic of the cultural spirit itself: decline is due simply to the exhaustion of a cultural spirit. Early evolutionary theories, too, failed to identify the mechanisms through which evolution occurs. Later evolutionists, influenced by Darwin's arguments, believed that they had found a mechanism in the Darwinian theory of natural selection. Social evolutionism developed in Britain as a particular view of cultural development. Sir Edward Tylor (1871, 1881) was its leading figure after Spencer, holding that cultural similarities between societies could be interpreted as resulting from uniformities in human nature and from similarities in their material and social conditions. Although each society has its unique history, societies may thus show similarities in their language, forms of calculation, technology, mythology, and religion. Sir James Frazer followed this approach in his comparative studies of totemism (1887, 1910) and in a major study of folklore and religion. First published in two volumes as *The Golden Bough* (1890), the latter was later expanded to many more. Tylor showed that cultural items were subject to natural selection and that it was possible to place them in a sequence of developmental stages. In the present state of knowledge, Tylor argued, only a fairly crude evolutionary sequence of whole societies could be established, and he distinguished 'savagery' (the stone age), 'barbarism' (the metal age), and civilisation. This echoed the earlier work of Ferguson and the Scottish theorists (see Gibbon 1776–81: Ch. 38) and an archaeological periodisation proposed by Lord Avebury (Lubbock 1865, 1870). Tylor's evolutionary schema remained an important organising principle for later British social theorists. Graham Clark (1946), for example, divided the 'lower' savagery of the 'old stone age' from the 'higher' savagery of the Neolithic and held that technological innovations in hunting and gathering had been the key mechanism of cultural advance from one stage to the next. Like many of his contemporaries (see Perry 1924, discussed below), Clark saw this transition occurring in Asia. As was noted in the previous section, contemporary views now favour an African origin for the human species.

Hobhouse focused on the evolution of whole societies. Rules and institutions are subject to natural selection and those that further the adaptation and survival of a society will tend to persist, while others fall into disuse. The selective retention of institutions is the means through which social systems become more or less adapted to their environments. Although Hobhouse identified similar patterns of evolution to those of Spencer, his use of the Darwinian mechanism of natural selection allowed him to explain the cultural pattern rather than merely to describe it. Hobhouse identified a branching pattern of evolutionary change leading from simpler to more complex societies. This ran from kinship-based societies, organised around 'primitive' thought and religious ideas, through 'civilised' societies with authoritarian states and complex religious systems, to modern societies based around scientific ideas and with 'civic' states and systems of social citizenship rights (Hobhouse et al. 1914; Hobhouse 1911). This view of modern society was later developed in the more famous account of citizenship given by Hobhouse's colleague, Thomas Marshall (1949).

Sumner, too, had constructed an evolutionary scheme, and his collaborator, Albert Keller, modified this – as Hobhouse had modified Spencer – by applying Darwin's mechanism of variation, selection, and transmission more rigorously to the social world. The habits that people follow in their routine actions, he argued, are subject to a process of social selection in which only those that promote adaptation will persist and become established as folkways and social institutions (Keller 1915; see also Keller 1923). Similar approaches to social evolution are those of Julius Lippert (1884, 1886), who drew on ideas from Johann Bachofen (1861), Richard Thurnwald (1931–5), and Franz Müller-Lyer (1908, 1912, 1913).[17]

The evolution of specific institutions and cultural ideas was also stressed by the Finn, Edvard Westermarck,[18] who spent part of each year with Hobhouse in London. He saw universal psychological and biological conditions as elaborated through learned cultural responses to form the elementary social institutions from which more complex ones evolve. Westermarck applied this to the evolution of kinship (1891; summarised in 1926) and morality (1906; summarised in 1932). His account of morality was emotivist, defining 'good' as that which arouses emotions of approval. The objectivity of moral concepts is a consequence of the socialised character of emotions. Thus, moral judgements are relative to the particular cultural contexts in which they arise. These arguments were followed by a number of his students and compatriots, such as Rafael Karsten (1905) and Gunnar Landtman (1909), the latter rewriting his book for its English publication in 1938. Similar evolutionary accounts were produced by Claudius Wilkens (1881) and Carl Starcke (1889) in Denmark and by Gustaf Steffen (1910) in Sweden. In China, Tao Lu Kung used the ideas of Westermarck and others to organise his ethnographic work on family organisation and living standards.

FOCUS: HERBERT SPENCER

The most influential evolutionary theorist was Herbert Spencer, who was considered in detail in Chapter 2. He set out his principal ideas in *Principles of Sociology* (1873–93), Part 1. A short statement of his position can be found in Chapter 3 of *The Study of Sociology* (1873).

The best available biography of Spencer is John Peel's *Herbert Spencer: The Evolution of a Sociologist* (1971), though Spencer's own account can be found in his *Autobiography* (1904).

Value Spheres and Practical Culture

A final idea considered in discussions of cultural formation is that societies can be analysed in terms of the relations between their values and their practical or material organisation. This was central to the so-called sociology of culture or sociology of knowledge. Alfred Weber, brother of the better-known Max, had turned from economics (1909) to general cultural sociology and saw the human world as a complex combination of levels or 'processes'. The fundamental levels are a 'social' process of actions and relationships and a 'spiritual' process of communicated meanings and institutions that grows out of it (1920–21, 1935). The spiritual process, in turn, has two autonomous levels. Practical, instrumental knowledge, such as science and its technical applications, comprises the process of 'civilisation'. Religion and other systems of values, on the other hand, comprise the sphere of 'culture' in the narrow sense of the word. Civilisation develops through a progressive 'rationalisation' in which formal principles of calculation and standardisation are applied to the economic and political relations of the social process. Culture change, on the other hand, involves creative variation in values and is the source of historical uniqueness. Weber (1946) diagnosed the contemporary social malaise of European societies as resulting from a dislocation of European civilisation from its cultural context. This gave economic and political activities an unprecedented autonomy and produced a level of rationalisation that hampered creative cultural activity. Europe in the early twentieth century, he held, had reached a stage of cultural crisis and, therefore, of social decay. In some respects, Alfred Weber can be seen as providing an alternative basis for the cultural critiques proposed by Spann, Freyer, and Spengler.

Max Scheler (1926) distinguished 'society' from the 'spiritual' constructions of science, art, and religion. Drawing on Husserl's phenomenological philosophy (1900–1, 1913), which proposed that the mentally constituted external world is experienced as an objective reality. Scheler argued that it derives its objectivity from the collective mentalities shared within particular groups. This led him to conclude that knowledge and spiritual constructions have to be seen as relative to the social groups that support them. Thus, the diversity of value systems in contemporary societies is a reflection of their racial, political, and economic stratification. Ideas and values arise from and remain bound to social groups, and their creative and innovative powers can be realised only through struggles to pursue their interests. Scheler argued, in particular, that the most important ideas originate in and are carried by creative 'elites' of individuals who must mobilise the intellectually more passive masses.

Karl Mannheim (1925a, 1925b, 1924), like Scheler, saw the diversity of world-views and artistic forms as rooted in a differentiation of lived experiences among social groups. Influenced by the Marxism of Gyorgy Lukács (1923), he saw class situations in modern societies as the most fundamental source of variation in lived experience and, therefore, as the crucial determinants of cultural forms and political outlook. Natural science is the only exception to this social determination of knowledge, though Mannheim (1929, 1931) did see rationality – and, hence, the rationalisation of the modern world – as the product of a specifically bourgeois class outlook.

Drawing on the conflict ideas discussed in the following chapter, Mannheim saw group struggles and conflicting interests as the driving force in social development, though interests are themselves shaped by the ideas of social groups and clashing forms of social consciousness. Mannheim (1942, 1947) was close to and strongly influenced by Alfred Weber, but he did not share his view of cultural decline. He argued, nevertheless, that the rationalisation of contemporary societies, expressed in ever more complex systems of social planning, was producing a standardisation and 'democratisation' of culture that threatened intellectual creativity. Echoing Saint-Simon, he saw a need for an 'elite' of intellectuals to bring about a social reconstruction.

Similar ideas are apparent in the early 'critical theory' of Theodor Adorno and Max Horkheimer (1944; see also Horkheimer 1947; Marcuse 1941). In a study of what they called the 'culture industry', they argued that the rationalised sphere of practical economic and political action had distorted the sphere of culture, transforming the production of music, art, and literature into standardised objects of mass production. Popular culture, produced, distributed, and consumed as commodities, had become a new means of domination. In the stage of 'mass culture', people's aesthetic creativity is subject to alienation, and they are unable to develop a critical approach to the structures that dominate them.

FOCUS: KARL MANNHEIM

Karl Mannheim is the leading contributor to the development of this view of the social, which was set out most clearly in his long essay on 'The Problems of the Sociology of Knowledge' (1931). The interesting, but difficult, extension of his argument in Adorno and Horkheimer's essay on 'The Culture Industry' has been very influential. It can be found in *Dialectic of Enlightenment* (1944), pages 120–67.

 A short biographical and critical account of Mannheim can be found in David Kettler et al.'s *Karl Mannheim* (1984).

Social Systems as Organisms

Theorists of cultural formation saw cultures forming 'wholes' within which individuals find the meanings and ideas that inform their actions. For many of these theorists, such cultural wholes could be seen as 'systems' of ideas that produced a systemic organisation of social life. In many other theorists, the idea of a social system became their central topic of analysis and they proposed methods for studying the systemic interdependence of individuals without entering into a detailed consideration of particular cultural ideas.

The idea that societies could be seen as 'systems' took two forms, with relatively few connections between them. The dominant view from the middle of the nineteenth century was that they could best be understood as social organisms with autonomous properties irreducible to those of their individual members. Constituted as cultural entities, they could be studied in relation to the specialised 'organs' that comprised their parts and in terms of trends and processes occurring at the system level. The most important contributors to this point of view took up the idea of the social organism set out in Comte and Spencer.

Organicism and Social Functions

The word 'sociology' is firmly associated with Comte, but the first books to use the word in their titles were published not in France but the United States. In newspaper articles republished as *Sociology for the South* George Fitzhugh (1854), set out a defence of southern slavery, and in the same year Henry Hughes (1854) published his *Treatise on Sociology*. Both writers challenged the enlargement of an unregulated market society and defended slavery as a natural and integral condition for stability and order. One of their principal targets was Carey (see below), who had been an early critic of slavery.[19] Under the paternalistic protection of their white masters, slaves were integrated into southern society and enjoyed living conditions superior to those in Africa. Hughes based this view on a model of society in which the various 'organs' of a community help to integrate their members into it. Modifying Comte's scheme, he identified the economic and political systems as the 'foundation' of society, and the 'hygienic', 'philosophic', 'aesthetic', 'ethical', and 'religious' systems as the 'secondary' supports to this foundation. The various classes or 'orders' result from the circulation of power through the social system.

Versions of organicism influenced by Spencer were produced in Germany almost simultaneously by Pavel Lilienfeld (1873–81, 1898) and Albert Schäffle (1875–80, 1903). Lilienfeld, who spent his working life in Germany, was a

Russian citizen and sometime provincial governor in Latvia. He published his major book simultaneously in Russian and German, but it was the German edition that received the greatest attention. Schäffle's earliest book, published in 1861, was a study of the social framework of commercial and productive activities. He spent much of his life in Austria. Both writers saw biological individuals as the material foundations of social organisms, but saw social organisms as real superorganic entities above and beyond them and, like all other bodies, capable of growth, maturation, and death. Social organisms are formed from the mental or spiritual 'tissues' of communication that run between individuals. These are the connective relations that tie them into cohesive and integrated social structures. Lilienfeld saw a cohesive social whole resulting when individuals purposively but unintentionally adjust their actions to each other. Families, groups, organisations, and institutions are the 'cells' of a society and are formed into larger 'organs', each carrying out a different 'function' within the social body. Schäffle shared this view, adding that family households are linked into the complex circuits of commodity production and circulation that comprise national 'economies'. This 'economic organ' is the means through which the 'digestive' and 'excretory' functions of a society are carried out. Families are also linked into the circuits of power that comprise the unifying organ of government that functions as the 'brain' of the society.

Whole societies were seen as differentiated systems adapted to their environments through their various specialised organs. Lilienfeld identified economic, juridical, and political differentiation, while Schäffle held that an 'outer' or practical sphere of institutions is concerned with production, trade, and transport, while an 'inner sphere' is concerned with education, science, art, and religion. The overarching sphere of the state is responsible for coordinating the inner and the outer systems. For both writers, social evolution is a process in which the functional parts of a society become ever more differentiated and specialised, though all the while remaining integral parts of a unified social whole.

The growth of organicist theory in France owed a great deal to these German writers. René Worms (1896, 1910), founder of the International Sociological Institute, took the strong view that social organisms are systems of social facts with distinct characteristics unique to themselves and irreducible to any facts about individuals.[20] They are 'structures' with the capacity to reproduce themselves and so to contribute to the reproduction of the larger society. Worms initially set out a static social 'anatomy', identifying the social groups that are the 'cells' or elements of a social body and that combine into larger segments and organs. The most important forms of connection among these groups are 'functional' and hence a dynamic 'social physiology' is also needed to investigate the vital, functional processes through which social organs operate together as specialised parts of a body. Worms identified specialised social organs concerned with 'nutritive', 'integrative', and 'reproductive' functions. In his later work (1921), he turned to the processes of socialisation through which individuals are formed into cells and organs, using ideas from Gabriel Tarde (discussed below).

The organicist viewpoint was also taken by Alfred Espinas (1877, 1897) and Jean Izoulet (1894). Espinas studied the early stages of human social evolution, seeing the development of social institutions as an expression of the collective mentality of a society. Institutions such as technology, for example, are established as collective habits of thought and action as a result of the practical actions of a population in relation to the material world. Izoulet elaborated on this, stressing that the basis of all collective mentality is not individual mentality but the 'association' of individuals with each other in social groups. Human association generates the shared habits and practices that bind individuals into an organic unity capable of collective achievements – such as those of technology – in ways that would not be possible for purely self-contained individuals.

The organicism of the Belgian Guillaume de Greef (1886–93, 1908), a close associate of Pierre Proudhon and an active syndicalist of the First International, introduced some novel ideas.[21] De Greef saw societies as combinations of 'factors' or subsystems and social activity as confined within 'frontiers' or boundaries that define its limits. Each social factor establishes its own frontier, which may or may not have a physical basis, and the various frontiers of a society may not coincide exactly. The economic frontier, for example, may be far more extensive than the political frontier with the expansion of international trade. The various frontiers are constantly shifting as societies develop, and the study of frontiers and frontier communities is, Greef argued, the key to understanding social change.

Bronislaw Malinowski's work combined highly detailed ethnography (1922, 1926, 1929, 1935) with poorly worked-out statements of systematic theory (1939, 1941) that, nevertheless, made an important contribution to the organicist view. The 'functions' of social practices and institutions, he argued, may relate to the biological needs of individuals for food, reproduction, safety, and health, or to the 'derived' imperatives of the culture itself. These latter imperatives are those of production, regulation, education, and authoritative control, and Malinowski suggested that institutions are likely to become specialised around one or other of these functions. In addition to these 'institutional imperatives', Malinowski also alluded to 'integrative imperatives' concerning symbolism and the cultural tradition, but he barely developed this idea. He concentrated his attention on the claim that any society that achieves a degree of integration and persists over time must be meeting the biological needs of its members and the specific imperatives of its culture; a society that does not adapt in this way will not persist. There will, therefore, be certain similarities among societies as a result of their functional organisation.

FOCUS: BRONISLAW MALINOWSKI

The person most closely associated with the 'functionalism' of the organicist position is Bronislaw Malinowski, who trained generations of anthropologists in ethnographic fieldwork techniques. He summarised his theoretical standpoint in the essays printed in *A Scientific Theory of Culture* (1941) – for all its limitations a very influential argument. The essay on 'The Functional Theory' (pages 147–76) gives a short overview of his argument.

Only the early part of Malinowski's life has been covered in a full biography, by Michael W. Young in *Malinowski: Odyssey of an Anthropologist, 1884–1920* (2004). His contribution to anthropology has been reviewed in Adam Kuper's, *Anthropology and Anthropologists* (1996).

Social Solidarity and Social Constraint

The most sophisticated and influential version of the organicist view was that of Émile Durkheim and his followers. Central to the institutionalisation of sociology in the French universities, Durkheim became the leading figure in a school of thought that bore his name and had an impact far beyond the disciplinary boundaries of sociology. He became the dominant intellectual figure in French social theory, lecturing from 1887 on solidarity, the family, suicide, law, and ethics. The Durkheimians formed a tight research cluster, connected through training, employment, and a cohesive pattern of research and publication in Durkheim's journal, the *Année Sociologique*.[22]

Durkheim saw himself as a follower, though not a slavish adherent, of Comte. He saw human societies as interconnected social wholes with distinct properties of their own, properties that are 'social facts' *sui generis*, or unique, to them (1895). Social facts comprise the mental representations shared by individuals and the actual relationships through which these individuals are associated. Individuals are born into particular societies and are constrained to act according to the prevailing collective representations and within the established social relations. They have no free choice about the language that they speak, the currency that they use, the religion that they practise, and so on. In lectures delivered between 1898 and 1912 and posthumously published as *Moral Education* (1912b), first published in France in 1925, Durkheim argued that it is through their socialisation into cultural representations that individuals acquire a sense of moral obligation towards them, and their conformity is further reinforced by sanctions that others impose on their actions. The connections between social facts and the natural environment define a particular sub-specialism of 'social morphology', based on his view that social relations are physically embodied in material forms, and that sociology has to attend to the constraints these natural conditions impose on forms of social relationships and the collective representations that arise within them. Durkheim drew a number of important methodological conclusions from this and constructed an influential account of the logic of empirical investigation. He illustrated these ideas in his concurrent investigations into suicide (1897) and the division of labour (1893).

The study of suicide showed that even such an extreme and highly individualistic act was shaped by social facts. Each society exhibits a particular rate of suicide, seen as a social fact, and the rates in different societies are associated with variations in other social facts. Durkheim explored the co-variation of these social facts, showing the relationships that exist between suicide, religious participation, marriage, economic activity, and so on, and treating these as indicators of deeper relations that characterise the state of social solidarity. Fundamentally, suicide rates vary with the nature of social solidarity. Durkheim also showed that individual suicidal acts can be explained by the solidarity that people have established. He looked at their degree of integration into the various groups of their society and the amount of regulation that group norms are able to exercise over them. Low levels of integration and regulation, which Durkheim referred to as states of 'egoism' and 'anomie', create a pattern of constraints that predispose people to suicide. Excessively high levels of integration and regulation – states of 'altruism' and 'fatalism' – also generate a tendency towards suicidal behaviour. Suicide is at its lowest when these social forces are balanced.

Durkheim's account of suicide was intended to illustrate the relationship between social facts and individual behaviour: all individual action, he argued, is constrained by social factors external to the individual. His most general term for this constraint was social solidarity, of which he recognised two polar forms.

There is the 'mechanical solidarity' of 'elementary' tribal societies, organised around similarity and homogeneity, and there is the 'organic solidarity' of societies with an extended division of labour and patterns of interdependence. Population growth in primitive societies increases social differentiation, reducing the possibility for mechanical solidarity by weakening traditional customs and the practices that held them together. An extension in the division of labour tends to be accompanied initially by increases in egoism and anomie, though Durkheim saw this as a transitional phenomenon. Social differentiation around specialised functions produces a growing interdependence of individuals, and this is the basis of a new form of social solidarity. This organic solidarity is achieved whenever a complex division of labour and high levels of individualism are associated with a moral regulation of contractual and exchange relations and of the relations among different occupations. Durkheim (1917; and see 1895–6) saw the disruption, suicide, and class conflict of his own day as things that would be overcome with the full establishment of organic solidarity. In the lectures delivered during 1895 and 1896, and intended for eventual publication as part of a larger book, Durkheim saw this as an idea that he shared with socialism. The lectures were not published in French until 1928.

Durkheim's work emphasised collective representations and the 'collective conscience', the mental structures and ideas shared by individual members of a society. In his final major work (1912a) he turned to the question of the origins of these representations. They have, of course, a social origin, and Durkheim held that this could best be demonstrated in the simplest possible situation. This he found in the 'totemistic' patterns of religion of the most primitive forms of social organisation. Representations and regulation are 'religious' phenomena in all societies, and the sphere of the 'sacred' is recognised as something set apart from all other social phenomena and to be approached in an attitude of reverence and awe. Modern societies are secularised ones in which the prevailing religion is a 'cult of the individual' and their overall religious pattern is highly complex. In primitive societies, however, matters can be seen more clearly and the processes at work can be illuminated. Durkheim used field evidence on Australian totemism to show that the religious categories of such societies can be seen as representations of the social relations in which their members are involved. Durkheim relied on the fieldwork of the British anthropologists Spencer and Gillen (1899). He examined collective representations further in his lectures on *Educational Thought* (1913), delivered every year from 1904 to 1913 but published for the first time in 1938.

Marcel Mauss, Georges Davy, and Paul Fauconnet applied Durkheim's ideas in their own studies. Mauss was Durkheim's nephew and collaborator (see Durkheim and Mauss 1903); he had helped by collecting and organising the statistical data used in Durkheim's study of suicide. Mauss applied Durkheim's ideas to gift exchange and magic (Mauss 1925, 1902), while Fauconnet (1920) applied them to law and crime. Davy (1922) constructed a powerful account of contractual relations on the basis of a strong conception of the collective mind or mentality, and he was the key defender of Durkheimianism in public disputes. Like Mauss, Davy was particularly concerned with 'primitive' societies, and he collaborated with Alexandre Moret in a comparative study of primitive and ancient types of social organisation (Moret and Davy 1924).

Among the most original and independent articulators of Durkheimian sociology were Maurice Halbwachs, Celestin Bouglé, and Lucien Lévy-Bruhl. Halbwachs's earliest work (1912) was concerned with the differentiation of social classes and he went on to relate class milieus to forms of class awareness (1938b). He was particularly concerned with the collective representations involved in class consciousness and undertook pioneering investigations into the part played by collectively shared memories in the cultural constitution of classes (1925).[23] Groups that live through the same events will, nevertheless, experience and remember them differently. They will each construct myths and narratives that owe as much to their solidarity as a group as they do to the actual events that are remembered in them. Halbwachs also extended Durkheim's studies of suicide (1930) and social morphology (1938a). His account of suicide related differences in suicide rates to the morphological differences between villages and cities, and he paid rather more attention to individual differences than had Durkheim.

Bouglé undertook studies of egalitarianism (1899) and democracy (1904) in which he showed that the increases in population that result in social differentiation also lead to higher levels of individualism and a greater degree of equality. It is the overlapping and intersecting of group memberships and the absence of strong and exclusive sectional attachments in modern societies that are the basis of their organic solidarity, and that favour both democracy and equality. In a study of the Indian caste system, Bouglé (1908) showed that the mechanical solidarity inherent in the hierarchical structure of caste relations confines people within specific social groups and allows them far less freedom of action. Bouglé (1922) later wrote a more general account of political values as objective cultural products.

Lévy-Bruhl's exploration of morality and knowledge (1900, 1910, 1921) reconstructed Comte's stages of social thought into a simpler dichotomy. He identified a specifically 'primitive mentality' that is quite distinct from the modern, rational and scientific mentality. The magical and animistic beliefs that

Comte had referred to as 'theological' forms of knowledge involve specifically 'mystical' forms of thinking. This primitive, pre-logical thought, Lévy-Bruhl argued, is unconstrained by experience, evidence, or logical connection. For this reason, he claimed, primitive and civilised mentalities define totally different conceptual worlds for their members. Primitive and civilised people may live in the same place, but they inhabit different worlds.

Durkheimian views were also influential outside the sociology departments. Antoine Meillet's studies in comparative linguistics (1903, 1921–36), Marcel Granet's studies of Chinese thought and society (1922, 1929), Maurice Bloch's account of feudalism (1938), and Henri Hubert's investigation of Celtic society (1932b, 1932a) were all strongly Durkheimian in character. In economics, François Simiand showed that money, production, wages, and currency could all be seen as social facts whose interrelations expressed collective judgements of social values. Echoing Durkheim's methodology for the study of suicide rates, Simiand (1932) argued that movements in prices, wages, and currency rates depend upon rates of gold production and shifts in social values.

FOCUS: ÉMILE DURKHEIM

Émile Durkheim was, of course, the key figure in setting out this organicist approach to social theory and exercised a great influence globally, as well as in France. A good illustration of this approach, in addition to Durkheim's own works, is Marcel Mauss on *The Gift* (1925). The key statement of the position is that in Durkheim's *Rules of the Sociological Method* (1895), Chapters 1 and 2.

The definitive biography of Durkheim is Steven Lukes's *Émile Durkheim: His Life and Work* (1973), which gives a thorough account of his approach to the subject.

Social Systems, Forces, and Energy

The second form of system theory in the formative period relied mainly on ideas from mechanics to produce models of societies as systems of forces or energy in a state of equilibrium. This took its inspiration from the 'social physics' mooted by Adolphe Quételet (1835, 1848), whose aim was to provide a firm foundation for the statistical study of social facts. Through this means, he hoped to advance the idea of society as a law-governed system of interdependent elements in a state of equilibrium. The specifically statistical version of this was developed in Italy by Enrico Morselli (1898, 1879) in studies of suicide and health and by Corrado Gini (see the following chapter). Mechanical systems theories were especially influential among economists who sought to cast their arguments into a broader economic sociology. These writers did not deny the subjectivity of human action or the meaningful character of social life. They held that in so far as individuals act rationally in pursuit of self-interest – as they do in their economic activities – then certain determinate consequences follow. These consequences can be modelled, and perhaps predicted, without the need for direct investigation into the cultural meanings that inform people's actions.

Force and Energetics

Friedrich List (1841) and Herman Gossen (1853) were among the earliest to propose a system model of the economy in which 'force' was the central concept. In their view, labour – physical human 'effort' – was the economic form of force. The most systematic writer was Henry Carey (1858–9), influenced by List, who saw his economic theory as part of a larger theory of forces. He analysed the attraction and motion of individuals using concepts of mass, distance, and gravitation, which he saw producing centrifugal and centripetal processes in social systems. Carey proposed a law of 'molecular gravitation' according to which social attraction among rational, self-interested individuals varies directly with 'mass' and inversely with 'distance'. The concentration of individuals into urban areas, for example, reduces the physical distances that separate them and increases the overall mass of people within a particular space. This, in turn, increases the gravitational attraction among individuals and tends to draw in others from neighbouring areas. The coexistence of rival urban centres within a system of cities defines patterns of migration and conquest, and the system eventually settles into equilibrium.

Carey (1872) proposed the ultimate unification of psychological and sociological theory with the natural sciences through a unified theory of force. He argued that forces of all kinds – light, heat, electro-magnetism, gravity, chemical bonding, and psychological attraction – are forms of the same basic force and can be seen as mutually convertible one into another. The principal force at work in social affairs is that of 'gregarious association', which he regarded not merely as analogous to physical gravitation but as an actual form of gravity itself.

Social equilibrium, then, can be modelled directly on mechanical equilibrium. The circulation of energy through an economy, for example, expands national wealth and power, and any obstructions and disruptions to this flow generate the pressures and strains that change the system state towards or away from equilibrium.

Eugen Dühring (1873) took his inspiration from Carey and saw force as the basis of all social activity, equating violent and coercive force with the forces of physics. The central institution of force in any society is its state, which establishes the conditions under which other social institutions must exist. Institutions such as slavery, wage labour, and property, as 'constitutional forms', are the infrastructure or 'frame' within which 'secondary' economic laws operate. Economic activity, then, is embedded in a framework of institutions sustained by the force of the state.

Friedrich Engels (1876, 1888) developed many of his own views through a critical dialogue with Dühring's social physics. His pamphlet on *Socialism: Utopian and Scientific* (in Engels 1876) forms a section of his larger work on Dühring, and Marx himself had helped to draft some parts of the book. The argument was most fully developed in the *Dialectics of Nature* (Engels 1886), but this work remained unfinished at Engels's death. Some parts of it were published in 1896 and 1898, but a complete text was not published until 1925. As he developed his argument, elaborating on Marx's famous 1859 *Preface* and its associated texts, Engels came very close to the social physics that he was criticising. Marx's system model, then, was assimilated to mechanical systems of forces or vectors in equilibrium, producing an economistic view of history that allowed little autonomy for cultural phenomena.

Physics was transformed in the last part of the nineteenth century through the work of James Joule, James Clerk Maxwell (1865, 1877), and others who moved from force to energy as the fundamental concept. The German physicist Georg Helm (1887) suggested some applications of these ideas to economic systems, but the most influential advocate of this new view of 'energetics' was Wilhelm Ostwald (1909, 1914).[24] Ostwald, a chemist, saw energy as the foundation on which to build a sociology (1912). Social order, he argued, makes possible the efficient transformation of raw energy into 'useful energy', and material wealth is a form of useful energy that can be accumulated and put to productive purposes in the economy, the state, and the wider social world. Equilibrium processes, following thermodynamic principles, reflect the flow of energy through the system.

Similar arguments were advanced by Ernest Solvay (1904, 1910) in Brussels and by Spirou Haret (1910) in Paris. In his sole venture into social theory, published only in French, Haret, a Romanian mathematician and engineer, saw all social systems as shaped by economic, intellectual, and moral variables. An individual can be represented by a magnitude on each of these three variables, which define their economic condition, their intellectual capacity, and their moral standing. The three variables together constitute the axes of a three-dimensional social space within which these individuals can be plotted by their coordinates. Each individual, therefore, occupies an overall social position in this space, and their behaviour can be explained by changes in the factors that alter their position along each of the axes.

Carey's work inspired some later economists to pursue the application of social physics to the study of social problems (Carver 1924; Sims 1924), echoing the 'energetics' of Ostwald, but this, too, had little influence outside economics departments. Social physics had some impact on American sociology through George Lundberg (1939), who agreed with Vilfredo Pareto that association and dissociation, understood as the motion and energy of individuals and groups, produces a force field that can be studied mathematically without reference to subjective states of mind. Economic equilibrium models, with their quantified variables, are simply the clearest examples of such mechanical systems.

Systems and Equilibrium

The most sophisticated formulations of these equilibrium models from within sociology were those of Lester Ward and Vilfredo Pareto. Both came to sociology from a background in the natural sciences, yet constructed comprehensive statements of social theory that showed the potential for using the social physics approach.

Ward was greatly influenced by Comte, and his sociology encompassed both the structural features of social systems (1897, 1903; and see Dealey and Ward 1905) and their change over time (1883). He also produced a related account of the social psychology of human action (1893). He saw the 'social forces' at work in structures and institutions forcing systems into a state of equilibrium, or what he called 'synergy'. Because the balance of forces alters continually, change in a system follows a 'moving equilibrium' as it adapts to its environment.[25] The achievement of an equilibrium state cannot be understood without reference to the meanings and purposes that individuals give to their actions, as it is the actions of individuals in relation to the problems generated by the system that drives social change. For much of the time, individuals reproduce established social institutions unreflectively, in routine, habitual actions. As they acquire a rational understanding of their lives, however, they increase their capacity for conscious collective control or 'social telesis' (Ward 1906).

Pareto (1916) used the language of the social organism, but he owed far more to mechanics than to biology. Taking up the suggestions of Helm, he saw social wholes as systems of interdependent social forces in a state of equilibrium that can be described in a set of simultaneous equations. Social theory must identify the forces to be measured and represented as variables in the equations.[26] Pareto's main concern was to measure the variables that define the distribution of motives and resources and to use these variables to construct social laws. He recognised that such variables were difficult to quantify, but he felt this was possible in the case of economic action. Individuals act rationally in pursuit of consciously determined economic purposes, so economic theories can use quantitative scientific methods to study them (1896–7). In the case of these 'logical' actions, all variables can be quantified in monetary terms. The laws of economics, therefore, are mechanical laws that describe the contingently rational forms of action that have, in modern societies, achieved a precarious autonomy from the more irrational elements in social life. Pareto saw his ideas as complementing neo-classical economic theory (see Chapter 4), to which he contributed a law describing the shape of the curve of income distribution. Pareto's views were taken up and promoted by Lawrence Henderson (1935) as the basis of the sociological system that he hoped to establish at Harvard. Participants in his seminar joined in this attempt to establish a new synthesis (Homans and Curtis 1934; Parsons 1937: Chs. 5–7), but they had little impact beyond Harvard.

Perhaps the strongest version of social physics was produced in Russia by Aleksandr Bogdanov (1913–22), real name Aleksandr Aleksandrovich Malinovskii.[27] Influenced by Ostwald's energetics, he also drew on some of the ideas of Dühring and combined these with an extreme positivist philosophy (1904–6) that led to the ruthless suppression of his work by the Bolsheviks (see Lenin 1909; and see also Plekhanov 1908) and minimised his influence.[28] His central concept was that of a system or 'organised complex', consisting of interdependent elements with emergent, self-organising properties in relation to their environment. An organised complex is an open system in a state of dynamic equilibrium with respect to its environment. Bogdanov saw this as a generalisation of ideas that he had earlier applied to the social world in a study of economics (1897).

Despite its suppression, Bogdanov's work had some influence on Bukharin (1921), who was one of the few orthodox Marxists to take 'sociological' ideas seriously. He saw the interchange of energy among the parts of systems as the means through which equilibrium is gradually established. The 'dialectical' aspect of Marxism was seen, as in Engels, as a way of describing the disturbance and re-establishment of equilibrium in successive modes of production. Although this rapprochement with sociology was initially encouraged under Bolshevik rule, Bukharin was later marginalised and eventually discredited and executed when Lenin's works were codified as the ruling ideology of the Soviet Union under Stalin. Bukharin (1919) had, however, previously made some use of Lenin's arguments in his criticisms of the equilibrium models of conventional economics.

The various views on social systems were attempts to explore the systemic properties of social relations and cultural ideas that result from the cultural formation of individuals. The nature of social systems has been understood differently in the various theorists, but they share the view that these systemic properties can be studied as phenomena in their own right and without detailed consideration of the cultural meanings that inform them. This was sometimes over-interpreted as a claim that nothing other than social systems need be studied, but I have sought to show that their arguments depend closely on an awareness of the mechanisms of cultural formation. System ideas are an important and integral part of sociological explanation, finding their place alongside the other themes highlighted in this chapter.

FOCUS: VILFREDO PARETO

Among the diverse writers exploring the idea of the system of forces, Vilfredo Pareto stands out for the scope of his work and his influence within sociology, economics, and political science. His large and rambling book, *A Treatise on General Sociology* (1916), contains his main ideas, and the key to his view of the social system can be found on pages 1433–58.

Although a number of biographical remarks are contained in the generally positive reviews produced by Henderson and by Homans and Curtis, there is no definitive biography of Pareto. A good overview of his ideas can be found in Charles Powers's *Vilfredo Pareto* (1987).

Socialisation and Enculturation

Ideas of cultural formation and systemic organisation worked closely together. In each case, there was also a recognition that individuals must learn the ideas and meanings through which their social relations can be systemically organised. Many of these theorists, however, assumed this to be a relatively unproblematic process and so gave little detailed attention to it: some were quite hostile to what they saw as explanations in terms of individual ideas. A significant number of theorists, however, saw a need to directly explore the processes of socialisation through which individuals are made, or fail to be made, into fully cultural persons with the capacities to generate the systemic, structural properties of social life.

Those who studied the processes of socialisation identified a variety of mechanisms of cultural acquisition. The most common approaches stressed socialisation through imitation, identification, and feelings of sympathy, while a further approach examined the social pressures that operated in both small groups and large crowds to reinforce these. A further theoretical approach focused on the shaping of the inherited responses and skills of human beings into conscious and purposive acts, producing an evolutionary psychology of mind and social action. Some theorists reflected on the diversity of human beings and suggested means through which individuals could be formed with distinct racial or sexual characters and, despite any common biological inheritance, exhibit much diversity of perspective and experience. A final set of theorists explored emotional and cognitive development in relation to the complex and changing balance between inherited capacities and social context at different stages in the life course.

Imitation, Diffusion, and Pressure

The earliest of the theorists who focused on imitation and social pressure was Walter Bagehot (1872). Drawing on suggestions first made about imitation by David Hume (1751), Bagehot argued that most human behaviour is the result either of inherited and unreflective behavioural reactions or of habits acquired through training and frequent repetition. In either case, instinctive responses must be seen as culturally formed, with imitation being the key mechanism at work in this cultural transmission. Bagehot was an early advocate of Darwinian ideas and saw this imitation as the means through which natural selection operates on cultural traits. Ways of acting and thinking originate because they are useful or adaptive in some specific circumstances, but they are perpetuated only when they are imitated. Through copying the successful actions of those around them, individuals ensure that these actions are 'selected' and become shared habits of action within a community. Imitation was seen by Bagehot as rooted in an innate 'copying propensity', but this is reinforced by passive group pressure to conform. People wish to act and feel like those around them because this appears to be the natural or normal way to act or feel. Thus, Bagehot saw most actions as the routinised, habitual results of imitation. Innovative actions are found only among a minority of 'great minds' who become influential leaders of fashion. Their actions and opinions become the models for others to follow.

The best-known exponent of the idea of imitation was Gabriel Tarde (1890), who also held that there is an inherited instinct or propensity for imitation and saw all cultural phenomena as the results of imitative acts. People who observe and understand the behaviour of those around them will instinctively copy this. The so-called collective mentality is simply communication and imitation among individual minds. As a result, cultural traits and practices are established and reproduced through the repetition and replication of actions from one person to another.

Like Bagehot, Tarde saw most people as followers and imitators, and very few individuals as truly creative or innovative. When innovations do occur, however, they spread through imitation, and Tarde (1901) posited a process of 'imitative radiation' through which 'waves' of diffusion spread innovations through a dense 'network of radiations' that follows the contours of social relations. Where such waves intersect, they may weaken or reinforce each other, or they may completely obliterate each other. The task of sociology is to formulate laws to describe innovation, imitation, and diffusion (1898, summarising 1895, 1897).

Tarde's emphasis on the individual level brought him into conflict with his compatriot Durkheim, though Worms (1921) tried to combine this socialisation theory with an organicist view of society. Émile Waxweiler (1906), at the Solvay Institute in Belgium, also stressed the importance of mutual influence, including imitation, as the means through which inherited biological conditions can produce the altruism that underlies social solidarity. His ideas, however, minimised properly social influences and were closer to the physicalist behaviourism then emerging in the United States (Watson 1919).

The principal theorist of social pressure was Gustav Le Bon. His early studies on Indian and Arabic cultures (1884, 1887, generalised in 1895b) were followed by an attempt to use psychological ideas to explain cultural conformity (1895a). He saw the 'racial' or ethnic spirit of a culture as an essentially conservative force and saw innovation occurring through the contacts among populations. This meant that, as Tarde pointed out, innovations in a stable society are produced by a creative minority and spread to the passive majority through processes of imitation. He saw crowds and social gatherings as the principal means through which imitation is facilitated. What Durkheim called the 'social effervescence' of collective activity encourages conformity and people are swayed by mass opinion. Le Bon (1912) used this idea to explain revolutionary mobilisation and change through mass action. Similar crowd psychologies were developed by Scipio Sighele (1891, 1903b; see also 1903a) in Italy, Herman Visser (1911, 1916) in the Netherlands, and Endo Ryukichi in Japan.

A similar approach was taken by Franklin Giddings, for many years Head of Sociology at Columbia University. Following Adam Smith, Giddings (1896, abridged in 1898; see also 1922, 1924) saw human sociation rooted in a natural 'sympathy' and gregariousness. Individuals relate to each other in terms of perceived similarities that make it possible for them to identify with each other. Through linguistic communication among those who identify common concerns, 'reflective sympathy' builds a 'consciousness of kind'. Actions are regulated by a desire to conform to the social expectations of those with whom a person identifies, and this is what makes imitation such an important mechanism

Edward Ross (1908) worked along similar lines, arguing that 'suggestion' is a means through which people can manipulate the motives and meanings of others, though his early work (1901) had held to a simple enculturation thesis. He identified a number of ways in which collective influences can control and shape individual actions, ranging from the loosely organised influences of 'crowd' pressure to the more structured formations of public opinion. Even in a modern society organised around 'publics', the 'mob mind' and suggestibility can make themselves felt in such 'irrational' phenomena as fads, crazes, and fashions.

An alternative approach to social pressure was taken by Kurt Lewin. Trained in physiological psychology under Wolfgang Köhler (1917), originator of the idea of the physiological 'field' (*Gestalt*) that structures perceptions. Lewin (1936a, 1936b) transformed this into a social concept and saw the collective mentality of a group as a 'psychic field' that shapes individual perceptions and motivation. This psychic field is shaped by forces of attraction and repulsion among the members of a group and with outsiders.[29] Lewin took the terminology of the field from Albert Einstein's work on the mathematics of electromagnetic fields ands explicitly addressed the need to build a social physics of socialisation. Internalised perceptions of social relations generate the psychic strains and tensions that make any group a field of interpersonal forces. This creates pressures on individual group members that cause them to change their attitude and orientation towards their group and the wider society. Thus, conformity and consensus result from pressures imposed by group members on each other.[30]

Instinct, Habit, and Purpose

Hobhouse (1901) had pursued some of Bagehot's arguments in his evolutionary psychology, holding that a common biological inheritance of instincts and impulses can be expressed in a variety of culturally specific ways. Linguistic communication, as the means of cultural transmission, is the basis on which impulses, drives, and the available means for their satisfaction can be reflected upon and subjected to control in purposive actions. Similar views were proposed by his colleague Graham Wallas (1908, 1914), who defined cultural values and ideas as the 'social heritage' that complements the biological heritage and shapes actions into the habitual, routinised forms that make predictable social activities possible.

The mechanisms involved in the social construction of instincts were more fully elaborated by William McDougall. Having devised a folk psychology of the 'group mind' (1920) to explain the fieldwork data collected during Alfred Haddon's anthropological expedition to the Torres Straits, he turned to the mechanisms through which individuals can be socialised into such a collective mentality (1908; see also his general psychology of 1905). McDougall's collective psychology (1920) was published shortly before he left Britain for the United States, where he published a general psychology (1923) and became the great rival to Ross (1908).[31] He saw action as purposive or 'hormic', but, nevertheless, driven by the impulses and emotions formed in the course of biological evolution (1919; see also Ginsberg 1932; Sprott 1937). All inherited dispositions are expressed in instinctive responses to environmental stimuli, but the particular ways in which these responses are manifested depend on social learning. Cultural knowledge and expectations, transmitted from generation to generation, shape the inherited impulses into purposive actions and into habits and forms of emotional expression. There is a social construction of impulses and instincts into actions and practices.

McDougall's theory also gave strong support to the claims made by Tarde and Giddings. He held that sympathy for others could be explained as originating in instinctively based emotions of 'fellow feeling', and Wilfred Trotter (1908, 1909) suggested that all social solidarity is grounded in such a 'herd instinct'. McDougall emphasised that, like all other instincts, this identification with others is culturally shaped. Interaction involves one person 'impressing' another by suggestion or example and so calling forth a sympathetic or imitative response in the other. It is through such processes of impression and imitation that children develop a specifically social sense of self. Children identify with those others with whom they interact and come to judge their own behaviour by these standards.

Leon Petrazycki or Petrazhytski (1908–10), a Pole who spent many years in Russia, produced an instinct-based theory of socialisation in which emotions are the ultimate driving forces behind legal institutions. One of his students in Russia, Georges Gurvitch, lived for much of his later life in Paris and produced important texts on legal institutions (1932, 1942), though he did not follow this socialisation theory.

The Relativity of Perspectives

McDougall's work on the social construction of instincts had been inspired by field studies that highlighted cultural relativity: no theory of socialisation, it would seem, could rely solely on inherited biological mechanisms. This also applied, of course, to cultural variations within societies, though he gave these relatively little attention. Marxism had highlighted class differences in consciousness and outlook, but gave no significant attention to how these were acquired. Around the turn on the nineteenth century, things began to change as theorists began to pay more attention to the nature and effects of race and sex differences.

William Du Bois (1903) explicitly theorised race as a social category, based on his ethnographic study of a black district in Philadelphia (1899). He rejected the idea that race is merely an innate, biological condition, arguing that it had to be seen as a social construct imposed on individuals through their socialisation and determining their identities in the eyes of others. Those designated the same race share a sense of identity as part of a community, and the shared cultural traits of a racial group are the products of their shared history and experiences. It is important also to mention Anna Cooper (1892), now seen as a precursor of black feminism, who argued for the full inclusion of black men and women in American society.

Charlotte Gilman (1898, 1911) and Olive Schreiner (1899, 1911) produced strikingly novel accounts of female standpoints and experiences. Gilman saw the economic dependence of women on men as a historical product that confines them to domestic work and motherhood. It originates, she argued, in the 'excessive sex-attraction' that had developed in the human species and had been crystallised and reinforced through cultural evolution. As a result, women and men inhabit different social worlds and acquire different outlooks on life. Schreiner, too, saw practical experiences of distinctive ways of life underpinning the socialisation of women and men. In particular, she stressed the 'sex parasitism' that produces the distinctive male and female personalities and points of view, alluding also to class and race parasitism . The psychological characteristics of men and women, she held, are not purely biological matters but follow from the particular social relations in which they are involved. Women are involved in particular kinds of paid and unpaid labour, most particularly in mothering and caring within the home, and this produces their restricted and skewed participation in the labour market.

FOCUS: CHARLOTTE GILMAN

The work of Charlotte Gilman is at last being recognised as a major contribution to the analysis of gender difference and social standpoint. Her most systematic statement is in *The Man-Made World* (1911), and a clear summary of key points can be found in Chapters 1, 2, and 14.

The standard biography of Gilman is Ann Lane's *To Herland and Beyond* (1990), but there is not yet any comprehensive critical assessment of Gilman's contribution to social theory.

Social Difference and Social Construction

These arguments had some limited effect on those producing theories of socialisation, but only a very few theorists attended to individual variations in socialisation or their consequences for structured variations in social consciousness. The most influential of these new theories of socialisation was that developed at the University of Chicago. William Thomas stressed that action is oriented as much by a 'definition of the situation' as by the actual situation, and this implies the need for a theory of the processes through which the meanings of situations are constructed. This was provided by George Mead, who studied with Wundt, collaborated with Cooley, drew on James's (1890) theory of self formation, used John Baldwin's (1897) account of imitation, and drew on McDougall's view of the instinctive basis of behaviour and on childhood and the self (see Mead 1909). He planned to publish his 'social behaviourism' in book form, but his text (1910) was lost and not published until long after his death. His ideas appeared in a series of papers, but the most systematic statement was in a collection of lecture notes (1927) published, posthumously, in 1934.[32] One of his students, Herbert Blumer, was famously to christen this theory 'symbolic interactionism' (1937).

Mead took the pragmatist position that ideas acquire their meanings and significance from the practical consequences to which they lead. He held that individuals act on the basis of the meanings that objects and situations have for them and so are involved in an ongoing process of 'interpretation' through which they define and negotiate these meanings. This occurs symbolically, using words and other conventional forms of expression. Social institutions are established as the common and recurrent symbolic responses of the members of a social group to the particular situations that they encounter in their actions. Conformity with institutions occurs because people anticipate the likely reaction of others to any deviance. Most importantly, they anticipate the likely reaction of the 'generalised other' – their image of the community as a whole or of the particular section of the community with whom they frequently and typically interact.

Mead saw socialisation as a process through which children learn to see the world as others see it as they 'internalise' the viewpoints of others. Central to this is the building of a sense of self that, as in Cooley, 'reflects' the attitudes taken by others. The evolving conscience of a child, for example, is a result of its internalisation of the attitudes of the generalised other. Through learning to see the world as others see it and taking on their attitudes, people come to develop a sense of the self – of 'me' – which derives directly from the ways they are seen by others. Through conscious reflection, their identities and proposed actions can be appraised and new actions planned – plans for how 'I' should act. Thus, the mind is structured socially as a self, as an 'I' and a 'me', and people are able to sociate as true members of their society, rather than simply as those who happen to occupy the same physical space.

This approach had many similarities with the ideas developed by Mead's colleagues John Dewey (1930) and Charles Ellwood (1927; see also 1917, 1925). In Iceland, Guðmundur Finnbogason (1912) produced an account of socialisation and imitation that drew on William James and Henri Bergson and had anticipated some of Mead's ideas. He held that imitation makes possible a 'sympathetic comprehension' through which the meanings of situations can be constructed.[33] Another related view is the 'differential association' theory of crime developed by Edwin Sutherland (1939), which showed that people tend to conform to the behavioural examples of those with whom they associate most frequently, and that variations in behaviour can be explained by the barriers and obstacles that exist to association and communication.

The concern for difference and diversity in socialisation was taken furthest by Karl Jaspers (1913; see also 1919, 1932b), who focused on those extreme individual variations that are often described as pathological. Jaspers trained in medicine at Heidelberg, moved into psychiatric work, and pioneered the use of existential phenomenology to interpret the psychiatric symptoms and cognitive processes of his patients. Like Martin Heidegger (1927), he saw human interpretations of the world as resulting from practical engagement in it. Mental life is experienced through the body, and in addition to delusions, dementia, amnesia, false memories, and dreams, Jaspers looked at speech disorders, involuntary gestures, and other forms of 'somatic expression'.

Although the meanings of objects are situationally negotiated, many everyday objects are pre-defined and made ready-to-hand for practical purposes. This limits the extent to which they can be re-defined by participants. Definitions and interpretations are intersubjective reflections of the assumed perspective of a larger 'they' and are the basis of 'normal' socialisation. Those labelled as mentally ill, on the other hand, have often arrived at idiosyncratic, and apparently bizarre, everyday meanings, and Jaspers sought to make sense of such psychiatric symptoms through a process of *Verstehen* or understanding. An interpretative psychology, he argued, must uncover the meaningful connections made by psychiatric patients and interpret them in relation to their particular biography and social situation. The mentally deranged have built meaningful worlds within which their thoughts and actions make sense to them, if not to others. Psychiatric symptoms arise within a family context as problems of communication and misunderstanding and are reinforced when actions are misinterpreted by others. This led Jaspers to question the sharp distinction between 'health' and 'illness', relativising these terms and relating them to the organisation of the medical profession.

FOCUS: GEORGE MEAD

The key to understanding symbolic interactionist ideas is to understand George Mead. Although he published many papers, the book for which he is best known is the posthumous compilation of his lectures that was published as *Mind, Self and Society* (1927). Parts 3 and 4 contain his central ideas, but they are more accessibly presented in his 1913 essay on 'The Social Self' in Reck's (1964) collection of *Selected Writings*, pages 142–9.

A brief biography of Mead can be found in Gary Cook's *George Herbert Mead: The Making of a Social Pragmatist* (1993). The best of the available commentaries is Hans Joas's *G.H. Mead* (1980).

Sexuality, Cognition, and Development

Sigmund Freud's psychoanalysis, too, sought to make 'pathological' psychological processes meaningful, but it did so by stressing the 'unconscious' aspects of mind. Freud's studies of nervous disorders led him to conclude that it is the mental processing of biological influences, rather than the biological conditions themselves, that produces the psychological problems experienced by neurotic patients. He gave particular attention to childhood experiences and their continuing effects on adult mental health. While his initial view was that repressed memories of childhood seduction result in hysterical symptoms (Breuer and Freud 1895), he soon came to conclude that *imagined* sexual experiences in childhood were crucial: children misunderstand or misinterpret events that nevertheless become 'real' memories for them.

Human activity is driven by the search for the pleasurable satisfaction of desires rooted in 'libido' or instinctual psychic energy. During normal sexual development, individuals repress desires that are felt to be inappropriate. Failures of sexual development involve the 'return' of these repressed drives as slips of the tongue, dream symbolism, and hysterical symptoms (Freud 1900, 1901, 1905). Dreams, for example, are narratives constructed according to rules of symbolic expression, though both the rules and the underlying repressed desires that they encode are unconscious. Dream contents, therefore, are not transparent expressions of their real meanings. The interpretation of dreams, Freud argued, is a means for understanding the repressed memories and, therefore, of freeing people from their effects.

Freud (1923) used the term 'id' to refer to the unconscious and impulsive drives that influence people without their conscious awareness. This psychological structure is oriented towards seeking pleasure and avoiding pain. The conscious mind – the 'ego' – must give meaning to experiences of these drives without having a full knowledge of them. Freud saw human action as resulting from the interplay between the 'pleasure principle' of the impulsive id and the 'reality principle' of the reflective and controlling ego. Social life depends upon the ability of the ego to repress or defer immediate gratification in order to achieve practical goals. During socialisation, a part of the ego is split off as the moral conscience, or 'superego', and Freud saw this internalised system of social values as the 'introjected' authority of the father.

Some developments of psychoanalysis took place in Britain. Wilfred Trotter (1915) had introduced his brother-in-law, Ernest Jones, to the work of Freud, and Jones became the 'principal populariser' of Freudian ideas in Britain, making great efforts to integrate Freud's account of the unconscious with McDougall's analysis of instincts (Jones 1924, 1936). McDougall (1936) integrated some arguments from Freud into his later work, seeing this as concerned with the specifically sexual instincts. William Rivers (1920) followed a similar direction in his clinical work on 'shell shock' during the First World War, having previously undertaken investigations into kinship structures (1914, 1924) that influenced his student Alfred Radcliffe-Brown.[34]

Melanie Klein and Anna Freud, both of whom settled in Britain, reiterated Freud's emphasis on the biological origin of unconscious desires and the central importance of sexuality. Melanie Klein had moved to Britain in 1927, publishing her first book on child psychology (1932) in both Vienna and London. Klein stressed the importance of aggression as a driving impulse, seeing this as producing the destructive envy that underpins emotions of jealousy and greed. Such envy, turned back upon itself, results in depressive and obsessive conditions. The Freud family left Vienna in 1938, following the *Anschluss*, and they also moved to London. Anna Freud's approach was close to that of her father, though she gave particular attention to the psychic defences and unconscious aggression that result from the 'denial' of libidinal impulses (1936).

Carl Jung (1921) broke with Freud in 1913 and developed a concept of libido as less exclusively sexual than Freud had claimed. His main contribution, however, was to complement the idea of the collective mentality with that of the collective unconscious. This unconscious repository of shared symbols and meanings he saw as inherited biologically as a 'racial' characteristic of particular populations. A more extreme formulation was that of Wilhelm Reich (1933a, 1942), who stressed the biological basis of sexual energy and saw psychoneuroses resulting from the build-up of this energy whenever there are physiological disturbances in sexual function. The failure to develop an adequate 'genital' character and to express this in a mature orgasm, he argued, was one of the causes of the authoritarian character type that sustained fascism (1933b).

Other psychoanalysts who broke with the Freudian orthodoxy gave far more attention to the cultural shaping of personality than had Freud. Alfred Adler (1914, 1928), for example, saw the formation of an 'inferiority complex' in individuals whose desire for recognition and acceptance leads them to judge their own actions as inadequate. He exercised a great influence on the work of Karen Horney (1937, 1946), who explored the 'basic anxiety' that results from a lack of parental warmth in childhood and saw a link between neuroses and particular patterns of cultural socialisation. Harry Sullivan (1939) drew on Adler's ideas and converged with aspects of Mead's view of the self. His concept of the 'self system' was differentiated into the 'good-me', the 'bad-me', and the 'not-me'.

Abram Kardiner, who worked alongside many of Boas's students, added elements of Freudian theory to provide a firmer basis for their enculturation thesis. His approach saw the 'basic personality structure', the core element shared by the members of any particular society, as resulting from childhood socialisation (Kardiner 1945; see also Linton 1945). The 'character' of each individual is a variation on the personality structure shared within the culture. Cora Du Bois (1944) developed a related idea of the 'modal personality structure', holding that key personality traits may be common to most, but not all, members of a particular culture. This approach came to be called the 'culture and personality' approach.[35]

The developmental psychology of the Swiss theorist Jean Piaget drew on Durkheim and on Lévy-Bruhl's ideas on collective mentality. His particular innovation was to see children developing through a sequence of stages, at each of which they exhibit a particular mentality common to all of that same age. He explored this through studies of intelligence, knowledge, and moral judgement (1924, 1936). Movement from one mental stage to the next, he argued, depends on both biological maturation and interaction with the surrounding world. Although the biological aspects of maturation are universal, the types of encounters that children have with their physical and social environment are quite variable and can advance or retard their progression through the stages. Mental structures are established and periodically reconstructed, as children become involved in more complex practical engagements with the physical world and with other people.

Each stage of mental development is distinct and the child's thought operates according to *sui generis* principles appropriate to that stage. Each stage of intelligence, for example, involves specific and distinct principles of reasoning through which knowledge about the world can be built. Infants initially operate in purely sensory ways, through their own physical explorations of the world, and are unable to form representations of objects not immediately present. After age two, however, their brains have matured enough for them to form representations of unseen objects, but they are unable to deduce anything about their properties or behaviour. These powers of deductive reasoning develop between age 6 and 11, when children acquire the ability to imagine different states of the world – they come to understand, for example, that others see the world from a different point of view than their own and so can take the standpoint of the other. The final stage, lasting from age 11 into adulthood, is one in which the ability to think in formal and abstract terms may be acquired. The particular form of intelligence achieved, and the level of formality and abstraction that is possible, depend crucially on the social context of the child's motivation.

The earliest attempts to build a Marxist theory of socialisation made use of Freudian psychoanalysis (Fromm 1941; Horkheimer et al. 1936), but a more original attempt was the developmental psychology of Lev Vygotsky (1930–4, 1934). Initially trained in literature and linguistics, Vygotsky moved into psychology in the 1920s and drew on Durkheim, Halbwachs, and Lévy-Bruhl to build a distinctively Marxist approach. He sought to show that the historical development and transformation of social facts is associated with similar developments in thought and consciousness. Consciousness is shaped by social relations and is mediated through the 'instruments' used in purposive action. The two fundamental dimensions of social development are labour and language, and the corresponding instruments used to mediate consciousness are productive technologies and sign systems.

Socialisation occurs through the communicative use of signs to influence the behaviour and mentality of ourselves and others. This operates through 'internalisation', by which Vygotsky means the transformation of external actions into internal representations and the direct internalisation of collective representations and symbolic codes. Speech, therefore, is the basis through which thought systems are produced. This occurs through a series of stages in which conceptual thinking gradually develops as an autonomous adult capacity. Where Piaget saw the social element in thought as a relatively late development, Vygotsky saw speech – and, therefore, thought – as intrinsically social. The ideological disputes of the 1930s limited Vygotsky's influence and left much of his work unpublished. His *Mind in Society*, consisting of essays, lectures, and papers written between 1930 and 1934, was translated into English only in 1978. The work of his colleague Luria remained unpublished in Russia until the 1970s.

FOCUS: SIGMUND FREUD

Sigmund Freud's analysis of unconscious processes and the levels of the mind were explored in numerous studies. He applied his general approach most famously in *The Interpretation of Dreams* (1900). An accessible statement, based on his later views, can be found in his essay on 'The Ego and the Id' (1923).

The standard biography of Freud is that of Ernest Jones (1953–7). A comprehensive critical assessment of his ideas can be found in Richard Webster's *Why Freud Was Wrong* (1995).

Discussions of culture and socialisation and of the ways in which cultural factors are shaped into social structures with systemic properties led to an explosive growth in our understanding of the social world during the nineteenth century and the first half of the twentieth century. Behind the diversity of contending theories was a cumulative growth in understanding based on an awareness of the interdependence of diverse approaches. These arguments were not, however, the only important strands of sociological debate in this period. In the following chapter I will look at the ways in which issues of interaction, conflict, and nature were handled.

NOTES

1. See Webb (1960).
2. Some German ethnographic work equated *Volk* with 'race', though this term was always used in the sense of 'people' or 'folk' rather than in any biological sense.

3. Pavel Vinogradov (Paul Vinogradoff), who migrated to Britain and became a leading legal historian (1892, 1905, 1908), studied with and was a close associate of Kovalevsky in England and France.

4. Some extracts from Masaryk's works can be found in Woolfolk and Imber (1994).

5. Some of Gökalp's work is extracted in Berkes (1959).

6. Czarnowski's book was first published in Paris, in French, and was published in Polish translation only in 1956.

7. On the connection between sociology and Fascism in Austria see Mozetič (1992).

8. Some of his papers have been brought together in Codere (1966).

9. Whorf published an important series of essays during the 1930s, reprinted in Whorf (1956).

10. The word 'sociation' was later used to translate a similar idea in Simmel's work. Stuckenberg himself spent fifteen years in Berlin during the 1880s and 1890s and may have had some contact with Simmel.

11. See Den Otter (1996), Vincent and Plant (1984), Milne (1962) and Inglis (1982).

12. See also Boucher and Vincent (1993).

13. Urwick's book of 1927 was published shortly after he left the LSE to work in the United States with Robert MacIver, who had left Britain some years previously. On the work of the Bosanquets see McBriar (1987).

14. However, some of his colleagues and supporters – most notably Morris Ginsberg (1921) and Robert MacIver (1917) – contrasted Hobhouse's view of society with what they described as the 'group mind' posited by the Oxford idealists. They also attributed this 'group mind' view to Durkheim, as Talcott Parsons (1970) discovered when he studied at the LSE.

15. The methodological implications of this argument were later drawn out by Winch (1958), who stressed similarities with the arguments of the later Wittgenstein (1953).

16. See Herf (1984).

17. Müller-Lyer produced a six-volume 'System of Sociology' with the general title 'The Developmental Stages of Humanity'. Only Volumes 1, 4, and 5 have been translated into English, at the suggestion of Hobhouse.

18. See Allardt (2000), Pipping (1982), and various essays in *Acta Philosophica Fennica*, 34 (1982).

19. On pro- and anti-slavery views in American social thought see Ross (1991).

20. Worms maintained close contacts with sociologists in Germany. The copy of his main text (1896) in the British Library of Political and Economic Science has a handwritten inscription from Worms to 'mon cher et savant collègue M. le Prof. Ferdinand Tönnies'.

21. Volume 3 of Greef's *Introduction* was translated in eighteen articles published in the *American Journal of Sociology* between 1903 and 1906.

22. See Clark (1973, 1972) and Besnard (1983).

23. This book has been partially translated in Coser (1992).
24. See Stokes (1995: 128–39).
25. See the discussion of equilibrium models in Russett (1966).
26. See also Bellini (1934).
27. Bogdanov was also a writer of science fiction (Bogdanov 1905).
28. See the discussion in Biggart et al. (1998).
29. Lewin's essays of the 1920s and 1930s were collected together in book form and published in 1936, shortly after he moved to the United States.
30. Lewin's arguments were, in some respects, attempts to elucidate the psychological consequences of the formal sociologies of Alfred Vierkandt and Leopeld von Wiese, discussed in the following chapter. In a related vein, the Viennese psychotherapist Jacob Moreno developed ideas about the effects of group structure on individual mentality, publishing his work (1934) after arriving in the United States.
31. On McDougall see Hearnshaw (1964: Ch. 12). Ginsberg's (1921) critical comments on the group mind thesis are presented in the context of what is, otherwise, a favourable outline of similar views to McDougall on the socialisation of biological impulses.
32. Many of Mead's essays are collected in Morris (1938) and Reck (1964).
33. See Hauksson (2000).
34. See the biography of Rivers in Slobdin (1978) and the fictionalised account in Barker (1992).
35. This approach had little significant impact in the United States until much later, when Parsons began to develop a Freudian account of internalisation. See Parsons and Bales (1956).

4

Action, Conflict, and Nature: Formative Views

The arguments of formative theorists on nature, action, and conflict are examined in this chapter. It is shown that numerous writers converged around the exploration of

- subjectivity, creativity, and rationality in human action

- interaction as the formation of social relations and larger structures of relations

- class and ethnicity as bases of social struggle and social power

- plurality, diversity, and the clash of cultural differences

- environmental and technological influences on human activity

- the spatial differentiation and location of social activities

It is shown that, despite striking political and philosophical differences, social theorists established a substantial common ground of analytical concerns and that these ideas were seen as complementary to those concerning cultural formation, systemic organisation, and socialisation.

Formative theories of the social set out the basis of sociological analysis. In the previous chapter I looked at their explorations into cultural formation, the systemic character of social activity, and socialisation. Theoretical work in this area showed how social structures are composed and how individual commitment to and involvement in these structures are sustained. The arguments to which I turn in this chapter are concerned with the ways in which systemic cultural processes are related to the natural, material conditions under which they are found, how individual actions and processes of interaction are situationally constructed, and how larger collectivities of individuals come into being and, through their conflict, restructure social systems.

Virtually all the formative theorists recognised that, to a greater or lesser extent, social activities are conditioned by the natural environment in which they take place and by the biological characteristics of human actors. For many social evolutionists this was a particularly strong theme, especially when Charles Darwin's discoveries about biological evolution stimulated attempts to examine processes of 'adaptation' and natural selection. This argument was rarely pursued in detail, however. The effects of the environment and human biology were more typically explored through investigations into the various habitats in which people live and the constraints that these set for human activity. Technologies were seen as socially organised ways in which human activities might, in turn, shape and control natural conditions.

Debates between theorists of cultural formation and theorists of socialisation sometimes took the form of a hostile opposition between 'holistic' and individualistic approaches. Action theorists were often hostile to what they saw as the exaggerated claims of 'structural' theorists, and many opposed any reference to social 'systems'. For others, however, an analysis of action and interaction was seen as a necessary complement to structural and systemic concerns: social structures are, after all, produced and reproduced through human actions, even if they may also have properties that can be analysed without having any direct reference to these individual actions. Actions could also be recognised as shaped by social structures without this requiring that actions and individual actors be treated as mere puppets of system-level processes.

Many theorists recognised distinctive forms of action in the struggles of whole nations, classes, and ethnic groups. Where individuals, on their own, had limited and indirect effects on social change, individuals united into collectivities could have major and rapid effects, From this point of view, historical transformations of cultures and social structures could be seen as the outcome of such conflicts and not simply the results of either individual interaction or the strains and tensions inherent in the systemic connections of social institutions. Such work emphasised that social systems are not always cohesive and solidaristic, and cultures are not always consensual. Social structures are internally pluralistic, formed into contending social groups, whose struggles must be a major topic of sociological investigation.

Action, Interaction, and the Interpersonal

Theories of action initially developed in economic theories that carried forward the work of Adam Smith, Jeremy Bentham, and James Mill on self-interested actions. Economic theorists saw social structures, such as markets and systems of trade, as the emergent outcomes of the rational pursuit of individual interests in production, distribution, and consumption. Late nineteenth-century advances in economic analysis encouraged the construction of broader theories in which both rational and non-rational forms of action were seen as means through which complex structures could be built. This discovery of diverse human purposes had been foreseen in earlier theories of action that stressed the creative character of action and the distorted forms of consciousness that result when human concerns are narrowed down to purely self-interested actions and embodied in objective structures of social relations. This latter view of action had its primary advocate in Karl Marx, while the former theory is particularly associated with Max Weber.

Action, Subjectivity, and Reification

The Marxian theory of action was concerned with purposive activity and the building of the social structures through which people live their lives. These structures are products of human action that tend to be perceived by their creators as things existing independently of them and to which they must adapt. Thus, people's actions are constrained by their own products. The key elements in this view originated with the 'Young Hegelian' writers with whom Marx and his collaborator Friedrich Engels were closely associated. Moses Hess, Arnold Ruge, Bruno Bauer, David Strauss, and Ludwig Feuerbach adopted Hegel's view that human spirit is realised in action, but saw this occurring through creative acts in which individuals could potentially achieve a greater control over their own creations. Forms of social life are 'externalisations' or 'objectifications' of spirit and only a critical consciousness can prevent them from becoming coercive constraints on individual freedom and autonomy. Social forms that were once progressive may become restrictions on individual action, and emancipation from this 'alienation' of the human spirit requires the cultivation of a critical stance towards them. Philosophy, as the critical voice of the human spirit, must challenge ossified institutions and so help to bring about their transformation. History thus involves a negation and transcendence of structures through constant critical acts; it is an ongoing spiral of creation, ossification, negation, and renewal.

The Young Hegelians saw this critical outlook as an aspect of spirit that could be realised in action under certain circumstances. Hess (1841) had located the greatest potential for critical self-awareness among the poor and the dispossessed, seeing their disadvantaged social position as the standpoint from which an authentic critical consciousness and a rational unity of thought and action could develop. The spirit informing their self-conscious actions can be articulated by philosophers, who can thereby promote a community of equals in which human capacities are developed free of all alienation, constraint, and oppression. Feuerbach (1841) added a stronger materialist dimension to this argument, holding that humans do not relate to the world in purely contemplative ways but engage with it through practical, sensual actions and under definite material conditions.

These were the ideas that Marx carried with him into exile in France. His encounter with the Parisian socialism of the 1840s convinced him that all political conflicts are expressions of the economically driven struggles of social classes. Working through the implications of Young Hegelian philosophy for these practical struggles, Marx produced a massive and, at the time, unpublished exploration (1844) of the organisation of labour in capitalist societies and, in his first published works (Marx and Engels 1845; Marx 1847), began the construction of a 'materialist' framework of social analysis. Subjectively oriented economic activities, he argued, are objectified in relations of commodity exchange and property ownership that limit human freedom by alienating people from their own activity. Mere philosophical criticism of alienation will not overcome it, as critical ideas can have a practical effect only if embodied in the consciousness of the alienated and disadvantaged members of society. Hence, the Marxian theory of action led to the conclusion that individual freedom from the alienating structures produced through social action could be achieved only through the *collective* action of the most alienated classes.

This theory of action found echoes among the Russian 'subjectivists' Pytor Lavrov (1868), Nikolai Kareev (1883–90, 1918), and Nikolai Mikhailovskii (1870). Their social theory, characterised as 'Westernism', challenged the cultural theories of Slav nationalism with ideas inspired by French radicalism and populism and by the philosophy of Feuerbach. The subjectivists rejected the extremes of determinism and free will, seeing individual action as a natural, biologically driven phenomenon shaped by subjective values.[1] Social reality is constructed and transformed through the imposition of subjective interpretations in purposive action. They stressed that the cultural creativity of individuals was exercised through their actions, within limits set by the specific social and physical circumstances in which they act, and they engaged in a protracted debate over limitations on the role of individuals in historical change.

Closely related to this view was that of Florian Znaniecki, who applied German Kantianism in his cultural theory of action. Like the Russian subjectivists, he saw social reality resulting from the creative imposition of meanings on the world. The values that inform social actions are historically relative, but acquire an objectivity through the part they play in this socially constructed reality. Znaniecki's influence in his home country of Poland was limited by the fact that much of his work took place in the United States, where he worked with William Thomas at the University of Chicago (Thomas and Znaniecki 1918–19) and where most of his work (Znaniecki 1919, 1925, 1936) was eventually published in English. His work complemented the socialisation theory of George Mead and was echoed in the general orientation to action that Chicago sociologists derived from the pragmatism of William James. Thus, John Dewey (1922) held that most actions are the results of habitual dispositions acquired through immersion in the established customs and social meanings of social groups. These habits are produced through the cultural shaping of impulses that orient people to the situations in which they find themselves. Actions are likely to change when conflicts between impulses and habits become the objects of conscious reflection and deliberation. Such reflective, 'intelligent' action involves choice, as a directed expression of subjective meanings.

Jean-Paul Sartre (1943) produced the most innovative form of this theory of action, drawing on the existentialism of Martin Heidegger (1927), Karl Jaspers (1932b), and Emmanuel Levinas (1930) to depict human actors as faced with the inevitability of choice in the face of 'nothingness'. There is no ultimate foundation for meaningful choice and individuals must take ethical responsibility for their choices. Any attempt to avoid choice and to assign responsibility to those others from whom meanings may have been acquired (to society or to culture) is an act of 'bad faith' that signals an inauthentic existence. People must make their choices on their own, without guidance from outside, and they must live with the 'nausea' they experience when faced with the moral emptiness of the universe. The individual is all, and 'hell is other people' (Sartre 1944). All actual societies, nevertheless, can be seen as massive assemblages of bad faith in which individuals act freely but convince themselves that they do so from moral compulsion or in conformity with social expectations.

FOCUS: JEAN-PAUL SARTRE

The most systematic formulation of these phenomenological and existentialist ideas is that of Jean-Paul Sartre, whose major work is *Being and Nothingness* (1943). This is a difficult work that concentrates on wider philosophical issues. Sartre had a great influence in the post-war period. His argument on nausea and nothingness draws on some of the implications of Marx's theory of alienation from his early manuscripts (1844), and the best way to grasp the importance of this approach is to look at the chapter on 'Estranged Labour' on pages 106–19 of the Lawrence and Wishart edition (widely reprinted elsewhere).

A favourable commentary on the sociological implications of Sartre's work is Ian Craib's *Existentialism and Sociology* (1976). Marx's view of human action is discussed in Vernon Venable's *Human Nature: The Marxian View* (1946) and in Istvan Meszaros's *Marx's Concept of Alienation* (1970).

Rationality, Calculation, and Choice

These critical theories of action arose in reaction to utilitarian theories. The latter saw the 'hidden hand' of the market mechanism as a creation of human actions that, nevertheless, can coordinate those actions and shape their outcomes. The first advance on this position from within economic theory came from John Mill. Given a highly disciplined utilitarian education by his father, James Mill, he broke with its overemphasis on cognitive rationality and began to build a theory that would give greater recognition to emotion and power. Originally intending to extend the psychology of Bain (1855, 1859) into a comprehensive sociology of action, Mill succeeded only in producing a new *Principles of Political Economy* (1848).

The most important advances in economic theory occurred during the last third of the nineteenth century, when Carl Menger (1871, 1883; see also Böhm-Bawerk 1896), Léon Walras (1874), and William Jevons (1871) simultaneously broke with the labour theory of value that dominated earlier economic theory. Accepting that individuals are rational economic agents, concerned to maximise the 'utility' received in their productive activities and exchange relationships, and that social regularities are the 'resultants' of complexes of individual actions, they introduced concepts of 'marginal utility' and 'marginal cost' to explain the allocation of resources to given ends.[2] Central to this 'marginalist' or neo-classical theory was the argument that, for any given commodity, rational actors attach progressively less value to each successive item that they attain. They will, therefore, maximise their value by ensuring that the additional utility gained from an extra unit of consumption is equal to the additional cost of attaining it. Transactions are regulated by principles of supply and demand, with exchanges taking place at an equilibrium point at which each participant has equalised his or her marginal utility on the items gained. Continual incremental adjustments in economic transactions produce observable fluctuations around this equilibrium price. Some detailed improvements to the theory were made by Henry Sidgwick (1883), Alfred Marshall (1890), Arthur Pigou (1912), and Irving Fisher (1919, 1926) – Marshall's key advance being the analysis of demand and supply through intersecting curves on a graph.

Menger saw marginalism as offering a general model for social science. Action, he argued, can be understood and explained *only* in so far as it is rational, and so the marginalist account of action provides a paradigm for the study of all human action. Although action may not seem to be rationally motivated, it should, nevertheless, be explained *as if* it were rational. This emphasis on theoretical fictions and 'as if' explanations is rooted in the neo-Kantian revival that underpinned much action theory and was elaborated by Hans Vaihinger (1911). The wider implications of Menger's claim were drawn out by Ludwig von Mises in Vienna during the 1920s and early 1930s. Mises, a staunch anti-socialist (1922), advocated a rigorous individualism and argued that the marginalist transformation of economics from a science of wealth to a science of choice opened up the possibility of a general theory of rational action – 'praxeology' – that focuses on conscious, purposive, and rational action oriented to the attainment of diverse ends (1949). Real actions, he recognised, involve both conscious and unconscious elements, but praxeology constructs an idealised analysis of the conscious and meaningful structure of purely rational forms of action. It begins from the goals and considerations of real actors and the particular logic of the situation in which they see themselves operating in order to construct an account of what the actor would do if acting with full rationality. A second part of his theory – 'catallactics' – was concerned with the formation of collective entities, such as market mechanisms, through a concatenation of the unintended consequences of actions. Social collectivities have no substantial reality of their own but exist only in and through the actions of the individuals who participate in them.

FOCUS: LUDWIG VON MISES

In the formative period, purely rational theories of action were largely confined to economics. The writer who did the most to systematise this framework as a general theory of action is Ludwig von Mises in his *Human Action* (1949). An accessible summary of some of the key ideas can be found in von Hayek's 1945 essay on 'The Use of Knowledge in Society', reprinted in his *Individualism and the Economic Order* (1949), pages 77–91.

Actions, Relations, and Structures

The dominant approach to action in German sociology placed the marginalist model of rational action within a more general conception of action. Its leading figure was Max Weber, originally an economist and legal historian, with related work undertaken by those such as Georg Simmel and Ferdinand Tönnies who were more closely identified with sociology as a discipline.

Weber's work began from the individual and the subjective meanings of individual acts. His emphasis on the need to show that social structures and historical change must be seen as complex patterns of interweaving acts has led to him being described as a 'methodological individualist'. Social entities such as markets, churches, states, and classes have a reality only as concatenations of individual acts; the task of sociological analysis is to produce explanations of social phenomena in terms of the actions that produce them. Weber's methodology and theory of action had been seen by Mises as providing a broader intellectual basis for the marginalist account of action, and one of his students, Alfred Schütz (1932; see also Kaufmann 1936), was encouraged to undertake a phenomenological reconstruction of Weber's view of the meaningful structure of action. His account saw actual social situations involving the coexistence of both rational action and unreflective or habitual conduct, the rationality of the latter being limited by taken-for-granted and unexamined expectations. Although Schütz had explored aspects of this argument in a number of related papers during the mid-1920s (see Schütz 1924–7), these were published only much later, in 1972, when he began to have his major influence on social theory.

The fundamental concepts of sociology, Weber argued, are built around the models of meaningful individual action that he termed 'ideal types' (1904; see also Simmel 1892). In the unfinished encyclopaedia of sociology on which he was working at the time of his death (1920a; see also 1914),[3] he set out a conspectus of sociological concepts rooted in this view of social action. The most easily understandable forms of action are the instrumentally rational forms analysed in marginalist economics, and Weber extended the application of these models from modern economic and economically relevant actions to legal and political actions. The most important form of action that he recognised alongside the rational type was the 'traditional' or habitual type that underpins customary practices and much routine everyday action.

Arguing against the extreme forms of organicism that prevailed in Germany, Georg Simmel also emphasised that structures were to be treated as configurations of interaction and not as substantive collective entities with their own capacities for action. Between writing on social differentiation (1890) and the money economy (1900), Simmel produced a series of essays, later collected into a book (1908),[4] in which he explored the ways in which interaction generates particular types or 'forms' of social relation. The form of a social relationship is distinct from its content or purpose, and the same form may appear in quite different historical contexts. While sociologists can engage in a number of diverse historical and cultural investigations, their specific subject matter is these 'pure forms'. Thus, Simmel described relationships of superordination and subordination, enmity and alliance, competition, conflict, exclusion, secrecy, individuality, and so on, and he showed how the character of these forms can vary with formal aspects of group structure such as size. These elementary social relations are, in turn, formed into more complex structures such as states, parties, classes, churches, and markets, and it is in these that they acquire their specific cultural contents as economic, political, religious, and so on.

Alfred Vierkandt (1923) and Leopold von Wiese (1924–9) built more systematic sociological accounts along similar lines to Simmel and Weber.[5] Vierkandt's roots were in folk psychology and cultural theory (1896, 1908), but, influenced by the phenomenology of Brentano (1874) and Husserl (1900–1), he began to explore the ways in which social forms are experienced in the consciousness of individuals. Where Vierkandt gave particular attention to the emotional aspects of social experience, Wiese took a highly formalistic and almost geometrical approach to classifying the forms of social relations. Using concepts of approach and withdrawal, he built a complex typology of elementary relations and larger 'formations', summarising each of these in mathematical formulas.

Formal sociology had a significant international influence. In the United States, there was a great deal of secondary interest in the work of Simmel, which was translated in the *American Journal of Sociology* in the 1890s and 1900s. Late in his career, Ross (1921) took up Simmel's formal sociology, and set out a more concrete version of von Wiese's argument. The Austrian émigré Jacob Moreno (1934) used these same ideas in the construction of his 'sociometry'. The early work of Gyorgy Lukács (1910), who moved between Germany and his native Hungary, also drew heavily on Simmel's theory of the forms of interaction in order to develop an account of cultural forms. Piet Endt (1931) made some attempt to popularise von Wiese's version of formal sociology in the Netherlands, while Theodor Geiger (1928, 1939) made some important contributions in both Germany and Denmark. More widely, the Russian theorist Bogdan Kistiakovsky (1899, 1916) applied ideas from Simmel and Weber in the development of his sociology of law, Panayiotis Kanellopoulos published commentaries on both Simmel and Wiese for a Greek audience, and Francisco Pontes de Miranda worked on the formal sociology of Wiese in Brazil.

Ferdinand Tönnies (1931a, 1931b) also saw social entities as products of social interaction.[6] The basic social entities – social relations consisting of the reciprocal interactions of individuals – can be formed into 'social collectives' and 'social corporations'. 'Collectives' are intersecting social circles of interaction whose participants have shared traits and a common way of life. Examples are local communities, ethnic groups, nations, and social classes. 'Corporations', such as states, parties, and churches, are organised entities with a capacity for unified social action. They arise from and recruit from collectives, and the actions of the individuals and corporations that comprise a collectivity are normatively organised through the customary habits that define its way of life (1909).

The analytical relationship between rational actions and other types of action, explored by Weber, Simmel, and the other formal sociologists, is also a historical relationship. Modernisation, as a process of rationalisation, involves an increase in the significance of rational actions and structures of action at the expense of traditional actions. The most influential discussion of this was in Tönnies's (1889) identification of *Gemeinschaft* (community) and *Gesellschaft* (association) as two polar ways of life. Actions involved in the 'communal' relations typical of traditional communities, villages, and rural localities are motivated by a spirit of traditionalism and are built around sentiments of solidarity that bind people tightly together into cohesive and consensual social groups. Actions involved in the 'associative' relations typical of modern capitalism are motivated by purely rational considerations and place people in competitive, anonymous, and fragmented situations.

Weber's view of the shift in European societies from communal to associative relations formed part of his influential account of the part played by religion in modernisation.[7] His early work had documented the historical diversity of capitalist activity through studies of Roman agrarian and property relations (1896b, 1909), medieval trading enterprises (1894a), agricultural labour in contemporary Germany (1892), and the modern stock exchange (1894b, 1896a). His aim was to uncover the specifically rational characteristics of modern capitalist forms, and he took as his central task the explanation of why and how these rational forms arose. In studies of the world religions (1904–5, 1915a, 1916, 1917) he investigated the ways in which religious orientations promoted or inhibited the development of rational forms of action. Only in Europe, he argued, was there the combination of religious orientation and political conditions that made possible a break with tradition and the growth of rationalism. The Protestant social ethic that arose in the wake of the great religious changes of the Reformation was especially conducive to the spread of that rational approach to economic matters that constitutes the spirit of modern capitalism. This was able to trigger the building of capitalist markets, however, only because the absolutist states of western Europe had already begun to introduce rationalised forms of administration and rational, calculable law (see also 1919–20). This argument was amplified by Ernest Troeltsch (1906, 1912), who later (1922; see also 1924) articulated the methodological basis of this historical method.

Weber's argument was supported by that of Werner Sombart (1902; see also 1911, 1913a, 1913b). Like Weber, he saw the 'spirit of capitalism' as the primary driving force in economic change. He argued, however, that the specific source of the creative dynamism of capitalism was the 'industrial' spirit of the entrepreneur that marked German bourgeois character. The commercial, acquisitive spirit that had destroyed the *Gemeinschaft* communities of feudalism he linked to the culture and religion of the Jewish merchants active in medieval Europe. Sombart took a negative view of the destructive effects of this acquisitive spirit, and his anti-Semitism and anti-socialism (1906, 1908) made him an enthusiastic – if unconventional – supporter of Hitler.

FOCUS: MAX WEBER

Max Weber was the towering figure among the writers considered here. His key statements on his approach to action and social relations can be found in the first part of his *Economy and Society* (1920a). This can usefully be compared with the arguments of Simmel's *Soziologie* (1908; see Wolff 1950). The core of Weber's argument can be found on pages 4–56 of his book.

The standard biography of Weber is that written by his wife Martianne as *Max Weber: A Biography* (1926). The secondary and critical literature on Weber is extensive, but the best general account remains Reinhardt Bendix's *Max Weber: An Intellectual Portrait* (1962). The most useful commentary on Simmel is also the earliest: Nicholas Spykman's *The Sociology of Georg Simmel* (1925).

Conflict and Collective Action

Marx's theory of individual action led him towards a theory of collective action and class conflict. He was not, however, the first to seek a theory of collective conflict. This initially arose with the recognition of collective political action as a phenomenon in need of explanation. Lorenz von Stein (1850; see also 1856) undertook a pioneering study of the socialist movement, inspired by his contacts with early Parisian socialists. He explained the rise of a socialist movement by the emergence of new forms of social division. Societies, he held, are differentiated by wealth and status, forming classes and estates. Social estates originate in the conquest of one population by another, more powerful one, and their economic differences are clothed in cultural differences of status. The power differences that produce classes in complex societies, on the other hand, are rooted directly in internal divisions of property ownership. State policies can be explained not simply by the preferences of policy makers or the cultural spirit that informs them but also by the estate and class interests that drive policy preferences. Political ideas are tied to the defence or promotion of social interests, and conflict between groups is the means through which political differences are pursued. Western societies had evolved from closed, patriarchal systems of social estates into open and achievement-based 'civil societies' divided by class, and it is economic divisions that produce the proletarian class of propertyless labourers that underpins the rise of the socialist movement.

Class Struggle, Parties, and Hegemony

Marx's theory of class conflict had been suggested by his own experiences among the Parisian socialists of the 1840s, when he also became aware of the early ideas of Stein. He and Engels set out a clear and systematic statement of this theory in the *Communist Manifesto* (Marx and Engels 1848), produced as a policy statement for the Communist League. All history, they argued, is driven by the conflict between classes formed through the ownership or non-ownership of the means of production. In feudal societies, class divisions appeared as divisions between social estates defined by their relative status. In capitalist societies, on the other hand, traditional and status ideals had been stripped away and classes appeared in purely material form *as* classes. Modern capitalism is organised around a conflict between a bourgeois class of property owners, forming its 'ruling class', and a propertyless proletariat that is subject to its power. The proletariat – the 'working class' of wage labourers – is an exploited class whose members gradually achieve a consciousness of their shared oppression and develop a political organisation that allows them to pursue the overthrow of the class that exploits them. Their revolutionary efforts are aided by the intellectuals who align themselves with the class through the Communist Party.

The elaboration of the Marxist theory of class conflict owed a great deal to the populists and anarchists with whom Marx and Engels became involved in the International Working Men's Association (later known as the First International). Mikhail Bakunin, closely associated with the Russian subjectivists, contended that bonds of habit and custom normally tie people into organic communities that limit their freedom of action. Creative collective action becomes possible only when they are liberated from tradition and develop a capacity for critical reflection (Bakunin 1873). Plekhanov, in the mainstream of orthodox Marxism, drew much inspiration from Bakunin and from the subjectivism of Mikhailovskii and Kareev. Though he came to see populism and anarchism as forms of 'utopian socialism', he followed their emphasis on the creative, collective action of the proletariat as the key factor in social change (see also Tugan-Baranovsky 1905).

The creativity of collective action was also emphasised by Antonio Labriola in essays that were published (1896) in France and appeared in his native Italy only in 1902. Deeply rooted in Hegelian philosophy, he combined a politically orthodox Marxism with a critique of its deterministic view of history, but he nevertheless responded vigorously to Georges Sorel's emphasis on spontaneity (Labriola 1898). Rejecting the strong economic determinism that he found in his fellow Italian Achille Loria (1886, 1901, 1921),[8] he held that Marxism must see collective action – 'praxis' – as the crucial link between economic conditions and the 'social psychology' or collective mentality of a class. All change is the outcome of praxis and historical materialism is the 'philosophy of praxis'.

Georges Sorel (1906) was, for a time, closely associated with Marxist politics, but he set out a theory of collective action and conflict that broke radically with the orthodox view. Sorel emphasised 'movement' as an integral feature of free action and saw the actions of radical social movements and political parties as spontaneous, free acts. Their revolutionary strategies involve conscious and deliberate acts of will aimed at the achievement of goals defined in the political 'myths' through which they organise their political demands.

Taking a similar view, Leon Trotsky (real name Lev Davidovich Bronstein) glorified spontaneous mass political awareness as the driving element in history

(1904), while Rosa Luxemburg (1906; see also 1913) saw the collective mentality of workers developing spontaneously through strikes and industrial action to the point at which they are able to take advantage of whatever opportunities are opened up by economic dislocation.

Vladimir Lenin (real name Vladimir Ilyich Ulyanov) was critical of such emphasis on purely spontaneous conflict and stressed the role of a disciplined organisation of professional Communist revolutionaries as the 'vanguard' of working-class consciousness (1902). Lenin rejected the 'tailism' implied by theorists of spontaneity: the 'tail' of working-class action cannot wag the dog of class consciousness. Party intellectuals who detach themselves from their class situation and acquire a scientific knowledge of society become the embodiment of true, revolutionary consciousness, into which they can educate the workers. The relationship between intellectuals and social movements was the central concern of Antonio Gramsci, who also explored the cultural basis of ruling-class power. Working in the tradition of Labriola's philosophy of praxis, he became leader of the Italian Communist Party, was imprisoned by the Fascists in 1926, and spent the rest of his life in prison. His main theoretical ideas (Gramsci 1929–35) were produced in secret and remained incomplete and unedited when he died. They were not widely known until many years after his death.

Gramsci argued that political power involves the establishment of 'hegemony', the building of a determined and conscious political force organised for leadership and command. The principal means of ruling-class hegemony is the state, but it involves also a whole array of associated institutions, in which its culture is embodied: schools, churches, and the mass media, for example. It is through such ruling-class hegemony that economic power can be buttressed with mechanisms of socialisation and social control. Gramsci also emphasised that for the proletariat to engage in successful revolutionary action, it must organise itself in a 'counter-hegemony'. It must challenge the ruling class on cultural and political grounds as well as on the terrain of the economy. To achieve this counter-hegemony, it must form cultural and political institutions that will help to build and inculcate its consciousness and political outlook. It is through the proletarian party that the theoretical consciousness of communist intellectuals can be aligned with the practical consciousness of the masses to forge a revolutionary political consciousness. It is the 'organic intellectuals' – those who emerge from within a particular social class – who are best able to formulate the ideas that promote this hegemony. Intellectuals not organic to the proletariat may, nevertheless, be 'assimilated' by it when their ideas are particularly conducive to its social conditions.

FOCUS: KARL MARX

The arguments on class conflict have the ideas of Karl Marx as their main point of reference. These are most directly and succinctly summarised in Karl Marx and Friedrich Engels *The Communist Manifesto* (1848), especially the section on 'Bourgeois and Proletarians'.

The best available biography of Marx is David McLellan's *Karl Marx: His Life and Thought* (1973). There are numerous secondary discussions of his work, and the most comprehensive discussion of the whole Marxist tradition is Leszak Kolakowski's encyclopaedic summary (1978). Marx's views on class conflict are considered in John Scott's *Stratification and Power* (1996), Chapter 3.

Racial Struggle, Power, and Conflict

Stein's arguments had a great influence among socialists and Marxists. They were also important for the development of the theories of ethnic conflict of Ludwig Gumplowicz (1875, 1883, 1905) and his followers and of Gustav Ratzenhofer (1893, 1898, 1907). Both held that 'racial' groups were the key actors in the earliest stages of human history and that contact between racial groups led to struggle and competition. They saw this as the basis of all conquest, exploitation, and slavery. Over time, such conflicts gradually become less violent and more focused around economic matters. Contemporary societies, therefore, are organised around class divisions that no longer have any clear ethnic basis. It is class relations that underpin the formation of political states as the principal mechanisms of control and coordination in advanced societies. The continual rise and fall of powerful ethnic groups and classes determines the succession of states in history.

The Dutch ethnographer Rudolf Steinmetz (1892, 1899, 1900) used ideas from Gumplowicz to organise his 'sociographic' data into a model of warfare, state formation, and nation building. The conflict ideas of Ratzenhofer were particularly popular in Japan, where they were expounded by Kato Hiroyuki and Hozumi Noboshige. It was the translation of Gumplowicz into Italian, however, that produced the most influential approaches in Michelangelo Vaccaro (1886) and Gaetano Mosca (1896, 1923).[9] Mosca focused on the ruling elites that he saw dominating all societies. Initially based on undifferentiated ethnic groups, ruling elites become more specialised as they recruit, to varying degrees, from military, religious, wealthy, and intellectual categories. The policies and strategies pursued by a ruling elite reflect the balance between these 'social forces' within it. Ruling elites depend upon force and constraint but justify their rule through legitimating doctrines that Mosca called 'political formulas'. Conflicts between elites and masses have driven European societies away from violence and militarism and have established democratic regimes with systems of citizenship rights that involve an institutional regulation of the power of the ruling elite. Oliver Cox (1948), working in the Political Science Department at the University of Chicago, developed this view more radically and incorporated an analysis of racial divisions into a broader conflict theory of social development that drew on both Mosca and Marx.

Yacov Novicow (1894, 1897, 1898), closely associated with the Russian School in Paris, saw human conflict beginning as a purely 'physiological' struggle for survival oriented towards the attainment of food. Cultural development, however, subsumes these within larger economic struggles concerned with wealth rather than food, and within political struggles for conquest and domination. These, in turn, have been supplemented by ideological struggles. European societies had, by the nineteenth century, become more 'rational' and had a potential for conscious and peaceful control over international affairs. Novicow predicted that political alliances would, eventually, result in the formation of a European federation that would prevent further warfare and allow an increase in justice and social solidarity. The publication of his ideas (1912) on the eve of the First World War perhaps undermined their credibility.

Franz Oppenheimer (1914, 1922)[10] traced the origins of class relations to the conquests made by pastoral nomads. The Germanic invasions in Europe, for example, led to the collapse of the Roman Empire and established feudal class relations. The absolutist nation states of Europe developed on the basis of the feudal aristocracy and exhibited many residual aristocratic features. Oppenheimer did not go as far as Hans Freyer (see Chapter 3) in connecting aristocratic privilege with the maintenance of European cultural achievements, and he did not share his political views, but he did see all states as shaped by their histories. Carl Schmitt (1932), however, combined Freyer's cultural organicism with conflict ideas to produce a view of all political struggles as involving the conflict of organised groups in pursuit of their interests. Like Freyer, these views led him to support the Nazis.[11]

In Japan, Takata Yasuma (Takata 1922; see also 1926)[12] drew on Simmel, Weber, and Durkheim and saw actions driven by two socialised 'desires': the desire for 'gregariousness' and solidarity and the desire for power. The pursuit of power – in the form of political command, economic wealth, and prestige – leads to the formation of social classes, and these classes become real social groups, capable of collective action, only when the gregarious desires of their members generate the necessary solidarity and class consciousness. This analysis of social-class conflict, though owing much to Marx, was seen by Takata (1925, 1940) as the basis of a 'third view' of history that is neither idealist nor materialist.

A novel twist to the conflict view was given by the Spanish social theorist José Ortega y Gasset. Where Mosca's conflict theory had given most attention to the formation, rise, and fall of ruling elites, Ortega (1929) was concerned with the social and cultural consequences of the enhanced power of the 'masses' in modern societies. While using some ideas from Le Bon and Sighele, he was more concerned with large-scale processes of massification that eliminated or minimised class differences and resulted in a cultural uniformity. Like the cultural theorists Othmar Spann and Hans Freyer, Ortega saw a 'revolt' of the masses taking place in the name of democracy and as leading, in fact, to a new barbarism in which the cultural achievements of aristocratic elites would be lost.

The most strikingly original American social theorist, Thorstein Veblen (1899, 1915), proposed a conflict theory that was much cited but attracted few immediate followers. He held that the struggle and migration of racial groups in Europe had led to complex and diverse societies with racially 'hybrid' populations. While losing their initial racial basis, these societies had become divided along economic lines according to their roles in production. The ruling classes do not themselves engage in productive labour and so must be seen as 'leisure classes' that depend on the productive work of their subordinates. A leisure class acquires its social status from its lack of involvement in work and from its ability to consume things it has not produced. To function as an effective symbol of status, Veblen argued, consumption and leisure must be obvious and visible, and he invented the term 'conspicuous consumption' to describe the economic goals of a leisure class.

Veblen (1904, 1919, 1923) pursued in some detail the economic organisation of the United States, pointing to the division between, on the one hand, the predatory and leisured captains of finance and, on the other hand, the subordinate managers and skilled workers who actually operate the industrial system. This led him to the more general point that social change must be understood in relation to the 'discrepancies' that arise between the institutions of a society and its material conditions (1911). The habits and customs that form a society's institutions are the result of the struggles that brought it into being. They shape the development of its technology of production but can also become fetters on its further development. Veblen (1918) illustrated this with reference to the persistence of the dynastic or patrimonial state in Germany and the ossification of liberalism and private property in the United States. In America, he argued, the leisure class restricts the opportunities available to the truly productive industrialists and engineers, not least through its control over the educational system and the curriculum of the universities. A similar view of institutions was taken by John Commons (1899–1900, 1924), who, with Veblen, was associated with the development of institutional economics in the United States.

FOCUS: GAETANO MOSCA

The key figure in non-Marxist approaches to conflict is Gaetano Mosca, whose works of 1896 and 1923 have been published together in English as *The Ruling Class*. His main ideas can be found on pages 5–69 and 329–37 of this translation.

 The best general introduction to the work of Mosca and his compatriots is Richard Bellamy's *Modern Italian Social Theory* (1987).

Conflict and the Clash of Cultures

For some, it was cultural conflict, rather than the sectional conflicts of classes and elites, that was the centre of attention. Sharing much with idealist theories of cultural 'spirit' and integrity, they focused also on the inter-societal conflicts that lie behind the expansion and contraction of particular cultural spheres. This was seen as a principal mechanism of cultural influence and diffusion. A leading exponent of such a theory was Benjamin Kidd (1894), who held that collective conflict occurs only when groups are able to suppress the purely self-interested drives of their members through cooperation and solidarity. Conflict is a consequence of altruism, solidarity, and 'social consciousness', as these are the means through which groups are able to constrain their members to act in support of each other and of the group as a whole. Kidd saw the ultimate source of this altruism in religion, with the specific 'spirit' of a religion determining the adaptive possibilities of a culture. The clash of societies and their cultures is a process of natural selection that ensures the survival of those cultural items that provide adaptive advantages. The rise of western Europe, for example, was a result, in large part, of the adaptive potential inherent in the Christian spirit. Christianity underpinned a strongly sanctioned ethic of altruism that had encouraged the growth of collective welfare, collective obligation, and the extension of equality (Kidd 1903).

Kidd argued that a society is weakened and liable to decay whenever individual rationality is not held in check by collective altruism. Thus, the decline of religion in contemporary European societies meant that struggles had become increasingly individualistic. In a posthumously published book, Kidd (1918) saw this decay as responsible for the growth of the militarism and imperialism that led to the First World War. He rejected the socialist solution to excessive individualism, holding that only religion could convince people to sacrifice their self-interest for the greater good. Western society could evolve towards a greater collective organisation and purposive regulation only if an altruistic religion could be re-established.

William Perry (1923, 1924) took a broader view of cultural conflict and diffusion. He saw migration and contact as mechanisms of cultural diffusion that operated alongside the actual political conquests stressed by other theorists. Perry held that civilised forms of culture arose spontaneously only in Egypt and spread from there across the world. The ancient Egyptians invented irrigation and farming technologies, statecraft, religion, metal working, shipbuilding, calendrical measurement, and writing. A chain of trading communities stretching from India to America were the centres from which Egyptian culture and civilisation spread into neighbouring areas that were still organised around hunting and gathering. Struggles and alliances between ruling 'aristocracies' in each community, along with mass migration, trading and military expeditions, were the means through which this cultural diffusion took place (see also Elliot Smith 1929, 1932; Clark 1946).

This approach to cultural diffusion was systematised by Arnold Toynbee (1934–9).[13] He followed Nikolai Danilevsky's view of cultural values as the sources of unity (see Chapter 3) and identified twenty-one dominant 'civilisations' in world history, five of which (Egypt, Sumeria, China, Maya, and India) were innovators of ideas and practices that were subsequently transferred to other cultures through diffusion, alliance, and conquest. Toynbee saw the spread of civilisation and values as driven by a process of 'challenge–response'. Civilisations face challenges posed by changes in their natural environments and by pressure from neighbouring societies. The most effective responses to these changes originate in a 'creative minority' or elite. If a civilisation is to survive, its elite must control its 'internal proletariat' and expand its territory at the expense of their civilised neighbours (the 'external proletariat'). A civilisation breaks down when its elite can find no effective solutions to challenges faced, and it is during a period of breakdown that civilisations are most likely to come under attack from other – more vibrant – civilisations and so to collapse completely.

FOCUS: ARNOLD TOYNBEE

The leading writer on the clash of civilisations was Arnold Toynbee, whose massive *Study of History* was not completed until the publication of its tenth volume in 1963. His argument is best approached through the abridged summary of Volumes 1–6 published by David Somervell (1946). Pages 35–47 of the abridgement give the flavour of Toynbee's approach.

 A biography of Toynbee has been produced by a contemporary advocate of his views: William H. McNeill, *Arnold J. Toynbee: A Life* (1989).

Pluralism, Conflict, and Ecology

A final form of conflict theory was particularly concerned with conflict among small groups within societies. This was largely the work of Albion Small, founder of the Sociology Department at the University of Chicago. Small studied in Germany and, like Cooley, his early work was heavily influenced by Schäffle (Small and Vincent 1894). Discovering the work of Ratzenhofer, however, Small (1905) recast his own work to take greater account of the conflict and competition among individuals and groups. Like Ratzenhofer, he saw conflict as motivated by individual 'interests' and psychological drives. Interests in such things as health, wealth, sociability, knowledge, beauty, and morality are the bases on which social groups are formed and are drawn into struggles over the resources required to pursue them. Small was especially concerned with the competition of socially organised interests at the local level, seeing larger-scale social processes as outcomes of the struggles among these small groups. His colleague Arthur Bentley (1908), in the Political Science Department at Chicago, began to formulate similar ideas into a 'pluralist' theory of political representation according to which political power in modern societies rests far more on the struggles of organised interest groups than on the votes of individuals in elections.

Small sought to draw others into a comprehensive research programme based around his ideas, and this was set out in a handbook of sociological thought and practice – known as the 'Green Bible' – edited by his colleagues Robert Park and Edward Burgess (Park 1921; see also Small 1910, 1924).[14] This was a defining statement for the sociology undertaken at Chicago, where Park, Burgess, and the social psychologist Ellsworth Faris oversaw a mass of ethnographic research into city life. The research combined Small's conflict theory with an 'ecological' view of the city as a material environment. This ecological argument was elaborated by the Chicago geographer Harlan Barrows (1923), who held that the interactions of social groups could be studied using ideas of competition, succession, and selection drawn from biology, but requiring only minimal reference to the physical environment itself. According to the Chicago sociologists, social groups enter into conflict on the basis of the resources and opportunities provided by their urban location, and the morphological structure of the city itself results from competition among social groups as they attempt to take advantage of their material circumstances (Park and Burgess 1925). The conflict of ethnic groups was seen as a particularly important determinant of urban structures and processes in a migrant city such as Chicago.

FOCUS: ROBERT PARK

The inspiration behind much of the work that applied conflict ideas to the study of Chicago was Robert Park. His students and colleagues produced numerous ethnographic studies of social groups and social types in the city. Park produced the *The City* (1925) with Edward Burgess, where his ecological model of the city was described by Roderick McKenzie in Chapter 3.

 There are many discussions of Chicago sociology, one of the best being Dennis Smith's *The Chicago School* (1988).

Nature, Environment, and Bodies

Two aspects of the impact of nature on human life have attracted sociological attention. There is the relation of social life to the external nature of the physical environment and there is its relation to the 'inner nature' of the human body. Evolutionary theory did a great deal to popularise these concerns, stressing that human bodies have evolved as adaptations to specific environmental conditions.

Social evolutionism elaborated the argument that social groups must adapt to their environments and to 'human nature' if they are to survive. More broadly, environmental theorising took up this idea of 'adaptation' and explored the mechanisms that allow it to occur. The central question examined was that of 'determinism' or 'possibilism': do environmental conditions directly determine particular social relations or do they simply open up or close off possibilities of action for those who live under them? There was a parallel argument over the question of 'heredity' or environment as the determinants of human nature: are human characteristics shaped by environmental conditions (including those of its social environment) or are they determined solely by inherited biological characteristics? The main focus of this debate was the relative importance of biological inheritance (recognised from the early twentieth century as genetic inheritance) and cultural representations in shaping human characteristics.

The principal means through which societies adapt to their environments was widely recognised as the material technology through which the members of a society secure their material needs and sustain a particular way of life. The relation between social activities and their 'economic' conditions, therefore, became a central question for many theorists. It was also recognised that the human populations that engage in particular ways of life are able to transform themselves as they transform their social relations. The demographic distribution of individuals is also a distribution of biological and social characteristics, seen as an ethnic or 'racial' distribution. Such matters of distribution were also explored as distinctive questions of the spatial location of human populations: to what extent do human societies gain advantages or disadvantages from their location in relation to other societies rather than simply from their physical conditions?

Climate, Landscape, and Society

The most influential of the early writers on environmental influences were Carl Ritter (1817–59), Adolf Bastian (1860, 1881), and Friedrich Ratzel (1882–91, 1887–8). Ritter drew heavily on the work of the von Humboldt brothers, combining the physical geography of Alexander with the cultural analysis of Wilhelm. His mammoth project of an *Erdkunde* ran to nineteen volumes but covered only Asia and Africa. Though he was a vociferous advocate of environmental determinism, his illustrations were largely descriptive and he used environmental ideas as an organising framework for data rather than as true explanatory principles. His aim was to break with mere reportage of cultural differences and present an integrated picture of the whole way of life of a people. To this end, he depicted the physical environment as comprising distinct 'areas' (*Raumen*) within which human life was constrained to follow specific patterns. Bastian took a similar approach in his ethnology, focusing on 'geographical provinces' or regions defined by interdependences of environment and culture.

Ratzel took this work in a more systematic direction, arguing that human activities were causally related to their particular physical context (*Landschaft*). Settlements and population movements are most directly shaped by the environment, with social organisms adapting through these morphological conditions. Ratzel was aware of the complexity of social influences, and one of his final works (1897) incorporated an analysis of conflict into his environmentalism. States with large populations, he argued, are both expansive and militaristic, though their external conflicts mean correspondingly fewer internal conflicts. Small states, on the other hand, are marked by strong 'nationalistic' tendencies. Although this argument found some echoes in Simmel's work on group size, it has greater similarities with the work of French writers such as Adolphe Coste, considered below.

A strongly determinist view of the environment was also taken by Élisée Reclus, who extended his physical geography (1867–8) into an investigation of the relationship between human beings and their physical environments (1876–94). His arguments were summarised in a posthumously published text (1905–8), where he postulated three levels of causation: the physical environment determines the material way of life, while this, in turn, determines all other aspects of human life.[15]

The most analytical of the early theorisations of the natural environment was that of Henry Buckle in the methodological introduction to his *History of Civilization in England* (1857–61). The most important environmental factors, he held, are climate and soil, which jointly influence food supply and the productivity of land. The latter, in turn, determine the rate of growth in production and the level of surplus available for consumption. The mental characteristics of individuals and the cultural traits they share reflect their practical experiences of living in a particular environment. What Buckle termed the 'aspect' of nature – the perceived aesthetic character of the environment – is also major element in determining mental imagery. Environmental influence is not, however, a simple one-way determinism, but a process in which the natural environment sets the limits within which human choices and decisions must be made.

Buckle argued that the causal effects of the natural environment vary inversely with the society's level of technological development: environmental effects are greatest in those societies that are technologically the least advanced. The growth of technology gives humans greater control over nature and, therefore, allows a greater autonomy for their cultural development. European civilisation, Buckle argued, had reached a technological level at which its environment posed fewer constraints on human action than ever before. Physical laws had less significance for explaining human action, and 'mental laws' were of correspondingly greater importance.

Somewhat later, Andrew Herbertson (1905) returned to a more deterministic view of what he called the 'natural regions' of the world, arguing that the climatic factors of temperature, pressure, and rainfall determine the nature of the soil and vegetation, which, in turn, shape the mode of subsistence, the distribution of the population, and the 'mental and spiritual' aspects of the population. Thus, the distribution of physical ecosystems – tundra, temperate forests, savannah, and equatorial forests – defines the distribution of natural regions within which various nomadic, hunting, and pastoral ways of life are found (see also Herbertson and Herbertson 1920).

Ellsworth Huntington and Ellen Semple developed this mix of ideas at Chicago, where they had a great influence on the ecological arguments of Small and Park. Huntington (1907), like Herbertson, took a strongly determinist position and invoked climate and climate change to explain the migration of pastoral nomads and their spread across prehistoric Europe. He suggested (1915; see also Huntington and Cushing 1920) that civilisation arises autonomously only in temperate regions and that it is incompatible with mentalities shaped by tropical climates.

Semple (1903, 1911) wanted to introduce Ratzel's ideas to an American audience and was far less deterministic in her approach than was Huntington. She saw the natural environment as determining the possibilities open to people and so conditioning or constraining their activities. Environmental analysis can, therefore, discover tendencies and potentials by tracing the distribution and movement of populations in history and by charting the differentiation of the habitats in which they find themselves. These human habitats reflect differences in climate (together with its effects on soil and vegetation), physical topography, natural resources, and the 'psychical effects' of lived experiences within a particular environment. People are driven to move from one habitat to another by pressures such as population growth, and, as they move, their cultural traits and social organisation must be applied in a new habitat. In these changed circumstances, there is a tendency for their cultural traits to be transformed. New environmental conditions may be disregarded in the short term, allowing people to continue act as before, but practices incompatible with the new environmental conditions will be perpetuated in the longer term.

Environmental influences were explored more loosely by a range of theorists and ethnographers. Among the most interesting were the Polish ethnographer Ludwig Krzywicki, who explored environmental influences on tribal societies (1914, 1934), and the Chilean comparativist Agustin Venturino, who saw cultural differences among Latin American countries resulting from differences in their physical environments, despite their common experience of European colonialism (1927–8, 1931).

FOCUS: ELLEN SEMPLE

Among the earliest environmental theorists, the most interesting work was that of Ellen Semple. In her *Influences of Geographic Environment* (1911), she systematises and elaborates Ratzel's argument into a clear statement of 'possibilism' that also owes a great deal to the arguments of Buckle. Her basic position is set out on pages 33–50.

Contemporary summaries of these environmental arguments can be found in a summary article by Louis Bernard (1925) and in Franklin Thomas's *The Environmental Basis of Society* (1925).

Region and Habitat

Frédéric Le Play (1855) took a more focused view of environmental effects, tracing the ways in which the physical milieu of a locality shapes the economic activity of its residents and how their work patterns, in turn, shape forms of family and community life. He studied family relationships through descriptive statistics and evidence on budgeting decisions that disclosed variations in whole ways of life according to physical environment. Le Play was not, however, an environmental determinist. He saw the environment merely as conditioning the choices that people can make, and he saw patterns of social change as outcomes of both environmental conditions and the cultural organisation of choices.

Le Play contrasted the 'patriarchal' family of eastern nomad and peasant societies with the 'unstable' family found in western manufacturing districts. Distinct from both was the 'stem' family, a highly individualised form found in Britain and the United States and in more isolated rural and mountainous districts in France. These family forms are related to the cultural spirit that emerges under particular environmental conditions. Where the static nomad and peasant societies of Eastern and Central Europe are organised around 'the spirit of tradition', the dynamic industrial societies of the West are organised around 'the spirit of innovation'.

Le Play's theoretical orientation was pursued by many followers and was consolidated in a new journal and an encyclopaedic summary volume of research findings (Vignes 1897). Theorists such as Edmond Demolins (1897, 1901–3) and Henri de Tourville (1904) extended the approach to study the effects of migration patterns on national solidarity. This work had a great influence on the disciplinary development of *geographie* as well as *sociologie*, and the geographers, who were particularly concerned with patterns of spatial distribution in relation to the physical environment, combined these arguments with those of Ritter. Le Play's environmentalism was developed by Sylvio Romero in Brazil.

Patrick Geddes was a biologist who discovered the work of Demolins and, through him, Frédéric Le Play. He may also have been influenced by Paul de Rousiers's study (1895) of English workers. Taking an evolutionary approach, Geddes argued (1915: 194) that human beings had evolved with a greater freedom from environmental constraints than any other animal. The character of the 'regions' in which people live are the cumulative outcomes of the social evolution of their inhabitants. Geddes emphasised the particular importance of the city as a unit of analysis, introducing the term 'conurbation' to describe the city and its hinterland. His interests had some echoes in the statistical studies of labour and poverty carried out by Charles Booth (1901–2), Seebohm Rowntree (1901), and, in the United States, William Du Bois (1899). Also in the United States, he influenced Lewis Mumford's work (1934, 1938, 1944) on the physical morphology of cities. The ideas of both Le Play and Geddes were promoted in India by Radhakamal Mukerjee (1926).

Le Play's focus on regional and comparative analysis informed the human or social geography of Paul Vidal de la Blache. In a series of articles and a posthumously published book (1922), Vidal argued that people must be studied in relation to their *milieu*, their immediate surroundings as determined by physical conditions. These milieus – small regions with distinctive soil, drainage, and vegetation patterns – are the natural areas that Vidal called '*pays*'. A physical landform is shaped by its soil, drainage, climate, and natural resources, and these constrain the way of life by setting limits to what it is possible for people to do. A 'way of life' comprises the customs and practices of a people, especially as these relate to their material mode of securing a living and to subsistence, settlement, and movement. John Unstead (1935) further developed Vidal's concept of the *pays*, defining 'tracts' as consisting of contiguous and interrelated 'stows', the latter being the specific river valleys, plateaux, and other localised milieus in which people live. Vidal made the physical basis of his scheme more plausible by emphasising that choices are made within limits set by particular milieus, and that these choices may exert a reciprocal influence on the landform of the milieu.

Vidal (1908) illustrated his approach in a major study of France, identifying the ways of life associated with such *pays* as the *Massif Central*. He saw his approach as especially well suited to the study of rural, agricultural societies, it being implicit that an environmental theory would have less explanatory power in urban and industrial societies, where technology allows a greater autonomy. Vidal's approach was developed further by Jean Brunhes (1910) and Camille Vallaux (1908, 1911), and it inspired numerous local and regional ethnographic studies. (See the summary of these ideas in Vallaux 1925; see also Bloch 1931.) Much of this work followed Vidal's view of a society as a mosaic of milieus, but Brunhes focused, instead, on the transportation, urbanisation, irrigation, production, and other processes that connect milieus into organised systems. Descriptive environmentalism following the lead of Vidal was apparent in the British regional work of Alan Ogilvie (1928), Dudley Stamp and Stanley Beaver (1933), and Clifford Darby (1936). In the United States these ideas were consolidated into a broad statement of regionalism by Howard Odum and Harry Moore (1938) and they were systematised as a charter statement for human geography by Richard Hartshorne (1939).

Lucien Febvre (1922), later involved with Marc Bloch in founding the 'Annales School' of history, forged the ideas of the Vidalians into a historical geography. Critical of the strong determinism of Demolins, he sought to clarify the causal influences that link environment and society. Physical areas, identified by their geology, meteorology, and hydrology, are 'regional frames' that set 'possibilities of action'. The particular possibilities activated depend upon the culturally formed ideas that people bring to bear in securing their subsistence and pursuing a particular way of life. Economic activities form modes of production, defined by the uses that people make of their environments, and Febvre classified societies into those of hunters and fishers, shepherds and husbandmen, and farmers. The mode of production is the most important element in shaping other social institutions and the mentality or spirit of a society. A descriptive approach using these ideas was set out in Daryll Forde's (1934) work on 'habitat' and its influence on social life.

FOCUS: FRÉDÉRIC LE PLAY

The most influential of the early theorists on environmental influences was Frédéric Le Play, whose ideas spawned numerous empirical studies in the tradition of research on family and community. His work is best approached through the selections included in *On Family, Work, and Social Change* (Silver, ed., 1982). His key work on family types is discussed on pages 257–80 of this book. Silver's 'Introduction' gives an excellent overview of his ideas.

Technology and the Mastery of Nature

One of the most powerful views of the relation between society and nature was, undoubtedly, that found in Marxism. Recognising the role of technology as the means through which societies could adapt to and exercise some control over their material environment, Karl Marx sought an account of the social organisation of technology into modes of production and the impact of these social structures on other aspects of social life. Marx recognised a parallel between his argument and that of the American anthropologist Lewis Morgan (1877), whose theory of matriarchal and patriarchal kinship relations in primitive societies was later taken up by Friedrich Engels (1884).

Marx's 'materialism' was an attempt to show that provision for material needs, especially through the production and distribution of food, was a basic precondition for all other human activities. Recognising that the production of subsistence took place under culturally formed conditions, he nevertheless felt it necessary to conceptualise the causal relations that hold between activities in relation to the material world and all other social activities. In his most general statement (1859), he conceptualised this through the relationship between an economic 'base' and an intellectual and political 'superstructure'. Social structures tend to be organised into two interdependent levels, one of which – the economic – is causally more significant and determines, over the long term, the whole pattern of social development.

The economic base comprises the technological 'forces of production', through which production actually takes place, and the relations of effective control – the 'relations of production' – through which they are organised. Together these constitute a particular mode of production. Although the relations of control depend upon legal and customary norms, they are also the outcome of a whole complex of political and intellectual conditions and cannot be reduced to any particular set of norms. The political and intellectual conditions for production form a part of the 'superstructure' that is able to prosper only because economic production makes this possible. People are able to pursue their vocations as politicians, lawyers, scientists, and so on, only so long as others are producing the goods and services on which they depend. On the other hand, production can take place only if technical knowledge can be applied to human labour within specific forms of property relations and under the protection of state power. Thus, base and superstructure are causally interdependent, with the economic base having ultimate causal primacy.

Social change is driven by changes in the economic base, which are the result of attempts to expand the technology of production and achieve a greater human mastery of the natural environment. For much of the time, the forces of production and the relations of production work closely together and generate the economic growth that sustains the superstructure. This superstructure, in turn, underwrites the expansion of the base through the cultural forms involved in the relations of production. Each mode of production, however, has a limit to the economic growth that it is able to sustain and there comes a time when this relationship is disrupted. The continuing attempt to expand the forces of production brings them into 'contradiction' with the relations of production, and if productive activity is to be sustained the relations of production and the superstructure that underwrites them must be transformed and a new mode of production established. This transformation is brought about only if social classes disadvantaged by the existing economic relations become conscious of the need to overthrow the structures that disadvantage them, and Marx held that his theory was to become an integral element in this 'revolutionary' struggle.

Marx (1858) traced these historical transformations through a sequence of stages, each characterised by a specific mode of production. In the 'primitive communism' of tribal societies there is no structural differentiation of base and superstructure, though economic activities are fundamental. With the emergence of the class and political relations of the ancient civilisations, a sharp structural differentiation emerges and the contradictions of these ancient societies impel them towards feudal modes of production that, in turn, are transformed into capitalist modes of production. It is in capitalist societies that class divisions and the differentiation of the base from the superstructure achieve their sharpest expression, and Marx diagnosed the society of his own time as marked by the growing contradictions of the economic base that were making its revolutionary overthrow inevitable.

The core of Marx's theory was a specialised economic theory of the production and distribution of goods and services within the capitalist mode of production. This theory was to provide the key to understanding the economic base and would form part of a larger theory of both base and superstructure. By the time of his death, however, Marx had managed to publish only the first of the volumes on *Capital* (1867) from his projected multi-volume *Economics*. The rest of his social theory existed only in sketches and drafts. Acting as Marx's literary executor, his lifetime collaborator Friedrich Engels completed and published the second volume of *Capital* in 1884 and the third volume in 1894 (Marx 1865–78, 1864–5). Engels – 'the first Marxist'[16] – also sought to systematise Marx's thought into a science concerned with the 'laws' of economic development through which the material environment is mastered. Engels's theoretical efforts, together with those of Franz Mehring (1893), Karl Kautsky (1887, 1918, 1927), and Georgy Plekhanov (1895, 1912–13), produced the 'orthodox Marxism' of the Second International, in which some definite advances were made.

Kautsky, who saw to the publication of Marx's *Theories of Surplus Value* (Marx 1862–3) in 1905–10, made important contributions to understanding the evolutionary sequence of modes of production, seeing primitive communism followed by a variety of forms of sedentary agriculture driven forward by the migration and conflict of nomadic herders. He also undertook a study of German agriculture (1899; see also Lenin 1899) that countered the influential account given by Max Weber (1892). His most systematic statement was first drafted in the 1870s and 1880s. He began to make revisions in the years following the break-up of the SPD in 1917, producing various drafts during the 1920s and a final text in 1927. He described this as 'the quintessence of my life's work' (Kautsky 1927: lxviii). The archaeologist Gordon Childe (1936, 1941) adapted the orthodox model to understand the development of prehistoric technology through the stone age, the bronze age, and the iron age.

So-called 'revisionists' sought to modify Marx's account of the economic base to reflect contemporary realities at the end of the nineteenth century, although they retained much of the orthodox model. These revisionists included Eduard Bernstein (1899) in Germany and the British 'Fabian' socialists (Shaw 1889; see also Webb and Webb 1923; Shaw 1928), who examined the consequences of the growth of industrial monopolies and imperial expansion. Closely linked with the Fabians was the liberal theorist John Hobson, a colleague of Hobhouse (see Hobson 1931) and an influential theorist of monopoly and 'imperialism' (1894, 1902, 1914). Most important were the Austro-Marxists, among whom Rudolf Hilferding (1910) built an influential account of the fusion of industrial and banking monopolies into the new economic form of 'finance capital'. Orthodox Marxists such as Nikolai Bukharin (1915, 1920) drew on Hilferding's account and saw nation states entering into a new stage of 'state capitalism' as they coordinated the monopoly enterprises in their economies and engaged in a world-wide imperialist struggle for commodities. Lenin (1917) drew on this work to build a similar account of imperialist expansion.

FOCUS: KARL KAUTSKY

Karl Kautsky was a leading figure in world Marxism and produced a major state-ment of the position in *The Materialist Conception of History* (1927). This general statement – not published until 1988 – summarised and elaborated the widely held Marxist developmental sequence and the historical materialist approach. The key ideas are contained in his discussion of 'Marx's Preface' on pages 224–46.

 Kautsky's life and intellectual activity are recounted in the biography produced by his son, John Kautsky: *Karl Kautsky* (1994).

Population, Heredity, and Race

Explicit consideration of the distribution of population and its relation to social activity was a relatively late development of the nineteenth century and emerged first in a number of statistical studies of the relationships between biological influences, mental characteristics, and social conditions. This early work moved towards Darwinian models of population. The question of the relative impor-tance of heredity and environment was central to the so-called 'positive school' of criminology in Italy, with Cesare Lombroso (1875, 1899; Lombroso et al. 1886), Enrico Ferri (1884, 1901), and Raffaele Garofalo (1891) all exploring this directly. Lombroso saw social conformity as 'normal' and deviance as resulting from the inheritance of 'degenerate' biological characteristics, though the others placed more emphasis on economic circumstances and class conditions. The balance between genetic inheritance and class situation was also central to the 'eugenics' of Francis Galton (1869; see also 1881; Pearson 1909), which proposed selective breeding as a means for improving the general level of intelligence in a population. Wilhelm Schallmayer (1891, 1903) and Otto Ammon (1895) in Germany also developed 'eugenic' theories of selective population control. Eugenic ideas were incorporated into the positive school of criminology by Alfredo Niceforo (1910), but these ideas were taken up most forcibly by Corrado Gini (1914, 1921, 1930) in his use of advanced statistics to study population and inequality, the rise and fall of nations, and warfare (see the summary statement by Franco Savorgnan 1936; and see also his 1918 and 1924). Gini's eugenicist sympathies led to his appointment by Mussolini as head of the state statistical service. In a similar vein, the Dutch sociologist Willem Bonger (1905) emulated the statistical work of Ferri and Garofalo on crime and economic conditions, but he also drew on Marxist class theory to broaden this. He showed (1913), for example, that observable religious and cultural differences in criminality actually reflect differences in economic conditions. The strongest form of hereditarian argument treated populations as 'racial' groups with shared biological characteristics. In France, Paul Jacoby (1881) and Georges Vacher de Lapouge (1896, 1909) defined any distinct and inter-breeding human population as a racial group, and saw the survival of its culture as dependent on its population dynamics and processes of social selection. The rise of an 'Aryan' or Nordic culture in Europe, they argued, could be explained in this way.

These arguments reflected a growing interest in the work of Arthur de Gobineau (1853), who had held that the biological characteristics of populations predispose them towards certain ideas and make it difficult or impossible for them to accept others. Publishing his work in four volumes in 1853–5, only the first volume of which has been translated into English, Gobineau set out a phylogenetic account of the origins of human 'races', assuming the independent evolution of racial groups in various parts of the world rather than their development from a single common stock. Relying on pre-Darwinian biology, he saw any mixing of strong with weak races as a 'dilution' of the racial attributes of the strong race that would result in a loss of its cultural 'vigour'. Cultural decline was seen as the inevitable result of such racial mixing. Thus, migration and conquest that had mixed strong 'white' populations with weaker races had led to 'racial degeneration' and had been responsible for the collapse of the Greek and Roman Empires and for what Gobineau saw as the decay of contemporary western civilisation.

Racial ideas were not a major theme in German social thought in the nineteenth century until Gobineau's work began to have an influence in the 1890s. The composer Richard Wagner had been one of the first to popularise Gobineau's ideas in Germany, and his son-in-law, Houston Chamberlain (1899), produced an influential formulation of the Aryan theory. His theory provided the intellectual basis for the eventual rise of Nazism (Hitler 1925) and the collapse of German academic life and social theory in the 1930s.

The use of 'racial' terminology was quite widespread in social theory, reaching well beyond racial theory itself. This term was generally used as a way of conceptualising the cultural differences that had become apparent through ethnographic fieldwork, as in, for example, the ethnographic surveys of Charles Letourneau (1880, 1888, 1889). 'Race' was simply a category for describing these cultural differences and relating them to the distribution and movement of populations; contemporary sociologists have preferred to use the term 'ethnicity' to describe this. In the racial theories of Gobineau and Chamberlain, however, 'race' was seen as a biological characteristic that constituted the genetic inheritance of a population. Such ideas have been thoroughly discredited by contemporary biology, where genetic differences between populations are recognised as neither rigid and immutable nor capable of sustaining cultural differences between populations.[17] More viable approaches to the effects of individual biology were produced in some of the theories of socialisation considered in Chapter 3.

If racial theorising proved to be a pernicious dead-end in social theory, the broader study of population characteristics has proved more fruitful. While this has largely consisted of the empirical study of population measures, some more theoretical refelections have been produced. Émile Levasseur (1859–67, 1889–92) and Arsène Dumont (1890) explored the links between population growth, social mobility, and economic productivity, while Adolphe Coste (1899, 1900) saw the growth and density of population as shaping both 'social' relations and 'cultural' or ideological phenomena. Coste showed that the formation of urban centres follows inevitably from the spatial concentration of an expanding population. With further concentration, these centres become cities and metropolises and underpin state formation. This political enlargement is made possible by the increased division of labour and easier communication that is possible in concentrated populations. Such arguments were taken up in Durkheim's (1893) account of the division of labour and were the basis of his advocacy of 'social morphology' as a specialist subject at the interface between structural sociology and human geography (see Halbwachs 1938a).

Spatial Location

Frederick Turner (1893, 1896) was an early advocate of the attempt to use the purely spatial characteristics of a society as an important variable in social analysis. He saw institutions and constitutional forms as expressions of the 'vital forces' within a population as it expands across a territory and enlarges its boundaries. Illustrating this for North America, he saw the expansion of the settler population as having opened up its 'wilderness' and transformed it into a manufactured, urban environment. Turner traced this expansion with the concept of the 'frontier', the spatial boundary 'between savagery and civilization' at which 'pioneering' conditions are found. The constantly shifting frontier of an expanding population, he argued, had shaped American character and institutions and helped to create its culture of openness and opportunity. In Europe, by contrast, the time of expansion had long passed: there is no expanding European frontier and, therefore, no tendency towards openness.

Herbert Fleure (1919, 1922) used similar ideas in his exploration of the 'border zones' where initially distinct populations come into contact with each other. Celtic culture in Wales, for example, had been suppressed after the English conquest, but this culture and the physical attributes of the Celtic people had better survived in the more isolated western and rural regions of Wales than they had in the large towns and cities (1923, 1926; see his critique of biological racism in Fleure 1930–1).

In a broader view of spatial relations, Sir Halford Mackinder (1902, 1904, 1919) argued that the physical position of a society in relation to others was an important determinant of geopolitical arrangements and strategies. He saw the world as centred on the 'World Island' of the Eurasian landmass, with its 'geographical pivot' lying in the northern and interior parts of the Tibetan Plateau and the headwaters of the South East Asian rivers. This immense 'heartland' was virtually immune from sea attack and could, itself, be the base from which a civilisation might dominate the rest of the world. The main threat to European security, he held, was Russia, the ascendant power of the early twentieth century. Russia had the capability to organise the states of the heartland into a power base and pose a major political challenge to western Europe. Mackinder concluded that a North Atlantic alliance of western Europe with North America might counteract this threat. Mackinder's geopolitics of space was an underdeveloped area of social theory, highlighting issues that were not posed for another fifty years.

FOCUS: HALFORD MACKINDER

Halford Mackinder's *Democratic Ideals and Reality* (1919) exerted a major influence across the social sciences and in political and military circles. His emphasis on the geopolitics of space is something that has been rediscovered in recent years. His key argument is set out on pages 53–81 of the book.

An intellectual biography of Mackinder can be found in Brian Blouet's *Halford Mackinder: A Biography* (1987). Blouet provides an elaboration of Mackinder's position in *Geopolitics and Globalization in the Twentieth Century* (2001).

In this and the previous chapter I have shown that strong and diverse approaches to social theory developed across Europe and more widely in the Americas and Asia. Pursuing a number of theoretical ideas arising from the Enlightenment discovery of the social, a large number of theorists helped to build a sociological discourse. This emerging social theory gradually became a global phenomenon.

The Second World War of 1939 to 1945 marks a natural punctuation point to this intellectual development. Warfare disrupted the flow of ideas and put an almost complete halt to the development of German sociology. The transnational discourse that had been built up in the universities and in Marxist political agencies was significantly disrupted by the build-up to military conflict and the immediate consequences of six years of warfare. The sociological world that emerged in the second half of the twentieth century was very different. The growth of US hegemony in the global political economy underpinned the dominance of an American conception of sociology, while Marxism had dwindled to a stifling orthodoxy sustained by Soviet power politics. In the following chapters I will examine the development of social theory in this period.

NOTES

1. On Mikhailovskii see Billington (1958).

2. On marginalism generally see Howey (1960).

3. The two parts of what is known as *Economy and Society* were compiled at different dates and Weber never integrated them into a single text. Much content is repeated in slightly different ways between the two parts. In broad terms, the first part (1920a) is more analytical and schematic, while the second part (1914) is more historical and comparative.

4. Simmel's book of 1908 has been partially translated, with some additional essays, by Kurt Wolff (1950).

5. See the summary and elaboration of von Wiese's book published in the United States by Howard P. Becker (Wiese-Becker 1932) and various essays collected and published in Mueller (1941). Von Wiese and Vierkandt are discussed in Abel (1929). A useful critical commentary on Vierkandt is Hochstim (1966).

6. Tönnies's book of 1931 summarises and draws together ideas that had been set out in a series of papers published during the 1920s. His interactionist ideas were implicit in his earlier study (1889) of 'community' and 'society' but were not drawn out until after Simmel's work had appeared.

7. Weber's essay on the Protestant ethic was first published in 1904–5 in journal form. It was subsequently revised in 1920 for publication in his collected volumes in the sociology of religion. The 1920 version is contained in Kalberg's edition

(Weber 1920b), which is a new translation of the same text used by Parsons in his 1930 translation. The original essays have been translated in the Baehr and Wells edition (Weber 1904–5).

8. Loria is often seen as a Marxist, but his arguments on land ownership owe a great deal to Henry George (1879).

9. See Burnham (1943) and Bellamy (1987).

10. Oppenheimer's work on the state (1914) was enlarged as Volume II of his *System der Soziologie*. Volume III of the *System* also updated an earlier book on economics. Other volumes covered the general methodological issues behind economic and political sociology.

11. See Gottfried (1990) and Balakrishnan (2000).

12. An English translation of the 1950 revised edition of Takata's *Shakaigaku Gairon* was published in 1989.

13. In addition to the six volumes of his *Study of History* published before 1939, Toynbee published a further four volumes between 1954 and 1963.

14. On Small's influence at Chicago see Hinckle (1994).

15. Élisée Reclus was involved in the anarchist movement and spent almost the whole of his life outside France, living principally in Switzerland and then in Belgium. He should not be confused with his brother Élie, the author of an ethnographic study (1885).

16. See Carver (1981: 31).

17. See Jones (1993) and the 1964 Unesco 'Statement on the Biological Aspects of Race' in UNESCO (1969).

5

Culture, System, and Socialisation: Developments

Theorists of the last fifty years have taken up formative ideas and developed them further. In some cases this has involved a rediscovery of earlier ideas that had been forgotten or ignored, while in other cases there is genuine advance. The key areas on which discussion is focused are

- the formation of cultural ideas into persistent and constraining social institutions

- discursive and symbolic aspects of cultural communication

- cultural organisation of the routines of everyday life

- differentiation of culture and social institutions into causally interdependent levels

- contradictions and complexity in social systems

- the development of sexual difference and moral concerns

- self formation in relation to the responses of others

While intellectual differences have been sharpened and writers have often been antagonistic towards each other's positions, this chapter shows that there remain crucial areas of agreement amongst quite diverse theorists.

The fundamental dimensions of sociological analysis were firmly established by the formative theorists as the foundations for all social theory. The new directions and new approaches proposed and pursued by contemporary theorists have sometimes obscured the achievements of their predecessors. Many contemporary theorists – especially those unfamiliar with the history of social theory – have simply restated or rediscovered their ideas. The most interesting contemporary theories, however, have built on the formative view and explored its gaps and lacunae, filling out its detail and complexity. Many such theorists have taken the formative ideas for granted and have felt no need to reiterate them or even to explicitly reaffirm them. As a result, their detailed accounts of cultural processes have often been seen by commentators and students as proposing radical alternatives to earlier arguments and implying, or requiring, their abandonment. It is not recognised that contemporary theorists are standing on the shoulders of the intellectual giants of the past and that their new approaches and new directions are viable only so long as the theoretical foundations remain in place. Yet it is only by recognising the continuing dependence of contemporary departures on their intellectual foundations that sociology can grasp the new social forms that have emerged during the twentieth century.

Contemporary theoretical work has been concerned with a much wider range of social phenomena than ever before, and sociologists have had to become more specialised in their interests. Developing their intellectual interests within a broad intellectual division of labour, it has been all too easy to lose sight of the relevance and validity of alternative theoretical approaches: disputations between 'system' and 'action' theories, between 'cultural' and 'naturalistic' approaches, and so on, have become sharper and more doctrinal. The proliferation of specialist theories has sometimes led to the view that sociology is no longer – if it ever was – a unified discipline. It comprises a number of more or less distinct and competing theoretical orientations. An unbiased examination of this theoretical work, however, discloses the continuing complementarities in diverse theoretical approaches, and it is this that I shall try to emphasise in my discussion. I will show that different theoretical approaches may often provide complementary bases of social understanding.

The number of those involved in the development of social theory has increased massively in the contemporary period, and it is impossible for any overview to pursue even a small fraction of the work produced. My account of contemporary theory will, therefore, be even more selective than that of the formative theorists. I will be able to consider only the more powerful and influential contributions and will be unable to give an adequate indication of the range and diversity of writers engaged in social theory. In this chapter I will look at those who have explored the cultural formation of social structures, the systemic organisation of social life, and the socialisation of individuals into social systems. In the following chapter I will examine the works of those concerned with interaction, with social conflict, and with the natural factors that condition social life.

Culture, Social Structures, and Lifeworlds

I showed in Chapter 3 that the formative theorists in sociology set out a view of culture as the central element in the structuring of social life and that, on this basis, they explored the systemic character of social structures and their development over time. In the reflections of Wundt, Boas, Croce, Cooley, and many others, culture was shown to be a distinct and autonomous network of communicated ideas – a system of shared meanings that results from interpersonal communication and is the pre-condition for the formation of individual minds and the organisation of actions. Diverse theories pointed in a similar direction and allowed much important empirical work to be carried out. The principal features of culture and its role in structuring social systems had been set out as a fundamental framework for sociological analysis. In this section, I will look at the ways in which Talcott Parsons enlarged the inherited view of culture and social structure and how, in turn, his work has been critically enlarged in the structuralism of Claude Lévi-Strauss and Roland Barthes, the post-structuralism of Michel Foucault, and the phenomenological work of Alfred Schütz and Harold Garfinkel. Such work articulated the implications of the idea that culture operates through discursive codes and that a central feature of social order is the establishment of a secure everyday lifeworld. I will look at attempts by Louis Althusser and Jürgen Habermas to draw on the Marxist tradition to explore the ontological depth of social structure through the idea of a differentiation of 'levels'. While these writers differ on matters of detail – and often disagree sharply – they all presuppose the key tenets of the approach to cultural formation developed by the formative theorists.

Culture, Norms, and Institutions

Talcott Parsons dominated American sociology for much of the second half of the twentieth century. Trained in Europe during the 1920s, he was more strongly influenced by Durkheim and Weber than by American predecessors such as Sumner, Giddings, Cooley, or Mead. Parsons is often considered – and denounced – as a 'functionalist' whose abstract models dehumanised sociology. In fact, his account of the social system was rooted in a view of cultural formation that, for all its limitations, placed values and subjectivity at the heart of sociological analysis. The formative theorists had seen culture as the basis of institutions and folkways, but they did not specify in any detail how these are formed and how they operate. Some insights into the formation and operation of kinship institutions had been gained by Radcliffe-Brown, but it was Parsons who really began the task of exploring social institutions. He did this through an array of concepts centred on the idea of the social 'roles' formed through cultural expectations and that constitute the basic elements of social structure.

For Parsons, individual action is 'voluntaristic', as individuals have the ability to choose how they will act.[1] The choices that they make, however, are not simple acts of unfettered free will but are constrained by cultural meanings. Cultures consist of signs or symbols arranged into the collective representations through which actions can be organised. Symbols are internalized objects that can be transmitted with minimal change from one person to another (Parsons and Bales 1956: 397). The symbolic patterns of a culture are analogous to the genetic patterns of an organism, and Parsons recognised an explicit parallel between the symbols and the gene. Where the gene is the unit of heredity in biological systems, the symbol is the unit of inheritance in cultural systems. Richard Dawkins (1976) and his followers (Blackmore 1999) have recently claimed this idea as their own, arguing that the concept of the 'meme' can be regarded as the unit of cultural transmission and that social scientists have failed to realise the fundamental parallel between genes and the cultural meme. Parsons not only made this point himself, but emphasised that the parallel between genes and symbols had first been made explicitly by the Chicago biologist Alfred Emerson during private discussions in 1956.

The parallel between the gene and the cultural symbol became central to Parsons's cultural analysis. The development and behaviour of biological organisms, he argued, depend upon the genetic code of the organism, stored in its DNA, and Parsons saw the development and behaviour of social systems resulting from the cultural codes that societies sustain in existence. A cultural code is a set of rules that defines the use and combination of symbols and that, therefore, allows the generation of collective representations (Parsons 1968: 189). A linguistic code, for example, is a particular type of cultural code and comprises the rules that define correct sentences and so allows the formulation and transmission of spoken and written messages. The cultural pattern of a society comprises a whole array of such codes.

Despite its European origins, Parsons's view of culture was very similar to that of Boas and his followers in the United States. Cultures can be compared, he argued, by identifying the 'value patterns' around which they are organised. Such value patterns are determinate combinations of certain universal value orientations that vary in strength from one culture to another. These value orientations are described in relation to 'pattern variables' that define the limits within which cultures can vary. Thus, cultural relativity can be seen as differentiation and variation within determinate limits that comprise the range of possible value orientations that humans can take towards the world.[2]

Cultural codes are the basis of the social institutions through which actions are concretely regulated. Social institutions had long been recognised as central to social order, and Parsons' main contribution was to show exactly how they are formed and how they operate. Institutions are constructed from meaningful symbols of numerous kinds, but those to which Parsons gave particular attention are the values that comprise a 'common value system'. These values underpin the commitments that people have to wider cultural patterns and they define the legitimate 'expectations' that people build about each other's behaviour.

Actors may anticipate the actions of others in purely pragmatic, cognitive terms – based on what they may have done in the past or what it is in their interest to do – and base their own actions on these cognitive expectations. The most important expectations, however, are 'normative' in character. Through sharing certain values, actors learn what they may legitimately expect others to do and what they are obliged to do in turn. The normative structuring of action ensures that force and coercion need only ever be secondary elements in social order (Parsons 1951: 15). The socialisation of individuals into a common value system provides them with an overall image of their society from which they can identify how they should act in specific situations and how they may expect particular others to act towards them. In this way, their actions are guided by 'norms' or rules of behaviour. Expectations tend to be formed into sets of complementary expectations, and this is what ensures that actions will interlock or 'interlard' smoothly. Expectations about the actions of students towards teachers, for example, complement those about the actions of teachers towards them. Complementary normative expectations, therefore, define complementary 'roles': expectations concerning behaviour appropriate for those engaged in particular kinds of activity and occupying particular social positions. Roles, in turn, are clustered into the social institutions (schools, families, businesses, states, etc.) whose interconnections constitute the social structure. They are the fundamental 'parts' of any social system, and it is on this basis that a degree of predictability and order is possible in social life. This idea was further elaborated in Merton (1957), Gross et al. (1958), and Dahrendorf (1958).

It is this socialisation that gives social institutions the solidity and taken-for-granted character through which conformity to established practices can be ensured. Parsons's reliance on a socialised conformity to inherited folkways has led to criticisms of his 'oversocialised' view of individuals and their actions

(Wrong 1961). He has been seen as having difficulty in explaining deviance, conflict, and innovation because of his emphasis on the conformity that results from socialisation into shared values. However, Parsons did not mean that all societies were actually to be seen as perfectly integrated social systems. The members of a society share a pool of collective representations to which they may be differentially committed. These are the symbolic means through which cultures regulate their relations with each other and inform any value judgements they make. Exploring the conditions under which perfect integration may occur – value consensus, integrated role expectations, and perfect socialisation – illuminates the more typical situations in which one or more of those conditions do not hold. Parsons's application of his general theory – for example in Parsons (1954) – uses his general model of social order to examine deviance and conflict as well as consensus.

Cultural value patterns, argued Parsons, are difficult to observe. They are 'latent' in the social institutions of a society and are rarely manifested in any direct way. They are 'genotypes' that are merely the templates from which are produced the 'phenotypical' character of the social systems in which they are institutionalised and the personalities by which they have been internalised. As latent, virtual realities, they legitimate recurrent actions, but are not consciously drawn on in individual actions. They are, rather, inherent in those actions, being deeply rooted in the unconscious as templates for action.

The most important line of criticism against Parsons's cultural analysis has taken up precisely this view, arguing that his analysis of mechanisms of cultural organisation faltered at precisely its most crucial point: Parsons failed to show the mechanisms through which latent cultural patterns can structure social actions. Claude Lévi-Strauss, Roland Barthes, Alfred Schütz, and Harold Garfinkel have, in their differing ways, attempted to resolve this problem of the structuring capacity present in latent cultural patterns.

FOCUS: TALCOTT PARSONS

Talcott Parsons was the major theorist to build on the formative work and construct a systematic account of the normative organisation of social activity. He set out a paradigmatic, if extremely dense, statement in *The Social System* (1951). Reading Chapter 10 (pages 428–79) of this book, on doctor–patient relations and the 'sick role', is the best way to appreciate the importance of his ideas.

(Continued)

Useful biographical information on Parsons can be found in Uta Gerhardt's *Talcott Parsons: An Intellectual Biography* (2002). From among the voluminous critical literature, some useful extensions of Parsons's scheme can be found in Jeffrey Alexander's *Theoretical Logic in Sociology* (1982–3), Volume 4.

Codes, Narratives, and Discursive Formations

Lévi-Strauss is widely recognised as the founder of a distinctively 'structuralist' approach to social life, an approach that he developed in reaction to the work of earlier theorists. In fact, his ideas are firmly rooted in those of Durkheim and his followers, and most particularly in Mauss's analysis of collective representations. The structuralist label attached to Lévi-Straus's ideas reflects his concern to explore below the level of the concrete meanings and relations that form the everyday 'surface' of social life in order to identify the underlying and latent structures that generate them. He developed this view using ideas drawn from the linguistics of Saussure and his followers, among whom Roman Jakobson was the most important. Jakobson was a leading contributor to the development in Russia of a 'formalist' approach to literature during the 1920s and he developed the linguistic aspects of this at Prague. The formalists treated literary production as a particular type of language that had to be analysed in terms of its formal or structural properties, as governed by tacit rules and conventions that structure literary texts. Jakobson and Lévi-Strauss both worked in New York during the Second World War, and it was there that Lévi-Strauss took the crucial step of combining formalist principles with the sociology of Durkheim. He began to develop these ideas in a number of papers from the 1940s and 1950s that have been reprinted in the first volume of his *Structural Anthropology* (1958).

Where Durkheim had seen structures of collective representations as shaped by structures of social relations, Lévi-Strauss emphasised their origins in the following of specific structural principles by those who produce and communicate them. As cultural systems are linguistic products, they can be analysed by direct analogy with linguistic systems. The flow of cultural signs and symbols that constitute a pattern of communication or exchange is analogous to what Saussure called 'speech' and can be seen as a product of the systems of rules and conventions that structure the use of signs. Such structures – equivalent to the 'tongue' of a language – are combinations of signs that acquire meaning only through the relations they have with other signs. Lévi-Strauss (1949a) initially applied this view to his fieldwork data on kinship in tribal societies, arguing that collective representations concerning kinship relations generate a structure of economic exchange and marital relations within which women circulate between patriarchal clans and lineages.

He developed his work through analyses of primitive thought and religion (1962a, 1962b) – revisiting themes explored by Lévy-Bruhl and Durkheim – and began a long series of investigations into Central and South American tribal mythologies (1964, 1967, 1968, 1971). This work makes it clear that Lévi-Strauss sees the structural principles as reflecting fundamental properties of the human mind. The deep-structure principles of a particular culture are organised around binary oppositions in which diverse cultural elements are combined according to a series of fundamental contrasts. The things contrasted are specific to particular cultures, but the logic of thought involving the making and combining of binary oppositions is a universal human attribute. The mind operates according to definite, innate rules, whose application in particular contexts results in the production and reproduction of the particular cultural systems observed in field studies. Latent structural principles organise social life because they are inherent in the human mind: human beings can act in no other way.

This argument echoed similar ideas that Noam Chomsky (1957) was developing in linguistics. Chomsky saw the infinitely varied speech patterns that humans produce as dependent upon the application of the finite system of rules that constitute the grammar of the language. The human ability to use a grammar – whether that of English, French, or Japanese – depends on an innate 'linguistic competence' common to all individuals. For Lévi-Strauss, the norms and meanings of which people are conscious and that figure in their collective conscience are not the real operative principles in social life. Sociologists should not privilege the subjectively shared meanings of actors, as conscious representations are always remote from the real causal factors at work (Lévi-Strauss 1953: 282). Drawing on the distinction between conscious phenomena and the unconscious 'infrastructure' made in Troubetzkoy's linguistics (see Lévi-Strauss 1945), he argued that cultural production depends on the unconscious models available within a culture and that generate observable cultural patterns. The conscious mental models espoused by participants comprise the codified norms and mental images through which they seek to describe their relations with each other. As accounts, these are, invariably, retrospective reconstructions and are, to a greater or lesser extent, inaccurate and partial guides to the real, unconscious processes at work. It is the job of sociology, furthermore, to discover the unconscious models that are actually operative. As systems of rules and relations among cultural signs, they are analogous to the grammars studied by linguists. Our ability to use them is rooted in an innate cultural competence.

Kinship systems, myth narratives, and other social phenomena result from the application of the rules of a particular cultural code as the mind operates, unconsciously, on the raw materials available to it. Lévi-Strauss held that the unconscious forms are fundamentally the same for all minds and so an understanding of the principles underlying any one institution or custom provides the basis for understanding all other institutions and customs (1949b: 21). This led him to postulate a number of deep-level similarities of structure among cultural systems. There are, for example, parallels between linguistic forms and kinship terms. Such structural similarities in language and kinship are found among the cultures of the Indo-European language area, the Crow-Omaha cultures, African cultures, and so on. Each of these, in turn, possesses deeper-level similarities with all others because of the universal principles by which human minds operate. Lévi-Strauss also proposed strictly analogous methods for analysing each cultural code: language was to be understood as a system of 'phonemes', mythology as a system of 'mythemes', and cookery as a system of 'gustemes'.

Lévi-Strauss recognised that the observable pattern of relations and representations in any society cannot be reduced to a single unconscious model. A number of structures are always at work, even within a single sphere of activity, and concrete realities must be understood in terms of the complex intersection of a plurality of structural principles, rooted in often contradictory cultural codes. The implications of this coexistence of a plurality of cultural codes were concurrently being explored by Roland Barthes, who developed his work specifically as 'semiology' and undertook a rigorous application and extension of Saussure's principles. Closely associated with Barthes was the work of Algirdus Griemas (1966, 1976), and similar ideas, owing more to Charles Peirce than to Saussure, were set out by Umberto Eco (1976, 1984). All of these writers owe much to the pioneering work of Louis Hjelmslev (1943). They also have certain parallels with Mikhail Bakhtin (1929, 1940), an early critic of formalism whose argument on discourse as 'dialogue' complements the general approach taken by Barthes.

Unlike Lévi-Strauss, Barthes did not seek an ultimate grounding of cultural variation in universal properties of the mind, and he has been seen as heralding the move to a more relativistic 'post-structuralism'. His central point is that cultures comprise a diverse plurality of 'systems of signification', only some of which take a linguistic form. Literature and other written texts can be analysed through the linguistic signs that they use, as Jakobson had argued, but this is not the case for music, pictures, food, clothing, furniture, urban design, sport, travel, and so on. The latter are 'second-order' systems that presuppose linguistic analyses but also depend upon systems of non-linguistic signs for their intelligibility (Barthes 1957).

The analysis of such cultural systems begins from the 'denotative' signs used. These are the signs that denote or point to some specific object and label it in some way. An analysis must then trace their 'connotations' or the implicit associated meanings invoked. Barthes illustrates this with a photograph of a black Frenchman saluting the French flag. The denotative meaning of this is 'Negro saluting French flag', but its connotations include 'colonialism', 'nationalism', and 'militarism'. People typically encode and decode the connotative meanings unconsciously from the objects presented to their consciousness, and so these wider connotative meanings have to be uncovered through semiological analysis. The connotations are ideologically effective precisely because they affect people below the level of their conscious awareness.

Barthes has applied his approach in a number of areas. He shows, for example, that food preparation is the product of cultural codes ('alimentary taboos') that limit the permissible combinations and transformations of foods (1964). In furnishing a house, systems of rules define the furniture appropriate to particular types of room and house, and the way in which furniture is actually arranged is an application of these rules. Similarly, fashion writing in magazines and newspapers employs a cultural code that allows the writer to create a 'simulacrum' of the actual clothes and to write about this new object in such a way as to obscure and distort the consciousness of the consumer (1967). Such discourse is central to advertising as a system: advertising is a form of 'mythology' in which ways of thinking and talking are structured in such a way as to convey a message that goes beyond the obvious surface denotations to the insidious hidden connotations. The rules employed may be those of a 'deciding group' (designers, manufacturers, advertisers) rather than those of the 'speaking mass' that actually consumes the meanings produced. The mass of consumers tend to be passive recipients of meanings, decoding them according to codes imposed upon them through relations of power.

Cultural analysis is only one part of social analysis for Barthes. It is a precondition for sociological analysis, not a substitute for it. Semiology uncovers meanings inherent in the mythologies through which people's lives are structured, but the task of relating these to 'socio-economic' forces remains. It is in this sense that Barthes's analysis of 'mythology' can be seen as a reformulation of the Marxist analysis of 'ideology': as in the sociology of knowledge, cultural narratives and their generative codes must be related to the material forces that organise them and sustain them. Important distinctions are to be made between the mythologies of dominant groups and the discourses of the oppressed. The former has a legitimating, 'naturalising' role, while the latter aims at a 'transformative' practice (1957: 149). The images of new cars, holiday venues, bottles of wine, and so on, that appear in the mass media provide the stereotypes and archetypes through which people live, in distorted ways, their everyday experiences. Such imaginary symbols deflect the transformative potential of oppressed groups and deepen their oppression. Barthes's ideas (1966) were influential for Louis Althusser's (1971) analysis of the ideological apparatuses.

Discussions of cultural formation had frequently been undertaken on the assumption that societies could be characterised by the possession of a single, overarching culture. It was in the work of Lévi-Strauss and Barthes that it was finally recognised that this was the case only for a very limited number of societies. In almost all cases, there is a diversity of cultures, whether these be the competing cultures and 'subcultures' of classes and ethnic groups or the intersecting symbolic systems that constitute different aspects of social life. The structuralists established the importance of investigating the actual diversity of 'systems of signification' involved in the cultural formation of individuals and their societies. In the wake of their arguments a group of theorists often characterised as 'post-structuralists' made this diversity their central topic and began to investigate its wider implications. Such ideas were elaborated by Jacques Derrida and Michel Foucault, and they underpinned some of the claims made by Jean Baudrillard.

Jacques Derrida (1967a, 1967b), along with Gilles Deleuze (1962, 1969), developed novel approaches to the analysis of literary texts, but their arguments were widely seen as carrying implications for other forms of cultural production and, therefore, for the whole process of cultural formation. The interpretation of a textual discourse is seen as a process of 'deconstruction' that uncovers the 'differences' or structural oppositions around which the discourse is organised and which produce its characteristic gaps (the 'absences' or 'silences') and contradictions. Any text is the product of a diversity of systems of signification, and it is the interplay that leads to the inevitable contradictions and incoherences that mark any text. According to Deleuze, these contending systems in a discourse comprise 'semiotic regimes' that structure its contradictory meanings. Thus, a text always conveys contradictory messages and will only superficially appear to be unequivocal or uniform in meaning. Textual analysis must uncover the hidden structurings at work. These arguments can be extended from a single literary text to collections of texts and to whole cultural systems. Exploring these possibilities, Deleuze emphasises that cultural systems must be seen as dispersed and fragmentary structures of signification and coding that can most usefully be seen as 'rhizomes' – as deep, horizontal assemblages of meaning without any central organising principle or hierarchical authority (Deleuze and Guattari 1972). Cultural influences spread rhizomatically, much as the fibrous roots of the Lily of the Valley spread below the surface of the ground.

For those influenced by Derrida and Deleuze, all the discursive systems through which humans live their lives must be deconstructed in order to be understood. Taking up the idea of semiotic regimes, Luc Boltanski (1993; Boltanski and Thévenot 1991) has argued that social life is structured through regimes of affectivity, regimes of justification, and regimes of familiarity that allow people to invoke particular discourses of meaning and constitute areas of life as those in which specific narratives and criteria of relevance should operate. Within each area there may, nevertheless, be a plurality of constitutive orderings that underpin diverse and conflicting interpretations to be made and offered to others. In the later work of Jean Baudrillard (1979, 1981, 1983) it is argued that the sign systems and collective representations generated in the mass media have become the key constituents of reality itself. The 'text' of social life has been written by the mass media, and it is the 'simulations' and images of media discourse that must be analysed for insights into contemporary life experiences.

Michel Foucault (1966, 1971), like Derrida and Deleuze, held that cultural systems have no essence or unity and cannot be treated as integrated 'totalities'. They must, instead, be seen as decentred and pluralistic. Foucault applied a historical approach to the emergence and transformation of diverse 'discursive formations' and the codes that generate the particular texts, narratives, and ideologies through which identities are built and social activities organised. These discursive formations – as Barthes had recognised – cannot be understood in cultural terms alone but are rooted in the material power relations that constitute social groups and their struggles for dominance (Foucault 1975–6).

Foucault saw rationality as central to modern forms of discourse, epitomised particularly in the 'scientific' worldview. Modern worldviews sharpened the idea of the 'irrational', and Foucault's early empirical work (1961, 1963) examined how, from the middle of the seventeenth century, new forms of medical and psychiatric discourse forged rational approaches to understanding madness and irrationality. A parallel discourse of criminality formed the categories of the 'criminal' and the 'deviant' (1975). These modern worldviews also gave birth to the apparatuses of power through which irrationality could be controlled: the clinic, the asylum, and the prison. Medical, psychological, and sociological discourses also formed ideas of sexual 'normality' and deviance and established a disciplinary regulation of pleasure (1976, 1984a, 1984b). This extension of apparatuses of surveillance and discipline was the result not of a central plan or strategy but of the interplay of groups of experts, state and private agencies, and other dispersed structures of power. The growth of modern states and their apparatuses of control is, in every sense, an unintended consequence of the purposive actions of groups pursuing their sectional interests in their struggles for power.

FOCUS: ROLAND BARTHES

The writers explored in this section are very diverse and differ subtly from each other. However, the works of Roland Barthes provide the key point of reference and underly many other contributions. Barthes has written on numerous topics, and the core of his position is set out in *Mythologies* (1957). Pages 36–8, 41–2, and 58–61 of this book give a clear exposition of his views.

Louis-Jean Calvet has produced a biography, *Roland Barthes* (1990), and a good critical introduction can be found in Jonathan Culler's *Barthes* (1983).

Everyday Lifeworld and Practical Methods

A different line of theoretical development was inspired by phenomenological philosophy. This approach to understanding everyday experience was used to extend and enlarge Parsons's account of the social context of interaction. Alfred Schütz's early work had been a phenomenological reconstruction of Weber's concept of action. His later work, in New York, turned to Parsons, whom he saw as owing a great deal to Weber. Though he became progressively more alienated from Parsons's highly generalised theory, Schütz saw his later work as complementing Parsons's view of cultural formations.[3] He produced a phenomenology of the social world that uncovered the actually experienced reality of cultural wholes and social structures, developing this in a series of papers and in the outline of a book that was completed by his student Thomas Luckmann (Schütz and Luckmann 1973; 1983).[4]

His central concept was that of a socio-cultural 'lifeworld', derived from Husserl's concept of the *Lebenswelt*. The lifeworld comprises the symbolic representations that shape and organise people's lived and directly experienced reality. It is a collective, inter-subjective reality or cultural tradition, consisting of the various religious beliefs and technical knowledge, literary and artistic ideas, fantasies and dreams, through which everyday experiences are internalised as mental representations. The lifeworld is constructed from symbolic elements that pre-exist each individual, are modified by the actions of associated individuals, and are passed on to the next generation. From the standpoint of each individual, it is an external, pre-given reality, experienced as a social fact. Such a reality is all too easily 'reified' – perceived and treated as an objective 'thing' – and is experienced by individuals as a *constraining* reality (Berger and Luckmann 1966; Berger and Pullberg 1966). Individuals accept the definitions and meanings contained in their lifeworld as unproblematic and self-evidently real or 'true'. These meanings are solidified through the reciprocal acts of reification in which people engage, each participant assuming that all others see the world in the same way. Their individual reality is normalised and naturalised as *the* reality.

This lifeworld is, nevertheless, an internally differentiated cultural framework that makes possible a range of experienced realities. As people move from one sphere of activity to another, their focus of attention shifts to those particular phenomena that are now most pertinent to them. They draw upon that particular zone or 'province' of meaning relevant to their current activity to interpret their experiences. The previous reality fades and a new reality forms. For example, on waking from a dream, its reality fades as the waking reality engulfs consciousness. Similarly, on returning home from a holiday, the reality of the holiday rapidly fades as the practical requirements of home and work are once more attended to.

Schütz gave particular attention to what he termed the 'everyday' lifeworld. This is a 'subuniverse' of meaning concerned with the practical actions of day-to-day encounters. It is the 'paramount reality' or foundation of all social life and provides the 'familiar' framework of 'common-sense' or 'taken-for-granted' knowledge in terms of which everyday expectations are built (Schütz and Luckmann 1973: 17–18). It comprises a 'stock of knowledge' derived from memories of the solutions devised for problems encountered in the past and, as such, it makes possible the predictability through which people can carry on 'as normal' in their day-to-day routines. Their actions are 'routinised' as habits that can be performed, without any need for rational and conscious reflection. The role expectations that form the social institutions of a society, for example, are reciprocal typifications, expressed in habits of action. They ensure social order and predictability because they are taken for granted as defining normal or natural ways to behave in particular situations.

Harold Garfinkel built on Schütz's work to develop his 'ethnomethodology' for studying the interpretative processes or methods involved in reality construction. Garfinkel's earliest inspirations, while a student, were Parsons (1937), Znaniecki (1936), and Mills (1940), together with the literary critic Kenneth Burke (1935). Discovering the published work of Schütz, while undertaking his doctoral work with Parsons, his interests crystallised around a critical consideration of the Parsonian view of social order. He has published his ideas in a series of empirical studies (1967, 2002).[5]

Garfinkel's main criticism of Parsons was that he treated actors as cultural or judgemental 'dopes' who passively enact learned cultural norms. His alternative view was that actors are active participants in the construction of social reality. Culture does not provide normative 'scripts' that can be unquestioningly followed in performing actions. Rather, it provides sketchy outlines that must be creatively improvised in the diverse and unpredictable situations in which people find themselves. Although social roles and expectations may be experienced as objective realities, as Durkheimian social facts, they are practical achievements of individuals acting together, and a sense of their objectivity can be sustained only if this is continually worked at. Everyday life is inherently uncertain and participants must build a sense of what is going on and how to act. This rarely involves conscious deliberation but is undertaken in practical and unreflective ways. Actors must respond to cues from which they can infer what rules and meanings might be invoked to account for what they have experienced and to legitimate their own actions. Thus, observed actions and other experiences are interpreted as 'indexical' expressions of deeply embedded cultural patterns that they cue or document (T. P. Wilson 1970).

In making these inferences, actors draw on their stock of taken-for-granted knowledge, which tells them what, for all practical purposes, they might expect to observe. Garfinkel saw culture as providing the rules through which actions are organised. All actions are rule-governed, but these rules are deeply embedded and taken-for-granted principles that make themselves felt as unconscious generators of actions. The conscious norms of which people are aware are mere codifications of the actually operative principles that remain latent, as Parsons put it, within the cultural codes acquired by individuals.

A similar view had been taken by Ludwig Wittgenstein (1953). Though he died in 1951, his posthumously published book was compiled from the notes and drafts that he left behind and his ideas were advocated by followers such as Peter

Winch (1958). Wittgenstein's central idea was that the culture of a society comprises the 'concepts' that define its 'form of life', and that the world encountered in human experience must, therefore, be grasped by understanding the particular sets of concepts around which it is organised. Wittgenstein made the apparently obvious point that these concepts must always be formulated in language and, therefore, that all human experience is mediated through particular languages.[6] A culture can be considered, ultimately, as a linguistic structure, as what Wittgenstein termed a 'language game'. It comprises a system of rules that regulate the ways in which the words and concepts of a language can be properly used. These rules – like the grammatical rules of a language – are only very unusually made the objects of conscious awareness and reflection. To understand a society, according to Wittgenstein, it is necessary to understand the rules or principles that comprise the various language games possible within its culture. A knowledge of the constitutive rules of a culture is the first step towards understanding the society and the actions of its members.

Garfinkel recognised that, for all its sophistication, the Wittgensteinian idea of rule-following remained too close to the idea of conscious norm-following. He argues that social activity should be seen as methodical conduct, as the pursuance of particular 'methods' of acting that have become deeply rooted and unconscious ways of behaving. Conformity to norms is a result of the application of shared and taken-for-granted *methods*. Actors learn ways of behaving and of accounting for their behaviour and so produce a sense of order in their everyday actions. By acting methodically they reproduce this sense of order and make their social encounters routine and predictable. Where such routinisation is achieved, the Parsonian model of explanation has much to offer, but it must be seen as having its foundations in the practical, and tentative, interactional achievements of everyday life. The 'member's methods' that actors follow are deeply embedded in individual minds, far removed from discursive consciousness, and they are applied routinely and almost without thought in everyday actions. They are skills and dispositions that, like the skills involved in riding a bicycle, embody knowledge, definitions, and expectations that are not normally accessible to conscious scrutiny.

The skills involved in the reproduction of the orderly character of everyday life are raised to consciousness only when questioned by others or when they fail to achieve their expected results. Thus, Garfinkel held that they could be studied experimentally by engineering disruptions to normal expectations that lead people to speculate about the reasons for the disruptions and to re-establish a sense of reality and order. When people attempt to reflect on their methods in consciousness, it is in order to 'account' for their actions and those of others. They attempt to invoke a plausible narrative to explain why certain actions have taken place in the ways that they have. Accounts are retrospective reflections on activities and must not be seen as direct reflections of the actual methods that produced them. Ethnomethods and ethno-accounts are distinct phenomena that are, nevertheless, reciprocally involved in the reproduction of social order. It is through their accounting practices that actors create and sustain the sense of an objective social reality that informs their methodical actions (Zimmerman and Wieder 1970: 293–4). Cultural patterns, to the extent that people formulate them in consciousness, have a rhetorical function rather than a motivational one. This has led some to draw the radical conclusion that cultural patterns should not be seen as having any existence independently of the accounting practices that invoke them (see Turner 1994).

Aaron Cicourel (1968, 1970, 1972) has drawn on structural linguistics to model ethnomethods. These methods, he argues, comprise the deep structure of grammar or syntax that makes possible an orderly flow of social activity. They are ingrained 'procedures' that structure thought, speech, and action. He highlights the 'interpretative procedures' that allow people to build a sense of social structure, and so to know how to act and which norms it is appropriate to invoke in accounting for their actions. Role behaviour, as described by Parsons, is possible only because it is the surface expression of the deep-structure ethnomethods through which people interpret the world.

Ethnomethodologists have studied such diverse areas as courtroom decisions, medical diagnoses and treatments (Emerson 1970), policing practices (Cicourel 1967), educational counselling (Cicourel and Kitsuse 1963), walking down the street, and telephone use. The interactional use of ethnomethods involves a 'conversation' in which accounts are proffered and accepted (or rejected) and underlying cultural codes are reinforced (or undermined), and particularly important extensions of the approach have undertaken conversation analysis , studying the actual flow of talk in everyday encounters (Sacks 1965–72; Boden and Zimmerman 1990).

A similar line of argument has been followed by Anthony Giddens, who uses it as the basis of his theory of the 'structuration' of human life. Arguing that much sociological debate revolves around an opposition of 'structure' and 'action' (1976, 1979), Giddens attempts a theory in which the two can be reconciled. Structural and systemic sociologies, he argues, have focused on the objectivity of social institutions and their external constraining power over individuals. Sociologies of action, on the other hand, have focused on the face-to-face encounters in which individuals construct their identities and present themselves to others. Very often, Giddens argues, the two sociologies can coexist as parts of a larger intellectual division of labour, but their mutual implications mean that there is a need for a theory in which they can be combined and form a single framework of explanation,

Giddens's solution is a recognition of the 'duality' of structure: individual actions are shaped by social structures, but systemic patterns are the outcomes of these individual actions. 'Structure' must be reconceptualised as both the *means* through which actions are produced and the *result* of such actions; as both 'medium' and 'outcome'. Giddens follows both Garfinkel and Lévi-Strauss in seeing a social structure as a system of rules that is 'instantiated' in social systems but has only a 'virtual' or latent existence (Giddens 1981). Rules are unconscious, programmed dispositions to act, think, or feel in particular ways, and people rarely have any accurate conscious awareness of them. Structural rules are central to what Pierre Bourdieu (1972) has called the habitus.

Giddens recognises three categories of rule, defining three capacities in human agency. These are the semantic (concerned with communication and significa-tion), the regulative (concerned with sanction and legitimation), and the trans-formative (concerned with the allocation and coordination of resources). The application of these rules generates the systemic forms of, respectively, discur-sive formations and ideology, legal and customary institutions, and political and economic institutions (1984).

FOCUS: HAROLD GARFINKEL

Phenmomenological ideas received their most forceful formulation in the ethnomethodology of Harold Garfinkel. His work, presented in *Studies in Ethnomethodology* (1967), is often quite complex, but a good introduction can be found in his account of Agnes, a transsexual, in Chapter 5 and the Appendix.

Some biographical information on Garfinkel can be found in Anne Rawl's introduction to his *Ethnomethodology's Program* (2002), while a critical secondary discussion can be found in John Heritage's *Garfinkel and Ethnomethodology* (1984). An excellent introduction is Kenneth Leiter's *Primer on Ethnomethodology* (1980).

Levels of Social Structure

Formative theorists had explored the differentiation of societies into distinct types of social activity. This was at its sharpest in the Marxist view of a differentiation between an economic base and a political and ideological superstructure, an integral aspect of the Marxist tendency towards economic determinism. Orthodox Marxism has continued to stress this distinction, which has been systematically explored by Gerry Cohen (1978). Among Marxists such as Lukács, Adorno, and Gramsci a far greater autonomy was accorded to the political and cultural spheres and forms of social consciousness. The insights of Gramsci, largely unknown until the 1950s, have been especially influential among those who developed Marxist approaches to literature and culture (Williams 1977, 1981; see also Hall 1977). These arguments paralleled earlier work in the sociology of knowledge and the sociology of culture, where writers such as Scheler, Mannheim, and Alfred Weber had explored the distinctiveness of 'real' or 'material' activities from cultural or 'spiritual' ones. Among contemporary theorists, Althusser has set out an analysis that owes its major debt to Gramsci, while Jürgen Habermas has drawn on both Adorno and Alfred Weber to completely recast the base and superstructure model and to relate it to systemic ideas of subsystem differentiation.

Althusser's (1963) argument was that any society, or 'social formation', can be seen as comprising three levels of 'practice' or practical activity. A practice is any process in which initial conditions and materials are transformed into new outcomes through specific and distinctive means, and specific forms of practice are distinguished by their particular materials and means and the 'apparatuses' into which these are organised. They are the activities that define lines of structural differentiation. Economic practice is social activity in which natural raw materials are converted into useful products and objects of consumption through the exercise of labour power. The social apparatuses involved in economic practice are the households, markets, property relations, business enterprises, and banks through which the production, distribution, and consumption of goods and services takes place (Althusser 1965). Political practice, on the other hand, transforms social relations – and especially class relations – into new forms of social relationship through collective action. This takes place through such apparatuses as parties, states, legislatures, armies, and other agencies of coercion, repression, and mobilisation. Finally, ideological practice is a distinctively cultural or discursive practice in which established cultural representations are converted into new systems of representation through intellectual or theoretical activity. The apparatuses involved in ideological practice are the families, schools, mass media, and churches in which are produced the collective representations through which people structure their lives and that may be formed into the discursive systems of religion, philosophy, morality, law, and art (Althusser 1971). Ideological representations do not 'correspond' to the real conditions under which people live but are 'imagined' simulations of them. Their connection to the real world can be judged only by their practical capacity to inform successful actions.

A social formation as a whole does not consist of an economic base and a political and ideological superstructure but of these three relatively autonomous levels of practice. Each level is a field of activity that operates according to its own logic and set of principles but is, nevertheless, interdependent with all others. A social formation is a complex articulation of reciprocal causal influences between levels and its overall shape is 'overdetermined' (Althusser 1962a): each level affects all others to produce the cumulative, reinforcing causal influences that bring about historical transformations. A social formation is a 'structure articulated in dominance' (1963), in the sense that one level will always have a dominant influence on the outcomes of historical action. Thus, in some societies the political level will be dominant and social relations will be regulated by political command and coercive force. In other societies, the ideological level may be dominant and people's actions will be defined by religious beliefs or traditional conceptions of social status. In no society, however, can the social formation be reduced to the effects of a single level; all three operate interdependently and social analysis must uncover the specific concatenation of causal influences at work.

Althusser followed Engels in holding that the economic level is, in the last instance, the basic determining influence in any social formation. The nature of the economic level determines which of the three levels is able to exercise a dominant causal influence. Social theory must, therefore, begin from an understanding of the historical sequence of modes of production through which economic activity is organised. Through most of human history, economic influences have been obscured by the dominant political or ideological relations made possible by particular modes of production. Modern societies, however, are organised around capitalist modes of production and the economic level is dominant as well as ultimately determinant. Althusser, therefore, has reformulated the idea of the economic base as the fundamental, long-term influence on social development.

Habermas trained under Adorno and was a key figure in the development of the new forms of Marxist theory often called 'critical theory'. He also engaged in debates with sociologists, such as systems theorists and phenomenologists, in his attempts to explore the relationship between material processes of labour and processes of communication (Luhmann and Habermas 1971). Social life, he argues, involves both the instrumental forms of action on the material world that Marx analysed as 'labour' and the communicative interactions through which symbolic representations enter into the constitution of social relations (Habermas 1968, 1968–9). Habermas sought to integrate the arguments of Parsons and Niklas Luhmann into a larger scheme that would retain the Marxian emphasis on the centrality of economic systems but recognise also the cultural formation of economic actions and the changing historical forms through which labour and communication are interrelated (Habermas 1981a, 1981b).

Habermas sees the earliest forms of society as relatively undifferentiated lifeworlds in which all human activity can be contained and given meaning. Such 'primitive' societies are organised exclusively through relations of family and kinship. Social evolution is a process in which the lifeworld is differentiated into specialised spheres of cultural discourse that become more numerous and distinctive as they evolve. Spheres of science, morality, and aesthetics may be formed, and these may differentiate into education, research, literature, music, art, and so on. Habermas draws heavily on the hermeneutics of Gadamer (1960) for his understanding of communication and the lifeworld, and he sees the discursive spheres comprising that area of human life that Alfred Weber (1935) designated as 'culture', with each sphere organised around its distinctive cultural code.

Economic and political activities – Weber's 'civilisation' – also tend to be differentiated from the lifeworld, which becomes a residual sphere of undifferentiated activity focused in family households and local communities. It becomes the intersubjective sphere of *Gemeinschaft*, of integrative norms and values. The 'uncoupled' *Gesellschaft* of adaptive economic and political activities comprises 'system' processes, using this word in a narrow sense that distinguishes it from the cultural 'spheres' and the residual lifeworld. The systems have substantive primacy as the driving or 'steering' forces in social life. They become progressively more significant foci of action, organised around work and domination through the production and mobilisation of money and power. Marx, Habermas argues, recognised the growing significance of the economy in modern social systems, but failed to appreciate its close association with the nation state and died long before such states had acquired the importance they have in late modernity. Money and power are now the generalised means through which whole societies come to be organised as they exert a growing influence over cultural activities and the lifeworld. The process that Habermas describes as 'colonisation' is one in which mechanisms and processes appropriate to the economic and political systems prevail in the culture and in the lifeworld. They become the yardsticks by which all other activities are organised. The system, as the reconceptualised 'base', shapes the autonomous development of the 'superstructural' lifeworld. Where Marx saw modern societies as those in which the base could be understood in exclusively economic terms, Habermas sees them as founded on the formation of a truly political economy, a combination of economic and political structures that has become the driving force in historical development.

FOCUS: JÜRGEN HABERMAS

Views on levels of social structure within a broadly Marxist approach have been explored by Jürgen Habermas in many publications. Working within critical theory and drawing on both functionalism and phenomenology, he set out his ideas in his *The Theory of Communicative Action*. His ideas are best approached, however through the essay on 'Technology and Science as "Ideology"' (1965).

There is a massive secondary literature on Habermas. The standard source (though now rather dated) is Thomas McCarthy's *The Critical Theory of Jürgen Habermas* (1978), but the most accessible introduction is that in Michael Pusey's *Jürgen Habermas* (1987).

General Systems, Functions, and Complexity

Two forms of systemic arguments were developed in the formative period, each ascribing *sui generis* properties to social wholes. As 'social physics', mechanical ideas of forces and energies were used to explore social systems. Social life was treated as a space or field of forces among elements that are connected in determinate ways, following linear patterns of motion that disturb, establish, or restore equilibrium. Such 'closed systems' could be completely explained by their internal properties. Forms of this social physics were strongly developed by Howard Odum (1971, 1983; Odum and Odum 1976) in his ecological models.[7] As 'organicism', biological ideas were used to study the internal flows and vital circuits of social systems and their subsystems. Some sought direct analogues of the heart, brain, and circulation, but most used only the idea of specialised 'organs' with more specifically social 'functions'. Such 'open systems' are involved in complex adaptive relations with their environments.

From the middle of the twentieth century, both approaches were transformed as theories of general systems were developed and applied to social theory. Advances in control engineering, through which low-powered equipment could control large-scale, high-energy industrial processes, produced the mathematical theories of self-regulation that led to further advances in computing and automation. Ludwig von Bertalanffy and Anatol Rapoport formed a research group in 1954 to develop this mathematics, and the ideas of Bertalanffy (1950; Bertalanffy et al. 1951) and Norbert Wiener (1948, 1950) were the basis for 'cybernetics' and 'general system theory' (see also Ashby 1956; Beer 1959; and the later systematic statement in Bertalanffy et al. 1968).

This theory recognised that most systems are 'open' to the effects of their environment through a constant flow of energy and information. Energy is characteristic of flows in physical systems and is involved as a carrier of information in other systems. Information may be coded into a physical form (as in the DNA of the genetic code) or is purely symbolic information conveyed linguistically. Even linguistic information, of course, requires a physical base – paper, tape, or air waves – but the distinction remains valid. Open systems move towards a 'homeostasis' or 'steady state', a dynamic state achieved through 'feedback'. Such systems evolve ways to monitor fed-back information and ensure it contributes to the maintenance or development of the system, making 'purposive', goal-oriented activity possible. In this relational view, system properties are irreducible to the properties of the parts; they are shaped by the relations through which parts are connected into 'organised' wholes. The parts are not fixed and closed entities but owe their properties to these same relations.

Systems, Functions, and Contradictions

The leading figure in applying these ideas in social theory was Talcott Parsons (et al. 1953, 1961, 1970, 1975).[8] Cultures can be understood in systemic terms, but must also be seen in relation to the systems of social relations and personality systems that they constitute. Parsons's starting point was the 'functional significance' of the structural subsystems or parts of a system, which make varying contributions to the survival or continuation of the system. Any system that survives for any time must have managed to establish mechanisms through which its structural parts have become geared to specific 'functions'. There have been a number of attempts to detail the functional 'needs' or 'requirements' of social systems, one of the most influential being that of Aberle and his colleagues (Aberle et al. 1950). Parsons himself initially distinguished two requirements on the basis of the two broad functional problem areas found in any social system: the 'external' processes of 'adaptation' through which people respond to problems posed by their environment; and the 'internal' processes of 'integration' through which adaptive activities and relations are held together and a degree of cohesion or stability is achieved. Adaptation and integration, then, are universal functional requirements of systems. They are the foci around which social systems are differentiated into functionally specialised subsystems. These are adaptive or external systems and integrative or

A adaptation	G goal attainment
L latency	I integration

Figure 5.1 *The Parsonian four function scheme*

internal systems (Parsons 1951; see also Homans 1950; Williams 1981). Failure to meet these functional requirements leads to the breakdown or 'death' of a system, and all surviving systems must have evolved ways of meeting them. Functional requirements may not always be met, and they may have no direct causal effect on people. They are necessary constraints or conditions with which people must deal. Only if, contingently, they respond effectively will a social system persist.

Parsons later subdivided the external and internal functions to produce a more subtle scheme. Externally oriented activities were seen as comprising 'adaptive' and 'goal attainment' activities. The narrowly defined adaptive activities are those through which necessary resources are secured from the environment, while goal attainment activities are those through which people are mobilised to attain them. The internally oriented activities were seen as comprising the 'integrative' activities through which everyday life is normatively regulated and the 'latent' cultural commitments that underpin them. Parsons formed these four functions into a template for systems analysis, commonly termed the AGIL scheme (Figure 5.1). Each function is the basis of an analytical subsystem, a set of activities and transactions concerned with that particular function.

Social institutions and other structural parts of a social system, Parsons argued, are concerned with particular functions, though many activities may be multifunctional. The institutions described as 'economic', for example, are primarily adaptive, while the 'political' are primarily concerned with goal attainment. Economic and political institutions regulate instrumental, rationally goal-oriented actions involved in the allocation and use of resources to secure the system's conditions of existence. They involve the use of money and power to achieve production, distribution, and collective mobilisation. Integrative functions have their primary focus in institutions organised around emotional and expressive activities. The institutions of kinship, community, and social status are the principal means of integration and through them the boundaries and identity of a system are maintained. When cultural patterns form deep cultural commitments and competences, these function latently to sustain the norms that constitute other social institutions. A latent subsystem of cultural pattern maintenance is the means through which the cultural system and its symbolic codes articulate with actual patterns of social relations.

Parsons saw social development as constrained by the need to respond to functional problems and so also as a process in which societies tend to become structurally differentiated along functional lines. Economic and political institutions tend to become more sharply separated and distinguished both from each other and from the integrative 'societal community' and its latent religious and ideological beliefs. Functional activities may split off into organisations regulated by specific institutions: money and productive activities regulated through banks, corporations, and market institutions; decision-making and coordination regulated through states, bureaucracies, political parties, and pressure groups (Easton 1953), and so on. Whenever such structural differentiation occurs, specialised structures – the 'organs' identified by earlier theorists – will correspond to the analytical subsystems: an 'economy', for example, may form as a structurally distinct complex of adaptive activities. This argument gives a functional underpinning to the forming of societies into distinct structural levels or spheres.

When social activities are structurally differentiated into specialised subsystems, these must maintain 'interchanges' with each other. Each subsystem depends for its capacity to function on the 'inputs' received from other subsystems. Resources can be secured from the environment, processed, and mobilised by specialised social groups and organisations, and can then be exchanged or transferred to groups and organisations operating in other structural subsystems. This is the means through which a social system accommodates and adjusts to its environment. The cumulative result of these separate transactions is a complex series of interchanges of energy and information among the four functional subsystems. Equilibrium in a social system exists when there is a balance or reciprocity in the interchanges of energy and information among the various subsystems. Changes in system states are results of imbalanced interchanges.

Parsons conceptualised these interchanges through the 'generalised media' of exchange – such as money and power – that allow them to take place (1963; Parsons and Smelser 1956). Money is a symbolic representation of economic value, a means of measurement that allows claims on economic value to circulate. It develops when exchange systems become true market systems through the introduction of free-floating monetary tokens independent of any metallic base. When modern states claimed a monopoly over the issue of such 'currency' it became possible to build impersonal mass banking systems and credit mechanisms through which money became abstract 'spending power'. Power – strictly 'authoritative power' – was also understood as a symbolic medium. It is a capacity to command others through symbolic resources, rather than simply through physical force. It is a collective and circulating resource for making binding decisions and for enabling those in positions of authority to promote their policies. Force stands to authoritative power in the same relation that precious metals stand to spending power. Both money and power have become independent of their material base.

At the level of the action system as a whole, interchanges are hierarchical. The information-rich cultural system 'controls' actions through its latent value patterns and their codification as norms of behaviour. The energy-rich environment and body 'condition' actions through technologies of production and organisation that make particular courses of action possible or impossible. It is the interplay of cultural controls and environmental conditions that generates the particular patterns of change in the social system that Parsons documented in an evolutionary scheme (1966, 1971).

David Lockwood's (1956, 1964) criticism of this argument made the point that system integration must always be seen as a variable. The structural parts of a system develop as separate adaptations to environmental conditions, and while they will show varying degrees of interdependence and interchange, there is no necessary or automatic state of stable and cohesive equilibrium. The parts may stand in contradictory relations to each other, with the adaptation of one undermining that of another, or they may coexist in relative autonomy and operate almost independently (see also Gouldner 1959). Social systems will, therefore, exhibit numerous strains and tensions among their constituent parts, and the degree of cohesion that exists among the members of a society depends upon its state of system integration.

Self-regulation in Systems

This emphasis on varying degrees of system integration was central to the neofunctionalism that emerged following a period of reaction against Parsons. Jeffrey Alexander (1988), Neil Smelser, and Shmuel Eisenstadt (1973, 1978) restated the Parsonian position and pushed forward a recognition of the contingency of system integration (see also Alexander 1985; Colomy 1990; and the application in Gould 1987). The most systematic elaboration of this, however, was the system theory of Niklas Luhmann, whose early work on legal and organisational sociology (1965) led to his first general statement of a system theory (1984)[9] and then a series of books that applied this to specialised areas (1968/1975, 1986, 1991, 1996, 1997).

Like Parsons, Luhmann saw the participants in social encounters as engaged in a communicative process aimed at securing mutual understanding. The construction of the role expectations through which actions are organised is the outcome of this process, and these expectations provide the 'code' in terms of which people organise their actions towards each other. Unlike Parsons, however, Luhmann saw the establishment of consensus as precarious. Individual differences are an ever-present source of disruption, and consensus is established through securing 'closure' and establishing a 'boundary' between relatively enduring spheres of social activity and the chaotic and disruptive environment in which they exist. The formation of social systems is a process in which the 'complexity' and uncertainty inherent in human life can be reduced by establishing islands of relative security and stability.

Social systems emerge at local points of interaction in an environment and may be quite diverse in character. They are geographically dispersed and, as they grow, they will merge and split – compound and differentiate in Spencer's terminology – to produce shifting kaleidoscopic patterns of closure and boundedness. Each sub-system is closed off and autonomous from others, operating according to its own code and following its own logic of development. The unity, cohesion, or identity of each subsystem is maintained through a process of 'autopoeisis' or self-creation: a use of information through purposive monitoring and feedback to control the system itself. Each subsystem also operates through a specific symbolic medium that serves as a common currency for internal transactions and interactions: science subsystems, for example, are regulated through ideas of 'truth', while the medium of communication in family systems is 'love'. It is possible, however, for certain media to become highly generalised and to play a part in inter-system relations. Money, for example, is the principal medium of a differentiated economy, but it can also be used to mediate the interconnections among many other systems.

Luhmann saw the formation of social systems as an evolutionary process that leads from segmented societies with 'mechanical' solidarity to functionally connected ones with 'organic' solidarity. Social differentiation, he held, takes three forms. There is, first, the 'segmentation' or horizontal differentiation of social systems. Each such segment is structurally similar to all others. Secondly, there is the hierarchical or vertical differentiation that creates forms of social stratification whenever segments differentiate around inequalities in resources. This produces divisions of status that underpin the customary practices and folkways of 'traditional' societies. Thirdly, there is the functional differentiation of social systems into specialised subsystems connected only through the transactions in which they engage. Thus, a church, for example, is specialised around religious and ritual functions but its members depend on farmers and merchants for their subsistence and for the means to finance their activities.

Luhmann recognised many more than the four lines of functional division that Parsons employed, holding that the number cannot be specified *a priori*.

In contemporary societies, Luhmann argued, there is a differentiation of economic, political, legal, educational, scientific, family, and other subsystems. The economic and political systems, nevertheless, have become critical to overall system integration. The capitalist economic system and the nation state crystallised as distinctively modern subsystems and have achieved a relative autonomy. Through their generalised symbolic media (money and power), they affect interactions across whole societies.

Luhmann's emphasis on the proliferation and complexity of social subsystems is reflected in the attempts of some theorists to abandon the terminology of 'system' and 'subsystem' altogether. Althusser (1962b, 1963) saw the 'levels' of a society forming a complex 'articulated whole' that cannot be reduced to the one-sided determinism of an 'expressive totality'. Each level has a relative autonomy and is associated with distinctive social forces. To conceptualise these levels, Althusser resorted to the metaphor of the 'field' advocated in the social physics of Engels and others.

This view of societies as force fields, rather than systems, became a leading idea among French social theorists such as Foucault (1971) and Pierre Bourdieu (1972, 1994). Bourdieu's starting point was that social structures must be conceptualised as existing in a 'social space' that is organised not into subsystems but into specialised fields of activity such as those of class (1979), gender (1998), education (1989), political, economic, and other relations. Each field is structured around the distinct locations that individuals occupy. The overall position of an individual in social space is a result of the complex articulation of his or her specialised locations. Fields are arenas of struggle over resources, and it is the flow of these resources – conceptualised as forms of 'capital' – together with their 'conversion' from one form to another that gives rise to the forces through which social structures are sustained and their distinctive 'logics' of action followed. A whole society, then, is a social space within which numerous overlapping fields of action coexist to follow their distinctive developmental dynamics. The space is a dispersed sphere that may have no coordination or controlling centre. Its degree of systemic integration is an outcome of the interdependence established among its autonomous fields.

Though eschewing the language of 'system', the arguments of Althusser and Bourdieu point in the same direction as the recent trends in general system theory that some social theorists have begun to use. Earliest among these was Walter Buckley (1967), who used the idea of 'positive feedback' to build models of structure-building, morphogenetic processes in which small changes in system state can be amplified into large-scale social transformations (Wilkins 1964;

Young 1971) and path-dependent social transitions (Stark and Bruszt 1998). This morphogenetic model has been further developed by Margaret Archer (1995).

Recent mathematical work in general systems has promised a firmer foundation for these arguments. These advances have come from physicists who have reconceptualised physical systems and drawn implications for biological and social systems.[10] Bertalanffy's system theory had seen complexity as a consequence of organisation in open systems, but Gregoire Nicolis and Ilya Prigogine (1977, 1989) saw it arising also in certain types of closed system. In such systems, the emergence of complex organisation is not a smooth, linear process but involves a sudden 'flip' or switch in system state. These transformations are 'chaotic' or 'catastrophic' (Thom 1972) outcomes of non-linear processes. The constituent parts of a system may act on the basis of simple procedures that, nevertheless, bring them to 'bifurcation points' at which a number of possible, and irreversible, outcomes are possible. The actual course taken will depend on very small changes in the key variables of the system. Where change occurs through a sequence of such bifurcations, the total number of possible outcomes from a given starting point will be immense and the actual outcome will be unpredictable. When these ideas are extended to open systems, the range of possible outcomes is even greater. Possible applications of these ideas to social systems have been sketched by John Urry (2003) and Dave Byrne (1998; see also Eve et al. 1997).

FOCUS: NIKLAS LUHMANN

Systems theory, or neofunctionalism, has been most comprehensively elaborated by Niklas Luhmann in a series of works. His *Social Systems* (1984) is very hard-going, and Jeffrey Alexander's *Action and Its Environments* (1988) is, perhaps, a clearer introduction. Luhmann's chapter on 'Entertainment' in *The Reality of the Mass Media* (1996) gives an idea of how he applied his approach.

Socialisation, Self, and Mentality

The theories of socialisation produced in the formative period were quite diverse. Enculturation – inherent in the idea of cultural formation – was the most common approach, but for many theorists of socialisation the social life of individuals was to be explained in terms of biological instincts and impulses. This was at its strongest in the instinct psychologies of Graham Wallas and William McDougall. This recognition of the importance of human biology was also central to psychoanalytic theories of personality, in which the range of views was defined by the tension between cultural and biological forces. Psychoanalysts popularised the idea that socialisation is a process of development through psychological stages, rather than a fixed, once and for all, acquisition of personality traits. Complementary developmental theories of intelligence and cognitive faculties were proposed by Piaget and Vygotsky. The cognitive issues were further explored in Lewin's field theory, which focused on the interpersonal influences on perception and the formation of motives. In the existential phenomenology of Jaspers and the symbolic interactionism of George Mead, the reactions of others in social interaction were seen as central to self formation and individual mentality.

All these theories have been taken further by contemporary theorists, and more areas of complementarity are apparent. For many theorists it has been the attempt to explain socialised differences of gender that has driven their theoretical work, and the success of such explanations has often been taken as the touchstone for their wider viability. In this section I will try to explore these issues through contemporary theorising on psychoanalysis, developmental psychology, existentialism, and on cognition and group dynamics. The work of contemporary evolutionary psychologists, which takes up some of the same arguments as earlier instinct psychologies, has focused on issues of the socialised body, and I will consider their arguments in the following chapter.

Personality, Culture, and Social Relations

The most influential approach to socialisation into gender roles in the middle years of the twentieth century was that of Margaret Mead (1935), who suggested that gender identities could differ markedly from society to society. Her argument was pursued more radically by Betty Friedan (1962), the inspiration behind the 'liberal feminism' that took the attainment of equal rights for men and women as its political goal. Friedan held that women in contemporary industrial societies had been socialised into domesticity and failed to realise that they had the capacity to break with socially imposed definitions and enter paid employment and careers. Female personality is a product of culturally relative construction as 'feminine', and women have the ability to challenge this and to combine marriage and motherhood with work commitments and participation in public life (see also Klein 1946). Friedan did not, however, extend this same principle to men, seeing no significant role for them in the family.

Friedan gave little attention to the mechanisms of socialisation. Mead herself (1950) had adopted psychoanalytic explanations similar to those adopted by Parsons (Parsons and Bales 1956). He recognised the sharp sex-role segregation in contemporary societies (in his early essay of 1942) and drew on Freudian theory to show how women are socialised into commitments to 'integrative' and expressive roles, while men are socialised into 'adaptive' and 'goal attainment' roles in which instrumental relationships prevail. However, Parsons made little reference to any advances being made in psychoanalytic theory.

One of the leaders in this theoretical advance was Erik Erikson, who trained with Anna Freud in Vienna but was influenced by the cultural anthropology of Ruth Benedict and Margaret Mead after he moved to the United States. His most important contribution to culture and personality theory was a study of child development (1950) that compared socialisation into the culture of white Americans and socialisation among the Sioux and other native Americans. This account was extended in a text on later identity formation (1968) and in psychobiographies of Luther and Ghandi. Related arguments can be found in the work of Heinz Kohut (1971, 1978).

Erikson's account of infancy and early childhood used the stages of psychosexual development identified by Freud but highlighted their culturally specific aspects. To this he added a sequence of adolescent and adult stages that comprise key transitions in the human life course. Erikson saw transition from one stage to the next as requiring a successful resolution of the 'crisis' specific to each stage. These crises are not consequences of biological maturation alone, but also reflect certain universal features of family and working life. All individuals experience similar life-changing situations that impel them periodically to reorganise their sense of self and recast their identities. The precise age at which these transitions occur, and the specific form taken by each stage, depend upon the particular forms of family and work life that shape the life course. Thus, personality development varies from one society to another, though all exhibit the same key stages.

Erikson described a number of psychosocial stages, running from infancy to puberty and then through adolescence, young adulthood, middle age, and old age. Social relations within the immediate family are the basis of socialisation in the early stages, but Erikson saw peer groups and participation in youth subcultures as especially important influences on the formation of adolescent identity. Young adulthood is marked by the search for close friendships through which intimacy, stable partnerships, and families can be formed. Middle adulthood is the stage of child rearing and career development. Finally, old age is triggered by children leaving home and by actual or imminent retirement from work: it is the stage at which people must come to terms with the approach of their own, inevitable death.

A psychoanalytic approach to early child development had been pioneered in the work of Melanie Klein, who elaborated her ideas on destructive aggression in a theory of the origins of envy (1957). The most important developments of her ideas, however, were the so-called 'object relations' theories of Ronald Fairbairn, Donald Winnicott, and Nancy Chodorow, as well as related work on group activity by Wilfred Bion. In all of these approaches, it is social relations, rather than cultural representations *per se*, that are the major explanatory variables.

Ronald Fairbairn (1952) abandoned the emphasis on the id and its instinctive drives to lay greater stress on the importance of the ego. Individuals are not motivated by biological drives towards tension reduction but by their focused striving for self-expression in relation to others. Fairbairn held that the ego relates to others (its 'objects') by attempting to defend its own integrity and establish an idea of personhood. These object relations are the source of the fundamental experiences from which people derive both their sense of the world and their sense of self. An ego is internally diverse and pluralistic, as it is defined by its relations to diverse others in the social relations it enters. People's social relations alter as their life circumstances change, and as they move from one situation to another; and their idea of self is modified and constantly reconstructed in response to these changing object relations. Actions are oriented by a constantly altering ego, which produces the changes in social relations that drive ego reconstruction. Similar views were elaborated by Michael Balint (1959) and Harry Guntrip (1961).

Donald Winnicott's work (1964, 1965a, 1965b) adopted this same general approach but stressed the particular relation between a child and its mother. He argued that a mature sense of self is formed in a child only if it has a close and enduring relation to its mother during its earliest years. Those without close maternal care develop a 'false self' that is incapable of full autonomy and individuality in its relations with others in later life. This view of 'maternal deprivation' was elaborated in the arguments of John Bowlby (1965, 1969–80), who investigated the implications of family break-up and female work patterns for child development. This initiated a substantial debate over whether 'maternal' care had to be provided by the actual mother or could be provided by a 'mother substitute' such as a nanny or a male carer.

Nancy Chodorow (1978) took up insights into femininity found in Karen Horney (1922–37) and combined these with object relations theory to construct a radical view of mothering and, especially, of the mother–daughter relationship. Her position is that children gradually develop their sense of self in relation to the attitudes and reactions of their parents, and so it is the differing roles of mothers and fathers in socialisation that provides the key to gender identities. Women have been socialised into gendered identities that involve a need for intimacy in close personal relationships and a close involvement in the caring and socialisation of their children. Mothers also identify more with their daughters than their sons and so treat their male and female children differently. As a result, close bonds of identification develop between girls and their mothers. While the 'Oedipal' stage for boys is one at which identification with their mothers ceases and they identify with their fathers, this is not the case with girls. Girls continue to identify with their mothers and grow up with the same socialised need for intimacy. Boys, like their fathers, grow up without this strong need for intimacy and so are less involved in the rearing of their own children. In these ways, motherhood – and fatherhood – are reproduced over the generations.

A final direction in psychoanalytical thought has been investigations into the effects of group membership. Wilfred Bion had adopted pioneering methods of group therapy during the Second World War and his theoretical work (1961) evolved as an attempt to combine this with Kleinian ideas.[11] He held that any social group has a particular 'group mentality' that provides a shared, but often unconscious, orientation to the world for its members. This shared worldview results from the socialised dispositions that people bring to the group and the actions of group members in relation to each other. It is the basis on which they are able to cooperate and pursue their goals, but it may also involve unconscious mechanisms that run counter to the conscious aims of group members and so prevent these from being achieved. These unconscious mechanisms are, typically, evasions and denials of threatening experiences.

The family is the social group most directly involved in the formation of basic personality characteristics. It is here that, during early infancy, an individual's underlying anxieties and defences develop. These unconscious mental 'positions' continue to influence people's adult activities and their participation in other social groups, as they tend to act on these deeply rooted character dispositions rather than in consciously rational ways. Bion gave a great deal of attention to the peer groups, work groups, and therapeutic groups in which people are involved as adults. Echoing the arguments of Le Bon, for example, he suggested that social groups dominated by a 'dependent' mentality, rooted in Klein's 'depressive' state, are likely to defer to the judgement of a leader and to act in submissive ways. Applying his work to industrial and organisational practice, he held that managers must identify the orientations that inform the behaviour of work groups and mobilise them in more 'positive' ways by encouraging them to bring their actions under more conscious control (see also Jacques 1955).

> ### FOCUS: NANCY CHODOROW
>
> The leading contemporary theorist in the object relations tradition is Nancy Chodorow, whose *The Reproduction of Mothering* (1978) has been a major influence within feminism and widely across the social sciences. Chapter 12 on 'The Psychodynamics of the Family' (pages 191–210) draws out her general position.
>
> The work of Chodorow has been critically considered in relation to other psychoanalytic theories in Juliet Mitchell's *Psychoanalysis and Feminism* (1974), which makes its own important contributions to the debate.

Cognitive and Moral Development

The developmental psychology of Jean Piaget has continued as a strong strand in socialisation theory throughout the contemporary period (1954, 1975; Piaget and Inhelder 1958), and this was strongly reinforced when Vygotsky's work was discovered by western theorists. Piaget's early work had established a developmental approach to intelligence and cognitive abilities, while Vygotsky had stressed the wider range of social factors involved in the development from one cognitive stage to the next.

The leading figure in furthering these ideas has been Jerome Bruner, who stressed that the characteristics of each stage of mental development persist into later life and, therefore, exercise a continuing influence on people's outlooks and expectations. He was particularly concerned with the processes through which children learn, and he had a major influence on educational theory and practice. Bruner's key idea was that knowledge is built through practical engagement in the world in actions involving progressively more complex cognitive skills (Bruner et al. 1956). These cognitive skills are adaptive methods for information processing and the construction of collective representations. Young children primarily employ 'enactive skills' of object manipulation and spatial reasoning. Older children, however, are also able to employ 'iconic skills' of visual recognition, comparison, and classification. In this way, as Piaget showed, they become capable of more complex forms of practical reasoning. By adolescence, they are capable of exercising 'symbolic skills' of abstract reasoning and inference from evidence. Later socialisation, then, can operate through making sources of evidence available for practical manipulation, rather than through mere didactic instruction (Bruner 1960, 1966; see also 1991).

Lawrence Kohlberg (1969, 1971) extended Piaget's approach into an account of moral development, drawing also on Dewey and Baldwin and converging with some of the ideas of psychoanalysts on moral pressure. He saw moral capacities developing through progressively greater cognitive understanding and traced three overarching stages. The first stage, comprising infancy and the first years of school, he terms the 'pre-conventional'. At this stage, children engage in egoistic calculation of the punishments and rewards offered by particular courses of action and by authority figures, They conform only because it is in their interest to do so. At the 'conventional' stage, typically attained in late childhood and adolescence, the ability to respond to the expectations of others develops. People are oriented to obligations that reflect a search for social approval and recognition. Conformity is sustained by the anticipated reactions of others. Moral judgements, therefore, reflect perceived social conventions. Most people, Kohlberg argues, develop no further than this. In a minority of cases, however, social circumstances are such that development to a 'post-conventional' stage becomes possible. This is a stage at which autonomous individual judgements are made on the basis of universal principles of justice. Thus, the level of moral development that it is possible for a person to achieve depends upon the particular social circumstances under which he or she lives. This conclusion echoes some of the much earlier arguments of Hobhouse (1906) about moral progress.

Kohlberg's arguments have been further enlarged by Carol Gilligan (1982), who holds that his account is too specific to male socialisation. The socialisation of girls, she argues, orients them towards a concern and care for the feelings of others, and their continuing orientation to others is a sign not of moral *inferiority* but of moral *difference*. Girls and women develop morally through their changing sense of self and not simply through learning more advanced cognitive skills. Those who enter the 'conventional' stage accept the importance of self-sacrifice in the interests of others, while those at the 'post-conventional' stage follow a principle of not doing harm to others.

FOCUS: LAWRENCE KOHLBERG

Lawrence Kohlberg has made particularly interesting advances in the approach discussed here. His main works have been brought together in the first volume of his *Essays on Moral Development* (1981). It is most useful to begin a consideration of his views through the critical discussion in Chapter 3 of Carol Gilligan's *In a Different Voice* (1982).

Self and Others

Issues of self formation have been explored in the theories of both George Mead and the psychoanalysts. Central to both approaches has been the key part played by the reactions of those others to whom an individual is closely related and the extent to which self-initiated actions can be seen as autonomous expressions of individuality. Despite the power and sophistication of the arguments offered by Mead and Cooley on the self, little advance has been made in specifically symbolic interactionist theories of socialisation. Perhaps the most important contribution has been that of Maines (2001; see also Denzin 1992; Plummer 1995), who has emphasised the importance of narratives in the construction and reconstruction of the self

Some related insights into the relations of self and others have come from existentialism. The early work of Heidegger and Sartre had highlighted the significance of existential philosophy for social action and for the understanding of bodily presence in social encounters, and some of the implications of this work for the formation of gender identities were explored by Simone de Beauvoir (1949). She held that women must be understood as the 'other', as the objects of a male oppression that results in a subordination of their own sense of identity to that imposed on them by men. They develop a sense of self only in relation to these male definitions and so experience an existential 'alienation' from their own being. This argument, echoing the earlier suggestions of Gilman and Schreiner, was elaborated, without its existential foundations, in Germaine Greer's (1970) programmatic statement of a radical feminist position.

The most important existentialist contributions, however, come from attempts to understand forms of selfhood that are described as mental illness. The pioneering work of Karl Jaspers on 'paranoid' reactions was elaborated by Ronald Laing (1959, 1961). Training in psychiatry at the Tavistock Clinic, he soon developed more radical forms of therapy that led him to define his approach as an 'anti-psychiatry'. His argument was that madness must be seen as a more or less rational response to maddening situations. The apparently confused and bizarre behaviours of those encountered as patients can be interpreted as distorted expressions of real anxieties about threatening situations, and they must be placed in the context of the social relations that produce them. People do not simply *think* that situations are threatening, they really *are* threatening if there is no realistic prospect of escape.

For Laing (1969; see also Laing and Esterson 1964), the key social relations are those of the family. Recasting Kleinian and object relations ideas from the standpoint of existential phenomenology, Laing argued that forms of mothering are crucial determinants of mental health or illness. Where mothers are absent or impose inappropriate or unattainable goals, their infants become totally oriented to the expectations of others and build a 'false self' or 'being for others' that is integral to their desire to be 'good' or compliant with external expectations. This publicly oriented false self is split off from a 'real self' that can be sustained only in an inner world of private experiences. A dominance of the demands of the false self over the real self produces high levels of 'ontological insecurity' among growing children. If this insecurity is resolved by an eventual rejection of external demands and the false self, the child's real self is left exposed and unable to cope with the practicalities of the external world. Their private ways of thinking and feeling are likely to be perceived by others as bizarre or even 'psychotic' forms of expression.

Laing developed this approach from the work of Gregory Bateson (summarised later in Bateson 1972), who saw the interactional 'bind' and 'double bind' as the basis of schizophrenic responses. A bind is a contradictory or discrepant expectation that can, typically, be resolved by altering the relationship that produces it. A double bind, however, comprises a set of multiple and reinforcing binds that constitute a 'no win' situation from which escape is difficult. Laing saw this as characteristic of many families, where parents see the growing autonomy and individuality of their children – and especially their daughters – as a threat to the control they have always been able to exercise. Individuality is seen as 'bad' or 'wrong' behaviour. When this occurs, children and their parents are drawn into a progressive cycle of misunderstandings and misinterpretations that leads the child to act in increasingly 'irrational' ways and, therefore, to be referred for psychiatric treatment. The child becomes a scapegoat for the problems of the family as a whole. Rather than treating the individual and his or her 'symptoms' – as in conventional psychiatry – Laing felt it important to treat the family as a whole in order to unravel the knots of misunderstanding in which all its members are entangled.

FOCUS: RONALD LAING

Ronnie Laing was the leading figure in anti-psychiatry and developed a powerful approach based in existential phenomenology. The case studies presented in *Sanity, Madness and the Family* (with Aaron Esterson 1964) are the best place to begin his work.

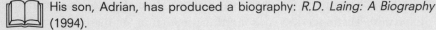 His son, Adrian, has produced a biography: *R.D. Laing: A Biography* (1994).

Balance and Dissonance

The works of Le Bon, Tarde, and Lewin helped build an awareness of the importance of group pressure and individual suggestibility in the formation of subjective imagery and definitions of the situation. The key insight to emerge was that individual mentality had to be treated as a dynamic field of forces in a state of tension and strain, with individual attitudes and actions reflecting intersubjective pressures. A key figure in developing this idea was Fritz Heider, whose pioneering work on psychological 'balance' was later summarised in an influential book (1958). Heider's ideas were taken up by Theodore Newcomb and others in their experimental studies, but the most systematic and influential approach was Leon Festinger's (1957) analysis of 'cognitive dissonance'. Festinger studied under Lewin and initially worked with him and with Dorwin Cartwright (see Cartwright and Zander 1953) on a theory of 'group dynamics', of the influence of group structure on individual mentality.

Festinger held that individuals find it uncomfortable to hold on to incompatible or inconsistent beliefs – to be placed in a 'bind' – and that they will attempt, subject to group pressure, to return themselves to a more consistent mental state. To investigate this empirically, he led a study of a flying saucer cult, showing that the failure of predictions concerning the imminent end of the world led to observable attitude changes among group members (Festinger et al. 1956). His theory of cognitive dissonance generalised the results of this empirical study.

Festinger's key idea was that individuals are motivated to seek a state of balance in their cognitive field. They find it subjectively uncomfortable to hold contradictory or inconsistent ideas. Whenever they experience such 'dissonance' they will also experience a psychological pressure to change their ideas or to minimise the dissonance in some other way. Festinger's method explored the pairs of elements – or cognitions – that constitute the mental field. These cognitions may concern the self, others, or the environment and are the representations through which definitions of the situation are constituted. If cognitions are not simply irrelevant or unconnected with each other, they will be either consistent or dissonant. A person who likes two others, for example, will hold dissonant representations if they dislike each other or hold contrary views about something important. We expect those we like to like each other and to like similar things to us, and we experience psychological discomfort if they do not. A person's total mental field is a complex combination of such cognitions, and the total dissonance he or she experiences is a cumulative effect of this overall state of dissonance. Festinger saw this as the proportion of dissonant cognitions, weighted by their importance. The greater the dissonance experienced, the more highly motivated will the person be to try to reduce it. The mental field is in a dynamic state, as the attempt to reduce dissonance in one set of cognitions is likely to increase it in another. Individuals pursue, but rarely attain, mental equilibrium.

Individuals may try to reduce dissonance by changing their own behaviour (e.g., by giving up one or other of their friendships or attachments), by trying to persuade other people to change their views, or by seeking out additional information that will allow them to redefine the situation. The failure of the world to end when predicted led members of the flying saucer cult to proselytise even more strongly than before, as each new convert could be taken as additional evidence that their underlying beliefs were well founded: their beliefs cannot be wrong if people are still willing to join them.

Although the theory of cognitive dissonance made it possible to draw certain conclusions about responses to dissonance, Festinger was unable to predict how any particular person would attempt to reduce dissonance. The method adopted depends on a person's commitment to a particular ideal or authority figure, and hence on his or her suggestibility and the persuasiveness of others. Here, it might seem, some other socialisation theories might have something to offer. Festinger's particular concern, however, was with the particular state of group influences (as interpreted and experienced in the mental field) that creates the social pressures towards one strategy or another. His work on this was directly related to work by Solomon Asch (1951) and, in particular, the experiments on group and authority pressures towards conformity undertaken in 1961 by Stanley Milgram (1974).

FOCUS: LEON FESTINGER

One of the most active theorists on balance and dissonance was Leon Festinger. While much of this work is highly technical, the study of a religious cult, presented in *When Prophecy Fails* (1956), is highly readable and has become a classic account of the theory. The book can easily be read in its entirety.

The undertaking of the Festinger study has been recounted in fictional form in Alison's Lurie's novel *Imaginary Friends* (1967). Although it is unclear how much of the book was directly inspired by Festinger's work, it is useful to read it alongside Festinger's own methodological appendix to his study.

The discussions of cultural formation, social systems, and socialisation in this chapter have already raised issues that are developed more fully in explorations of other themes in social analysis. In the following chapter I will pursue these through a consideration of extensions of the formative arguments concerning action, nature, and conflict.

NOTES

1. This was initially set out in his pre-war work (Parsons 1937).
2. These pattern variables are discussed in Chapter 7.
3. The correspondence between Schütz and Parsons from 1940 to 1941 can be found in Grathoff (1978).
4. His papers were published between 1932 and his death in 1959 and were brought together in three volumes of *Collected Papers* (Schütz 1962–6).The book was outlined in note form by Schütz in 1957–8, and he intended to incorporate many of his papers into the final text. Luckmann completed the work, adding ideas of his own to fill the gaps in the manuscript. An earlier draft manuscript (Schütz 1947–59) was published posthumously in 1970.
5. See Heritage (1984). Related ideas have been developed by Coulter (1979, 1989).
6. Winch's arguments on this point also owe much to Sapir (1921) and Whorf (1956).
7. Odum's work developed from his father's earlier work on regionalism (Odum and Moore 1938).
8. Parsons's work had its origins in the attempt of Lawrence Henderson, discussed in Chapter 3, to systematise the work of Pareto, drawing also on the Harvard physiologist Walter Cannon (1932) and his idea of 'homeostasis' in biological systems. See the early statement in Parsons (1945).
9. This was preceded by essays of the 1960s and 1970s collected in Luhmann (1982).
10. For applications in biology see Kauffman (1993, 1995).
11. The book published in 1961 is a revised collection of essays first published between 1948 and 1951. Some later work is presented in Bion (1963).

6

Action, Conflict, and Nature: Developments

Contemporary theorists have further developed and articulated formative ideas on nature, action, and conflict. There has, again, been some rediscovery of forgotten or ignored ideas, but theoretical advance is apparent. The chapter looks, in particular, at

- spatial arrangement and the morphological features of human activity

- the rediscovery of nature and the environment as critical factors

- nature and culture in the formation of bodies and the embodiment of social relations

- rationality and exchange as aspects of interaction

- self presentation, social reaction, and social definition in interaction

- classes, power, and historical change in social structures

Though debates among advocates of such contending positions as 'structure' and 'action' theories became more marked and hostile, it is shown that the issues raised involved a recognition of common concerns with theorists discussed in the previous chapter.

Constraints and conditions on individual and collective action had been recognised as mechanisms through which cultural socialisation is able to produce dynamically developing social systems. The natural environment and the natural heritage of the human body are the fundamental conditions under which all social activity must take place, and the relationship between culture and nature had been central to formative discussions. The actions of individuals and collectivities – interweaving, cooperating, and conflicting – are constrained by those natural conditions as well as by the cultural inheritance acquired through socialisation. Each of these themes was elaborated more fully in the contemporary period. The natural body appeared as an especially important object of sociological analysis, and cultural formation was recognised as involving a process of embodiment. Environmental conditions were given far less attention; the subject of spatial location emerged as the main focus for the explanation of natural environmental conditions. Symbolic interactionists became the basis of a social theory of action in which issues of power and constraint are central concerns. The analysis of power, however, was principally developed in theories of conflict and collective action, where the historical transformation of social structures has been a major concern.

Environment and Space

Environmental theorising had explored the organisation of different ways of life in relation to the climatic, geological, and other physical conditions that comprised their habitats and set the conditions under which the 'regional' structuring of human activity occurred. Movements of people and objects between regions and the consequent restructuring of the geographical pattern are shaped by the possibilities set by environmental conditions. It was also recognised that technology made possible a degree of independence from environmental constraints. Technologies of food production, building, and transportation increased the range of environments in which humans could live and reduced their particular dependence on local habitats. With increasing levels of technological development, social morphology became a *product* of social activity as much as a *condition* for it.

For many contemporary theorists, therefore, the natural environment increasingly came to be seen as apart from and external to social life and so no longer having a place in social theory. Environmental determination is a feature of premodern and non-modern societies with a low level of technology. Thanks to their technical mastery of the environment, modern societies could ignore natural conditions. Adorno and others associated with critical theory had seen this rational, technical control over nature as a major achievement of the Enlightenment (Adorno and Horkheimer 1944). Carl Sauer (1925) had concluded that the natural landscape of soil, minerals, and landform is merely the 'medium' through which the cultural ideas of a society produce a 'cultural landscape' of fields, crops, housing, and roads: the environment is an object of cultural formation.

Studies of localities in the 1950s and 1960s (see the review in Frankenberg 1967) led Margaret Stacey (1969) to conclude that the very idea of 'community' – tied to the idea of 'place' – had to be abandoned in favour of that of a 'local social system' firmly embedded within national and transnational economic and political relations. Descriptive regional geography was eclipsed by the differentiation of geographical work along thematic lines into economic geography, political geography, medical geography, and so on. Many who were engaged in the development of human geography as an academic discipline abandoned the search for environmental determinants and adopted theoretical ideas from other social sciences. Applying these ideas without a 'regional' focus, they became indistinguishable from the work undertaken in those fields.

Environmental factors have still been invoked in some broader studies of long-term historical change in pre-modern and early modern societies. Fernand Braudel (1949, 1979a, 1979b, 1979c, 1986–7; see also Le Roy Ladurie 1965), for example, used the ideas of Febvre and the *Annales* group to explore French history and its regional context. In a similar vein, Barry Cunliffe (2001) has related the development of European civilisation to its maritime location. Felipé Fernández-Armesto (2000) has recently used environmental categories (tundra, desert, savannah, steppe, etc.) to organise an account of the development of civilisation that restates environmental 'possibilism'. He bases his account on the assumption that physical and social factors interact closely to form the specific habitats that comprise the 'niches' around which social evolution takes place. Relatedly, Colin Turnbull (1976; see also 1961, 1973) has used the differentiation of grassland, river, forest, desert, and woodlands to organise African ethnographic material.

The determining role of the physical environment was invoked also in writings on pre-modern landscapes and townscapes, where *ad hoc* explanations were rarely drawn out as systematic theory. Thus, William Hoskins (1955) stressed the need to link geology and human activity as factors shaping the rural landscape and land use, and his work inspired a number of regional studies in the established tradition of historical geography (Scarfe 1972; Taylor 1973, Steane 1974). This approach was also applied to the form of early towns, enlarging the established concerns of urban geography with factors of 'site' and 'situation' (Aston and Bond 1976; Roberts 1982, 1987). From this point of view, the physical environment offers a range of locations where village or town development is likely to be favoured (river crossings, gaps in escarpments, natural harbours) and others where human settlement would be impossible. The actual sites of urban development depend on decisions made in relation to the regional context, including such factors as the nearness of other towns, the requirements of trade and industry, and existing transport networks. This approach stresses the *historical* importance of the environment rather than its contemporary role: initial location decisions are significantly shaped by the environment but, once established, a settlement develops mainly in accordance with its human activities. Continuing physical effects on the morphology of towns are likely to be minimal: towns in valleys, for example, are likely to spread along the valley before they spread over its ridges. The growing town or city becomes a humanly modified physical environment, and human activity is shaped by its 'manufactured environment' rather than by any purely 'natural' one.

Space, Capital, and Morphology

An important group of geographers sought a distinct disciplinary identity by abandoning regionalism in favour of a spatial analysis that took up and extended earlier approaches to location. Conceptualising 'space', rather than nature, they saw the spatial distribution of human activity as a distinctively social process without significant material constraint. They took up, more analytically, the idea of areal differentiation and variation by looking at the formal properties of spatial arrangement and location. This articulated the concerns of demographers such as Adolphe Coste and the formal sociology of Georg Simmel. Their aim was to construct a purely formal 'geometry' of social relations, detached from physical conditions and defining the parameters of a definite social space. Thus, Carl Sauer (1941) proposed the mapping of distributions of social phenomena in an abstractly defined space. The spacing of phenomena, he argued, occurs through relations of presence and absence, massing and thinning, time and space distanciation, spreading and diffusion.[1] Location in space is defined by coordinates in the mathematical frame of reference that maps the distribution.

Peter Haggett (1965) was the most important advocate of this view. He saw space as defined by the relations among the entities contained within it. The relations among human beings involve their movement and that of their goods and ideas through particular 'channels' that intersect and interweave in a network of linkages. Networks have a hierarchy of central nodes and a structure of 'surfaces' or zones, and a spatial theory can use tools of network analysis to examine the location of individuals and groups in space. Richard Morrill (1970) took a similar approach and defined social space in terms of the distances that separate people and their accessibility to each other. He sees these relations of distance and accessibility agglomerating people into structures that vary in size and location with respect to each other. Other advocates of this approach have incorporated ideas of 'direction' in space and the strength or intensity of the relations that define it. Such arguments often draw on social network analysis (Scott 2000), especially in so far as social networks can be plotted in a mathematically defined space by techniques such as multidimensional scaling or correspondence analysis. Both Haggett and Morrill (Morrill et al. 1988) show that the diffusion of innovations across the surface of a social space is shaped by its morphological features. They have constructed models of 'central places' and 'gravity' that echo the pioneering arguments of Henry Carey more than a hundred years earlier. These arguments have often been grounded in theories of rational action according to which relative location in space is simply another variable to be optimised by rational calculators.

Spatial ideas have been explored within a Marxist framework by Henri Lefebvre, an early advocate of a critical, humanist Marxism (Lefebvre 1939) who finally broke with the Communist Party orthodoxy in the early 1960s and went on to develop a novel approach to spatialisation (1968b, 1971, 1972, 1974). Lefebvre held that the human world is a physical distribution of things that is constructed as a social morphology because each person experiences it and defines it as a social reality. Social theory must, therefore, be concerned with 'lived space' rather than physical space *per se*. The space in which people live their everyday lives is a social space produced through the particular practices in which they engage. These practices – and Lefebvre focused on those of the mode of production and way of life it sustains – link physical locales with particular activities and distribute them as places of work, leisure, and private life that are connected through the specific patterns of movement and interchange that constitute villages, cities, and regions. These are socially constructed or created spaces (see also Soja 1989), and whatever effects that an external nature may have on human life are mediated through the lived everyday reality produced through prior attempts to control it. Nature is never primordially given. It is a material substratum that is the outcome of social production. Social relations of production are projected into the space they produce and so inscribe themselves in nature as embodied and morphological structures.

Lefebvre argued that productive activity in agrarian societies had been tied to the land and that space appeared as 'place'. The development of industrial activity began to liberate production from physical location. The activities of those who lived in cities were no longer so tightly constrained by their physical location, and social activity could become more detached from particular places. The expansion of technical knowledge and systems of technocratic state planning made possible the planned development of social space through town and city planning, urban regeneration, and the building of new towns. Old city centres and conurbations are weakened as foci for ways of life because developments in transport and communication allow urbanism to transcend the division of 'urban' and 'rural' that characterised the industrial cities. Urbanism as a mode of everyday life permeates whole societies (Lefebvre 1968a, drawing on 1947, 1961; see also 1981).

Manuel Castells (1972) took Lefebvre's ideas as his point of departure. Writing initially from the standpoint of Althusserian Marxism, he rejected the human-ism that he found in Lefebvre's view of urbanism as a purely disembedded way of life and emphasised the specificity of the city as a focus of the reproduction of labour power through consumption activities. State intervention and planning produce the objects of 'collective consumption' – housing, transport, education, and welfare – that constitute the 'urban' facilities required for the reproduction of the labour force. These must be spatially concentrated as they can only be con-sumed collectively. A corollary of this production of distinctively urban spaces is the rise or urban social movements that are loci of conflict and collective action in relation to collective consumption. Their activities complement those of the older labour movements concerned with issues of production. The struggles of urban social movements define the character of the city and contest its structure. Castells's later work (1978, 1983) owed more to Lefebvre's own position, as he saw urban processes as constituting the phenomenological realities of the every-day lives that people pursue.

A similar trajectory is apparent in David Harvey, whose initial explorations into the social production of space (1973) led him to turn to Lefebvre for the ideas that he set out on capital and city development (1982). Harvey sees the spa-tial configurations of activities as the outcome of historically specific forms of capital accumulation. The objects that comprise the morphological dimension of social life are subject to ownership relations and processes of labour that trans-form them in accordance with the larger dynamics of capital production. The dis-tribution of land and buildings, patterns of railway construction, and airline routes all depend on changes in rents and prices, company formation, and credit mobilisation inherent in particular systems of capitalist production.

Harvey (1985) went on, however, to produce a phenomenology of everyday life in urban locales. He argues that the creation of urban spaces is associated with distinctively urban forms of consciousness carried by the coalitions of classes that live in the differentiated and segmented localities of the cities. Such everyday urbanism is to be analysed in ways suggested by Simmel and Louis Wirth and by the early Chicago School.[2]

This approach to the social production of space has minimised the causal impact of physical nature on social relations and has emphasised the social construction of nature. It posits a distinctively spatial patterning of social life and sees its morphological features as aspects of a created or manufactured environment. The spatial constraints under which people act are consequences of social processes of production and not directly of physical determinants. The concentration of large numbers of workers in close proximity to their workplace, the concentration of mechanisms of capital mobilisation in financial centres, and the colonial expansion of modes of production constrain the location of economic and other social activities. The result is the production of urban areas and places of work as determinate physical spaces with limits defined by the extent of their labour markets and the temporal range of travel-to-work routes. Urban areas, as spaces of collective consumption, are differentiated into zones with distinct social characteristics, their zoning resulting from competition over resources and land market operations. Cities themselves have been differentiated on a global scale, with the relations among cities being shaped by flows of capital and information between them (Sassen 1991). The global flows between financial units based in the global cities sustain a particular pattern of territorial economies and national capitals and are associated with regional and global divisions of labour and, therefore, with patterns of regional growth and decline. At a global level, space may be structured as a world system with core, peripheral, and semi-peripheral zones and patterns of 'uneven development' between them (Frank 1967; Amin 1973; Wallerstein 1974, 1980, 1989).[3] Work on the world system has begun to build on the earlier spatial geopolitics of Mackinder.

FOCUS: HENRI LEFEBVRE

The most interesting and influential theorist of space considered here is Henri Lefebvre, who related the organisation of space to the structuring of everyday life. A key statement of this is *Everyday Life in the Modern World* (1968a), but a very accessible introduction to his ideas is *Rhythmanalysis* (1992), pages 3–69.

 The whole of Lefebvre's work is critically considered in Rob Shields's *Lefebvre, Love, and Struggle* (1999).

Nature Resurgent

Discussions of the production of social space have marginalised or ignored the question of the conditioned effects of natural forces originating in the physical environment. The natural environment has been treated – if at all – as something that is produced or constructed as an integral feature of the social production of space. The technological achievements that have given humans an unprecedented degree of control over their natural environment give much credence to this view, but it has come to be challenged as social scientists and others have become aware of the limits there are to human control over the environment.

A growing number of environmental problems have, since the 1960s, dented the economic optimism of the immediate post-war period and have led to a burgeoning of academic and political interest in environmental issues and ecological concerns. These fears have concerned such things as regular and recurrent famines across large parts of Africa; acid rain, smog, and other forms of pollution affecting agriculture and human health; accidents and disasters resulting from the use of nuclear energy; the eventual depletion of global resources of oil and gas; the erosion of the ozone layer that gives protection from the ultraviolet rays of the sun; the likelihood of long-term global climate change and its implications for weather patterns and sea levels; the rapid spread of new diseases and epidemics in humans and in the animals of the human food chain; the sustainability of economic development and the limits to economic growth; the extinction of many animal species in the wild; intensive farming techniques that maintain fertility only through the application of large doses of chemicals and that destroy wildlife habitats; and a myriad other dangers to human existence.

These concerns have highlighted the need to reconsider and reassess earlier ideas on environmental determination and to consider ways in which the formative theories might be reconstituted and enlarged to grapple with the environmental problems of an industrialised world. This work has barely begun, and only a very few theorists have started to explore the environmental impact on human life. The sociology of the environment has become an important option within sociology degree schemes, and the causal relations between 'nature' and 'society' have begun to be reconsidered. These arguments are introduced in such overviews as Yearley (1991), Dickens (1992), Martell (1994), Goldblatt (1996), Bell (1998), and Irwin (2001), but general theoretical reflections are few and far between.

The emerging view sees the causal effects of natural processes as real but mediated through the cultural meanings that people employ in their actions. Natural forces have an impact in and through the social relations through which people seek to understand and to control them. Thus, technology is not simply a means for mastering the natural environment but can also shape the ways in which the environment makes itself felt. This has been articulated most forcefully by Ulrich Beck (1986, 1988), who contends that nature is no longer – if it ever was – encountered directly in the raw. Nature has become a 'cultural product' to such an extent that the inevitable environmental disturbances and disasters that occur are generated in culturally defined ways.

The premise of Enlightenment science had been to improve human existence through an enhanced and rational exploitation of nature. Scientific knowledge informed the techniques of industrial production that underpinned the expansion of modern societies, but the rational application of science and technology has now reached the point at which the 'side-effects' of industrialism have become ecological problems that increasingly make themselves apparent at a global scale. Science is more and more concerned with defining and distributing the risks that it has itself produced. As they are the result of technology, they cannot be resolved through technology alone – the 'technical fix' risks generating further ecological problems. Attempts to resolve problems of food supply through genetically modified crops, for example, raise new and less visible risks of agricultural cross-contamination and the production of harmful foodstuffs. Beck's concept of the risk society aims to grasp the social consequences of this restructuring of the relationship between nature and society.[4]

Body and Embodiment

The formative theorists treated bodies, along with the environment, as natural conditioning factors in social life. Universal biological characteristics were viewed as resulting from the evolution of the species through adaptation and natural selection. These 'instincts', emotions, and abilities, however, were also seen as transformed into social competences and actions through socialisation. Theories of socialisation differed in the balance between nature and culture that they proposed and the specific mechanisms through which they saw socialisation occurring.

For much of the twentieth century the leading arguments to pursue this took genetics as their basis and tended towards a genetic determinism. Approaches such as 'sociobiology' and evolutionary psychology saw social differences and the inequalities of race and sex as due solely to the determining impact of biological conditions. Advances in genetics, combined with the marginalisation of environment conditions, meant that theories of the human body have emerged as an increasingly separate and distinct field of study within sociology. This has especially been the case since the rise of feminist theory highlighted the significance of bodily differences.

Evolution, Genes, and Society

It was the discovery of genes as the units of biological evolution, and, in particular, the discovery of the mechanism of genetic variation and replication, that drove the growing interest in biological determinism. In order to understand their position, it is necessary to understand something of the genetic mechanism.

All organisms are composed of cells clustered into the various specialised organs that comprise a body. Cells consist largely of proteins and nucleic acids (mainly DNA) that carry the information for building body parts. The units in which this information is stored are the genes, and the replication of the genes as cells divide and multiply ensures that the whole of the genetic information defining an organism – its genome – is contained in each cell of the body. It is through acting on this stored information that bodies produce the enzymes and proteins that are its physical expression and from which bodies are built. Particular importance is accorded to sexual reproduction, as this is the means through which the genes of distinct individuals can be mixed and genetic variations can enter the gene pool of a population. Variations that improve the survival chances of an individual – that are 'adaptive' – are more likely to be perpetuated in the gene pool; it is in this way that they are 'selected'. Such variation and natural selection is the means through which the biological characteristics of individuals alter over the generations and through which whole species evolve into new forms.

Genetic research has shown that certain characteristics of human beings (such as sex, hair colour, height, and susceptibility to some diseases) are, without any doubt, a direct consequence of genetic variation. It is very rarely that such characteristics can be traced back to one particular gene. The genes more frequently have their effects only in combination: each gene contains only very simple information and macro-level outcomes are the results of the operation of a whole array of genes under specific triggering conditions (Jones 1993; Ridley 1999). Sociobiology and evolutionary biology have suggested extensions of this genetic approach from the purely biological to the mental and social levels. Linguistic competence, emotional capacities, cognitive abilities, homosexuality, criminality, violence, and many of the routine behaviours of everyday life have all been attributed directly to genetic variation.

The earliest statements of sociobiology are those of Robert Ardrey (1961, 1967, 1970) and Edward Wilson (1975), and their arguments draw on earlier animal studies such as those of Konrad Lorenz (1963). Ardrey traced the emergence of humans as an individualistic, aggressive, and violent species with sharply defined sex differences, and Wilson, too, saw humans as evolving 'aggressive dominance systems' with a strong sexual division of labour, family unit, and pattern of male dominance (see also Maryanski and Turner 1992). Social differences between human populations are seen as resulting from the possession of 'genes promoting flexibility' that have allowed large-brained creatures to build complex cultures whose patterns can be passed on through the socialisation of children within human family units. Cultural variation is limited, as those cultures that prevent or inhibit their members from reproducing will, in the long run, decline. Human biology sets the limits to cultural variation.

Such arguments have much to offer. Evolutionary psychologists have, for example, produced powerful explanations of language (Pinker 1994) that begin to clarify the biological mechanisms behind linguistic competence. They have also suggested biological bases to sexual attraction and parenting. Their arguments, however, have often involved an extreme denial of any cultural differences and a claim that 'social scientists' – with whom they do not identify – have ignored biological conditions (Tooby and Cosmides 1992; Pinker 2002). Some, for example, have argued that genetic differences of 'race' between black and white populations can explain differences in levels of measured intelligence (Jensen 1972; Herrnstein and Murray 1994). Equally controversially, claims have been made about the genetic basis of rape. Male sexual competitiveness and female commitment to parenting, Thornhill and Palmer (2000) argue, are evolved genetic differences that lead men to engage in coercive sex. Thus, a willingness to rape is the genetic inheritance of all males. This drive can be mitigated, but not eliminated, only because men have also inherited a genetic willingness to respond to moral exhortation: societies in which strong prohibitions on rape are institutionalised may be able to minimise the amount of rape, but men with a genetic moral weakness will still be likely to commit acts of rape whenever the opportunity is presented to them.

As yet, however, it must be recognised that no specific genetic mechanism has been identified in any such studies, and the case for reducing social behaviour to fixed genetic characteristics remains weak. The only safe conclusion to draw about the work of the evolutionary psychologists is that they have produced some plausible accounts of the biological conditions affecting human behaviour, but they have seriously overstated their significance (Benton 1999).

Patriarchal Bodies

The claim of the evolutionary psychologists that 'social science' has ignored biological conditions is completely without foundation. The formative theorists, as I showed in Chapter 4, were very clear about their importance, and a number of very sophisticated instinct theories were proposed. Among contemporary theorists there has, if anything, been a growing interest in such matters, largely as a result of the growth of second-wave feminism since the late 1960s. This has forced a consideration of gendered bodies into the sociological mainstream and stimulated a wider consideration and re-consideration of 'racial' characteristics and individual differences as part of a larger sociology of the body.

Feminist arguments have been focused around issues of sexual difference but have moved beyond the terms of the conventional sex-role theory and properly traced the implications of the biological differentiation of men and women. While recognising the genetic determination of biological differences of sex, they have focused on the implications of these differences for biological functions and behaviour and the possibilities they create for cultural influences to operate. Their arguments can, therefore, be seen as analogous to the 'possibilism' of the formative theorists of nature. Shulamith Firestone (1970) and Kate Millett (1970) established the importance of seeing the 'patriarchy' through which men dominate women as deeply rooted in sex and reproduction. Human reproductive biology is the key basis for the dependence of infants on their mother and of the mother on a man willing to support her while she is engaged in maternal care. Men, for their part, are drawn into these social relations by their sexual needs. Andrea Dworkin (1981) holds that the male view of women is always 'pornographic'. The male orientation to women is a sexualising one, articulated in and encouraged by printed and broadcast pornography, and the sexualised relations between men and women are the basis of all other forms of domination and subordination. This pornographic gaze contrasts with the orientation of women to other women, which expresses their shared oppression by men and their resistance to male sexualised oppression. Nevertheless, women are constrained to enter into sexual relations with men and their standpoint and experiences are structured by this combination of 'compulsory heterosexuality' and resistance to male sexualisation (Rich 1980; see also Rubin 1975). Women's lives are also structured by the experience of pregnancy and childbirth and the bodily changes and cycles associated with menarche and menopause, which give them a more intimate connection with the natural processes of the body than men derive from their limited role in insemination. Patriarchal relations, expressed in the family relations of marriage and kinship through which men control women and children, are the bases of distinct male and female standpoints on the world and of the particular emotional and cognitive characteristics of men and women (O'Brien 1981, 1989).

It is through these patriarchal structures of the domestic sphere that larger patterns of patriarchy in the public sphere are generated. Women are subordinate not only in matters of sexuality and reproduction, but also in sexual divisions of labour. This limits and distorts their participation in the labour market and in political activity and it ties them to a disproportionate involvement in domestic work. For many such theorists, these patriarchal structures have a further basis in force. Men, it is argued, are inherently more aggressive than women, and their socialisation encourages violent responses. The pornographic sexualisation of women predisposes men to respond coercively in their sexual relations. The sexual objectification of women, then, makes rape an ever-present possibility in 'normal' sexual relations and a common form of male violence against women. The level of rape in any society is socially generated by such factors as militarism, which encourages higher levels of violence generally (Brownmiller 1975).

FOCUS: KATE MILLETT

Among the very diverse strands of feminist theorising, the work of Kate Millett in *Sexual Politics* (1970) has been particularly important. This was a key contribution to the early development of second-wave feminism. Chapter 2 sets out her theory of patriarchy, while pages 176–234 contain the core of her critique of psychoanalysis and the functionalist view of the family.

Discursive Constructions and Embodiment

The arguments of these theorists associated with radical feminism have led to a questioning of masculinity and femininity as sharply defined social identities. They have come to be seen as social constructions of biological differences rather than *necessary* consequences of those differences. Biology sets a range of possibilities but does not generate fixed and essential attributes or behaviour. Thus, Susie Orbach (1978, 1986) shows how cultural images of the female body distort women's perceptions of their own bodies and lead them to engage in behaviour that alters it in culturally approved or sanctioned ways. The stress on appearance encouraged by the fashion and diet industries and the push towards consumption by the advertising industry generate patterns of compulsive over- and under-eating that result in real, though often unintended, bodily changes (see also Wolf 1991).

Central to these arguments is a recognition of the importance of cultural representations of the body. Dale Spender (1980; see slso Daly 1978) produced an early work that pointed in this direction, arguing that the cultural codes through which language use is structured show a male bias. There are distinct male and female usages and vocabulary, and the dominant male form shapes the experiences and representations of both men and women. Language conveys patriarchal images and assumptions that, in turn, structure the cultural products through which people organise their lives. This is taken up by Julia Kristeva (1969, 1974),[5] who, along with Hélène Cixous (1975) and Luce Irigary (1974), drew on the literary psychoanalysis of Jacques Lacan (1966a, 1966b) to construct accounts of the discursive formation of gendered identities and emotions. Social constructions of identity reflect the diverse symbolic frameworks available and the asymmetries of power that underpin them. They are, therefore, as contradictory as any literary text. In western societies, for example, patriarchal male discourse and language prevail, even in constructions of femininity. Kristeva has applied this perspective to the social construction of emotions such as distaste (1980), love (1983), and depression (1987).

Where these post-structuralist theorists have emphasised the impact of cultural representations, Pierre Bourdieu explored the impact of social relations on bodily formation. Drawing on the general approach of Durkheim, and especially of Mauss (1934), Bourdieu (1972, 1979) looked at the ways in which structures of class and gender relations are associated with the formation of specific bodily skills and capacities that are, in turn, involved in their reproduction. Social structures are 'embodied' and are reproduced in the practices of individuals. Bourdieu's central concept is that of the 'habitus', understood as a socialised disposition to think or act in particular ways. Habituses are akin to Garfinkel's methodical programmes for action. They are internalised forms of the social conditions under which people act, each habitus corresponding to particular sets of social relations – class conditions, gender conditions, and so on. The acquisition of a habitus is a direct consequence of involvement in particular, recurrent social relations. A habitus embodies the structural principles around which social relations are organised and ensures the reproduction of these relations by habituated individuals. It is a means through which the systemic aspects of social structure are interrelated with the flow of individual agency.

This concept is used to provide a link missing from both the Marxist theory of class and the sociology of knowledge. Particular sets of social conditions provide distinctive and recurrent experiences that give their occupants a specific standpoint on the world and a basis for developing their unique social consciousness. While it is impossible for all members of the same class to have exactly the same experiences, each member of the same class is more likely than any member of another class to encounter similar situations. Generalising from their shared experiences, people build the conceptual schemes through which they can continue acting on the basis of their experiences (Bourdieu 1972: 85; 1979: 170). The habituses acquired by individuals through involvement in specific sets of social relations provide the cognitive and motivating structures through which they experience the world and organise their actions.

The structures that comprise the habituses are inscribed in the most automatic gestures and techniques of the body and operate below the level of consciousness. They comprise non-discursive forms of 'practical knowledge' that implement collective representations and rules by giving people a practical 'sense' for what to do in particular situations and how to do it (Bourdieu 1979: 470; 1989: 2). They are generative principles that allow people to act as if they were consciously following rules. Habituses provide ways of walking, eating, and talking, systems of tastes and preferences, forms of classification, and numerous other tendencies and dispositions. Grammatical ability, rooted in linguistic competence, is one such habitus, and where evolutionary psychology has seen this as a mere 'instinct', Bourdieu recognised the element of social construction through which such instincts are shaped.

FOCUS: PIERRE BOURDIEU

Issues of embodiment were central to the work of Pierre Bourdieu, initially set out in his *Outline of a Theory of Practice* (1972). The best introduction to his views on the embodiment of gendered identities is *Masculine Domination* (1998), where he revisits his work on Kabyle society. The whole book is very short, but Chapter 1 gives a good introduction.

There are numerous commentaries on Bourdieu, but especially useful is David Swartz's *Culture and Domination: The Social Theory of Pierre Bourdieu* (1997).

Action, Strategy, and Performance

Previous chapters have shown how Enlightenment theorists identified two forms of action – the egoistic and the altruistic – and the ways in which these were employed in a variety of theories of action that proposed certain common themes. Action was seen as sociologically comprehensible in so far as it is strategic in relation to the goals and perception of individual actors. Egoistic actions occur when actors make purely technical and practical judgements about their situation and their interests, while altruistic actions occur when actors recognise the legitimate demands of a wider circle of others.

Rational Choice and Social Exchange

The model of rational action was developed as an account of strategic action in the work of Fredrik Barth (1959, 1966) and Fred Bailey (1969; see also Firth 1951; Leach 1954), who took the metaphor of the game as the basis for understanding how particular cultural codes make rational action possible. Games are strategic contests regulated by sets of rules. The 'rules of the game' specify the general principles governing the choices that actors must make within the game, but they do not lay down precise and detailed prescriptions that eliminate all choice. Within this normative framework, game players can adopt purely technical and instrumental tactics and manoeuvres and engage in 'gamesmanship' aimed at competitive success. All spheres of social life can be modelled as 'games' in this sense, and a theory of action can trace the ploys adopted and the teams formed to ensure the attainment of 'prizes' or success in particular life games. Bailey has applied this view to politics, which he sees as a game in which leaders mobilise resources through their party machines in order to pursue political goals. Followers are attracted and their support is ensured through contracts and agreements that tie them into particular social relations.

The underlying assumptions of this viewpoint are those that Karl Popper (1945, 1957; see also 1968, 1967) derived from marginalist economics, and from the reflections of Ludwig von Mises and Friedrich von Hayek[6] Actors make their decisions rationally in relation to the particular 'logic of the situation' in which they find themselves. This is a definition of the situation and a judgement on the purely rational considerations that must be taken into account. Actors who define the situation in different ways are likely to act differently, but those who define it in the same way will, as rational agents, act in similar ways (see also Jarvie 1972; Goldthorpe 1998).

The most comprehensive and unambiguously rationalistic pursuit of the strategic model of action has been termed rational choice theory. The relative success of economic theories of market behaviour encouraged others to apply economic models to all forms of social action. Gary Becker (1976, 1981) has been an influential advocate of the use of rational action models to explain criminal behaviour and behaviour in the family, while Anthony Downs (1957) has applied the same approach to the electoral behaviour of parties and voters. From within sociology, James Coleman (1990, 1973; see also Fararo 1988) has formalised the argument as a general social theory. This work has converged with the arguments of a number of Marxists who pursued a theoretical unification between Marxist and marginalist economics and have drawn this out as a general theory of action (Elster 1983, 1989, 1999; Roemer 1988).

The most influential and powerful sociological account, however, is also the earliest. George Homans, working as what he describes (1984) as 'legman' for Henderson's Pareto seminar in the 1930s, developed a general sociological orientation (1950) that he then sought to reconstruct in purely individualistic terms (1961). His theory of rational action rejected any reliance on conscious choice and strategic calculation. Such things may occur – they may, indeed, be typical – but it is unnecessary for a social theory to make any reference to them. Rational responses are learned responses; they are routine dispositions and tendencies of action that will be pursued by any rational actor faced with a given situation. Social theory can formulate principles of calculation and apply them 'as if' actors were acting consciously in relation to them, but the actors themselves may be acting in purely routinised ways on the basis of deeply engrained responses to given stimuli.

Homans's basic model sees actors oriented by the rewards and costs they see attached to alternative courses of action and that reflect their interests and preferences. These calculations of rewards and costs are made in relation to the marginal rewards and costs secured, and individual actors are motivated to maximise the 'profits' they can accrue. Homans's particular concern was not isolated acts but social relations, which he conceptualised as exchange relations or transactions. No pattern of interaction will emerge or persist, he argued, unless all participants are making a profit (1961: 61). Those who make a loss in their interactions will withdraw from them and pursue more profitable courses of action. Homans further argued that exit and entry into exchange relations would continue until the point at which all participants are able to equalise the profits secured in a relationship and those that could be gained from available alternative actions.

The profits that people aim to secure are not purely financial. Through their interactions they may achieve love, recognition, loyalty, political support, and knowledge as well as monetary rewards, and they may experience violence, abuse, loss of time, tiredness, anxiety, and hate as well as making monetary losses. The overall profit secured in a relationship, therefore, involves a complex appraisal of diverse rewards and costs, and it is not surprising, perhaps, that money is often used as a common measure or yardstick on the grounds that everything has its price. Nevertheless, it is more difficult to predict equilibrium points in social interaction than it is in the purely economic case of a market transaction.

Peter Blau (1964) applied these ideas to the formation of work groups, showing that informal structures of social relations, concerned with social status and mutual aid, are built around purely formal employment structures organised in terms of the use of money and authority. Emerson (1962; see also French 1956; Cook 1977) has shown that it is important to examine the bargaining power that results from the dependence of one actor on another, as this shapes their involvement in social exchange. Thus, it has been shown that power differentials derived from household resources structure the domestic relations between husbands and wives and that wives will evaluate the profits gained from their marriage against the potential profits available elsewhere. For many women, a lack of employment outside the home means they are unable to withstand the cost of ending an unprofitable marriage (Blood and Wolfe 1960; Wolfe 1959; see also Vogler 1998).

FOCUS: GEORGE HOMANS

Rational choice theories have been a major growth area in recent social science, but they have gone little beyond the important insights of George Homans. His *Social Behaviour* (1961), for all its limitations, remains a landmark study in social theory. The core of his argument can be found on pages 51–82.

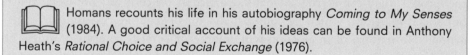 Homans recounts his life in his autobiography *Coming to My Senses* (1984). A good critical account of his ideas can be found in Anthony Heath's *Rational Choice and Social Exchange* (1976).

Presentation and Performance

The view of strategic action was broadened by Erving Goffman as a more general account of action. A student of Herbert Blumer at the University of

Chicago in the 1940s, Goffman later followed him to work at Berkeley. His work complemented Blumer's (1962, 1966, 1969) elaborations of George Mead's symbolic interactionism and Goffman drew, in addition, on the anthropology of Radcliffe-Brown and, above all, the formal sociology of Simmel. His published works began with a programmatic study of interaction (1959), followed by works on mental hospitals (1961a) and disability (1963b) and by collected essays on various facets and forms of interaction (1961b, 1963a, 1967, 1971).

Goffman's work has been described as 'dramaturgical' to emphasise his concern for the ways in which action involves the presentation of a performance in a particular role. Where Parsons saw role behaviour as the passive enactment of cultural norms, Goffman saw it as an active and strategic piece of improvisation. This was based on Mead's view of the self as combining the impulsiveness of the 'I' with the routinised social constraint of the 'me'. The way that a person appears to others is a product of that person's actions and of the reactions of others. The self as presented in public varies with the particular audience of others with whom the person is interacting. In order to give convincing performances to diverse audiences, people must employ particular techniques of 'impression management', ensuring that the 'setting' and the 'props' are appropriate to the intended performance. For example, a doctor dons a white coat, adopts a formal manner of address, and deploys instruments, notes, and equipment in order to sustain a particular definition of the situation. The aim is to convey an impression of expertise and of a purely medical encounter that will allow patients to permit the doctor to work on their bodies in intimate and intrusive ways they would not otherwise allow. While adopting the props appropriate to their current role, individuals may also adopt varying degrees of 'role distance', reducing their identification with the externally imposed expectations and emphasising that they are not merely a passive role occupant.

Structural sociologies depict social roles as distributed among differentiated spheres of activity, and Goffman saw this as showing the possibility of segregated performances. Individuals can present different images of self in the various situations in which they act because the audience for each performance is distinct. Goffman also recognised certain 'back-stage' settings where a degree of relaxation from normal 'front-stage' techniques is possible. Back-stage settings are segregated from front-stage ones – for example, home life is segregated from front-stage work performances – and back-stage audiences are those who are more intimate with the actor and among whom strategic impression management is less salient.

Goffman's concern, then, was with face-to-face interaction, and he summarised many of his ideas in a discussion of what he called the 'interaction order' (1983).

This is the sphere of face-to-face relations within which much day-to-day social life is grounded. It is in this part of the lifeworld that the self is constructed and presented to others. Its face-to-face character means that embodied performances may leave people 'vulnerable' in various ways. Failure and incompetence, for example, may involve a 'loss of face' in the eyes of others, and Goffman high-lighted the importance of emotions of embarrassment and shame in social inter-action. Breaking the conventions that surround interaction means running the risk of being discredited or stigmatised as unworthy of proper recognition. Anticipation of this social rejection generates specific physiological responses, both internal and external, that display anxiety towards the others whose reac-tion is feared (see also Scheff 1990).

This insight into the social construction of emotions through interaction has been very influential among those studying the sociology of the body. It has been extended in a specifically interactional context by Arlie Hochschild (1979, 1983), who has documented the 'emotion work' involved in giving convincing role performances. She has paid particular attention to employment relations in which managers require their subordinates to display particular emotions as an integral aspect of their work. Airline flight attendants, for example, must adopt a friendly manner towards their passengers, no matter what their personal feel-ings towards them may be.

Goffman is, perhaps, the central figure in the development of this approach to interaction, but others have made important contributions. Anselm Strauss (1959, 1978, 1993) explored the processes of negotiation through which definitions of the situation are consensually established and the continual work that must be done to sustain them. He saw Goffman's interaction order as the basis through which interactants can establish a 'negotiated order' in relation to which they each ori-entate their actions (Strauss et al. 1963). Freidson (1970a, 1970b) has explored such constructions as 'professionalism' and their part in sustaining claims to expertise.

Particularly important is Howard Becker's (1963; Becker et al. 1961) work on deviance and careers. Deviance, he argues, is simply an act that the members of a group define as a transgression of its rules, even though it may conform to the rules of another group. What is defined and 'labelled' as deviant depends upon the relative power of group members to impose their definitions on others (see also Goffman 1963b). The reactions of others, then, are crucial, and a person must accommodate to the definitions imposed by an audience whenever they have the power to make their definitions stick. When defined as a deviant, some opportunities (such as employment, education, or home life) may be closed off or restricted, while others (such as court appearances, psychiatric diagnoses, imprisonment) are required. The person enters a phase of 'secondary deviation' (Lemert 1967) in which they are confined to the life of a deviant rather than being able to drift in and out (Matza 1964). Their lives come to be structured in relation to their definition as deviant and they begin to pursue a deviant career; further deviant acts become more likely as a result of the continuing reactions of others. As Goffman (1961a) showed, an incarcerated mental patient exhibits a distinctive 'moral career' as their image of self is transformed, and Becker (1960) demonstrates how such individuals may build up commitments to their career. The person may even come to embrace the label as a description of their identity: they feel themselves to be a deviant and accept that the punishing actions of others are legitimate and appropriate, or at least understandable, responses to 'their' deviance.

Symbolic interactionism posits a view of action that is broader than that of rational choice and social exchange theory, and that can incorporate these as special, limiting cases. Its central claim is that action follows from the definition of the situation that the participating actors have negotiated. Where a situation is defined as one that is emotionally neutral and in which purely technical and instrumental considerations are relevant, actors who follow the logic of the situation will act in exclusively rational, self-interested terms. Where a situation is defined as one in which moral and emotional commitments are relevant, then its logic will require more altruistic and other-oriented actions. Strategic acts of impression management and self presentation enter into each of these polar types.

It was a recognition of this complementarity of the two principal forms of action theory that led Habermas (1965, 1967, 1981a, 1981b) to contrast instrumental action and communicative action as the fundamental elements in his typology of action. He models his view of instrumental action on Weber's concept of purposively rational action and sees it as central to labour and economic action. In such actions, objects and other people are mere means to the technical attainment of defined goals. Actors are motivated by calculations of alternative outcomes in relation to preferences that they pursue in exclusively technical ways. Communicative action, on the other hand, is discursively constructed through the use of cultural symbols that give meaning to the actor's world. It is organised around mutual understanding and is motivated by moral commitments and the institutionalised normative expectations of others. Such actions are susceptible to definition as deviance in the light of the reactions of others. These two analytical types of action enter into all forms of action in varying degrees, though they are the building blocks, respectively, of systems of economic and political relations and the lifeworld of communal relations.

FOCUS: ERVING GOFFMAN

Contemporary work on action and self presentation has received its most influential formulations in the diverse works of Erving Goffman. *The Presentation of Self in Everyday Life* (1959) is still the best way to understand his argument, though almost anything that he has written can be read with reward. Chapter 6 of *Presentation of Self* gives a short summary of his views on impression management.

A biography of Goffman is being prepared by Yves Winkin and some biographical information can be found in his contribution to Greg Smith's *Goffman and Social Organization* (1999). A useful overview of symbolic interactionism and Goffman's place within it is Joel Charon's *Symbolic Interactionism* (1979). A more comprehensive critical survey is Philip Manning's *Erving Goffman and Modern Sociology* (1992).

Conflict, Change, and History

A number of formative theorists had explored the basis of a comprehensive account of conflict. The writings of Gumplowicz, Mosca, and Toynbee set out theories of large-scale historical transformations in which the intra- and inter-societal conflicts of political, military, and economic elites were the driving forces, and cultural patterns spread as a result of this competition, conflict, and conquest. Marx and Veblen added a recognition of the economic divisions of societies into classes, which they saw as underpinning these conflicts. Small and others at Chicago scaled down these considerations into an analysis of the small-group conflicts and rivalries that shape urban processes and political struggles within contemporary states.

Contemporary theorists have recast and elaborated these views. John Rex and Ralf Dahrendorf modified the Marxist model of class conflict into a self-conscious 'conflict theory', and in Dahrendorf the institutionalised political conflicts of small groups also found a place in the theory. C. Wright Mills and Ralph Miliband were more strongly reliant on Marx, though in the case of Mills the elitist theory of Mosca was also a major influence. Marx had stressed that class conflict involves subordinate classes as much as dominant classes and elites, and the struggles of subordinate and excluded groups figured centrally in the work of those such as Alain Touraine who explored their involvement in transformative social movements. This amalgam of conflict ideas fed into the historical sociologies of Barrington Moore, Theda Skocpol, and Michael Mann, and into the developmental sociology of William McNeill.

Classes, Conflicts, and Elites

Dahrendorf's work (1957) has its roots in the criticisms raised by David Lockwood (1956) against Parsons's view of the social system. Immersed in Weberian sociology, Dahrendorf and Lockwood at the London School of Economics took the lead in constructing an account of conflict to complement the 'consensus' orientation of Parsons. At the same time, Rex was working at Leeds University on ways of conceptualising the ethnic conflicts of his native South Africa. This concern led to general statements of the conflict view (1961, 1981, 1970) that echoed some of the earlier contributions of Oliver Cox.

Dahrendorf holds that Marx's emphasis on property relations was a historically specific form of a broader view of 'authority' as the basis of social conflict. All societies are divided into dominant and subordinate groups, but it is only in capitalism that these divisions are organised through the ownership of property. European and North American societies since the second half of the twentieth century, Dahrendorf argues, are no longer capitalist societies and so can no longer be analysed in conventional Marxist terms.

Rex's view of conflict is very similar, though he remains closer to the concepts set out in Weber's classic statements on social stratification. The distribution of economic, political, and cultural resources, Rex argues, comprises a 'substructure of power' that divides dominant from subordinate groups and establishes a 'balance of power' between them. Parsons's theory of the social system had concentrated on those situations where these conflict groups have established a 'truce' or *modus vivendi*, and it loses much of its relevance in situations where the underlying power relations are unstable, highly skewed, or unregulated. Conflict theory, therefore, provides a more general account of social life in which the Parsonian model appears as a special, limiting case.

According to Dahrendorf, relations of authority generate clusters of dominant and subordinate roles. These are the 'classes' that provide their occupants with distinct experiences and conflicting interests. Occupants of the dominant roles, for example, have an overriding interest in maintaining the structure of authority from which they benefit. Class interests are the bases around which people organise themselves for collective action into one or more 'interest groups'. The solidarity of these interest groups and their effectiveness in conflict depend upon the unity and cohesion that class members are able to establish through their shared experiences and their patterns of association. Rex's theory saw the power of ruling groups as expressed in the imposition of institutions, ideas, and values on subordinate groups. The opposition of black and white ethnic groups in South Africa for much of the twentieth century, for example, involved just such a wholesale opposition of conflict groups. Overt conflict, then, is likely to express a clash of whole ways of life, and the outcome of such conflicts may well be the structural transformation of societies.

Dahrendorf focused directly on competition among the 'interest groups' that are recruited from authority or power classes. Thus, the competition of trades unions, political parties, pressure groups, lobbying agencies, cooperatives, and so on, has to be seen in relation to the underlying distribution of authority that gives rise to them. In a similar vein, Rex looked at the local-level struggles of neighbourhood groups, political parties, and others as expressing the systemic divisions of the class and ethnic groups from which they are recruited. Dahrendorf and Rex offer far more sophisticated views than those such as Robert Dahl (1957) who developed a 'pluralist' theory that takes account only of the struggles of interest groups and does not relate these to any larger structural sources of conflict (see Lukes 1974). Using the ecological ideas of the Chicago conflict theorists, for example, Rex investigated ethnic conflict in the British city of Birmingham (Rex and Moore 1969; Rex and Tomlinson 1979) in ways that go well beyond Dahl's study of New Haven (1961).

Alain Touraine's theory of conflict is an attempt to update Marxism to recognise the new conflicts and social movements of the contemporary period. Working on strikes and industrial conflict (1955), he elaborated on the Marxian account of the economic basis of the labour movement and extended this to take account of work relations in the more advanced technologies. New class relations were giving rise to the new social conflicts of new social movements (1965, 1966). A class with a common economic location has the potential to become a 'historical subject' and can realise this potential if its members are organised for collective purposes. This occurs through the building of a *conscience collective* that defines the members of the class as participants in a larger process of historical transformation. This consciousness underpins their participation in the organisations and groupings that constitute social movements.

Touraine (1969) shares Dahrendorf's view that social conflicts are now rooted in the distribution of authority in large organisations and that a dominant class of 'technocrats' exists in conflict with the intellectual workers who actually produce the technical knowledge on which the technocrats rely. His later work (1973, 1978) generalised this account to see conflict occurring in relation to power differences associated with age, gender, ethnicity, and consumption, each of which finds its expression in a distinct social movement. Actors in each of these spheres of activity develop a consciousness of their shared interests within a common framework of experiences, and the various social movements compete to control the norms that regulate their lives. (See also the articles of the 1970s and 1980s collected in Touraine 1984.)

A conflict orientation was developed in the United States by C. Wright Mills. He saw 'coordination' by a ruling group as a fundamental mechanism of integration in any social system (1953). Such ruling groups link together the various structural hierarchies of their society and ensure that they work in a coherent way to sustain the overall structure of power on which the ruling group depends. In the societies of North America and Europe in the second half of the twentieth century, Mills argued, political, military, and economic hierarchies are tied together through overlapping power relations that unify a 'power elite' and render powerless the mass of ordinary people (1956). This structure of power is the result of a long-term process in which older class relations have been superseded by the growth of bureaucracy in business (1951) and by the massive expansion of states and military apparatuses. The resulting power elite comprises the leaders of the largest business enterprises, the central political establishment, and the top military bureaucracy. Where pluralists saw the competition of groups as a democratic mechanism, Mills saw it as marking a minor division of opinion within an otherwise unified power elite.

Mills had a great influence. Ralph Miliband met Mills during the 1950s and his own development of a Marxist theory of the state owed a great deal to Mills's arguments. Miliband (1969; see also 1982, 1983, 1989) redefined the Marxist idea of the ruling class as a 'state elite' recruited from an economically dominant class. Also influenced by Mills and the European conflict theorists was Alvin Gouldner, whose early analyses of industrial bureaucracy and its structuring around conflicts between management and workers (1954a, 1954b) were followed by more wide-ranging accounts of the rise to power of a 'new class' of technical and humanistic intellectuals within western societies controlled by capitalist businessmen and eastern societies controlled by Communist bureaucrats (1979; see also 1976). This argument influenced the studies of East European societies undertaken by the Hungarian sociologist Ivan Szelenyi (Szelenyi and Conrad 1978; Szelenyi et al. 1998).

FOCUS: JOHN REX

Contemporary conflict ideas have most forcibly been developed by John Rex in his general work and in his studies of South African society. His *Social Conflict* (1981) gives a brief overview.

A critical review of Rex's ideas can be found in Herminio Martins's edited collection *Knowledge as Passion* (1993). The whole approach is outlined in David Binns's *Beyond the Sociology of Conflict* (1978).

Conflict and Historical Change

A specifically historical approach to conflict was taken by Barrington Moore (1966), whose arguments originated in an early critique of Parsons (Moore 1958). He saw the class division between aristocracy and peasantry in agrarian societies as rooted in their property relations. It is the historically specific class relations of these pre-capitalist societies that determines their routes into the modern world. There is, however, no single trajectory of modernisation, and so this process cannot be reduced to economic terms alone. Differences between liberal democratic, Communist, and fascist forms of modernisation reflect variations in the agrarian class conflicts and property relations that produced them (see also Skocpol 1979). The commercialisation of agriculture in England generated a growing economic surplus and was furthered through political conflict that broke the dominance of the feudal landowners to create a class of owner-occupying farmers. At the same time, this commercialisation strengthened the urban mercantile and manufacturing classes, which were able to mount an increasingly strong challenge to the aristocracy. This complex balance of power allowed the building of liberal democratic political forms. In societies that were late to industrialise, on the other hand, there was little agricultural commercialisation and only a weak bourgeoisie. In Germany and Japan, modernisation had been initiated 'from above', by a state that was still controlled by an old aristocracy and that laid the foundations for militarism, nationalism, and, eventually, fascism. In Russia and China, on the other hand, the aristocracy opposed change, and modernisation could be advanced only through the peasantry allying itself with industrial workers. This modernisation 'from below' produced the Communist regimes, headed by party administrators, of which the peasants were to become the principal victims.

A particularly wide-ranging basis for such arguments has been provided by Michael Mann (1986, 1993). He takes a view of societies as dispersed or fragmented systems within which the relations of groups and organisations stretch through various transnational networks to groups and organisations in other, similarly fragmented, systems. Central to these transnational networks are relations of power such as those analysed by Rex and others. Mann identifies four dimensions or axes of this power: political, military, economic, and ideological, and he traces the 'intensive' relations of closure and the 'extensive' relations of expansion and diffusion through which inter-societal systems are built.

Mann applies this general argument to the formation of early empires through the coalescence of hunting bands and the creation of vertical power structures headed by state elites (see also Gellner 1988; Hall 1985; and see Giddens 1981). He goes on to show the formation of the nation state and systems of states that underpin the expansion of the modern world system. Though he has not yet completed this argument with an account of the expansion of industrial systems, he has (2004) traced the formation of fascist regimes as specific conjunctions of class relations. Mass fascism, he argues, arose in the European power crises following the First World War and aimed to establish radical forms of statism that would transcend the class divisions that give birth to them.

The most comprehensive historical theory of conflict is undoubtedly that of William McNeill (1963, 1967; see also 1996; McNeill and McNeill 2003), who explicitly builds on Toynbee's model of challenge and response. He read both Spengler and Toynbee in the 1930s and worked with Toynbee in London after 1950, when he began to plan a systematic materialist approach to world history. A particular influence was Gordon Childe, though McNeill rejected his strong economic determinism. Nevertheless, technology and the diffusion of technological innovations are central to his argument. Technological advance, McNeill argues, is driven forward by economic and political competition over resources, expressed most obviously in inter-societal military conflicts. McNeill's arguments pre-figured those of the world system theorists (Wallerstein 1974), and he saw conflict as producing a global ecology of peoples and problems (McNeill 1976, 1982).

FOCUS: WILLIAM MCNEILL

William McNeill's view of conflict and historical change, largely set out in *The Rise of the West* (1963), owes a great deal to the earlier work of Toynbee. McNell rarely draws out general theoretical arguments, but some indication of his standpoint can be found on pages 726–62.

The previous four chapters have reviewed the principal themes in social theory and traced their patterns of development during the formative and contemporary periods. In considering these ideas it will have become clear that the theorists were not developing theories for their own sake but in order to understand their world and its development. Some of their substantive claims have already been glimpsed, but it is now possible to approach these more directly. Chapter 7 looks at the nature of the modern society that gave birth to formative social theory and with which much social theory has been concerned. In Chapter 8 I turn to consider the argument of those who have argued that fundamental changes in the pattern of modernity may be introducing new forms of social organisation for which new forms of theory may be required.

NOTES

1. There is a useful summary in Baker (2003: 38).

2. See Simmel (1903) and Wirth (1938). These ideas are also discussed in Katznelson (1981).

3. For a general overview of some of these issues see Smith (1984).

4. Beck's wider arguments about modernity are considered in Chapter 8.

5. Kristeva (1969) is partially translated in Moi (1986).

6. Popper's argument had appeared as a critique of 'historicism' in article form in 1944. Friedrich von Hayek, a student of Ludwig von Mises, moved to London in 1932 and developed the general implications of marginalism for a theory of action (1942, 1962, 1965, 1967). The background to this is discussed in Chapter 4.

7 | Modernity and Rationalisation

This chapter turns to the ways in which social theorists have used the analytical ideas introduced in this book in order to understand contemporary social change. These concerns have focused on issues of modernity and modernisation, understood as a move from traditional to rational cultural patterns, social structures, and processes of action. This has been seen in relation to

- political forms of statehood, bureaucracy, and citizenship

- inter-state relations and global political structures

- economic forms of markets, property, and management

- transnational economic relations and world economies

- plurality, cultural diversity, and disenchantment

- mass processes of cultural formation and social organisation

These key institutions of modernity have provided the point of reference for key debates in contemporary sociology.

Most of the formative and contemporary theorists saw the key substantive issue to which their theories were directed as the idea that their societies had undergone a transition from 'traditional' forms of social organisation to characteristically 'modern' ones. Sociology was seen as a product of modernity, as something that could not have emerged in a traditional social order. Those who did not themselves undertake empirical work saw their theoretical ideas as means to illuminate the investigations of those who did. In this chapter I look at some of the claims made about this transition. I discuss what it means to be 'modern', and I use the sociological concepts discussed in earlier chapters to explore the development of modern social institutions. In the following chapter I will consider the arguments of those who have claimed that the world today is undergoing a further transition from modern to 'post-modern' social forms.

The *Oxford English Dictionary* shows the word 'modern' to have derived from the Latin *modernus* (originally *hodiernus*), meaning 'just now' or 'of today'. Its meaning is closely linked with the ideas of the 'present day' and the 'contemporary'. To be modern, then, is to be up-to-date and of the current time. The word can also imply something that is fashionable – a usage encouraged by its similarity to the unrelated word 'mode', meaning a prevailing fashion or style. The word 'modern', then, is used to refer to the present and recent times, as contrasted with any more remote past, and to designate the specifically contemporary character of something. The 'modern' things referred to – pieces of music or works of art, items of clothing or furniture, ways of behaving and attitudes of mind – need share no quality other than that of being up-to-date: what it is to be modern will change as fashions and preferences change. In sociology, the word is often used in just this sense in such phrases as 'modern social theory', a phrase that alludes to the contemporary character of the theory and contrasts it with 'classical', 'nineteenth-century', and other older, perhaps 'out-moded', approaches to theory. It is similarly used in such phrases as 'modern Britain' to refer to the study of present-day British society, as contrasted with 'Victorian' Britain, 'pre-war' Britain, and so on.

The word 'modern' and its equivalents in other European languages came into use among the Renaissance scholars, who contrasted the contemporary rebirth of classical knowledge with the preceding 'dark ages' from which they were emerging. It was the philosophers of the Enlightenment, however, who transformed it into a term for use in systematic historical analysis. Constructing narratives of historical change, they used the word 'modern' to refer to the specific post-medieval character of the European world in which they were living. The philosophical discourse of modernity depicted 'modern' times as being radically different from immediate past times.

The analytical point of reference for this conceptualisation of difference was the social order that prevailed in western Europe until the collapse of the Western Roman Empire in the fifth century AD. The whole Graeco-Roman period was referred to as the 'ancient' world, and was seen as the world in which all that is of cultural value originated. Enlightenment thought organised itself around typologies of social development in which the 'ancient' and the 'modern' were separated by the medieval or 'middle' ages of barbarism, feudalism, and despotism (Bury 1955). As Enlightenment thought was deepened, this historical framework became one of progress or evolution: the modern age was seen as having surpassed the achievements of the ancient age and as holding the promise of yet further advance.

This historical usage led to a broadened meaning for the term 'modern'. Because a 'modern' society, like any other society, tends to change over time, its characteristics may vary quite considerably from one century to the next, and even from one decade to the next. As a result, those things that were once 'of today' will eventually come to be seen as unfashionable, out-moded things of the past: things 'of yesterday'. Things that were up-to-date in the seventeenth century were no longer so in the nineteenth or twentieth centuries. However, the historical usage of the term 'modern society' sought to characterise a longer-term and more enduring social condition. It was a form of social life that came into being in the seventeenth century and that, despite many superficial changes, persisted in all essential respects as a non-traditional social order. A 'modern society', for historians and sociologists, is no longer simply a society of the present day; it is a society defined by certain substantive characteristics.

Substantively, a modern society came to be seen as one that had broken with ignorance and tradition. A modern society is governed by increasingly rational considerations. The modern social condition is a rationally organised way of life. It is one in which social institutions and practices are discursively established and justified through rationally grounded knowledge and critical appraisal. Actions tend to be organised as techniques or strategies that use the most appropriate and exact means for attaining goals or pursuing values in all areas of life. At the heart of this rationalisation are 'political' principles of statecraft and of the purposes of governance, together with the 'economic' and 'industrial' techniques through which people secure their means of subsistence. The Enlightenment ideal, however, had been to achieve a comprehensive and thorough-going rationalisation of life, and a modern society was seen as one in which all aspects of human existence were equally subject to rational considerations. The Enlightenment theorists could see no possibility for any way of life to surpass the modern condition. Once humans properly exercise the powers of reason that set them apart from all other beings, there would be no turning back: they would always be modern. While a move away from modernity was logically possible, it could never be the sensible choice for rational beings to take.

Modernity became the central object of sociological debate. The formative social theorists, however, had more complex and nuanced understandings of the human condition. They were, on the whole, less attracted by highly optimistic views of the inevitability of human progress through intellectual rationality. Nevertheless, most social theorists did tend to see the modern condition as inescapable, and so treated the rationalisation of the world as a relentless and virtually unstoppable process. It was generally assumed that all societies would follow a similar developmental process of 'modernisation'. All societies that made the transition from a primitive to a more complex form would, by adopting rational techniques of state-building and production, be compelled to extend rational control to other areas and so to set off on a path of modernisation towards the kinds of societies that had been pioneered in western Europe. Thus, modernisation was also 'westernisation'.

My aim in this chapter is to explore the idea of rationalisation and the kinds of institutions and practices that are generally seen to define the modern condition. I will also assess the extent to which the process of modernisation can be seen as inevitable. This will allow me to answer the question of what it means to be modern and whether human beings are, in fact, condemned to particular institutional forms of modernity. If these institutional characteristics change, then a society may cease to be modern and the inevitability of modernity can be questioned. If rationality is expressed in particular institutional forms and these are not inevitable, then it is possible that these institutions might change to such an extent that it is no longer sensible to continue using the word 'modern' to describe them. If this were the case, modern societies would have to be seen as entering a new, non-modern condition. In these circumstances, the term 'modern' would, paradoxically, become a purely historical designation: modern societies would simply be certain societies that once existed in the past! I will look at this question in Chapter 8, where I assess whether recent changes are such that modernity has given way, in the contemporary world, to a new 'post-modern' condition.

Modernisation as Rationalisation

The first intimations of modernity during the Renaissance set out a broadly 'humanist' conception of rationality. This was at its clearest in such thinkers as Desiderius Erasmus of Rotterdam (lived 1466–1536), François Rabelais (lived 1483–1553), and Michel de Montaigne (lived 1533–92). Their aim was to promote toleration and reasonableness in all things and, to this end, they advocated a critical and sceptical challenging of all established and authoritative ways of acting (Toulmin 1990). Tradition could no longer be seen as the justification for human actions. The human world was to be placed firmly at the centre of attention and was to be the primary object of speculation, replacing religious authority and speculation about the nature of God and his will. Human needs, powers, and interests were to be the bases of all values, and social life was to be transformed in accordance with these. Human life was, therefore, to be self-organised through the exercise of reason alone: there was to be a move towards a society in which the sovereignty of God would be replaced by the sovereignty of reason.

A pre-condition for this rational transformation was a weakening and eventual dismantling of the institutions of established religious authority. The Lutheran Reformation and reform movements within the Catholic Church made this possible by challenging the liturgy and dogmatism of the established religion and opened up greater possibilities for a more comprehensive rationalisation of life. Protestantism undermined the social hierarchy of the Church, making the individual the ultimate arbiter in all matters. Individuals might hope to hear the direct and unmediated guidance of God, but they must, on an everyday basis, rely on their individual powers of reason in deciding how to live. Individuals had been made in the image of God, and by acting in a specifically human – rational – way, they could best achieve his purposes. The Enlightenment thinkers took this one step further. Even when the idea of God was not rejected, they nevertheless recognised a strict demarcation between questions appropriate to the religious life and those appropriate to the practical organisation of life in this world. Practical considerations were to be governed exclusively by individual rationality. Religion, like myth, superstition, and traditionalism of all kinds, prevented the establishment of reason as the universal and impersonal criterion for handling practical problems.

The Enlightenment, then, established the idea of rationality as an inherently superior mode of thought to all others, whether those of the medieval and ancient West or those of 'primitive' non-European societies (see the debate on rationality of African societies in B.R. Wilson 1970; see also Lévy-Bruhl 1921). In doing so, however, they narrowed down the idea of rationality. Where Renaissance humanists had seen this as an intensely practical criterion, rooted in enduring human values, the Enlightenment project emphasised its purely formal principles. There was a stress on 'abstract, timeless methods of deriving general solutions to universal problems' (Toulmin 1990: 34–5). The idea that reason was a condition for universal freedom and autonomy was lost from the mainstream of Enlightenment thought, which emphasised the purely technical mastery of nature, other people, and oneself. The ethical discourse of reason was, therefore, abandoned as Enlightenment thought came to emphasise power, technique, and decision.

This narrowing down of rationality was seen as the means for providing greater certainty in human affairs. The Renaissance had challenged medieval absolutes in the name of rational scepticism, encouraging uncertainty and doubt. The science of Newton and his contemporaries, however, seemed to promise a new certainty, but a certainty only of technique. This was rooted in the power of reason itself to generate absolute and unchallengeable knowledge of the external world. Within its own sphere, science had re-established a degree of certitude, and so long as the limits of this rationality were recognised, it was possible to achieve some certainty and to avoid many of the cultural schisms and conflicts opened up by the Renaissance and the Reformation. The rationalisation advocated in the Enlightenment project was a scientific rationalisation focused on instrumental techniques and reforms, and the claims of science were promoted as a means for extending its principles and gurantees to other spheres of human action. Seventeenth-century science, then, was the keystone in the modern worldview or the 'framework of Modernity' (Adorno and Horkheimer 1944: Ch. 1; Toulmin 1990: 108; see also Latour 1991).

It is important not to isolate these intellectual developments from wider social changes. No purely idealistic account of rationalisation would be satisfactory. Enlightenment ideas were encouraged by certain *prior* changes in social structure, and they embodied and carried forward particular social interests and concerns. They were promoted and encouraged largely by those from a 'bourgeois' class background who were excluded from participation in many established social institutions. Their growing economic wealth gave them the power to challenge this exclusion, and demands for political citizenship in reformed states and for a clear recognition of the rights of individual property owners were integral elements in their challenge to religious authority. In eliminating religious dogma from 'secular' affairs, it was intended that the interests of the bourgeoisie could be more rationally pursued. The rational individual was, implicitly, a bourgeois individual (Tawney 1926; Macpherson 1962).

Hence, the impersonal and universal claims of reason were tied to very specific class relations and class interests. The intellectual claims advanced in the Enlightenment project had their foundations in practical processes that were already under way. The commercialisation of agriculture, the growth of trade and markets, and the shifting political balance between aristocracy and bourgeoisie had long histories and were closely tied to the slow emergence of individualism and rationalism within declining feudal and patrimonial structures (Macfarlane 1978). What makes the Enlightenment so important is the self-consciousness with which its programme was pursued and the rapidity with which the changes that it advocated took place. The Enlightenment project was formulated when conditions were ripe for its implementation. The seventeenth century saw the true birth of modernity, following its long gestation during the preceding centuries.

The great theorist of this process was Max Weber, who aimed to describe and interpret the rationalisation undergone by European societies and transferred to other parts of the world. Weber rejected the views of developmental theorists who saw the growth of rationality as an inevitable outcome of a unilinear and universal process of social evolution. There is no inevitability about the rise of modernity. Nevertheless, he argued, there had observably been a long-term growth in formal rationality, which it was important to explain. Weber saw this as a growth in practical rationality in all aspects of social life, producing an enhanced mastery and control over nature, society, and self. Practical rationality is the rationalisation of the means for achieving particular, given ends. It is realised in purposive or instrumental action in which the technically most appropriate means through which particular goals can be achieved are calculated and methodically pursued. The criteria by which actions are judged are those of effectiveness and success. The paradigmatic example of rational action for Weber was economic action, understood in marginalist terms in relation to consciously chosen preferences: economically oriented actors are those who act strategically, using appropriate techniques to attain their goals. The purposes involved in rational actions are arbitrary, but they may be regarded as rational purposes if they are chosen deliberately and in relation to some specific value. The values themselves, however, are irreducibly arbitrary and without ultimate foundation. Once tradition and the unreflective acceptance of values have been dethroned and denied any role as foundations of values and knowledge, value judgements are seen to be rationally unjustifiable commitments through which human beings attempt to give some meaning to an intrinsically meaningless world. They are the 'warring gods' among which individuals must choose without any guidance from hierarchy, traditional authority, or foundational beliefs.[1] Rationalisation, therefore, involves the elimination from public discourse of unreflective prejudice, and, in consequence, fewer actions shaped purely by emotion or tradition.

Weber (1903–5) stressed the particular importance of the religious factor in triggering this rapid rationalisation of the world. While many of the institutional preconditions for rational political and economic action had developed elsewhere, it was only in northwestern Europe that this take-off occurred so rapidly and introduced a new, modern age (Weber 1915a, 1916; and see the general summary in 1919–20, 1920b). The Protestant, and especially the Calvinist, sects that arose in the Reformation were particularly congenial to the outlook of the bourgeoisie, and it was in their religious communities that the modern outlook was nurtured. The Calvinist theology of salvation and predestination generated an inner anxiety and psychological loneliness in the collective mentality of its adherents, encouraging its pastors to formulate a social ethic for the conduct of life that stressed the rational, diligent pursuit of practical goals. In following this ethic in those vocations that were open to them – most notably in banking, trade, and manufacture – Calvinists achieved vocational success. He argued that this pointed to an inner or 'elective' affinity between Calvinist social ethics and those ideas that could ensure practical vocational success. He stressed, in particular, the 'spirit of modern capitalism' that developed among Calvinist businessmen in Protestant Europe during the seventeenth and eighteenth centuries. The business success of Protestants resulted in competitive pressures that compelled others to pursue their businesses in the same spirit. Merton (1938) argued that the spirit of modern science had similar origins and that the Protestant encouragement of rational inquiry into God's purpose and the nature of the world that he had made also encouraged the development of a secular science that was ultimately to devalue all religious values.

The spirit of rationality and technique, then, was diffused through science, business, and politics, making possible a comprehensive rationalisation of social life. The secular spirit of rationality, detached from its original religious inspiration, spread widely, contributing to a progressive 'disenchantment' of the world as religion, superstition, and myth lost their compelling and all-embracing character (Brubaker 1984). As 'traditional' justifications for action lose their force with this dissolution of belief, so societies become 'detraditionalised'.

The transition from traditional to modern society, then, can be understood as a process of rationalisation in which the value standards that define people's orientations towards each other show an ever greater degree of formal rationality. The nature of this shift was described by Talcott Parsons (1951, 1960b) using the 'pattern variables' that he derived from his readings of Weber and Tönnies. These pattern variables are the dimensions along which formally rational value patterns can be measured. They refer to the 'dilemmas of choice' that face individuals in their actions and to which their culture provides a solution. Ascriptive,

Figure 7.1 *The pattern variables*

Traditionalism	Modernity
Ascription (quality)	Achievement (performance)
Affectivity	Neutrality
Diffuseness	Specificity
Particularism	Universalism

affective, diffuse, and particularistic standards give way to achievement, neutral, specific, and universalistic ones (Figure 7.1).

A shift from ascriptive to achievement standards involves a move away from the categorisation of others by their personal qualities. Each participant in a rationalised social relation defines others by how effective or successful they are in attaining their goals. They are judged on the basis of what they have actually achieved or what they may achieve in their future acts. The important consideration is not *who* they are but *how* they perform in practical contexts. A shift from affectivity to neutrality is an alteration in the emotional content of social relations. Affective social relations are impulsive and emotionally engaged, allowing an immediate satisfaction of each participant's wants and wishes. In affectively neutral social relations, on the other hand, an impersonal and disciplined cognitive orientation is adopted, allowing a calculative, long-term orientation to the satisfaction of desires. In the shift from affectivity to neutrality, sentiment and emotion become less salient and acts and their consequences come to be judged in purely pragmatic terms. When social orientations are diffuse, the overall character of each person as a whole is of interest. In a specific social relation, on the other hand, the focus is on a single aspect of the other. Specific orientations restrict expectations and interests to narrow and limited aspects of the other: actions are functionally specialised. Particularistic orientations are subjectively biased in accordance with the unique significance they have for participants. Universalistic orientations, on the other hand, judge people in relation to what they share with others: they are regarded as members of a class or category of persons with common characteristics.

The contrast between traditional orientations and modern orientations is the same contrast made by Tönnies (1889) between *Gemeinschaft* and *Gesellschaft* and by Morgan (1877) between *civitas* and *societas*. Rationalisation produces a shift along one or more of the pattern variables, with changes along one dimension reinforcing and promoting change along the others.

In modern societies, the public worlds of the state and the market are dominated by rationalised orientations, becoming ever more disciplined and organised around formal and impersonal standards. Emotion and sentiment become mere secondary elements in these spheres and are increasingly subordinated to rational control. The range of actions subject to non-rational orientations shrinks and is largely confined to the personal and intimate spheres of family, kinship, and locality. Even here, however, they become subject to discipline and manipulation, as individuals are concerned with the calculated impressions that they make on others (Goffman 1959). The spontaneous expression of emotion becomes evermore repressed and denied in even the closest relationships.

The rationalisation of value standards, then, is at the heart of modernisation. It is a process in which key social institutions are transformed in the direction of a greater formal rationality in the standards by which they operate. This is focused on certain crucial aspects of social life that come to be seen as the central institutions of modernity. These are the institutions of the nation state and the capitalist economy, together with those of communication and education with which they are closely articulated.

Rationalisation and Political Structures

A state comprises the set of apparatuses through which political rule is exercised over those living within a given territory. This is secured through authoritative, binding commands backed up by organised physical force (Weber 1914: 952; 1920a: 54–6; Mann 1993: 55; Held 1989: 11; Scott 2001: 33–4). Rationalisation has culminated in the institutional arrangements of the modern nation state, in which the elites that stand at the apexes of its various institutional hierarchies collectively form a state elite that operates through the rationalised legal and administrative orders of constitutionalism and bureaucracy.

European states took this recognisably modern form from the late fifteenth and early sixteenth centuries as the traditional structures of the medieval world broke down. Medieval states were systems of strong and often despotic power with very limited internal penetration (Mann 1993: 59–60). The centre of gravity in these states was the royal court (Elias 1969; Poggi 1978), where the monarch had complete control over dependent nobles and courtiers. It was through the court that monarchs built rudimentary departments of government – councils and chambers responsible for particular practical matters that were no longer a mere prerogative of private landownership. The key innovation was the building of hierarchies of paid officials in a power apparatus that would generate more in revenue than it cost to maintain, and revenues could be further increased by the selling of official positions. Competition among states created pressures on each state to emulate the successful innovations and practices of others (Hall and Ikenberry 1989: 39), leading to a long-term convergence of structures and practices. State after state established large civil bureaucracies and standing armies through which they were better able to 'pacify' and administer their own populations and to extend their territorial scope. The 'absolutist' states that resulted were the focus of the rationalised structures that were to be central to political modernity, though it is doubtful whether this would have proceeded very far without the additional stimulus provided by the cultural spirit of the Enlightenment (Anderson 1974).

Bureaucracy, Democracy, and Citizenship

Central to the modern nation state are its mechanisms for the making and enforcing of laws and regulations. Rational law-making occurs through a specialised sphere of decision-making, a 'legal order' that rests on purely formal procedures. There is neither arbitrary interference from political rulers nor customary limitation on the scope of the law. Legal formalism involves those at the head of the state operating through formal procedures and placing themselves under the legal order. Legislation consists of the conscious and deliberate enactment of new legal norms through this formal process. Laws are cast as abstract and general rules that may be formally codified. Judicial decisions in a rational legal order involve the universalistic application of these general legal norms to specific cases. Within such an order, contractual and other legally defined relations allow a high degree of predictability and calculability.

The 'administrative order' of a state comprises specialised means through which laws and legal decisions are sanctioned and implemented. In rationalised states, this exists as a formally rational bureaucracy in which impersonal rules are applied to particular situations. Administrative decisions are detached from sentiment and emotion and are no longer subject to the arbitrary intervention of a traditional authority. Administration is no longer an adjunct of personal or family position but rests on a formal separation of the 'official' from the means of administration. Administrative officials are employees, and the means of administration are owned by the administrative body itself and are regulated by abstract and general rules. Each official has a specific jurisdiction within which he or she is empowered to act. Each office is part of a hierarchical structure of delegated authority. The levels of the administrative hierarchy consists of officials constrained to exercise technical expertise without regard for the personal characteristics of those subject to their authority. There may be a separation between the experts who formulate the rules and the officials who enforce them, but officials act, nevertheless, as the enforcers of rules that can be given a rational justification. This is the key to the rational-legal authority that Weber saw as characteristic of modern bureaucracies (Albrow 1970).

The states of the modern world define themselves in relation to their distinctive 'national' territories, each exercising its national sovereignty vis-à-vis other states. These territorial bounds are defined by frontiers and borders across which the movement and migration of people are policed. Entry conditions are established and enforced through passports, visas, and administrative requirements, allowing 'citizens' and non-citizens to be treated differently. Citizens are to be treated on the basis of formal legal equality, without regard for personal characteristics; non-citizens can be denied the rights possessed by citizens. The French Revolution of 1789, directly inspired by the Enlightenment project of a rational politics, was seen by Parsons (1971: 79) as central to this idea of legal citizenship and its spread as a democratic ideal. The legally defined status of national citizen has come to involve not only rights of exit, entry, and movement, but also rights to political participation and to participation in the wider public life of the nation (Hobhouse 1911; Marshall 1949; Lockwood 1996; Morris 2002). Mann (1993: Ch. 3) discusses this in terms of a link between 'representative' and 'national' issues, though the discussion here departs from much of his wider account. Political systems organised around citizen representation in the political process secure popular support for governments through a conception of the mass of the population as active and participating citizens rather than merely passive subjects of a king or emperor (Bendix 1964; Mann 1987). Thus, citizenship involves a 'democratisation' of political authority. The potential power of all adult members of a society, understood as its 'citizens', is enhanced through their formal political rights and through forms of mass participation and representation in national politics. Legitimate rights are accorded to the collective mass of citizens, understood as the 'people' and the embodiment of the 'nation'.

The crucial period for the rationalisation of states was the so-called long nineteenth century, from around 1760 to 1914. It was in this period that absolutist states made the transition to constitutional states, sometimes peacefully but more often through violence and revolution (Moore 1966; Skocpol 1979). The landed aristocracy, the emerging bourgeois classes, the traditional peasantry, and free wage labourers engaged in struggles to negotiate their relationships to the new states, and thereby shaped the forms taken by those states. By the end of the period, the leading states of Europe and America were modern states in an increasingly modern world.

Rationalisation of social control and state activity produces 'politics' as a sphere of decision and of power in the service of decisions. Perhaps the most significant feature of the French Revolution, however, was its legitimation of collective political action (Halliday 1999; see also Tilly 1978; Skocpol 1979). Made possible by improved communications and by the political and economic transformations themselves, collective action became a means through which conscious and comprehensive plans of social reconstruction could be implemented (Stein 1850). Politics now largely operates through 'parties', a term that Weber proposed to describe the groups, factions, and alliances exercising and influencing power within a state (Held 1995: 36, 48–9). Mass-based parties became competitors in elections for the right to participate in legislation, and an array of interest and pressure groups compete to influence both legislation and executive decisions. Political activity is organised around elections and plebiscites that operate as 'political markets' for mobilising popular support. Citizenship involves a right to influence state decision-making through participation in the electoral contests of parties and through office holding within state agencies. Where a differentiation of government and 'opposition' parties has been institutionalised, voting mechanisms may allow a regular social circulation in the exercise of power. Elections are central to democratic legitimation, as the individual act of voting binds the citizen to acceptance of collective decisions.

Struggles over state policies and practices are not confined to political parties. They occur in other formal 'associations' and organisations. The replacement of customary regulation in 'communities' by authoritative regulation through formal associations is what Tönnies (1889) saw as central to the *Gesellschaftlich* character of modern social orders. Historically pre-existing associations, such as churches, business enterprises, universities, and hospitals, adopt formally rational principles of administration, operating under the law and in terms of their own internal rules and procedural mechanisms. New types of association, such as trade unions and interest groups, operate in similar ways, and whole societies acquire an associational character based on formal bureaucratic administration under a legal or quasi-legal order. The mobilisation and articulation of interests in this way means that political decisions reflect whatever power balance exists among the various interests. A key argument of pluralist writers, such as Robert Dahl (1971; see also Bentley 1908), is that modern democracy differs from classical 'direct' democracy by virtue of the indirect competitive mechanisms of group pressure that are the only possible basis for democratic representation in large and complex political units (Held 1987). Critics of pluralism (Bachrach and Baratz 1962, 1963; Lukes 1974) have argued that the competition of pressure groups may be systematically biased by underlying power differentials and so may not involve an equal representation of all points of view.

The importance of these forms of political association had been recognised by early sociological observers of American society (Tocqueville 1835–40; Martineau 1837). They noted also that American political parties were less centralised and less tightly linked to class interests than their British counterparts, and that central state regulation was, as a result, far more limited. Hence, politics was localised and fragmented, and trade union activity came to be confined to work-based issues. Parties operated as broad class alliances (Sombart 1906).

A major limitation on citizen representation in many modernising societies has been property ownership. For the earliest theorists of representative democracy (Locke 1689), a modern state required a property-based franchise, as the capacity for rational reflection and deliberation was seen as solely an attribute of propertied individuals (Macpherson 1962). In Britain, this formal limitation had largely been removed by the second half of the nineteenth century and a full adult male franchise was established. Citizenship and political representation continue to be divided by class – the two systems are, in Marshall's (1949) words, 'at war' – but this is not incompatible with modernity. To the extent that class inequalities are a normal and natural result of the operations of a rationalised capitalist economy, there are no 'rational' grounds for limiting their influence on political decision-making. The privileges of property *per se* might be challenged, but not the *de facto* inequalities that result from a fully marketised system.

A more serious restriction on rationalised political participation has been the continuing exclusion of people on the grounds of religion. Rationalisation involved a progressively declining salience of religious and secular ideologies, as politics became more instrumental, pragmatic, and 'realist'. Religion was, however, rather slow to disappear from formal politics. Religious exclusion remained a contentious matter well into the nineteenth century in Britain, and the British state still has an 'established' Church with direct representation in parliament. In Northern Ireland, religious differences are the basis of the most fundamental political divisions and continue to inhibit the establishment of a democratic constitution.

Moral and *de facto* exclusionary practices around gender and race have been even more persistent as limitations on rational constitutional principles of citizenship. They continue as fundamental limits on the extent to which modern nation states can be regarded as fully rationalised. To the extent that states, otherwise modern, deny citizenship rights and other rights of political participation to women and to members of specific ethnic categories, they cannot be considered fully modern. The enfranchisement of women was quite late, even in the core states of modernity: women achieved full voting rights in the United States in 1920, in Britain in 1928 (though women over 30 had received the vote in 1918), and in Switzerland not until 1971. Women's rights remain inferior to those of men in such areas of social citizenship as welfare and pensions (Voet 1998; Pateman 1988). The most notable examples of racial exclusion have been the United States and South Africa. In the US, full citizenship rights were effectively denied to African Americans until the 1960s (Myrdal 1944), and colour remains a fundamental limitation on public participation. In South Africa, racial segregation formed the central pillar of the 'apartheid' state until 1994. Actually existing modern states also restrict citizenship by age, and this could be regarded as a non-rational limitation to their modernity. This would be justified on the grounds that only adults are capable of autonomous rational deliberation, much as the exclusion of women was once justified on the grounds that only males possess the rational capacities required for modern citizenship (and see the arguments of Astell 1694; Wollstonecraft 1792 discussed above). In the case of infants and juveniles, however, the limitation seems to have more foundation (Piaget 1924), even if the precise age at which rights are acquired might be arbitrary. Related considerations apply to the 'rights' of animals (see Benton 1993).

Sovereignty, Centralisation, and Geopolitics

Rationalised states are defined by their sovereignty, by the establishment of a clear distinction between internal 'friends' and external 'foes' (Schmitt 1932). Such states are foci of autonomous and unrestrained power. They rest upon the internal pacification of their populations and a willingness to pursue external military exploits in defence of territorial autonomy. Within its boundaries, a state claims a monopoly over the legitimate use of force, removing sources of violent disturbance and of opposition to its policies and intensifying its power by reserving such coercive force to itself. The use of force is the ultimate sanction through which a state can, in the last instance, enforce its legal order and discipline its population.

Nation states intensify their use of power within their boundaries through what Mann (1993) describes as an increase in 'infrastructural power'. This is the capacity of a state to penetrate the full extent of its territory and to implement its decisions. As a result, a modern nation state shows a 'territorial centralisation':

despite its extended territory, all social relations within its boundaries become subject to centralised 'national' policies rather than local or long-range inter-territorial considerations. This spatial centralisation of decision-making is the principal means through which local and regional differences, which often have an ethnic or religious basis, can be transcended.

Most importantly, rationalisation has involved a tendency towards greater centralisation and coordination. The purposive element in societal decision-making has become more extensive as the scale of the administrative machinery and the scope for planned intervention have increased. A growth in centralised power in Britain began with the emergence of strong, centralised political parties representing specific class interests. The growth of working-class representation around the beginning of the twentieth century helped to build a 'New Liberalism' that supported a limited growth in central regulation aimed at collective provision for health, education, and pensions as the basis for inclusive national citizenship (Hobhouse 1911; see also Middlemass 1979). The gradual extension of these rights to social citizenship produced the twentieth-century welfare state (Marshall 1949) – a state in which the right to welfare was institutionalised, and in which welfare was delivered primarily through juridical, administrative mechanisms. Many policies pioneered in Britain's New Liberalism of a generation before were introduced in the US 'New Deal' of the 1930s, which also anticipated some features of a more comprehensive social citizenship. In addition to these changes, the New Deal introduced a degree of central regulation over business and labour affairs (Skocpol 1980; Skocpol and Finegold 1982; Quadagno 1984; see also Skocpol 1992). Economic activity was subject to a greater degree of central planning by states that had the capacity to determine and implement effective economic and social policies. The economic theory of Keynes (1936) provided the tools through which states could use tax and expenditure to alter levels of investment and demand.

The adoption of centralised forms of political control in the short-lived fascist regime of Germany was seen by some commentators as evidence of a drift towards rationalised systems of dictatorship that would make totalitarianism the political future for all modern states (Burnham 1941; see also Rizzi 1939; Adorno and Horkheimer 1944). Mann (2004) has shown, however, that such regimes are alternate forms of modernity characterised by a particularly extreme emphasis on the principles of the nation state. By combining an organic nationalism with authoritarian statism, and carrying this project through with a 'bottom-up' paramilitary force, fascist regimes established highly modern forms of politics. The rise of Stalinist dictatorship in the Soviet Union and Eastern Europe confirm the idea that totalitarianism and its extremes of political terror are one of the possible forms that can be taken by modernity (Giddens 1985: 295–310; Bauman 1989). They are far from being 'pre-modern' in character, and the eclipse of such systems does not mean that they may not arise once more.

In their external relations, states face a constant threat from other states, and violence and the threat of violence have been a more frequent and routine feature of inter-state rivalries. The building of sovereignty within national states involved a recognition that each other nation state had a similar right to its own sovereignty (Poggi 1978: 87–92). There could be no inter-state regulation, as this would limit the sovereignty of the states involved. Inter-state relations, therefore, became increasingly 'anarchic' as the growth of nation states undermined the surviving remnants of Western Christian unity. Although an 'international society' of states was recognised, there was no recognition of any moral framework behind this. Legal rules in the international sphere had to be limited to those that facilitate the coexistence of sovereign nation states, and any international structures can reflect only the current balance of power among those states.

The rationalisation of international relations depended on an alignment of interests and coercive power, expressed ultimately in the military balance. The internal tensions of the state system generated numerous territorial and colonial disputes as each state sought to include its identified 'national' ethnic community within its 'natural borders' (rarely corresponding to its actual borders) and to extend its reach to 'unclaimed' colonial territories and places of settlement (Giddens 1985: 233). The military aspects of modern states were more thoroughly rationalised from the second half of the nineteenth century. Military technology developed rapidly with the shift from wooden to steel ships, with improved armaments, and with the development of radically new technologies such as submarines, tanks, and then aircraft (McNeill 1982; Kaldor 1982; but see also Kennedy 1987: 185). Growing international conflict was marked by extensive mobilisation of the mass citizenry in support of military systems. While the core of the regular army, and especially its higher levels, became highly professionalized and dependent on the technical expertise of its officers (Huntington 1957), protracted conflicts relied on the conscription of recruits. In many societies, conscription became a regular basis of military recruitment in peacetime. Wartime conscription and the mobilisation of populations in defence of the 'home front' led to 'total war' in which whole societies were organised as 'nations in arms' (Marwick 1977: 27). Two wars in the twentieth century involving virtually the whole of the modern world – in 1914–18 and 1939–45 – were the consequences of this military build-up in a competitive state system, and peacetime state forms maintained many of the administrative systems established during war. In the eighteenth and nineteenth centuries a stable international order was provided by British dominance – the so-called *Pax Britannia* – but the twentieth century was marked by British decline and a growing American hegemony. Debates over the European constitution show the difficulties involved in establishing fully rationalised political constitutions, as national differences within the EC remain the single largest obstacle to political centralisation within a European state (compare the earlier views of Novicow 1912; and see, for example, Meyer et al. 1997).

FOCUS: MICHAEL MANN

Michael Mann's views on states, warfare, and international conflict can best be approached through Volume 2 of his *The Sources of Social Power* (1993). You will find it useful to look back to the section on 'Conflict, Change, and History' in Chapter 6 above and then read his 'War and Social Theory: Into Battle with Classes, Nations and States' in *States, War, and Capitalism* (1988).

Economic Rationalisation

Rationalised value standards in the material production of subsistence and the way of life involved with this have produced a characteristic 'capitalist spirit', and the pursuit of actions initially motivated by this spirit have produced institutions that, despite the later declining salience of the spirit, have continued to constrain people's actions within characteristically modern channels.

Rationalisation of the production of goods and services has involved the formation of an 'economic' sphere in which consumption and investment choices are implemented and monitored through purchasing power. Economic action is action that involves impersonal, technical calculations oriented towards the acquisition of profit. The pursuit of profit is the maximising of returns relative to costs, and taking account of the practical alternatives available. The subjective motivation behind such actions is the calculated maximisation of the individual return that it is anticipated will follow from particular courses of action.

Markets, Labour, and Management

The pursuit of profit through the balancing of rewards against costs involves the establishment of formally free markets as the institutional mechanisms through which the exchange of goods and services can take place. Markets are not specific to modernity, but Weber saw modern markets as having certain specific characteristics. He held that the rationalisation of economic activities involves the elimination of all customary and traditional restraints on market exchange, allowing purely instrumental and calculative exchange relationships to prevail.

Participants in a rationalised market are able to calculate the opportunities for exchange open to them and so base their decisions about production, distribution, and consumption on their perceived self-interest. This is made possible by the existence of money, which, as an objectified means of impersonal accounting, allows the unfettered expression of rational self-interest (Simmel 1900; Poggi 1993; Ingham 2004). Money establishes a purely quantitative measure of value that is essential for the exercise of formal rationality in economic life. It allows all goods and services to be seen as commodities that can be bought and sold on the market (Carrier 1994).

The market system of commodity production and exchange allows goods and services to be processed through chains of exchange that, in turn, make possible an extensive specialisation of production and, therefore, an expansion of the technical division of labour. Rational market exchange depends upon systems of pricing, wage payment, and accounting, together with money in virtual form as bank accounts. This makes possible a banking and credit system that becomes central to the organisation of production.

Equally important, however, is the transformation of labour itself into a commodity. This rests on a separation of labour from the means of production, a division between those who own the land and tools necessary for productive work and those who control only their own capacity for labour. When this division is generalised across a society, those with labour power alone can secure their means of life only under conditions determined by the owners of the means of production (Marx 1864–5). In a rationalised economic order, this relationship between labourer and owner is mediated through a labour market in which labour power can be freely bought or sold and so made available for productive use. Labour is undertaken as industry: literally as 'industrious' or diligent work towards a definite end. Whether agrarian, manufacturing, or commercial in character, work is 'industrial' and the capitalist labour process an industrialised one.

The organisation of work as employment creates pressures towards the mobility of labour – changes of residence in order to find available work and the undertaking of training or specialised education in order to enter better-paid work. Work is specialised in relation to the changing technology of production, and there is a progressive shift from primary sector work in agriculture and the extractive industries, through secondary sector (manufacturing and commerce) work, to tertiary or service sector work (Clark 1940). Industrial institutions – those specifically associated with technology and the division of labour – make high levels of productivity possible within a capitalist system. Industrialism involves, above all, a transformation in the basis of productive energy from animal and human energy to inanimate mechanical energy. Water, steam, oil, and electricity have provided the main sources of energy for industrial activity, allowing the building of ever more complex machines (Giddens 1985: 138). As the level of mechanisation increases, machines are used to produce machines. Work itself is organised into occupational roles: technical work tasks, institutionally separated from roles in family households, are undertaken by employees who depend on their performance and achievement for a monetary income (as a wage or salary).

Labour acquired through the labour market must be controlled by the owner through practices of management. Weber saw this as underlying the extension of rationalised bureaucratic administration to economic life. Systems of discipline and surveillance allow the technical division of labour to be expanded within coordinated factory and office systems. Employers exercise their authority through systems of surveillance and discipline that control recruitment, promotion, and the termination of employment. Both raw materials and labour can be secured through market mechanisms, but they must be regulated through bureaucratic hierarchies of management in ever-larger business enterprises. Business managers, like state officials, are separated from the means of managerial administration, allowing an increasingly effective mobilisation of labour power in pursuit of trade and production. Management is the focus for the incorporation of technical expertise into production. The competitive struggle for profit and the employment of free wage labour can be combined through systems of accounting and financial measurement, while mechanical knowledge can be applied in expanding the productive forces.

The institutional characteristics of industrialism and capitalism give economic activity a specifically collective organisation. Work is undertaken in large units and establishments by concentrated and disciplined workforces. Collectively organised work is the basis of workplace solidarity among employees and their collective organisation into trade unions. Prototypically, corporate enterprise was *factory* production, bringing together ever larger numbers of individual workers into a complex division of labour to carry out their work industriously in a single place and under close supervision. Changes in management and technology were associated with changes in the sectoral distribution of occupational roles. The proportion of the population employed in manufacturing work peaked at around one third in most countries, remaining at this level through the first half of the twentieth century. Only in Britain did the proportion rise to a half (Kumar 1978: 202). The expansion of commercial and managerial work, and the later expansion of service employment, led to the growth of *office*-based work organised along similar lines (Braverman 1974). Employment in commerce and services has shown a great increase. By 1950, more than 50 per cent of the US labour force was employed in the service sector. While there may have been much movement of labour from manufacturing to services, by far the greatest change in all societies has been that from agriculture to both manufacturing and services: the proportion of the labour force employed in agriculture had everywhere declined during the first half of the twentieth century.

This concentration and transformation of production occurs within specifically capitalist business enterprises. Capitalist business is organised through 'corporate' property holdings based on share capital: each member of a company or corporation makes a financial subscription to it in the form of a shareholding. The totality of such subscriptions form an investment fund, and the members can be paid a dividend from the profits of this investment. This joint stock capital is supplemented by interest-based lending by banks and other financial enterprises, whether private or controlled by a state. The scale of business activity, therefore, comes to depend on the scale of credit that is available (Hilferding 1910). Corporate property allows an expansion in the scale of economic activity, manifest in the horizontal and vertical organisation of production and the amalgamation of enterprises into larger and more concentrated units. This concentration of economic activity lays the foundation for a further organisation of business into employers' associations and other business associations (Offe and Wiesenthal 1980).

A Capitalist World Economy

Weber traced the expansion of modern capitalist enterprise to the eighteenth century, when the disciplined vocational activity of Protestant entrepreneurs stimulated the expansion of self-sustaining capitalist activity. This was associated with an expansion of trade in new commodities, such as food and textiles, a consequent increase in shipping activity, and a growth of financial institutions that were geared to this international trade and distribution. The state-sponsored expansion of trade in Europe generated a characteristically modern world economic system alongside the system of competitive states. The nature and development of each national economy could not be considered in isolation, but only as part of a larger system of economic activity structured by the tensions that result from the conflicting forces that comprise it (Wallerstein 1974: 347).

The modern world economic system that emerged in the sixteenth century, then, was a true system organised around its own internal contradictions and tensions, structured by the conflict of classes and ethnic groups, and operating across a range of geographical environments. Its core lay in north-western Europe, which succeeded the Mediterranean societies as the dominant European powers. The states of the capitalist core pursued mercantile economic policies, aimed at expanding the national wealth and, thereby, the wealth available to the state. These policies were pursued through expansion into the Americas, with slave-trading and slave-based agriculture playing a key part (Williams 1944; Blackburn 1998).

The growth of capitalist activity produced the necessary pre-conditions for industrialism in many European countries, yet it was in Britain that rapid industrial growth first occurred. British agriculture was highly commercialised at an early date and prospered in the expanding international system of markets. Growth in wool and cloth production allowed a massive expansion of English overseas trade at the expense of the formerly dominant Italian and Hanseatic merchants. Agricultural and industrial improvements had been made possible by the growth of scientific knowledge, and enclosure, improved cropping systems, and manufacturing workshops transformed the rural scene. The 'take-off' to industrialism is conventionally dated to 1760–1830 and was so rapid that it has been referred to as an 'industrial revolution' (Toynbee 1881–2; Ashton 1948). The application of science to capitalist production and the resulting technological innovation fuelled a self-propelling process in which the economy grew as a system of interdependent industries organised around a vast network of instrumental actions. Compared with the Netherlands and France, Britain had both a strong base of natural resources and a relatively large number of non-conformist entrepreneurs. It also had a relatively 'open' and less tradition-bound stratification system with fewer restrictions on social mobility. In these respects, however, it was similar to the United States. A key factor in Britain seems to have been what Rostow (1960) termed 'reactive nationalism' – the insular hostility of the British state elite to the Catholic Church and to foreign power.

British industrialisation, then, owed a great deal to a class of entrepreneurs whose self-oriented actions unintentionally contributed to the transformation of the traditional way of life into a new and thoroughly rationalised one. Their actions had this consequence because of particular cultural and environmental pre-conditions that made it possible to generate a structurally distinct and self-propelling economic system. Industrialisation occurred in other countries, from 1850, largely as a response to increasing British economic power and competitive pressures in their domestic markets. British ownership of companies in foreign markets, where this occurred, exacerbated the perceived problem. Emulation of British practices and a consequent diffusion of technical and economic innovations generated a domino effect. The competitive struggles of entrepreneurial classes in different countries drove this process, but it generated a rapid industrialisation only where classes denied opportunities in existing political and economic structures were able to alter the balance of class power and use state apparatuses to pursue a deliberate strategy of 'modernisation'. Through subsidising and supporting domestic industries, engaging directly in production, and building the necessary infrastructure, active and interventionist states could promote the emulation of British innovations – often improving on them – without having to follow the historically specific practices that gave rise to them.

The 'late industrialisers' (Gershenkron 1962) of Europe, the United States, Japan, Canada, Australia, and parts of South America were able to advance rapidly because the growth of an increasingly industrialised world economy stimulated the growth of international capital and commodity markets. The emerging economic order was organised around primary industries and producer goods, though productivity in agriculture and resources (timber, oil, gold, rubber, silk) had all increased. New industrial technologies transformed production as traditional craft skills were more completely mechanised in large-scale production line processes that brought together workers in ever-larger numbers. These de-skilled workers (Braverman 1974) were subject to discipline and control in tightly regulated systems designed according to scientific principles. 'Taylorism' and 'Fordism' became the prototypical forms of the new division of labour. The technological requirements of military expansion encouraged an increase in the technical and financial scale of capitalist activity. Indeed, production line technology had been pioneered in armaments production and had then been emulated in other industries; and military bureaucracy had been a major influence on the building of managerial hierarchies in large industrial enterprises (Chandler 1963; Dandecker 1990). In addition to the expansion of military technology, there were rapid changes in communications and transport technologies. Steam power revolutionised shipbuilding and led to the building of extensive railway networks for the movement of people and freight, and transportation was further transformed with the introduction of oil-powered internal combustion engines that finally replaced horse-powered transport by the automobile and complemented rail networks with even more extensive road networks that transformed the urban scene. New communications technologies such as the telegraph and the telephone were followed by the more mass-based broadcast systems of radio, film, recordings, and television.

The 'liberal' form of industrial capitalism that prevailed in nineteenth-century Britain and in the early stages of industrialism gradually gave way to forms of 'organised' or managed capitalism under the cumulative impact of the economic and political changes of the early twentieth century. In liberal capitalism, entrepreneurial capitalists ran small-scale, single-factory enterprises in intense competition with each other. Market relations were such that no individual entrepreneur could affect the overall level of production or profit in its market, and each enterprise was a 'price-taker', as described by Adam Smith (1766). State economic activity was minimal and predominantly facilitative, states being concerned with creating and maintaining the conditions for the private pursuit of profit in competitive markets. In the organised forms of industrial capitalism, concentration and centralisation of production are combined with national states concerned to expand national power and prestige through business expansion (Weber 1895). This transformation in the economic role of nation states underlay the building of welfare systems and the expansion of public enterprise. Trade unions were more likely to be recognised or even sponsored by these states, and both unions and Labour or socialist parties came to play a greater part in wage bargaining at enterprise level and in the determination of state economic policies. The key agents in a system of organised capitalism are the financiers, based in the concentrated banking system and centralised credit mechanism. They build the financial groups, trusts, federations, and corporatist practices that constitute the system (Hobson 1902; Hilferding 1910; Bukharin 1915).

This system of organised capitalism arose first among the late industrialisers, but rapidly spread to Britain and other capitalist economies. The world economic system came to be centred on powerful imperialist states sustained by the financial groupings that dominated their industries. The system rested on an international currency system based on the 'Gold Standard' – the convertibility of sterling and other paper money into gold – and the financial and commercial institutions of the City of London were central to its global management

(Ingham 1984). The conflicts of 1914–18 disrupted the internationalisation of economic activity that had been built up before the war, and the economic depression of the 1930s strengthened specifically national economic institutions and practices. The world economy between 1914 and 1945 was fractured into rival imperial blocs to a far greater extent than in the preceding half century. The 1930s also saw the rise of fascist regimes in which highly centralised systems of business regulation were established (Neumann 1942; Brady 1943), and many of these economic structures persisted after the collapse of the political regimes.

Business ownership and control also became more organised and rationalised. Families and individual entrepreneurs found it more difficult to retain control of their expanding businesses and a larger proportion of capital was drawn from the expanding financial system. Ownership of company shares passed to banks, insurance companies, investment companies, and pensions funds, combining a degree of managerial autonomy with ultimate financial control. National economies consisted of large industrial and financial enterprises connected together through chains of interweaving shareholdings and interlocking corporate directorships (Scott 1997; Useem 1984). As enterprises became more transnational in their activities, so international networks of ownership and control tied them together at a global level (Fennema 1982; Fennema and Carroll 2002).

Along with the nation state, industrial capitalism becomes the principal mechanism through which human control over the natural world and over other human beings can be most rationally pursued. They are the central institutional manifestations of modernity. The technologies of violence and production contained in and articulated through these institutions manifest the continual expansion of scientific knowledge in physics, chemistry, and biology, and the core modern institutions both apply and became the objects of the newer social sciences. Political economy was the initial scientific matrix through which the political and economic institutions were organised and theorised, and the formation of more specialised institutions was associated with the appearance of more specialised sciences: most notably political science, jurisprudence, and economics. This complex of institutions and the sciences that enter into it comprise what Alfred Weber (1920–1) and many other German sociologists of the formative period described as 'civilisation'. For them, the growth of modernity through the rationalisation of the world was a growth of such rational civilisation. This involved a continual expansion of what Habermas (1981a) has described as the 'systemic' organisation of social life through instrumental techniques and procedures.

> ### FOCUS: IMMANUEL WALLERSTEIN
>
> The leading theorist of world systems today is Immanuel Wallerstein. The various volumes of *The Modern World-System* (1974, 1980, 1989) are the core of his work, and the section on 'Space, Capital, and Morphology' in Chapter 6 of Volume 1 provides a good starting point.

Rationalisation and Societal Communities

The recognition of structural differentiation and Marxist accounts of base and superstructure has been seen as an important pointer to emerging lines of division between distinct levels of social structure. From this point of view, rationalisation can be seen as a process occurring in the spheres of culture and the societal community as well as at the economic and political level. The transition from traditionalism to modernity has involved significant changes in these respects that occur alongside and interdependent with the development of nation states and industrial capitalism.

Max Weber identified a tendency towards a pluralisation of 'life spheres' as one type of activity after another splits off from its original communal context. Each specialised sphere of activity comes to be organised around specific and relatively distinct institutions and constitutive values (Weber 1915b). The formation of states and economies is one aspect of this process of social differentiation but this is merely a part of the overall process of differentiation. This institutional differentiation is highlighted in Talcott Parsons's pattern variable of diffuseness–specificity. In traditional societies, the social positions occupied by an individual are closely integrated with each other and conform to a single set of diffuse standards that relate to their personal, particular, and affective characteristics. In a rationalised society, on the other hand, this diffuse embedding breaks down. There is not simply a separation of distinct activities but also a growth in the diversity of roles held by each individual. What formerly existed as a societal community with differentiated state and commercial structures is further differentiated into yet more specialised institutions and a residual communalism focused in family households and certain other expressive and particularistic groupings. Because people occupy a variety of roles in different spheres, their position in each operating according to quite distinct principles and standards, it becomes ever more likely that individuals will experience a clash of values as they move from one sphere to another and will have to come to terms with mutually contradictory expectations. The competing demands of home, school, and work, for example, must be balanced by the various members of a family household (Merton 1957; Goffman 1961b).

Cultural Pluralism and Disenchantment

Weber saw the rationalisation of religious culture and the development of rational science as the bases for the growth of technology and of modern economic and political institutions. He saw the outcome of the rationalisation of religious worldviews as three forms of cultural rationalism (see also Habermas 1981a: 234–5). There is, first, the cognitive knowledge of the sciences in which an empirical and mathematical discourse, organised around the use of experimental methods, is elaborated to construct theories capable of explaining, and therefore predicting, events in the world. This rests on a methodical objectivation of nature and is the means through which industrial and political technologies are built. Secondly, there is the rationalisation of aesthetic expression found in literature, art, and music. The secular arts are culturally autonomous from religion and develop in distinctive rationalised ways: as the rational harmony, instrumentation, and orchestration of musical forms (Weber 1911), the narrative form of novel and drama (Lukács 1914–15), and perspective and composition in visual art (Berger 1972; Puttfarken 2000). The third form of cultural rationalisation involves the moral and evaluative representations that guide practical human relations. Here, formal law and formal ethics, organised around universalistic practical principles, become the key means of social regulation. These norms govern human relations in science – underpinning its objectivity and value freedom, and they are central to the legal order that underpins bureaucratic administration (Löwith 1932).

Both Alfred Weber and Jürgen Habermas stressed that as cultural spheres become differentiated, rationalised political and economic systems can exercise an ever-greater control and influence over them and over the societal community or lifeworld. Learning and creativity, art and popular entertainment, health, education, and welfare, the discursive frameworks of 'national' and collective identity, the neighbourly and communal forms of locality, and the domestic institutions of the family and kinship have increasingly been subject to these forms of rational regulation that originated in the institutions of the nation state and industrial capitalism. Habermas (1981b) describes this as a 'colonisation' of the 'socio-cultural lifeworld' by the political and economic systems.

Through colonisation, these collective practices and aspects of socialisation can be subjected to 'juridification' (or bureaucratic regulation) and 'commodification' (or market regulation), transforming them in the direction of the rational logic of the modern political economy. Provision for health, education, and welfare, for example, can be separated off from the household and the local community and transformed into a series of separate and specialised institutions that are regulated through bureaucratic organisations and that provide their services in the form of citizenship rights and entitlements or as purchasable commodities. Welfare states, public health systems, private medicine, and contributory pension systems exemplify this. Similarly, processes of social control over deviance and crime can cease to be purely customary, regulated through localised and informal folkways, and become the objects of direct surveillance and regulation. Prisons, orphanages, and psychiatric hospitals may form a network of carceral organisations that operate alongside other agencies, including those of health, education, and welfare, as a structure of disciplinary control over whole populations (Foucault 1961: 301; 1975). Medicalisation and welfarisation are characteristically modern forms of the surveillance and regulation of the lifeworld. The creation, dissemination, and enjoyment of music, literature, art, and science itself can also be brought within this same rationalised logic and given an 'industrial' form as processes of bureaucratic production and commercial consumption (Adorno and Horkheimer 1944: Ch. 2; Parsons 1960a). In this latter respect, popular music would become a standardised and homogeneous commodity produced for sale in a mass market, and the popular entertainment provided by radio and television would be provided either as a regulated public service or as a private venture sustained through advertising and sponsorship. This entertainment, through competitive pressures, would also become a homogeneous product supplied to a mass audience through means of mass communication.

The clear implication of these views is that modernisation involves both a cultural rationalisation and a further rationalisation through 'colonisation'. A culture is modern to the extent that these processes actually take place. Where such cultural modernisation has occurred, social integration can no longer be sustained through 'mechanical solidarity'. Societies can no longer be integrated through comprehensive and all-embracing communal structures encompassing all aspects of social life. The lifeworld or societal community shrinks away, and integration can be achieved – to the extent that it is achieved at all – only through the 'organic' interdependence of specialised systems in a vast division of labour (Durkheim 1893). Central to this organic solidarity are the 'steering mechanisms' of the economic and political systems – money and authority. The common denominator of the differentiated cultural spheres, all that prevents the complete fragmentation of social life around rival value systems, is formal rationality, which becomes the sole yardstick for comparing and evaluating rival claims and through which money and authority can be used to bring about their coordination.

In such a system, all cultural judgements would become standardised and homogenised around reified meanings. Choices would be made as rational calculations and not in relation to ultimate values, for which there would no longer be any authoritative foundation. Where rational calculation does not suffice, any remaining choice must be arbitrary and so without ultimate meaning. Ultimate values could no longer be sustained by any overarching canopy of religious narratives and certainties (Berger 1969), and they would be left exposed and unsupportable. Moral, emotional, and personal elements would be progressively eliminated from social relations, which would increasingly come to be organised around impersonality, formality, and the functional connection of means to ends. The meanings behind actions would be 'devalued' and reduced to immediate and material goals and purely instrumental considerations.

Culturally, modernity is also built around structures of secularism and individualism. Collective commitments decline, while individual interests and choices are strengthened. The secularism or disenchantment that results from the rationalisation of religion institutionalises reflexivity and critical questioning in all matters. This would allow no uncritical acceptance of given authorities and would lead to a correspondingly high concern for innovation and an active orientation to the world. This achievement or 'success' orientation would establish a concern for the practical outcomes of one's actions, especially individual actions, in whatever field is pursued (Riesman and others 1953).

Mass Media and Mass Society

The institutional forms of rationalisation in cultural spheres are diverse and cannot be summarised so easily as was possible in relation to economic and political rationalisation. The evidence suggests that cultural rationalisation can, indeed, be identified in all societies that have undergone an economic and political modernisation, but it also demonstrates the absence of any single pattern of cultural systems and modern societal communities. It is possible, nevertheless, to identify certain generic patterns of character and collective mentality and corresponding systems of cultural production and consumption. These can serve to illustrate the modern cultural pattern.

Mass participation in public life can be ensured through mass literacy and through the expansion of vocational education. Industrialisation and the strengthening of the idea of citizenship encouraged an extension of basic education to the whole population. The minimal level of education has gradually increased with the changing nature of work, and an extension of secondary schooling, further, and higher education has produced an educational system in which educational attainment is supposed to be based around ability and achievement. Creation of an educated and technically trained workforce provides the human capital required by the economy. Selection and employment according to measured educational attainments – credentialism – ensures a degree of correspondence with required occupational skills. Mass education and mass communications together sustain a mass culture of conformism.

Riesman (1950) undertook a particularly important investigation of the changes in 'social character' that he saw as generic to contemporary forms of modernity. He saw the contemporary character type as a consequence of the development, from the late nineteenth century, of large-scale, rationalised industry and of the urban neighbourhoods associated with this. The growth of mass production and mass consumption and the growth of large and extensive bureaucratic hierarchies are the basis of relative affluence and abundance for larger numbers of people and drive them towards new forms of social outlook that break with the character forms of early modernity.

The changes of the Renaissance and the Enlightenment had brought about a transition from a 'tradition-directed' to an 'inner-directed' character type. The tradition-directed character passively conforms to the folkways and customs of a particular age-group, sex, or social estate. Such people internalise detailed prescriptions and proscriptions and are sanctioned by feelings of shame. These traditions were 'splintered' by the forces of modernity, and individuals became more inner-directed characters that make choices between alternative sets of norms or 'competing traditions'. Socialisation in this period formed an individual guided solely by an internal 'gyroscope' and who would recognise the need to make autonomous life choices and to exercise self-mastery and self-discipline in enacting these choices. Such people are sanctioned by the guilt that they feel when they fail in this. Adherents to the Protestant ethic epitomise this character type, which Riesman sees as having been the principal object of Freudian theory.

The further rationalisation of social life, however, Riesman saw as having involved a superseding of inner-direction by an 'outer-directed' character type. This developed first among the middle classes and the more prosperous workers of the major cities of the United States and Western Europe. It is a characteristically urban outlook and is central to the urban way of life (Simmel 1903). The outer-directed person sees the views of his or her contemporaries as the most important guides to action. Such people internalise the expectations of others and strive to be sensitive to these. They must be attuned to picking up the nuances of expectations. They are oriented by the need for approval and recognition, and they will tend to imitate those things that they judge will earn them the recognition and approval they seek. The other-directed person 'seeks not fame, which represents, limited transcendence of a particular peer-group or a particular culture, but the respect and, more than the respect, the affection, of an amorphous and shifting, though contemporary, jury of peers' (Riesman 1950: 137). They are oriented towards the expectations of the generalised other and must learn the techniques of impression management (Goffman 1959).

Extension of the period of formal education makes teachers and peer groups a more important part of socialisation than before, but Riesman held that the mass media also became a more important source of information about the views of others. Children learn early to become consumers, and the media encourage them to see the world as other children see it – and, therefore, to conform to the consumption patterns followed by those others with whom they identity (Riesman 1950: 97). The rationalised, outer-directed character type is a creation of the ideological apparatuses of school and mass media.

The growing centrality of the mass media, and their overwhelming importance in contemporary definitions of reality, have been documented in a number of studies (Williams 1961; Winston 1998). Looking at the development of popular entertainment from the vaudeville and music halls of the 1890s to the records and films of the 1930s and 1940s, Adorno and Horkheimer (1944; Adorno 1938) saw the development of what they called a 'culture industry'. The music, films, and novels consumed by the mass of the population are the product of the same rationalisation process of organised, finance capitalism that had transformed the production of other goods and services. This was first apparent in the growth of popular newspapers from the end of the nineteenth century (Curran 1977; Murdock and Golding 1978) and then marked the growth of film, cinema, radio, and television broadcasting. Cultural objects came to be produced by large business enterprises, run by financiers, managers, and technicians, and are treated as any other commodity. Their colonisation takes the form of commodification. They are produced as standardised items, constructed according to stereotyped formulas that are judged to appeal to the largest possible audience (Miege 1989). They are promoted through marketing and advertising systems that make them items of mass consumption along with cars, cigarettes, soap powder, and all the other mass commodities on which monopoly capitalism depends. They form an expanded popular culture that Adorno and his colleagues referred to as 'mass culture'.

Adorno saw the products of the culture industry as responsible for an ever-deepening alienation among their consumers. Their alienation at work had increased, thanks to the development of monopoly capitalism and its rationalised logic of mass production; and they were now alienated in their leisure as well. Unable to enjoy autonomously created works, the masses are the mere passive consumers of items that have no intrinsic aesthetic value. Cultural commodities are valued according to their marketability: those that are bought become 'popular', and those that are popular become attractive purchases (Adorno and Horkheimer 1944: 167). Cultural commodities pander to 'false needs' generated by the advertising industry, which manipulates people's desires on the basis of their suggestibility and subjects them to an ideological oppression. Alternative viewpoints are suppressed and conformism is encouraged. Herbert Marcuse's (1964) discussion of the 'one-dimensional thought' that results from an expanded and deepened system of technological domination is an elaboration of this idea.

It is certainly clear, as Gitlin (1991) has shown, that media organisations produce their commodities in relation to constructed audiences, to particular images of the types of consumer to whom the products will appeal (but see also Newman 1991). However, audiences do not consume these products in a totally passive way. Cultural products are consumed from within the lifeworld by individuals 'embedded' in their particular interpersonal relations of family and community (Morley 1980; Ang 1985), and audiences are actively involved in reading and decoding them. These studies of audiences echo many of the arguments of Henri Lefebvre about everyday life (e.g., Lefebvre 1968a; see also de Certeau 1974). The range of possible readings is, nevertheless, restricted by operating criteria of 'newsworthiness' and 'entertainment value', themselves dependent on commercial criteria of profitability (Schlesinger 1978; Tracey 1977). Mass media output reflects a cultural hegemony (Hall 1982), an ideologisation of the lifeworld that ties its systematically distorted representations to the maintenance of the nation state and the capitalist economy (Thompson 1990; Mayhew 1997).

Adorno traced a growth of conformism and authoritarianism, and a consequent declining possibility for authentic individualism, to this mass culture. He saw this conformist character structure as central to modernity. His work adopted a Freudian approach to socialisation and he was critical of the cultural trend in Horney and Fromm on which Riesman had relied. Conformism is the basis of a mass irrationality that motivates the challenge to traditional authority disparaged by writers such as Spann (1928), Freyer (1930), and Ortega (1929). This character structure involves an extreme ethnocentrism, a defence of national culture from external 'foreign' influences, expressed most radically in the anti-Semitism and fascism that spread through Europe between the two world wars (Adorno et al. 1950; see also Adorno 1952–3). Conformism and the associated 'authoritarianism', Adorno held, involve a susceptibility to propaganda and cultural manipulation. In response to the anxieties induced by living in a modern society, people enter into an irrational search for meaning in a disenchanted world dominated by technological rationality. They willingly pursue the irrational consumption of the products of the rationalised system. Their alienated and dependent needs are met through their compulsive consumption of mass-produced consumer goods and the products of the culture industry: of soap operas, popular music, and movies. People are 'happy robots' satisfied by the gratification of merely false needs (see also Baudrillard 1978).

FOCUS: THEODOR ADORNO

Theodor Adorno's essays on 'The Culture Industry Reconsidered' (1964) and 'The Stars Down To Earth' (1952–3) update his earlier argument on the culture industry, discussed in the section on 'Value Spheres and Practical Culture' in Chapter 3 above.

The Inevitability of Modernity

I have shown that modernisation can be seen as an ongoing rationalisation of social orders that undermines traditionalism and increases the overall level of formal rationality in social organisation. The foundations of authority are thoroughly relativised and no system of values can be taken as an unquestioned guide to social action. Cultural modernity involves an increasing reliance on scientific knowledge, forged through the application of formal principles of rationality and applied in technologies that are judged by their practical success. The broader cultural framework of modernity is both secular and individualistic. Religious beliefs are more difficult to sustain, or appear as irrational in the face of scientific knowledge, and each individual must make his or her own choices without the authoritative guidance of tradition or established beliefs.

There is a comprehensive 'disenchantment' of life, an elimination of all that formerly gave human activities their overarching meaning or purpose. Human actions in a modern society can be sustained in their course only through a pragmatic acceptance of necessity. As Weber argued, sheer self-interest ensures that people conform to rationalised principles and practices. People are constrained to act in disciplined, rational ways and there is no longer any need for them to be individually committed to the Enlightenment project or even to the spirit of cultural rationalism. Individual workers and entrepreneurs, for example, have no real choice but to conform to the formally rational logic of the market, the division of labour, and bureaucratic regulation (Weber 1920c: 123; 1904–5). They must act instrumentally, as that is the way that others act towards them. To act in any other way would invite failure and disadvantage. Actions that result in such consequences will not persist or be imitated. Selective pressures operating through the competition of individuals and groups result in the perpetuation and routinisation of instrumentally rational actions, and these, in turn, cannot but reinforce the rationalising constraints faced by others. Individuals become virtual cogs in a vast machine: they are housed in 'hardened steel' structures that regulate and discipline their actions.

In concrete terms, modernity centres on the institutions of the nation state, industrial capitalism, and mass forms of societal organisation. States are oriented to territorial expansion and power intensification, operating through the articulation of the interests of a mass citizenry. This involves a democratisation of political power through elections and plebiscites that enable mass opinion to be mobilised in support of state strategies. High levels of regulation and surveillance are matched by high levels of popular participation in the exercise of power. Industrial capitalism operates through an extensive technical division of labour and through markets for goods, services, and human labour. Industrial and other forms of work are organised through employment relations and occupational structures and are coordinated through managerial structures that are embedded in the systems of control inherent in financial markets. Colonisation of differentiated cultural and social spheres has produced interlocking systems of communication and education organised around practices of mass production and consumption. Mass communications and mass education are the means through which collective opinion can be mobilised in ways that sustain support for the colonising political and economic systems. The routinised constraint described by Weber is reinforced by the cultivation of a submissiveness to authority through the socialised mass conformism of other-directedness. Thus, the interests that are articulated and mobilised in democratised states are 'false', unreflective interests rather than autonomously considered concerns. A cultural outlook of unreflective irrationality is encouraged as an 'escape' from the rationalised requirements of everyday life.

These features of modernity do not appear all at once. They are the results of an ongoing process of modernisation and appear gradually and unevenly as rationalisation becomes ever more progressive. The forms of modernity change over time as rational principles become more deeply embedded in cultural codes and habituses. There is no fixed set of modern institutions, only a continuing rationalisation, and the transcendence of modernity – a move to 'post-modernity' – would involve a break with these principles rather than the simple disappearance of a particular set of institutions.

It is sometimes argued that there is an inevitability to modernity. Clark Kerr and his colleagues, for example, famously made the claim that there are common and essential characteristics of any 'industrial society' and any society that adopts industrial technology must adopt these features if it is to continue to industrialise. These consequences follow from the 'logic of industrialism', from the 'imperatives intrinsic to the process' (1960: 42). According to this view, certain political and cultural forms are required by the very nature of the rational technology of industrialism. The logic of industrialism is an inexorable consequence of the use of rational technology, and wider social changes are mere reflections of this. There is, undoubtedly, a reciprocal influence among culture, politics, technology, and economics, but rationalisation cannot be reduced to a mere epiphenomenon of technological change.

Although it is not inevitable and is not a consequence of a technological logic, modernisation can be considered as a directional process that, once initiated, shows a tendency to increase. This was seen by Parsons (1937: 751) as an analytical law of increasing rationality. He held that any increase in the level of rationality in a traditional system will generate tendencies towards further rationality. Traditionalism cannot withstand the critical and reflexive consequences of a rational orientation to the world and will, eventually, give way to rationality in whatever sphere of activity it is introduced. Rationalised politics, for example, generates a tendency towards further political rationalisation, and it reinforces the rationalisation of those other spheres on which it has the greatest impact. These spheres, in turn, are subject to their own rationalising tendencies and will have reciprocal effects on the political sphere. The net result is an overall tendency towards the comprehensive rationalisation of social life, though its pace and precise character will depend on the particular historical conditions from which the process began, the environmental circumstances that ease or limit it, and the constraints involved in coexistence with other societies. Rationalisation is neither inexorable nor uniform in character, and it certainly does not conform to any unilinear process of 'evolution'. It is a complex, multi-levelled, and uneven process in which each society follows its distinct developmental pathway, combining the emulation of other societies with their own endogenous processes to produce their particular route to the modern world.

Modernity exists if the key institutions of a society are modern. Neither these nor the whole society has to be completely and fully rationalised for a society to count as 'modern'. It is in this sense that Latour's (1991) statement that 'we have never been modern' can be assessed. His claim is that we have never been completely and exclusively modern in all respects. In fact, any modern society will be modern only to a greater or lesser extent, and there will always be residual, non-modern 'survivals' and elements that are, in themselves, neither modern nor pre-modern. A society is modern if its key major institutions are rationalised in all key respects and its general logic of development tends to further or maintain this rationalisation.

NOTE

1. This view led Weber to be seen as providing an intellectual underpinning for emotivist and existentialist views of ethics (Jaspers 1932a; see also MacIntyre 1967).

8

Intimations of Post-Modernity

The most recent approaches to social theory have raised the issue of post-modernity: the idea of cultural and social forms beyond those of modernity. This chapter looks at the origins of post-modernist ideas and considers whether the postulated changes are as radical as sometimes supposed. This is considered through discussions of

- consumerism and monopoly production

- the centrality of knowledge and information to social order

- manufactured environmental risks and personal anxiety

- transnational, intersocietal links and globalisation

It is shown that these can be considered as *extensions* of modernity rather than alternatives to it.

Modernity is the outcome of a process of structural rationalisation through which high levels of formal rationality are built into the principal institutions of societies. The extension of formal rationality undermines the intellectual foundations of traditionalism as everything is subjected to the criteria of calculation, technique, and effectiveness. Formal rationality becomes the basis of a worldview – often decried as white, male, and bourgeois – that marginalises diversity, emotional expression, and non-rational motivations. People are passively attached to this worldview, conforming to modern practices because there seems no alternative. Modernity seems to be our fate. The intellectual and practical successes of formal rationality and its institutional forms are not unchallenged, but challenge and resistance have been weak and marginal.

Some have suggested, however, that the second half of the twentieth century saw a fundamental sea change in human existence and was marked by the entry of the western world to a new 'post-modern' world: modernity had, at last, reached its limits and was on the wane. Writers on post-modernism pointed to the end of such 'grand narratives' as those of 'history', 'progress', and 'truth' and held that no cultural framework could any longer generate integration and solidarity: the end of modernity is also the end of society. Individuals are now condemned to an enduring uncertainty and anxiety that prevents them from finding any meaning in their lives. An alternative modernist view was put by Francis Fukuyama (1992), whose work caught the imagination of commentators world-wide. Fukuyama also saw modernity as having achieved its ultimate stage at the end of the twentieth century, but he drew different conclusions from this: capitalism and liberal democracy had established themselves against all competitor systems and showed no prospect of ever disappearing. Modern societies had reached 'the end of history' and there could no longer be any prospect of 'advance' or 'progress' beyond

In this chapter I will explore both modernist and post-modernist views on contemporary societies and the radical transformations that they have identified in the structures of modernity. These rival views first made their appearance in aesthetic discussions in the early twentieth century, when commentators on artistic trends contrasted contemporary forms of art, literature, and music with those of the nineteenth century. An assessment of social theories of post-modernity must begin with a consideration of these aesthetic theories.

Aesthetic Modernism and Post-modernism

The rationalising spirit of the Enlightenment was the motivating force behind the dominant aesthetic forms of the eighteenth and nineteenth centuries. The dominant styles of art, architecture, music, and literature all embodied this cultural outlook. Representational realism in the visual arts, the classicism of form in architecture and music, and linear narrative and naturalism in literature were its principal expressions. The aesthetic desire to present a 'realistic' image of the world complemented the more instrumental forms of realism and objectivity found in natural science, in technology, and in economics and politics.

Many of those engaged in the arts were, however, committed to artistic innovation and differentiation. By the middle of the nineteenth century, these rational forms had become fetters that limited their creative abilities. The desire for novelty and invention became more difficult to express within the highly rationalised cultural forms and further artistic development seemed to require a move beyond them. This abandonment of Classicism and other rationalised forms motivated the cultural explorations of the Romantics: poets such as Samuel Taylor Coleridge, Percy Shelley, and John Keats, artists such as William Blake, and composers such as Ludwig van Beethoven, Franz Schubert, and Richard Wagner. The Romantics placed feeling, emotion, and sensibility above the formal reason and realism of Classicism. It was most strongly marked in the aesthetic tendency that, paradoxically, came to be called 'modernism'. This label was applied to those who rejected the reliance on classical forms and recognised the purely formal rationality of the modern world. What the modernists had in common was the self-conscious desire to explore the nature and limits of modern rational forms. This desire both reflected and contributed to wider philosophical explorations into the nature and limits of cognitive, technical knowledge. It embodied and encouraged a recognition of relativity, diversity, and fluidity in all cultural matters.

Aesthetic modernism saw structures and forms as the more or less transient outcomes of creative activity. No matter how fixed and permanent any structure may appear to be, it cannot be assumed to embody any eternal truths or principles. The 'modern' artists of the nineteenth century sought to draw attention to this transience and fluidity of form by making it the central theme in their own works. Art was no longer to be guided by the naïve assumption that artistic works are realistic representations of an external world to be judged by cognitive standards of accuracy and objectivity. Instead, it was to explore the diversity of ways in which aesthetic representations can be constructed and the purely 'abstract' interrelations of forms. The modern artist felt a need to make clear the arbitrariness of any cultural forms involved in the attempt to depict an external reality. Modern art was reflexive, aware of the arbitrariness of its own forms. This aesthetic modernism embraced the scepticism and reflexivity that are the hallmark of modernity and turned these against modernity itself to challenge the unquestioned foundations of technique and formal rationality. The modernists emphasised diversity, movement, and choice and used these ideas to radicalise the modern worldview. Abandoning fixity, certainty, the absolute, and order, they espoused flux, the contingent, the relative, and the fragmentary.

Modernist ideas were extremely diverse. The earliest examples of a modernist outlook can be found in the poetry of Stéphane Mallarmé, Arthur Rimbaud, and Charles Baudelaire, usually known as Symbolism. This used mystical and fantastic imagery to suggest larger ideas through the connotations that they evoke in their particular audiences and it was an influence on the later poetry of W.B. Yeats and Stefan George. Impressionist painters such as Edgar Degas, Claude Monet, and the early Paul Cézanne, like the composer Claude Debussy, sought to obscure the apparently firm boundaries of shapes and forms by showing that they could be understood as transient effects of subtle variations in light and sound. The novels of Fyodor Dostoevsky, August Strindberg, and Franz Kafka used extreme characterisation to give expressive emphasis to the alienation and dehumanisation inherent in technocratic and bureaucratic structures. This was also clear in the Expressionist paintings of Vincent van Gogh, Paul Gaugin, and Henri Matisse, who used vibrant, clashing colours and bold outlines without depth or perspective to emphasise the 'distortion' involved in any attempt at representation. Surrealist painters such as Joan Miró and Salvador Dali depicted clear sharp structures that, nevertheless, stood in chaotic relations with each other and dissolved or melted into fluidity. In literature, the so-called 'stream of consciousness' writings of Virginia Woolf, James Joyce, and Marcel Proust aimed to mimic the chaotic flow of subjective mental activity rather than its 'final', polished intellectual outcomes. D.H. Lawrence and Thomas Mann took a different tack and sought to show how 'natural' human feelings are subject to cultural distortion and repression. The chromatic and atonal music of Arnold Schönberg and Alban Berg began from a rejection of the ideas of key, tonality, and the symphonic form. They explored the fluidity of musical expression and, in Schönberg's later Serialism, the expressive possibilities of an abstract permutation of forms. The related work of Igor Stravinsky collated fragments of folk and popular melodies into musical collages, much as the literature of T.S. Eliot juxtaposed diverse images in a single work. Collage was also apparent in Cubist painters such as Pablo Picasso and Georges Braque, who used stylised patterns of geometrical forms to depict the multiple perspectives from which realities are constructed. The Functionalist architecture of Walter Gropius and Ludwig Mies van der Rohe were based around the view that a building must make the arbitrariness of its structure apparent by making visible and obvious the uses and purposes to which the building is put.

Such 'modernist' views also had an impact in wider cultural fields. In sociology, for example, the works of the classical theorists combined an emphasis on scientific explanation with an awareness of diversity and cultural difference. Initially involving a confrontation of scientific rationality with Romanticism (Nisbet 1966), the works of the later nineteenth-century theorists began to show a strong influence from modernist philosophy and aesthetics. Socialism and Marxism showed this same combination of elements: 'positivistic' and deterministic approaches were countered by those that emphasised creativity and revolutionary transformations in historical structures. Much modernism in the humanities and in everyday culture centred on the expression and remaking of the self in a context where no traditional guidance on meanings or social identities could be relied on. Its strongest expression here was found in Freudian psychoanalysis and approaches influenced by 'irrationalist' ideas (Hughes 1958). Self-realisation and self-actualisation were the principal themes, leading Daniel Bell to conclude that modernism is 'prodigal, promiscuous, dominated by an anti-rational, anti-intellectual temper in which the self is taken as the touchstone of cultural judgements, and the effect on the self is the measure of the aesthetic worth of experience' (1976: 37).

Cultural modernism took an explicitly adversary stance towards established culture, Modern artists saw themselves as an iconoclastic avant garde, pointing the way forward. Their concern to maintain the autonomy of the aesthetic sphere meant that modernist art was 'auratic' (Benjamin 1935), presenting original and unique 'works of art' as creative products to be contemplated and understood reverentially by cultivated individuals attuned to their significance. Modernism was, therefore, disdainful of much popular culture, which was seen to comprise mere standardised commercial products of formal rationality that pandered to the 'barbarism' of the masses. Some modernists saw themselves forming a creative intellectual 'elite' that would emancipate the masses from outside, while others thought it possible to find inspiration in popular views and to give expression to them. This same dilemma made itself felt in Marxist views of the Communist Party and the development of proletarian class consciousness. Lukács's aesthetic ideas, for example, were reflected in his view of Marxist theoreticians as an intellectual 'vanguard'.

The critical impetus behind aesthetic modernism was weakened as the twentieth century proceeded. Many modernists came to terms with established art and began to give more attention to formal technique and structure. The later architecture of Mies van der Rohe, Le Corbusier, and Frank Lloyd Wright, for example, made technique and function the basis for their harshly modern 'Brutalist' designs, stressing the simple patterns and stark structures appropriate to buildings that are 'machines for living in'. This accommodation with modernity was particularly apparent after the Second World War, when the rational planning of space became a central element in corporatist strategies of economic and political 'modernisation' (Harvey 1989: 37). Modernism as a critical project had exhausted itself. Any critical artistic and political intent had, therefore, to be directed against modernism itself.

The first intimation of anti-modernism was the 'counter-culture' of the mid-1960s (Roszack 1969). Hippies and political radicals mounted a politicised challenge to the technology and bureaucratic rationality of the 1950s and 1960s in the name of impulse and pleasure, psychedelic expressivity, and cultural freedom. This planted the seeds for the development of what came to be known as 'post-modernism' in the years between 1968 and 1972.[1] Post-modernism, with or without its hyphen, explicitly took up the radicalism of aesthetic modernism and pursued this even more relentlessly. The elitist, 'auratic' idea of the artistic van-guard was abandoned, leaving no grounds for maintaining a sharp boundary between 'art' and popular culture. Anti-auratic art stressed its own status as the 'reproduction' or reiteration of things already constituted in popular culture. The work of Andy Warhol became the exemplar of this outlook.

If no foundations for intellectual certainty can be established, then all activity must involve a rejection of what exists and a futile attempt to create new forms that will be equally transient and without foundation. Diverse worlds and images must be accepted without it being assumed that they must fit together to form a larger whole. There is no 'totality', no 'grand narrative', no 'big picture' that makes sense of the chaotic and ephemeral flow of meanings. The modernist idea of artistic collage was extended into a post-modernist 'radical eclecticism' that involved a constant search for a 'hybridity' of form. Post-modern aesthetic rep-resentations comprise only 'perpetually shifting fragments' (Harvey 1989: 52), each is a mere pastiche of elements drawn from anywhere and everywhere with no attempt at historical continuity or stylistic unity. The architecture of Charles Moore, Aldo Rossi, and Richard Rogers, the minimalist music of Philip Glass and John Cage, and the art of Robert Rauschenberg all took up these ideas as their explicit credo. They had a significant influence on the philosophical and literary theories of Jacques Derrida (1967a, 1967b), Michel Foucault (1971), and Richard Rorty (1980), and they have been responsible for a growing influence of ideas of the relativity of values and ideas.

These developments in the spheres of aesthetics and philosophy were not, of course, completely free-floating cultural developments. They occurred under specific social conditions and their rise and fall cannot be understood in isolation from these. The social basis of modernism, it is now recognised, was the devel-opment during the late nineteenth century of monopolised markets and the mass production systems of machinery and the factory, the associated expansion of mass circulation through advances in transport, communication, and urban forms, and the growth of mass consumption and mass culture. The social basis of post-modernism is less clear, though a number of rival proposals have been put forward for explaining this cultural trend and for exploring its social consequences. In this chapter I will examine these arguments and try to assess whether the cultural trend of post-modernity has been associated with a structural shift away from modern forms of social activity to a more specifically 'post-modern' way of life. I will look at a series of overlapping and intersecting theoretical interpretations that stress such things as the disorganisation and fragmentation of economic activity, the growing significance of technical knowledge and the hazards that have resulted from this, the enhanced role of consumerism and popular culture in everyday life, and the global extension and interconnection of human activities.

Late Capitalism, Disorganisation, and the Consumer Society

For many theorists it is developments within the capitalist mode of production that have driven the cultural changes described as post-modern. Adorno, Horkheimer, and their colleagues in the Institute of Social Research during the 1930s and 1940s originated the idea that the development of monopolistic, organised capitalism was associated with the growth of systems of mass communication and a standardisation of their cultural products. Ongoing rationalisation had brought about a transition from liberal, free-market forms of capitalism to more organised and monopolised forms of finance capitalism that were, in turn, responsible for a growing commodification and bureaucratic regulation of social life. Social consciousness took an increasingly technocratic form that reified human relations and cultural concerns, seeing them as expressions of objective and impersonal laws. The possibility of mass social criticism was much diminished by the growth of this 'one-dimensional thought' (Adorno and Horkheimer 1944; Marcuse 1964).

In parallel with the development of organised capitalism and mass culture, however, Adorno traced the development of more autonomous forms of artistic expression. This aesthetic modernism retained and promoted the possibility of a progressive, critical opposition to the cultural and political implications of rationalisation. These modernist artists challenged both the inherited 'bourgeois' forms of artistic production and the passive and alienated consumerism of the masses. Adorno had studied musical composition with Alban Berg and he saw the experiments of Berg, Arnold Schönberg, and Anton von Webern as the most progressive trends within this modernist cultural movement. Ambivalent about or hostile towards certain types of modernism, which he saw as overly relativistic and emotional, Adorno saw chromatic, atonal music as a powerful and critical attempt to move beyond the restrictions of classical forms by exploring their limitations. Adorno allied himself with the modernist view of the artistic avant garde, seeing the autonomous artistic activity of a cultural 'elite' as the means through which aesthetic and philosophical truths could be pursued through the opening up of new possibilities for creative expression. He saw his own theoretical work and that of his Frankfurt colleagues as carrying forward this same critical intent.

This cultural analysis was carried forward by Jürgen Habermas, who argued that further changes in the structure of industrial capitalism had transformed modernist aesthetics into post-modern forms that no longer had any critical orientation. Habermas (1973) argued that a stage of 'late capitalism', entered in the second half of the twentieth century, was the culmination of the monopolistic trends of organised capitalism. In this stage of capitalism, markets are regulated and controlled by ever more interventionist states. Tendencies towards economic crises had been eliminated through the ability of states to engage in focused public expenditure and to pursue fiscal policies that maintained levels of private expenditure and effective demand. The adoption of Keynesian policy prescriptions had all but eradicated the likelihood of the kind of economic slump envisaged by Marx (see also Mandel 1972). This had, however, been achieved at a price. Economic dislocations had been suppressed rather than eliminated, and they now made themselves felt in crises of the state itself. States had consistently to adjust their own expenditure and taxation and face periodic fiscal crises (O'Connor 1973) when they are unable to meet the growing demands placed upon them. Expenditure on health, welfare, and education – all pursued as supports for private capitalist production – must be cut back periodically. Late capitalism has encouraged a growth in consumerism, as recognised by Adorno, and contemporary states face growing legitimation problems, as reductions in public spending generate discontent among the growing numbers in the population who depend upon their expenditure. These states can no longer rely on traditional loyalties to sustain their authority, as the continuing rationalisation of culture has undermined this. Commitment to the achievement principles and possessive individualism of the work ethic (Offe 1970) and to the pursuit of consumer goods can be sustained only if states can maintain the flow of material benefits that allows consumption to be maintained – and it is this flow that is threatened by fiscal crises. Active opposition and resistance to this passive consumerism comes from the 'counter-culture' of artistic radicalism, which articulates the contrast between the motivational patterns required by the economic and political system and the more hedonistic principles inherent in consumerism.

With each successive withdrawal of legitimacy in fiscal crises, the influence of this outlook further radicalises mass consciousness. It is this logic of late capitalism that generates the post-modern response (Jameson 1984).

Habermas provides an interesting argument, but he does not show how the 'post-auratic' aestheticism of the counter-culture originated and grew. Nor does he show how it may influence and radicalise popular consumerism. The beginnings of an answer have been provided by Baudrillard, whose early work (1968, 1970, 1972) was cast firmly in the mainstream of the critical theory of Adorno and Habermas. He has developed this into a distinctive account of post-modernism. He sees this as a direct outgrowth of the consumerism that has increasingly replaced the commitment to productive activities, occupational work, and the work ethic. Consumption, he argues, is the consumption both of physical products and of the cultural symbols, meanings, and images that define them. In a consumer society, the circulation and consumption of meanings takes priority over material consumption. The advertising system makes products into objects of desire, and it is these commodities that people strive to attain. They desire not just a car, a soap powder, or coffee, but a particular brand of car, soap powder, or coffee. In a real sense, their consumption of the brand image is more important than their consumption of the physical object itself. People are concerned with what an object symbolises about them and their lives. The images attached to objects, therefore, have become central to the capitalist economy. People are bound to their societies through the signs communicated in the advertising imagery of the mass media.

Thus, the Marxian analysis of the commodity in terms of its use value and its exchange value must be complemented by an analysis of its 'sign value'. The value of a commodity to a consumer consists not simply of its material utility or the monetary value for which it can be obtained but also of the recognition and reputation that the consumer achieves through its consumption. The 'system of needs' and the 'system of products' are integrated into a 'system of signification' (Baudrillard 1968) that defines the products in particular ways. The discourse of advertising organises commodities as a system of brand names that denote the product while mobilising 'connotations of affect'. That is, they are given images and associated meanings that encourage people to identify with them and to develop an emotional attachment to them, despite the irrationality of this orientation towards the manipulated desires of the advertising system.

Class inequalities do not disappear in a consumer society, but their significance is transformed. Inequalities in the ability to buy particular objects are reproduced through ongoing processes of capitalist production and so there is still a differential class consumption of the commodities. Thanks to their social construction as objects of desire, the consumption of commodities comes to be perceived and experienced as a symbol of 'status' rather than of class (Baudrillard 1970: 60). The system of media advertising, therefore, becomes a means for the social distribution of status. Baudrillard suggests that the subjective experience of consumer choice is motivated by a desire for prestige and by rivalry and emulation.

Baudrillard's later work broke more firmly with the Frankfurt view to build on the ideas of Roland Barthes (see Baudrillard 1973) and he moved far closer to post-structuralism (1976, 1979, 1981). Mass media images become increasingly detached from any 'real' objects of reference and people orient themselves to these as pure images. They have, however, no secure basis for choosing among these meanings. The erosion of tradition and the comprehensive rationalisation of culture have removed any foundation for certainty in choice. This is the post-modern cultural condition. Despite his recognition of this cultural trend and the application of the post-modern label to him by commentators, Baudrillard has consistently refused to use the term 'post-modern' in relation to his own work. People must accept *all* meanings offered to them as equivalent to each other. There is no basis for choosing among them, and both established and counter-meanings become mere objects of 'spectacle'. They are 'simulations' that provide a sense of the world in terms of which they can act and think.

The media image of the politician, for example, becomes the yardstick by which media advisors, public relations experts, 'spin doctors', and others construct and reconstruct politicians and so organise public discussion and debate around photo opportunities and media events. Baudrillard also demonstrated this in his discussion of American society. People's knowledge of the world comes largely through the mass media. The images conveyed in television, Hollywood, and Disneyland, Baudrillard argues, define 'America' for us, and our actions in 'real' situations are constructed in terms of these definitions. The actual America encountered in everyday experience is reconstructed and reformulated to fit the image we have acquired through the mass media. The cultural template that defines extends itself through ever more simulated settings and encounters (Baudrillard 1981).

Evidence in support of these simulations is itself constructed from other simulations, and Baudrillard concludes that it is the interlocking of simulations that produces a strengthened sense of reality for the whole world of simulations. Simulations are reified and become 'hyperreal'. There is a cultural 'implosion' through which the boundaries between different spheres of activity are dissolved. Signs flow from advertising to entertainment to news and documentaries, and from these into everyday settings, to politics, and to business. Hyperreality is a single field with a constant flow of messages and simulations: differences of class cultures, political ideologies, and so on, disappear into a single mass culture.

This can be seen as Baudrillard's reformulation of the mass culture thesis. People appear as passive consumers of signs, as members of the 'silent majority' (Baudrillard 1978). Nevertheless, Baudrillard also sees possibilities for resistance and opposition. Cultural meanings are free-floating and available for appropriation, and people can choose – must choose – the meanings by which they will live. All social consciousness, therefore, is an eclectic bricolage of available meanings. People construct worldviews that have no external referent but merely 'internal', self-referential connotations with other systems of meaning. Any one person's consciousness is equivalent to any other and no construction can be presented as necessary, inevitable, or natural: all can be 'refused'.

Habermas, Jameson, and Baudrillard have set out a distinctive view of the cultural transformations that they see following from the development of industrial capitalism beyond the monopoly stage. They have made a strong case for seeing some of the central features of cultural post-modernism as consequences of the growing centrality of consumerism to the economy and of interventionism to the state. It is not shown, however, that these developments within the political economy involve any move beyond modernity. Indeed, Habermas and Jameson see the current organisation of the political economy as simply a *higher* stage of modernity – as *late* capitalism. The 'cultural logic' of consumerist capitalism may, indeed, be strongly post-modern in orientation, so far as aesthetics and everyday consciousness are concerned, but there seems to be no reason, on the basis of these arguments, for rejecting the view that contemporary societies are still modern societies. In order to show that the structures of modernity have crumbled and that a new stage of post-modernity has been entered, it would be necessary to demonstrate the occurrence of more far-reaching changes in the political economy than these writers have suggested. It is to those who have suggested exactly this that I now turn.

Knowledge Society and Post-modern Sensibility

A number of theorists have stressed industrialism, rather than capitalism, as the core element in modern economies and have traced the development of this industrialism into a new stage of post-industrialism. Writers as diverse as Alain

Touraine, Daniel Bell, and Jean-François Lyotard have each proposed variants of this argument, each tracing the transformation of industrialism to the growth of a 'knowledge economy'. This is seen as an economy in which knowledge and education have become the principal factors of production and capital ownership has ceased to be of any great significance. New classes, owing everything to the level of their education in these required skills, have expanded and have become the carriers, or the active supporters, of a distinctive post-modern sensibility.

The phrase 'post-industrial society' was first used by Daniel Bell in the early 1950s and was popularised in the futurology of Herman Kahn (Kahn and Wiener 1967). The idea was also taken up by Ralf Dahrendorf (1957) in his idea of a distinctively 'post-capitalist' society headed by a knowledge-based 'service class'. The French writers Serge Mallet (1963) and André Gorz (1964) developed related views in which the growth of a knowledge economy required a 'new working class' of engineers, professionals, technicians, and skilled workers.

Alain Touraine (1969, 1978) was the first to give this idea a systematic formulation. A post-industrial society, he argued, is a 'technocratic' or 'programmed' society. What he means by this is that technical knowledge has become the basis of the power relations that organise and control social activities and the principal driving force in economic growth. A post-industrial economy is one in which growing numbers of jobs in the leading sectors require a high degree of education in their occupants. As a result, its members become aware of their creative capacity and their ability self-consciously to produce their own society. The apparatuses through which this knowledge is produced, however, are organised around instrumental power relations that divide the dominant controllers from the subordinate creators. The creators are effectively excluded from effective participation in their own creativity. As a result, education and communication have been drawn ever more closely into the structures through which knowledge is produced and applied.

Industrial societies are organised around an opposition between capital and labour, while the class conflicts of post-industrial societies are organised around educational differences. At the top of the post-industrial class structure is the class of highly educated 'technocrats' who form the 'ruling powers'. Their knowledge derives from an advanced level of education of a 'generalist' kind, available, in France, at *Grandes Écoles* such as the École Normale d'Administration, the École Polytechnique, and the École Normale Supérieur. Thanks to their education, these technocrats are able to monopolise the top positions in apparatuses of economic and political decision-making. The class is defined by 'its management of the massive economic and political structures which direct development'

(Touraine 1969: 53), but Touraine rejects Dahrendorf's use of the term 'service class' to define them. Nevertheless, his argument has much in common with Dahrendorf's view of a new ruling class of managers rooted in relations of authority rather than property.

Those with less education and with highly specialised technical education are excluded from the ruling positions and participate in power, if at all, only as 'dependent participation' (Touraine 1969: 9). The subordinates form a large and diverse class, stretching from middle-ranking technicians, engineers, and other experts to various types of skilled manual worker. Workers and trade unions are now a secondary force that has an impact only in association with new social movements based on the new subordinate class.

In his earliest work, Touraine stressed the key part played within this class by students, whom he saw as the principal focus of opposition to the technocrats and the post-industrial system that they rule. It is students who are most exposed to technocratic power, both during their education and as they try to enter the labour market. It is for this reason that Touraine sees the universities as the principal bases for any opposition to post-industrialism. The student movement and various other new social movements in which students are active have replaced the labour movement to become the key agencies of social change. This was apparent, he holds, in the 'events' of May 1968 in France.

Touraine's view of the student movement reflects its unusual radicalism in the 1960s and its counter-cultural orientation. In later work he took a broader view, seeing its leading element as those with scientific and technical competence and who constitute the principal 'professional' fraction: 'They speak in the name of knowledge against the apparatus that seeks to subject knowledge to its own interests, and they ally themselves with those who are forced to the sidelines by a central apparatus and submitted to its power' (1978: 22).

Scientific professionals play a central role in the opposition to the ruling technocrats, becoming critical elements in the various new social movements that have adopted an anti-technocratic stance. Rationalisation of political and economic structures and their growing influence over other areas of life left, nevertheless, an autonomous basis for the cultivation of subjectivity and freedom in the lifeworld. It is this that fuels the resistance of the subordinate classes. While people still need to be socialised into the rationalised and instrumental attitudes to the production and application of knowledge that motivate their involvement in the technologies of power, education also generates attitudes and orientations that run counter to this (Touraine 1978: 14–15). People are no longer socialised unproblematically into attitudes of deferred gratification and the work ethic and it is their oppositional attitudes that are the roots of the growing opposition to the power of the technocracy.

This emergent form of opposition reflects a 'cultural crisis' of modernity that had its initial focus in the student radicalism of 1968 and was to lead to the emergence of other oppositional movements and began a process of 'demodernisation'. There was a broadening of movements of workers, which came to be concerned with the emancipation of workers from oppressive working conditions and their ability to act as subjects with individual freedom and a capacity for historical action (Touraine et al. 1984). There was also a whole array of new social movements, drawing on particular constituencies within the subordinate classes: feminist movements, for example, that promote the specific desires and identities of women, together with environmental, consumer, and peace movements.

This 'progressive' resistance is constantly undermined by the reassertion of more 'reactionary' opposition that roots itself in the residual traditionalism that also survives in the lifeworld. Opposition based on fundamental religious beliefs, for example, challenges formal rationality but also inhibits the desire for autonomy. Touraine (1992) sees the crucial political task in the subordinate classes as that of shifting oppositional conscience from reactionary to progressive forms.

FOCUS: ALAIN TOURAINE

Alain Touraine is a difficult writer to read, but the attempt repays the effort. The starting point for much that he has written is the argument of *The Post-Industrial Society* (1969).

One of the most influential theories of post-industrialism and the growth of a knowledge society has been that of Daniel Bell (1973, 1976). He holds that fundamental changes in the 'techno-economic order' of contemporary societies have posed problems and constraints for their political and cultural development and that these cultural developments, in turn, have posed problems and constraints for collective action. This techno-economic order – sometimes referred to simply as the 'social structure' – comprises the economic, technological, and occupational structure, together with the forms of social stratification associated with them. The key changes defining post-industrialism follow from the growing centrality of scientific knowledge and new intellectual technologies in the organisation of production and distribution. Codified and systematic theoretical knowledge that can be applied in a deliberate and rational ways as natural and social science has become more central to economic planning and practice and now determines the technologies of production and the principles by which economic activities are managed. It is for this reason that 'The post-industrial society ... is a knowledge society' (Bell 1973: 212). There has been, Bell argues, an exponential growth in the amount of knowledge produced in scientific work and, therefore, in the resources that are needed to organise it as libraries and IT systems. Intellectual fields have proliferated and the development and application of knowledge has become more specialised. The new intellectual technologies have required great advances in theories of strategic decision-making and games theory in order to grasp multi-dimensional systems and 'organised complexity' (Bell 1973: Ch. 5). The planning of technological change through systematic forecasting becomes an ever more important feature of economic activity.

These changes have produced a 'service economy' in which professional and technical occupations now play a more important part than manual occupations. Bell argues that a majority of the labour force now find employment in health, education, research, government, and other services. These are the people who produce, organise, and apply knowledge. Even in the production of goods, auto-mated systems embodying a high level of scientific knowledge depend on knowl-edgeable workers to keep them running. The fastest-growing occupations are scientists, engineers, technicians, and teachers, which require at least a college education. Occupations that embody advanced training and the application of technical knowledge are expanding, and there is a corresponding expansion in the university system to produce this knowledge (Bell 1973: Ch. 2).

Bell claims that the growing significance of knowledge has transformed capital-ist business enterprises. The corporate enterprises of the first half of the twentieth century had allowed a much larger number of shareholders to participate in ownership than was possible in entrepreneurial businesses. It also made it more difficult for family shareholders to maintain control, as they no longer had exclusive ownership. As enterprises grew in size, so the number of shareholders increased and the position of the controlling families and entrepreneurs became more precarious. The mergers and amalgamations that created larger national and multi-national units around the turn of the twentieth century, Bell argues, were crucial in bringing about a complete separation of ownership from control in large enterprises. The bankers who played a key role in these mergers were in a strong enough position to remove the old family owners from top management positions and to replace them with professional, propertyless managers. These managers saw through and benefited from the technological changes that required greater levels of education and expertise. The powers of the bankers declined as managers established their technical indispensability within the enterprise and built an independent power base. Because corporations were no longer so dependent on capital, property ownership became largely irrelevant to production (Bell 1973: 93; see also 1957). Those who had access to the new scarce resource of knowledge could now exercise the powers of control (1957: 43). Supporting the earlier claims of Bruno Rizzi (1939) and James Burnham (1941), Bell saw this as a 'managerial revolution' in contemporary industrialism.

By the middle of the twentieth century, Bell argues, this managerial revolution was well advanced. The large enterprises of industrial capitalism had operated according to the calculative 'economising' mode of allocation central to the spirit of capitalism. The large enterprises of post-industrialism, on the other hand, are 'sociologising' rather than economising: they are oriented towards the 'public interest' rather than sectional shareholder interest (Bell 1973: 283). For other writers, this is the 'soulful corporation' oriented towards 'social responsibility' (Drucker 1951). This makes post-industrialism an 'active society', its key agencies being oriented to active and deliberate social change through planning and guidance (Etzioni 1968).

The separation of ownership from control and the increased importance of knowledge, Bell argues, had major implications for class structure. The key class division in modern societies had been that between capitalist owners and propertyless workers. The declining importance of property relations weakens this class division and the old social classes begin to decay. As the old industrial classes decline, new knowledge-based classes emerge. Bell's discussion of the contours of this knowledge-based class structure is unclear and confused, but he seems to see it as having three levels. At the top there is a 'scientific elite' or 'educated elite' of creative personnel working in science and the top professions and administrative sectors. This is separated from a middle class of engineers and professors and a proletariat of technicians, junior faculty, and teaching assistants (Bell 1973: 214). These classes, however, have a far greater unity and solidarity than the industrial classes, and Bell holds that, in many respects, they form a single 'knowledge class' that is analogous to the 'industrialists' of Saint-Simon (1825) and the 'engineers' of Veblen (1919). The post-industrial society is not so sharply riven by the class conflicts that dominated industrial capitalism.

The expanding knowledge class is, for Bell, the focus of the cultural contradictions of the post-industrial society, as it is for Touraine. Though the class is concerned with the production and application of technical knowledge, Bell argues that there has been no simple consolidation of technocratic consciousness: although he does not mention specific writers, it seems clear that he has in mind the views of Adorno and Marcuse, discussed above and in Chapter 3. The 'cultural mass' within the knowledge class shows modernist and post-modernist modes of expression alongside the expansion of scientific knowledge found among technocrats. There is a divide between C.P. Snow's 'two cultures' (1959), a separation of the knowledge class into technocratic and more 'artistic' sections. The post-modern sensibility has its location within the artistic and humanistic sections of the knowledge class.

Post-modernism, then, is a product of post-industrialism and the 'knowledge society' but it does not itself define a new stage of social life. 'Post-modern', for Bell, does not refer to a new, non-modern way of life. The techno-economic order and the political order remain fully modern. Post-modernism, like 'modernism', is a cultural movement that exists in a contradictory relationship with political and economic modernity.

The post-modernist sensibility stresses hedonism, consumption, and status. While this hedonism feeds consumer demand for commodities, it also undermines the work discipline and the work ethic on which economic activity depends. Bell sees this as opening up the possibility of a radical challenge to post-industrial values. The growth of the 'cultural mass' means that what was previously the 'bohemian' life style of a minority is now that of a significant part of the population. The radicalism of the 1960s counter-culture, he argues, was a harbinger of this new sensibility and prepared the way for the emergence of lifestyle politics and of social movements organised around post-modern values (Bell 1976: 53; and see, for example, Inglehart 1990).

In a related view, Jean-François Lyotard (1979) has highlighted a transformation in scientific knowledge itself that can, he believes, be called 'post-modern'. Like Touraine and Bell, Lyotard sees a development from industrialism to post-industrialism, and he recognises that knowledge has become a commodity produced for its exchange value in the form of technologically useful 'information'. This knowledge, produced in universities, has become the principal productive force and so is the driving element in the development of post-industrialism. The dominant class in a post-industrial society comprises the 'experts' and technical decision-makers in positions of corporate leadership, high-level administration, and the top levels of major organisations. Lyotard departs from his predecessors, however, in seeing the rise of this managerial class of experts as rooted in the dynamics of a capitalist economic process. The expansion of technology has been driven by the efforts of multinational enterprises to bring about a 'reopening of the world market'. This has transformed the world order and has meant that many key matters can no longer be controlled by nation states. Transnational capital flows have increased and are an important condition for the generation and application of knowledge, which, like money, now flows far more freely as it circulates from one nation to another.

Lyotard's concern is for the ways in which such knowledge can be justified in the eyes of the non-scientists who use it and who rely on expert prescriptions for policy and practice. Any process of legitimation, he argues, depends on the construction of narratives that give a wider meaning to information by placing it within larger systems of meaning that are accepted as unproblematic and so provide it with a secure foundation. Knowledge in traditional societies was sustained by legends and myth narratives of the kind described by Lévi-Strauss (1964). Passing this on orally as the collective memory (Halbwachs 1925), the narrators are defined by traditional, ascriptive norms as those who can define criteria of practical competence and evaluate actions relative to these criteria. Scientific knowledge involved a rational challenge to such myth narratives. In an implicit echo of Comte's law of the three stages, Lyotard sees the Enlightenment project as involving an abandonment of all religious and 'metaphysical' forms of knowledge. Cognitive, empirical knowledge is valued above all other knowledge and develops its own internal criteria of objectivity and truth. Through the modern period, however, science has relied on certain traditional sanctions to sustain its own legitimacy and authority in the eyes of others. Non-scientists, and many scientists, predisposed to believe in overarching 'purposes' could justify an acceptance of science by its relation to particular secular goals. Scientific knowledge cannot be presented as true knowledge without a resort to narratives that, themselves, cannot form a part of science (Lyotard 1979: 29). Through the eighteenth and nineteenth centuries, university science legitimated its autonomy and power through two such narratives: the narrative of emancipation through the cultivation and education of humanity and the narrative of the cultural or spiritual mission of the university to pursue scientific knowledge for its own sake.

What Lyotard calls the 'post-modern condition' is a cultural condition in which all knowledge claims can be assessed in rational terms alone, marking a final abandonment of all reliance on unreflective and taken-for-granted meanings. The success of science in challenging all presuppositions has led to a growing 'incredulity toward metanarratives' (Lyotard 1979: xxiv). Overarching structures can no longer be accepted as unproblematic because their frameworks of legitimation have been challenged. The narratives that once legitimated science come to be seen as unjustifiable survivors of a pre-scientific discourse. For more and more people in the post-industrial societies, scientific knowledge and scientific authority can be challenged and the scientific enterprise faces a declining legitimacy. This, for Lyotard, explains the resonance that the arguments of Thomas Kuhn (1962) and Paul Feyerabend (1975) have had. Science can no longer sustain claims to objectivity and truth because the grand narratives through which it was formerly legitimated are no longer accepted as unproblematic foundations.

Science itself is pluralised as its various branches become more specialised. Disciplinary boundaries can no longer be sustained as markers of fixed and interdependent activities. The scientific landscape is a flat network of overlapping and shifting discourses (Lyotard 1979: 39) that overlaps with a similar landscape of non-scientific discourses. There is no meta-discourse that can define the relations among different forms of knowledge. What scientists claim as 'truth' is simply whatever each scientific specialism has come to accept as true within the terms of its particular norms and practices. The only possible basis for justifying any scientific venture is through its 'pragmatics' or 'performativity' – by the pragmatic success that its technical applications yield for those in power. Pragmatic technical success is the basis on which funding can be secured for research and education. Education becomes merely technical or professional training – a means to an end – as commodified knowledge contributes to the reproduction of a knowledgeable elite of expert managers.

The structural changes that Touraine and Bell have identified as producing the post-modern sensibility are not as far-reaching as they have suggested. Structurally, contemporary societies can still be regarded as modern, despite their 'post-industrial' characteristics. The shift from the production of goods to the performance of services has not eliminated the rationalised division of labour that characterises 'industrial' organisation, though it certainly constitutes a significantly new phase of industrialism. Bell also overstates the extent to which capitalist forms have been transcended. The managerial revolution and its separation of ownership from control are not as extensive as Bell suggests, and it is clear that capital and its ownership remains central to contemporary economic organisation (Scott 1997). Thus, the class structure remains more complex than Bell suggests, and it is important to recognise the continuing salience of 'old' capitalist classes (Bottomore and Brym 1989) and the subordinate positions of both the service class and the larger 'new middle class' of technical and intellectual workers (Erikson and Goldthorpe 1992). The cultural implications of the expansion of technical knowledge and educational systems must be seen as occurring alongside the persisting material inequalities of a capitalist class structure.

Lyotard, perhaps, offers a more nuanced account of these changes, recognising a continued linkage of knowledge production to the ownership and organisation of capital.

Reflexivity, Individualisation, and Risk

It is possible to conclude, so far, that structural changes in the economic and political institutions of modernity have not been so radical as to involve the demise of capitalism. The contemporary political economy remains thoroughly modern, both industrial and capitalistic. It has, nevertheless, seen changes in the organisation of education that have generated a growing post-modern sensibility alongside a continuing emphasis on the practical application of formally rational scientific knowledge. This is the key to the post-modern cultural condition that constitutes the cultural logic of late capitalism.

It remains to be seen, however, whether these cultural changes might not be associated with changes in the lifeworld and, therefore, with the beginnings of a post-modern form of social organisation. Touraine had highlighted the lifeworld as the crucial basis for initiating and sustaining a post-modern sensibility, and this argument was taken slightly further by Lyotard. According to Lyotard, people are involved in networks of communication that can be understood as particular 'language games' through which individual selves and lifeworlds are constituted. Following Goffman (1959), Lyotard sees contemporary societies involving people in strategic game playing through a number of separate and distinct 'flexible networks' of interaction (Lyotard 1979: 15, 17). Each sphere of activity operates according to its own criteria, and the principles of one cannot be assessed against those of another. There is a radical incommensurability, then, between the various spheres that they constitute.

This view of an incipient transformation of the social institutions of the lifeworld has been taken in a new direction by a group of writers who seek to show that traditional solidarities have been eroded and that contemporary societies are highly fragmented and individualistic. Ulrich Beck (1986, 1988, 1993) and Anthony Giddens (1990, 1991),[2] like the post-industrial theorists, see contemporary industrialism as radically transformed. Contemporary societies, they argue, have entered a new phase of 'radicalised' modernity. Neither writer posits this as a 'post-modern' condition, seeing radicalised modernity as a more comprehensively modern social structure. They do argue, however, that the radicalisation of modern structures has led to a cultural fragmentation and a growth of 'individualisation'. Zygmunt Bauman (1992) was, for a time, more sympathetic towards the idea of social structural post-modernity, but he, too, now refers to a 'liquid' or 'fluid' modernity (2000, 2001, 2002).

Beck (1986) argues that rational restructuring of traditional forms of production and power had, by the nineteenth century, transformed agrarian into industrial societies, and he sees these as having continued to develop through an ongoing challenge to traditionalism. The survival of traditional structures and practices, however, meant that such societies were, until recently, only 'semi-modern' (Beck 1993: 33). It was only from the 1970s that traditionalism really became an unimportant feature of contemporary existence. No significant elements of tradition remained to be rationalised and the process of rationalisation could operate only on already modern structures. This 'reflexive modernisation', Beck argues, is bringing into being the first purely modern forms of society.

Reflexive modernisation involves a self-transformation of industrial societies in which structures are constantly renewed and no fundamental narratives or foundational principles can legitimate them or justify their retention (Beck 1993: 15). As a result, people have become detached from stable norms and cohesive social bonds. They are 'individualised' and now face the many hazards of life without any guidance from established authority and, in their social isolation, experience a growing sense of insecurity and anxiety. People must face unprecedented existential choices and must reflexively build their own lives – make their own biographies – without guidance from taken-for-granted templates for action (Beck 1986: 135–6; 1993: 95–7). Beck sees these tendencies producing what he calls a 'risk society' that will be the ultimate form of modernity.

Beck holds that the key institutional structures of classical industrialism – work, family, and class – depend on traditional structures of gender, hierarchy, and loyalty to sustain people's commitments to them. These disappeared along with other elements of tradition at the same time that work, family, and class have themselves been restructured. For much of the twentieth century, industrial work was organised into standardised systems of full-time employment and the realistic expectation of secure continuity of work and, for many, a career. This, Beck argues, has given way to the flexible working patterns required by efficient post-Fordist production systems. Workers are now more likely to experience periods of casual, partial, and temporary employment, and much work is now undertaken at home or on the move, rather than at a single, fixed spatial location (Beck 1986: 140, 142). This temporal and spatial reorganisation of work breaks down the distinctions between work and home, it leads to high levels of underemployment and much insecure employment. Commitment to work as a central life interest is no longer viable and, as a result, more and more people experience an extreme anxiety over their income and future security.

At the same time, the patriarchal gender divisions that structured family life and that were a major limitation on the full development of modernity are undermined. Inequalities between men and women do not disappear, but they are no longer legitimated by the norms of a traditionalist patriarchy. Married women have been liberated from the narrowly 'feminine' roles of wife, mother, and housewife as they have been forced – by the insecurities of their husbands' work – to pursue employment outside the home. The woman's role in the family is no longer confined to the production and reproduction of healthy, well-fed male workers. Gender 'fates', for both men and women, are dissolved as people actively choose their intimate partnerships and begin to explore new ways of living together. The family becomes a more egalitarian 'negotiated family' that no longer pre-defines the separate spheres of men and women (see also Beck and Beck-Gernsheim 1995). In their work, women are exposed to the same insecurities and anxieties as men and this constantly frustrates the rising expectations generated by their greater freedom within the family.

Patterns of stratification are altering as a result of these changes in work and gender relations. Systematically structured inequalities of resources and life chances persist, but these are no longer experienced as the traditional work and gender relations that reinforced the shared identities and solidarities of class-based communities. Flexible working patterns and greater geographical mobility have fragmented the single-class communities in which most people formerly lived. Class membership recedes in people's awareness and there is less consciousness of sharing a class fate with others. Such people feel compelled to choose or to make an identity for themselves rather than to unreflectively take on identities inherited from the past. The new phase of modernity, according to Beck, is 'a capitalism *without* classes, but with individualized social inequality' (1986: 88) – in the words of Klaus Eder (1993), it is a thoroughly individualised class society.

The transformation of work and inequality is part of a wider set of economic changes that has exacerbated the insecurities of existence that Beck sees as characteristic of contemporary modernity. The continued application of science and technology to industrial systems of production has produced hazards – both physical and social – of a type and on a scale never before experienced. While technology has allowed many economic problems to be solved and has increased average standards of living, it has also resulted in many new difficulties and dangers. Nuclear radiation, chemical pollutants and toxins, genetic mutations, and similar 'side-effects' of medical, food production, energy, and other industrial technologies degrade the physical environment in which humans live and work, making 'catastrophic' environmental and bodily problems more likely. Insecure and precarious employment and the absence of any fixed guidelines for action render life uncertain and problematic, making it a source of chronic anxiety. Such hazards and insecurities are so novel that they cannot be interpreted simply as accidents and contingencies, as they are in conventional, insurance-based calculations of risk. New hazards result in new, incalculable and unpredictable perceptions of risk, and anxiety becomes all-pervasive (Beck 1986: 21–2; 1988).

Beck sees the production and distribution of these hazards and the risks of encountering them as a result of the economic structures of radicalised modernity and as working alongside and reinforcing the class-based distribution of wealth. The globalisation of industrial production leads to a globalisation of risk, and, as the wealthy are better placed to avoid many hazards that endanger the poor, there is an increasing likelihood that risks will appear disproportionately in the poorer districts of the world. Nevertheless, many hazards are more difficult for the wealthy to avoid and will be experienced and suffered by all. The radioactive fallout from nuclear incidents, for example, spreads indiscriminately, and the global warming that results from the emission of greenhouse gases changes the climate in every part of the world.

The effects of such global of hazards are often highly visible, but many risks may not be apparent to those who face them. They may be recognised principally through reports in the mass media of scientific investigations. The risks associated with global warming, for example, became apparent only after protracted enquiries into variations in weather patterns, alterations in the earth's ozone layer, and the emission of gases by automobiles, domestic equipment, and industrial processes. Even when people have direct knowledge of hazards, they are likely to depend on scientists to assess the risks involved. Awareness of risk is, therefore, 'knowledge-dependent': people are dependent on access to scientific knowledge for their recognition and understanding of risks and their own victim status. Risk awareness increases with the permeation of scientific knowledge into public consciousness (Beck 1999: 101), and the everyday consciousness of risk is a 'scientized consciousness' (1986: 28, 52). Despite this dependence on science, however, scientists have lost much of their authority, as recognised by Lyotard. It is increasingly concluded that those who identify risks are also responsible for the technologies that produce them and have no authority for imposing their views on others: 'The consciousness of modernization risks has established itself against the *resistance* of scientific rationality. A broad trail of scientific mistakes, misjudgements and minimizations leads to it. The history of the growing consciousness and social recognition of risks coincides with the history of the *de*mystification of the sciences' (Beck 1986: 59; 1993: 37).

Within nation states, bureaucracy and expertise have been strengthened at the expense of parliamentary and democratic mechanisms of control. Political issues are defined in increasingly technocratic terms and are seen purely as matters for technical solutions. Support for policies is secured through the corporatist involvement of organised interest groups and the mobilisation of vested interests. The 'scientization of political decisions' (Beck 1986: 188; 1988: Ch. 7) insulates the technical discussions of experts from any significant democratic scrutiny and control. Beck sees this producing a growth in media-constituted spheres of 'sub-politics' separate from states (1993: 97ff.). It is here – in the mass media, within social movements, on internet discussion forums, and so on – that debates over risk take place, with scientists, business executives, professionals, and others, each with their particular discursive frameworks for identifying and defining risks, competing to shape the terms of the debate. It is here, also, that participants in the new social movements contend with each other. Those who experience risks and suffer from the hazards of advanced technology must organise themselves in these movements if they are to bring their concerns into the arena of public debate and to challenge expert judgements. The growing debate over risks, therefore, develops as a confrontation of expert and lay views structured through the mass media rather than through the conventional political channels of the nation state. Beck's reflections on the likely shape of such politics in the future led him to conclude that they would develop as a 'third way' 'beyond left and right' (1993: 142, 148).

FOCUS: ULRICH BECK

Ulrich Beck has written extensively on the social character and consequences of risk. His books are dense and difficult, and they are often allusive. Chapter one of *Risk Society* (1986) forms the best starting point.

Bauman's reflections (2000) on the work of Beck and Giddens have led him into an attempt to understand how contemporary social life has gone beyond the technological domination and technocratic consciousness analysed by the

Frankfurt writers. He does this by distinguishing two forms of modernity, which he calls 'solid' and 'liquid' modernity.

Solid modernity is the modernity of nation states, industrial capitalism, and national societies. These prospered in the classic period of modernity: the era of bureaucracy, the Fordist factory, the panopticon, corporatism, and the incipient threat of totalitarianism (Bauman 1989). This stage of modernity involves an imposition of order and societal integration by bureaucrats and planners who build the physical and social machines that make it sensible to define this period by its solidity, as 'heavy', 'condensed', or 'systemic' modernity. An increased density of transnational flows of money and information has, since the second half of the twentieth century, weakened both national capitalism and nation states. This has undermined strategies of social engineering and the related practices of management, hierarchy, career, and planning through which lifeworlds could be colonised and societal integration sustained through the steel-hard social structures of the 'hardware era'.

Nation states were able to claim the complete and undivided loyalty of their citizens, overriding differences of religion, language, and ethnicity. Most states, of course, only ever realised this national solidarity incompletely and they faced the constant possibility of fragmentation. It was the maintenance of an ideological vision of an imagined national community, backed by the power of a nation state, that gave a solidity to their societal cohesion. Nation states were organised around ideas of nationalism and the building of a submissive population:

> The nation state was a grand vision of a nation blended into a polity ... Survival of the nation being identical with the unsapped and intractable might of the state, love of the nation manifested itself most fully in the meticulous observance of the law of the land and faithful service to whatever had been presented and recognised as being in a state's interest. (Bauman 2002: 9)

In the new era, nation and state have been separated far more radically than ever before. There has been a loss of confidence in the modern strategy of social 'telesis', of top-down rational planning and control. Many state activities have been transferred to non-political agencies, and the growth of transnational economic relations and 'extraterritorial' powers has weakened state sovereignty. As a result, national identity no longer has any special place; the nation is simply one of a number of imagined communities – others are based on ethnicity, religion, language, and gender – that compete for loyalty and emotional commitment. The sense of common 'citizenship' and citizen politics within a national arena is undermined.

Business corporations have become looser forms of economic organisation with 'dis-organisation' built into them. Large enterprises are formed into intersecting networks of communication through which information can move with great speed and that allow great flexibility in the organisation of economic activities (Bauman cites Boltanski and Chiapello 1999 on this). They no longer constitute the primary basis for social identity: work is no longer a 'central life interest' and cannot sustain societal integration.

Societal integration now depends far more on the flexible patterns of a 'software era', and Bauman argues that contemporary modernity is most usefully seen as taking a 'fluid' or 'liquid' form. People face great political and economic uncertainties and must cope with a growing sense of the ambivalence and insecurity of existence, of the contingency of events. People are sceptical of the grand narratives that once ordered their lives and now live in a state of heightened ontological insecurity. They are compelled to take control of their own lives, in the absence of external controlling structures, but they are anxious about how to do this. They are inescapably engaged in a process of 'self-constitution', reflexively building the self-discipline of mind and body that will, they hope, enable them to survive. There is no longer any safe and secure 'community' to which people can attach themselves. Family, class, and neighbourhood solidarities dissolve as effective bases of social solidarity. While it was previously possible to rely on structures to which commitments could be made and whose expectations and requirements provided a basis for social conformity, people are no longer socialised into ascribed, traditional identities (such as those of 'estate') and they are not confined to fixed and given identities such as those of class and gender. They now live in social worlds in which not only individual *placement* but also the very *places* have dissolved.

Systems of norms proliferate, dissolve, and are reconstructed with such speed that none can be regarded as 'obvious' or self-evident points of reference. Individuals are faced with such divergent and contradictory expectations that 'each one has been stripped of a good deal of compelling, coercively constraining power' (Bauman 2000: 7). They must actively make their own lives, choosing from within a 'supermarket of identities'. It is no longer a question of *how* to achieve a desired identity but of *which* identity to aim for. This process of 'individualisation' has been 'transforming human "identity" from a "given" to a "task"' (Bauman 2000: 31; 2001: Ch. 11). Individuals must choose the way they live their lives and must live by the consequences of their choices with only themselves to take responsibility. In an attempt to establish some certainties for themselves, they face a never-ending, open-ended search for the kind of authentic and meaningful identity that does not exist and so can never be achieved. This ontological uncertainty is the basis of their anxiety and insecurity. Thus, Bauman describes liquid modernity as an individualised or privatised society.

The insecurity and precariousness with which people must live makes it impossible for them to commit themselves for the long term or to have security or trust in anything beyond themselves. All things are transient, objects simply of short-term satisfactions that are to be used and enjoyed while available. There is a resort to objects of immediate consumption and a concern for the acquisition of goods through shopping. As Bell recognised, consumerism replaces the work ethic as the basis of social identity and social integration. The difference is that where Bell sees this ethic as a consequence simply of the growth of a privileged knowledge class, Bauman sees it as reflecting also the emerging risk society. The majority of the population in the technologically most advanced societies are relatively affluent consumers who find their identities in shopping and the pursuit of leisure. Consumerism allows people to forget and so to assuage their anxieties about the uncertainties and contingencies of their lives. People are bound together only as consumers, oriented by seduction and desires, with no fixed standards to guide their consumption. The desire to consume is unlimited and unregulated, subject to constant universal comparison and leading to 'compulsive shopping'. Although there has been a growing post-modern sensibility, contemporary society cannot be seen as non-modern: 'The society which enters the twenty-first century is no less "modern" than the society which entered the twentieth; the most one can say is that it is modern in a different way' (Bauman 2000: 28).

Bauman (1998) also recognises a growing global divide between the rich and the poor. The great mass of relatively affluent consumers are flanked by an expanding class divide between the global rich and the global poor. The global rich comprise the transnational executives and cosmopolitan jet setters who control the consumer economy and benefit from mass consumerism. They are able to achieve an integration and cohesion at the global level, as global 'nomads' who can rule without the need for any fixed spatial location. Constantly on the move, their communications technologies allow their extraterritorial power to move at the speed of the electronic signal that conveys it. The global underclass, on the other hand, are the poor who are excluded from consumerism and live on the fringes of the consumer society.

These arguments about the growing risk society and risk consciousness broaden yet further the understanding of contemporary society that have been explored in this chapter. The consumerist post-modern sensibility and growing individualism have been seen as associated with weakened mechanisms of societal integration. Beck and Bauman agree that the new stage of social life should still be seen as 'modern', albeit in a radicalised form. Their arguments enlarge on those of Durkheim (1897, 1895), who saw the expansion of the modern division of labour as associated with increasing levels of individualism as mechanical, communal forms of social solidarity are stripped away. Durkheim also diagnosed the depression and anxiety generated by this growth of individualism whenever new norms and bonds of social integration could not be built. Egoism and anomie were chronic 'pathologies' in an individualised society. Bauman has suggested, however, that underlying economic and political trends have weakened industrial capitalism and the nation state, which I have argued to be the central institutions of modernity. I now turn to look at those arguments that have made this their central topic of investigation. Might it be that institutional changes in economies and political systems have, after all, been so extensive that modernity has been radicalised out of existence?

Transnational Networks and Global Flows

The central figure to have discussed the possible 'disorganisation' of modernity is Manuel Castells in his major tripartite study (1996, 1997, 1998), where he sees this disorganisation as a consequence of integral features of contemporary globalisation. Castells recognises that information plays a key part in the organisation of economic activity in contemporary societies, but he does not adopt Touraine's and Bell's idea of the knowledge or information society. The application of knowledge and information certainly results in cumulative processes of technical innovation that have a significant and continuous effect on social organisation (Castells 1996: 16–17, 32), but what Castells adds to this argument is the claim that this reflects the close articulation of information with the global expansion of capital. The emerging society is one in which the use of capital has become subject to structured technical information and the dynamics of the two cannot be separated. It is not, therefore, an 'information' society but an 'informational' one. This informational society, Castells holds, is emerging in all the advanced capitalist economies, although it occurred initially in North America and northern Europe. Since the collapse of Communism it has developed apace in Russia and Eastern Europe, and it is also developing in the countries of Pacific Asia. Though each society has its own distinct historical starting point that creates its particular path dependent pattern of development, each is driven by the similar global logic of informationalism.

There are two elements to the mode of production in this emergent society. There is, first, a global expansion of business operations through the establishment of complex transnational linkages and, second, the fusion of economic networks with information networks. The fiscal crises faced by the leading states in the 1970s reduced state-generated demand and impelled businesses to seek new and larger markets overseas. This was the basis of the drive to globalisation during the 1980s. This global expansion coincided with the introduction and application in business of new technologies of information generation, processing and transmission. Although these technologies had a long history, it was only in the last part of the twentieth century that they came together in a transformative explosion of information technology. Advances in micro-processing and the networking of computers, together with the development of digital, fibre-optic, and satellite systems of telecommunications, built a mutually reinforcing complex of technologies with a massive potential for application in industrial and business control systems. Following the work of Imai (1990) on information networks, Castells argues that the application of these information technologies led to increases in productivity and efficiency and has generated dramatic organisational changes that allowed businesses to operate on a global scale in ways never before possible.

From the 1980s, the global expansion of business operations involved a new 'organisational logic' of the 'networked enterprise', characterised by flexible, post-Fordist operations. Castells actually writes of the 'network enterprise', but the phrase 'networked enterprise' better catches his idea. This networking of enterprises arose as a direct response to the endogenous requirements of the new economic situation faced by enterprises, but it also involved the emulation of established Japanese examples of networking and management that were adapted to these requirements. Indeed, these managerial changes were often described as a 'Japanisation' of western management. Organisations established systems of work that were built around the 'flexible specialisation' (Piore and Sabel 1984) or 'dynamic specialisation' (Coriat 1990) of their employees. Flexibility in both the manufacture of products and the processes used to produce them was pursued through the adoption of flexible forms of labour – which, from the employee's point of view, meant work and employment insecurity. This allowed a rapid response to changes in market demand for products and services.

In the leading markets of the major economies, the large self-sufficient and hierarchically organised enterprise is disappearing. 'Leaner', slimmed-down enterprises now tend to enter into financial and commercial alliances, agreements, and joint ventures with each other and form more horizontally structured organisations. At the same time, the autonomous divisional units that comprise an enterprise each establish their own links and connections to units and enterprises elsewhere. Through these means, financial, commercial, and technical relations are established with smaller enterprises that operate as sub-contractors, franchises, or subordinate suppliers (Castells 1996: 191). The enterprise becomes an 'articulated network of multifunctional decision-making centres' (1996: 166) operating across national frontiers and without regard for purely national economic considerations.

These organisational changes are transforming the existing world economy into a distinctively 'global' economy. The world economy described by Braudel (1967) and Wallerstein (1974) is a system of national economies structured into a division of labour in which core economies are separated from peripheral ones. A global economy, however, is 'an economy with the capacity to work as a unit in real time on a planetary scale' (Castells 1996: 92, emphasis removed). Thanks to information technology, networked enterprises can cooperate and coordinate their activities more rapidly, allowing the invisible hand of the global market to operate more effectively. Capital can circulate through integrated financial markets in real time, twenty-four hours a day, and enterprises can be connected almost instantaneously into this financial circuit. As a result, their marketing takes place at a global level, unconfined by the particularities of national markets. Labour, also, becomes a resource that can be managed on a global scale, partly through the migration of workers and partly through enterprises shifting the location of their activities. An increasing amount of production and distribution, Castells holds, is now organised through the global alliances and associations of networked enterprises. Thus, capitalism is fragmented and disarticulated at a national level, but remains a coherent capitalist system at the global level.

This growth of transnational linkages into extensive, interweaving networks of relations has reduced the powers of nation states to control the crucial economic factors for their national economies. The units of the global economy are not national economies, because these disarticulate as their sectors become intertwined in a variety of relations with varying strengths of attachment. As national economies become disarticulated, and so become less meaningful as units of analysis, so nation states become less salient sources for key political decisions. Nation states, nevertheless, remain important as foci of political decision and regulation, though having to cooperate more routinely with other states and political agencies (Castells 1997: Ch. 5). In an interesting echo of the earlier argument of Novicow (1912), Castells points to the building of the European Community and other European institutions and the consequent redefinition of sovereign state powers as epitomising a new state form – the 'network state' – in which alliances and coalitions bring about a degree of unification at the cost of a reduction in the sovereignty of the constituent nation states (1998: 311).

The dominant segments of economic activity have become linked into a 'global web' that is internally differentiated into a global-level regional structure with three core areas: North America, Europe, and Pacific Asia. This global web is sharply separated from the subordinate sectors of its peripheral and marginal economies. The 'Fourth World' of Africa, together with parts of Latin America and Asia, are excluded from any significant participation in running the informational economy that shapes their economic activities. This dualism or polarisation, however, is not fixed for all time, and neither is the triangular structure of the core. Although inequality and polarisation is a characteristic of the emergent informational economy, its particular patterns of inequality and polarisation may change over time: 'The global economy emerging from informational-based production and competition is characterised by its interdependence, its asymmetry, its regionalisation, the increasing diversification within each region, its selective inclusiveness, its exclusionary segmentation, and, as a result of all these factors, an extraordinarily variable geometry' (Castells 1996: 106).

It is on the basis of this view of global divisions that Castells constructs an account of class structure in informational societies that is more nuanced than that of Bauman. He foresees a progressive decline in both the capitalist class of owners and the capitalist working class at the national level. The informational economy puts a premium on technical knowledge, and those who possess this are able to benefit at the expense of those who do not. The declining importance of mere capital relative to information undermines the importance of property ownership and, as it does for Bell, makes the owners of capital less central participants in the productive process. Castells differs from Bell, however, in seeing that the new informational economy remains a capitalist economy. At the heart of the informationalised financial markets are the 'globapolitans' who are the core elements in a new global capitalist class (1997: 68; 1998: 342). The owners of shares and the top industrial executives are themselves globapolitans if they are also information rich, and the whole class is embedded in impersonal systems of capital. This capitalist class exists at a global level, as the global rich of mobile executives, and is separated off from the socially excluded in the marginal sectors of the global economy. Between the two global classes are the vast majority of people with varying degrees of education and, therefore, varying opportunities within the informational economy. All experience the anxieties and uncertainties of flexible working systems, but those with less education have the most precarious employment situations (1996: 277).

Castells links this change in class structure to a change from the mass culture of advanced industrialism to the segmented culture of the informational society. Television channels have proliferated with cable and satellite broadcasting, and this has segmented television audiences according to specialist interests and concerns. There can no longer be a single and uniform national culture, only a diversified mosaic of cultural meanings. The fusion of television with computing technology has allowed broadcasting to move away from one-way communication and towards interactive and multimedia forms. Information, education, and entertainment fuse together into a single yet highly differentiated symbolic environment. Drawing on Baudrillard (1972), Castells argues that the subjectively experienced lifeworld comes to be completely and comprehensively defined through available media imagery and all forms of cultural expression come to form a single 'culture of real virtuality'.

The building of this symbolic environment completely transforms popular perceptions and experiences of both space and time. Households and places of work alike become embedded in the informational flows of real virtuality. Cities become virtual, cyber spaces as well as mere physical spaces, and there is no longer a direct relationship between the everyday activities of work, shopping, leisure, and education and the physical proximity of people. All these activities can be pursued on-line, and the 'informational city' – and, especially, the 'megacities' that form the nodes of the global web (Sassen 1991) – can no longer be understood with models such as those of the Chicago School (Park and Burgess 1925) that are appropriate to the industrial city. Each city must be seen as a 'space of flows', not a human ecology. A city is a space within which flows of information, people, and objects take place (Castells 1996: 418). As a result, the meanings of the places within which people live is transformed through a dissociation between the unifying horizon of impersonal and public cultural flows and the fragmented and disconnected aggregation of physical places.

In the same way that the city as a physical space is disrupted, so the linear conception of clock time is transformed into 'timeless time' (Castells 1996: 435). The rapid, virtually instantaneous transmission of money through the global financial system removes all remaining temporal constraints on economic activity and allows a highly flexible time management. The culture of real virtuality brings about a temporal immediacy of distant events, by bringing them instantly to the television screen. The synchrony of events is presented as a collage and any idea of temporal sequencing disappears.

Castells does not ignore sources of opposition to the global informational order. The organisations of the labour movement cease to play any significant part in oppositional politics as the old working class declines. Conflict in the network society cannot, therefore, be understood with the old model of class politics. The institutions of liberal democracy and the 'public sphere' of debate and opinion also decline (Sennett 1978) and nation states cease to be the principal forums for discussion of transnational flows and their implications. Contrary to Beck's view of sub-politics, Castells does not see the media-induced culture of real virtuality making any effective political discussion possible.

Resentment about lack of control over global flows has often led people into defensive reactions as they unite around threats that globalisation poses to their religion, nationality, ethnicity, or locality. Castells holds, however, that these cannot be adequate bases for political projects of resistance to global informationalism. Effective political opposition must be proactive and involve forms of consciousness organised around projects of radical social reconstruction, and he sees the principal challenges to the globapolitans and the system from which they benefit as coming from those engaged in environmental and feminist issues (1997: Chs 3 and 4). These originated as resistance identities, but they alone have the potential to go beyond reactive opposition to projects of reconstruction. Although Castells is not explicit about the social sources of environmentalism, it seems clear that he sees it as generated by the technological risks and hazards of globalisation affecting ever larger numbers (see Beck 1997). Those who are most opposed to the risk society are the principal recruits for environmental movements. Feminism poses a challenge to patriarchy in family and sexuality relations and arose among women experiencing a contradiction between the increased economic and educational opportunities made possible by informationalism and the persistence of patriarchal oppression. Thus, the women's movement, too, can offer a challenge to global informationalism.

FOCUS: MANUEL CASTELLS

From his early work on urbanism, Manuel Castells has become a leading theorist of globalisation, setting out his ideas in the volumes of *The Network Society* (1996, 1997, 1998). A short overview of his argument can be found in his article on 'Materials for an Exploratory Theory of the Network Society' (2000).

John Urry (2000, 2003) relies on the arguments of Castells for his account of the fragmentation of society. Globalisation has brought about a massive growth in the transnational flows of people, signs, and the physical objects that are symbolically transformed into objects of social action. People move around on business and for politics, and they travel as tourists in ever-increasing numbers and with ever greater frequency; advertising images, scientific knowledge, films, and television programmes are distributed with little regard for national borders and at ever-increasing speeds; food products, cars, weapons, and money are all exchanged and distributed on a world-wide scale and as integral elements in a larger global circulation (Lash and Urry 1994).

This reflects a 'disorganisation' of national economic, political, and cultural structures. The growing internationalisation of production and finance means that large business enterprises are far less bound to particular national territories and are able to organise their activities on a global basis. Each locality becomes an intersection point of transnational processes and its economic activities are neither integrated nor coordinated. National markets are deregulated, and national economies are decentralised and disarticulated. The expansion of service sector jobs aids this spatial de-integration, as service work needs to be far less localised than productive work (Lash and Urry 1987; see also Offe 1985).

The social institutions of modernity can no longer be confined by established national boundaries. Social life in the contemporary world is no longer organised through centralised and hierarchical constraints that operate on a purely national basis (Urry 2000: 8). The flows of people, signs, and objects transcend national boundaries, rendering them increasingly irrelevant for most practical purposes. Urry explores this 'disorganisation' of societies and the emergent 'post-organisational' world by adopting and devising concepts geared to grasping its novelty. He notes that the flow of people, objects, and signs occurs through specific channels or 'routeways'. The movement of people and objects takes place through transportation routes: air, sea, rail, and road routes that use various forms of vehicular transport for passenger and freight traffic. The movement of signs, encoded as information and images, takes place through communication channels: wire and wireless channels, both terrestrial and satellite, using both person-to-person instruments and broadcast media to convey their messages. These processes of transportation and communication are socially organised into 'scapes' (Appadurai 1986), understood as the particular fields or spheres through which human life is patterned. People, objects, and signs follow 'time-space paths' through these overlapping and intersecting scapes, forming hybrid human–machine structures (Latour and Woolgar 1979; Latour 1999; Haraway

1991). Social structures must now be recognised, more than ever before, as horizontal, rhizomatic formations. They are networks of interconnected nodes comprising specific configurations of the intersecting channels through which people, objects, and signs flow from one place to another and with no obvious starting or finishing points.

The key phase in the transition from vertical and national structures of organisation to the horizontal and global structures of 'disorganised' modernity, Urry argues, was the middle of the twentieth century. National societies were a reality through the nineteenth century and most of the twentieth century. They had, in fact, been considerably strengthened by the drive towards organised capitalism and the building of national economic policies and welfare regimes in the 1930s. However, the institutions of national societies declined substantially during the second half of the century as capitalist production and finance extended more deeply to the global level and nation states lost power relative to international and transnational agencies. From around 1990, the development of new information and communications technologies began the complete transformation of modern structures. The social structures that formerly defined and sustained territorial integrity and solidarity became more 'fluid', more subject to frequent transformation. They became, therefore, less compelling and less constraining for those living in particular places. People were no longer socialised into a commitment to or acceptance of stable and quasi-permanent national structures. As Bauman argues, there has been an individualisation of human existence as societal bonds are weakened and individuals are 'liberated' to cope with the consequences of disorganised global scapes.

The transnational flows that constitute these scapes define a global space that is now the paramount reality for all who live in the modern world. This global space has no central structure and cannot be conceptualised as a global 'order'. Rather, it comprises 'dissipative structures, islands of new order within a general sea of disorder' (Urry 2003: 101). These 'islands' in the Foucauldian 'archipelago' are the results of the 'glocalisation' that Roland Robertson (1992) has seen as an integral feature of globalisation. Signs, flowing through the new channels of communication, become 'dematerialised from place' and so 'spatially indifferent' (Urry 2003: 84, 85). It is possible for anywhere to become a focus for network flows. Once such foci occur, however, they become gravitational points of attraction that concentrate and condense further flows. In the spirit of Coste (1899), Castells sees global spaces developing with multiple centres, each of which 'peripheralises' other parts of the space as it consolidates its own centrality. Such centres may become foci of opposition and resistance as often as they become foci of power, but always such processes are localised – fragmented – to a multiplicity of centres. Transnational structures and social movements exist as 'virtual communities', 'deterritorialised global entities', that are sustained by the flow of people, objects, and signs from one locality to another through television and the internet and that depend also upon the intermittent coming together of their members in particular places.

Urry's analysis sees particular importance in the movement of people across the world (see his early analysis of travel in Urry 1990 and in Chapter 10 of Lash and Urry 1994, significantly expanded in Urry 1995). There have been significant transformations in 'corporeal travel' and the associated 'object mobility' that runs along with this. The massive growth of car ownership and increasing ease of air transport have produced a greater mobility of people across national borders. Much of this travel is business-related, but the real growth in the advanced societies has been in travel as 'tourism'. International travel now accounts for a half of all world trade by value and for 10 per cent of both global employment and gross domestic product. Trade in producer and consumer goods has been supplemented by the movement of objects along with travellers in the form of means of transport and as 'souvenirs' of their travel. People spend more of their time 'on the move' and objects have less of a home base than ever before.

A key part has been played not only by improvements in transport technologies but also by developments in communications technologies that allow people to keep in touch with each other while on the move. The mobile telephone and the laptop computer allow virtually instantaneous communication anywhere in the world, and the availability of satellite television means that the traveller need not feel 'cut off' from familiar images and sources of information. Urry sees these technological changes as also bringing about completely new forms of movement, which he terms 'imaginative mobility' and 'virtual travel'. Television images allow people to visit distant places in their minds and without any physical movement from their own couch. Images of people and places that are physically far removed can be brought into their immediate field of view and so become as much a part of their knowledge of the world as those that they directly encounter. Vicarious participation in distant events becomes just as meaningful as face-to-face participation in local events, and the one sustains the other. This imaginative mobility – the mobility of images within the social imaginary – is complemented by the virtual travel made possible by the development of computer networks. Through e-mail and the internet – which are increasingly integrated with television and with other electronic systems – households and workplaces are tied into extensive cyber networks of communication and virtual interaction. Greater volumes of interaction and larger amounts of knowledge are now generated and transmitted through such channels than through more established routeways of communication. People's experience of the world is increasingly mediatised through such flows.

This transformation of movement is seen by Urry as leading to an altered conception of and experience of time and space. Each scape has its own characteristic temporality, and so each individual experiences multiple (perhaps contradictory) speeds of movement. Early modernity involved the dominance of mechanical 'clock time', the rationalised form of measurement through which the passage and use of time could be calculated and human activity could be monitored, regulated, and disciplined (Urry 2000: 114). Time and money were treated as analogues for one another, both being regarded as measurable resources, because the uses of time are geared to the availability and use of money. The expansion of monetary and financial systems, therefore, went hand in hand with the expansion of coordinated schedules, timetables, and other temporal regimes. The current phase of modernity, however, is one in which there can no longer be any predominant and all-embracing temporal framework, except at a very abstract level. There are, instead, the varying and competing times associated with the different scapes that people encounter, and these coexist with a generalised increase in the 'speed' or pace of social life (Virilio 1986). This results in fragmentary and chaotic perceptions of the sequences and flows of events, which are no longer structured around a linear conception of time. Citing the earlier work on experienced time of Halbwachs (1925) and Gurvitch (1964), Urry holds that 'instantaneous time' replaces clock time in people's everyday experience (2000: 126).

Spatially, human populations and their social activities have been detached from specific localities. Social life is no longer constrained by local environmental conditions, and environmental determination loses its explanatory power. Industrialism had extended people's 'imagined communities' (Anderson 1983) from the local to a metropolitan and national scale (Stacey 1969; Bell and Newby 1976), but the new communications, technologies have extended them to the transnational level and allowed them to become virtual solidarities. Localities are embedded in the virtual realities of cyber space and many can be regarded as 'non-places', such as airport terminals and railway stations, which exist solely in order to mediate global flows. Virtual communities are matters of choice and are entered into and left by people who are constantly on the move. Such floating solidarities are the bases for the new social movements concerned with lifestyle, environment, peace, and gender.

The transnational scapes of the globalised world do not generate only the flows of people, objects, and signs. They also generate a flow of the hazards and risks identified by Beck as a crucial feature of contemporary modernity. Chemical leakages, epidemics, nuclear fallout, and environmental pollution flow easily across the world thanks to the fast routeways opened up in the disorganisation of modernity (Macnaghten and Urry 1998).

Urry highlights important changes in nation states, which are not becoming simply powerless ciphers but are transforming their power relations. Some powers have been transferred or lost – to the EU and other international agencies – and states have responded by engaging with transnational flows and becoming intermediaries between peripheral areas and network centres. States develop more inter-state relations with each other, building yet further levels of transnational flow. They have, however, experienced an altered relationship with their own citizens. Urry notes that sociological accounts of citizenship (such as Marshall 1949) have tended to be 'societal' or national in character. In the global space, however, people have developed a stronger commitment and orientation to the transnational entities and practices in which they are involved. Nation states no longer contain their interests or solidarities. Rights are demanded of various national and international bodies as 'universal' human rights, rather than rights dependent upon a particular national identity. Demands for rights and political representation at this level, he argues, marks – as recognised by Hobhouse (1911) – an implicit demand for 'post-national' citizenship (Soysal 1994).

Urry draws out what he sees as the implications of these changes for sociology itself. Sociology developed along with modernity, and its central object of analysis – 'society' – was constructed as a way of grasping the building of modern institutions. Sociology's concept of the social, Urry argues, all but equated it with such nationally organised entities. When sociologists explored the nature of the autonomously 'social' reality, irreducible to individual minds and actions, they did so through a concept of national 'society'. This tendency was especially marked in the American functionalist sociology that dominated sociological debates world-wide for much of the twentieth century. The demise of such societies requires nothing less than the abandonment of conventional sociological theories and the construction of new accounts using concepts of mobility, fluidity, and global complexity. Urry undoubtedly has a point, but it is, perhaps, overstated. By no means all of the classical sociologists, as I have shown in Chapters 3 and 4, confined their attention to hermetically sealed national societies. Even some of the most strident organicists recognised the interdependence and interrelations of societies, and many paid explicit attention to their transnational relations. It is true, however, that empirical work has often failed to grasp the importance of the global level of transnational flows in structuring social processes.

In this book I have outlined and illustrated the numerous competing approaches to sociology. In reviewing them historically and cross-nationally, I have sought to bring out the convergences and interdependencies among them. Implicit in my discussion has been the argument outlined in Chapter 1, that the history of sociology is marked by frequent rediscoveries and restatements of key themes and that the differences among theoretical positions are rarely as great as is sometimes assumed. In particular, I have tried to stress that it is rarely a matter of having to choose between rival theoretical approaches as the sole defensible strategies for undertaking sociological research. Least of all is it necessary to advocate the absolute validity of one theorist above all others. Theoretical differences exist, for the most part, because theorists have been concerned with exploring different sets of issues, and all theoretical approaches can, in principle, find their place within a comprehensive sociology. So long as theories are able to secure empirical support for their central contentions, they must be recognised as having made a lasting contribution to the sum of sociological knowledge. It is in this light, too, that a historical approach to sociological theory can bring out areas of intellectual advance. The history of sociology is not simply a succession of divergent intellectual positions but shows real progress in understanding in which successive writers are able to build on the achievements of others. This is often lost sight of in discussions of competing schools of thought and the 'great thinkers' of the sociological tradition, and the present text has concentrated on the similarities and interconnections among theorists in order to rectify this unbalanced view. The discussion of the central institutional characteristics of modernity, and the possibility of a post-modern social order, brings this out very well. Often seen as radical critics of conventional sociology, writers who engage with post-modernist ideas are involved in a common effort of intellectual understanding and their powerful insights make sense only if seen in relation to wider views of modernity. Engagement with post-modernism is merely the latest stage in the broadening and deepening of sociological understanding, and the arguments of a Tocqueville, for example, are no less relevant or important than those of a Baudrillard. It is in this sense that I can reiterate my rejection of Alfred Whitehead's claim that 'a science which hesitates to forget its founders is lost': a science becomes truly lost when it does forget or disregard its founders and the many others who have contributed to making it what it is today.

NOTES

1. The first-known usage of the term 'post-modernism' was in Toynbee (1934–9), though he did not use it in the sense given here. The term was first used in its current sense by Ihab Hassan (1971). Jencks (1977) later set out an influential view. Spengler (1918–22: 428) did not use the word but predicted that the end of the twentieth century would see the end of modern art and the beginning of a period of 'meaningless, empty, artificial, pretentious architecture and ornament. Imitation of archaic and exotic motives'. For a general review of debates see Best and Kellner (1991).

2. The English translation of Beck's book on the risk society (Beck 1986) includes a revised translation of a German essay of 1993 in place of the original Chapter 3. The English translation of *The Reinvention of Politics* (Beck 1993) includes a translation of a 1996 paper in place of the early chapters of the German edition. For convenience I refer to both books by their original dates of publication.

Bibliography

In the chapters of this book and in the bibliography, works have been cited by the date of first publication or, in some cases, date of composition. The bibliography also shows the date of the actual edition or translation consulted where this differs.

Abel, Theodor 1929. *Systematic Sociology in Germany*. New York: Octagon Books, 1965.

Aberle, David F., Cohen, Albert K., Davis, Alison K., Levy, Marion J., and Sutton, Francis X. 1950. 'The Functional Prerequisites of a Society'. *Ethics* 60: 100–11.

Adler, Alfred 1914. 'Individual Psychology, Its Assumptions and Its Results' in Alfred Adler, *The Practice and Theory of Individual Psychology*. London: Routledge and Kegan Paul, 1923.

Adler, Alfred 1928. *Understanding Human Nature*. London: George Allen and Unwin.

Adorno, Theodor 1938. 'On the Fetish Character of Music and the Regression of Listening' in Theodor Adorno, *The Culture Industry* (selected and edited by Jay Bernstein). London: Routledge, 1991.

Adorno, Theodor 1952–3. 'The Stars Down to Earth' in Theodor Adorno, *The Stars Down to Earth* (edited by Stephen Crook). London: Routledge, 1994.

Adorno, Theodor 1964. 'Culture Industry Reconsidered' in Theodor Adorno, *The Culture Industry* (selected and edited by Jay Bernstein). London: Routledge.

Adorno, Theodor, Frenkel-Brunswick, Else, Levinson, Daniel J., and Sanford, R.N. 1950. *The Authoritarian Personality*. New York: Harper.

Adorno, Theodor and Horkheimer, Max 1944. *Dialectic of Enlightenment*. London: Verso, 1979.

Albrow, Martin 1970. *Bureaucracy*. London: Macmillan.

Alexander, Jeffrey 1982–3. *Theoretical Logic in Sociology* (4 vol). Berkeley: University of California Press.

Alexander, Jeffrey (ed.) 1985. *Neofunctionalism*. Beverly Hills: Sage.

Alexander, Jeffrey 1988. *Action and Its Environments*. New York: Columbia University Press.

Allardt, Erik 2000. 'A Sociologist Relating Nature and Culture', *Acta Sociologica* 43: 299–306.

Althusser, Louis 1962a. 'Contradiction and Overdetermination' in Louis Althusser *For Marx*. Harmondsworth: Allen Lane.

Althusser, Louis 1962b. 'Notes on a Materialist Theatre' in Louis Althusser, *For Marx*. Harmondsworth: Allen Lane.

Althusser, Louis 1963. 'On the Materialist Dialectic' in Louis Althusser, *For Marx*. Harmondsworth: Allen Lane.

Althusser, Louis 1965. 'The Object of Capital' in Louis Althusser, and Étienne Balibar, *Reading Capital*. London: New Left Books, 1970.

Althusser, Louis 1971. *Lenin and Philosophy and Other Essays*. London: New Left Books.

Amin, Samir 1973. *Unequal Development*. New York: Monthly Review Press, 1976.

Ammon, Otto 1895. *Die Gesellschaftsordnung und Ihr Natürlichen Grundlagen*. Jena.

Anderson, Benedict 1983. *Imagined Communities*. London: Verso.

Anderson, Perry 1974. *Lineages of the Absolutist State*. London: New Left Books.

Ang, Ien 1985. *Watching Dallas*. London: Methuen.

Appadurai, Arjun (ed.) 1986. *The Social Life of Things*. Cambridge: Cambridge University Press.

Archer, Margaret S. 1995. *Realist Social Theory: The Morphogenetic Approach*. Cambridge: Cambridge University Press.

Ardigò, Roberto 1870. *Psicologia come Scienza Positiva*. Mantua: V. Guastalla.

Ardigò, Roberto 1879a. 'La Morale dei Positivisti' in Roberto Ardigò, *Opere filosofiche,* Volume 3. Padua: Draghi, 1900.

Ardigò, Roberto 1879b. 'Sociologia' in Roberto Ardigò, *Opere filosofiche,* Volume 4. Padua: Draghi, 1886.

Ardigò, Roberto 1893. *La scienza dell'educazione*. Padua: Draghi.

Ardrey, Robert 1961. *African Genesis*. London: Collins.

Ardrey, Robert 1967. *The Territorial Imperative*. London: Collins.

Ardrey, Robert 1970. *The Social Contract*. London: Collins.

Asch, Solomon E. 1951. 'Effects of Group Pressure upon the Modification and Distortion of Judgement' in Harold Guetzkow (ed.) *Groups, Leadership and Men*. Pittsburgh: Carnegie Press.

Ashby, W. Ross 1956. *An Introduction to Cybernetics*. New York: Wiley.

Ashton, Trevor S. 1948. *The Industrial Revolution, 1760–1830*. Oxford: Oxford University Press.

Astell, Mary 1694. *A Serious Proposal to the Ladies for the Advancement of Their True and Greatest Influence*.

Aston, Michael and Bond, James 1976. *The Landscape of Towns*. London: Allen Sutton, 1987.

Azcárate, Gumersindo de 1881 *Programa de sociología*. Madrid: Ateneo de Madrid.

Bachofen, Johann J. 1861. *Das Mutterrecht*. Basel: Benno Schwabe.

Bachrach, Peter and Baratz, Morton S. 1962. 'The Two Faces of Power' in John Scott (ed.) *Power*, Volume 2. London: Routledge, 1994.

Bachrach, Peter and Baratz, Morton S. 1963. 'Decisions and Nondecisions: An Analytical Framework' in John Scott (ed.) *Power*, Volume 2. London: Routledge, 1994.

Baehr, Peter 2002. *Founders, Classics, Canons*. Beverly Hills: Sage.

Bagehot, Walter 1872. *Physics and Politics*. London: Kegan Paul, Trench, Trübner, 1905.

Bailey, Frederick George 1969. *Strategems and Spoils*. Boulder, Colo.: Westview Press.

Bain, Alexander 1855. *Treatise on the Mind: The Senses and the Intellect*. Bristol: Thoemmes Press, 1998.

Bain, Alexander 1859. *Treatise on the Mind: The Emotions and the Will*. Bristol: Thoemmes Press, 1998.

Baker, Alan R.H. 2003. *Geography and History*. Cambridge: Cambridge University Press.

Bakhtin, Mikhail 1929. *Problems of Dostoyevsky's Poetics*. Manchester: Manchester University Press, 1984.

Bakhtin, Mikhail 1940. *Rabelais and His World*. Bloomington: Indiana University Press, 1984.

Bakunin, Mikhail 1873. *Statism and Anarchy*. Cambridge: Cambridge University Press, 1990.

Balakrishnan, Gopal 2000. *The Enemy: An Intellectual Portrait of Carl Schmitt*. London: Verso.

Baldwin, J.M. 1897. *Social and Ethical Interpretation in Mental Development*. New York: Macmillan.

Balint, Michael 1959. *Thrills and Regressions*. London: Hogarth Press.

Barker, Pat 1992. *Regeneration*. Harmondsworth: Penguin.

Barrows, Harlan Harland 1923. 'Geography as Human Ecology'. *Annals of the Association of American Geographers* 13: 1–14.

Barth, Fredrik 1959. *Political Leadership among Swat Pathans*. London: Athlone Press.

Barth, Fredrik 1966. *Models of Social Organization*. London: Royal Anthropological Institute.

Barthes, Roland 1957. *Mythologies*. London: Paladin, 1973.

Barthes, Roland 1964. 'Elements of Semiology' in Roland Barthes, *Writing Degree Zero and Elements of Semiology*. Boston: Beacon Press, 1968.

Barthes, Roland 1966. 'Introduction to the Structural Analysis of Narratives' in Roland Barthes, *Image-Music-Text*. London: Fontana, 1977.

Barthes, Roland 1967. *The Fashion System*. New York: Hill and Wang, 1983.

Bastian, Adolf 1860. *Der Mensch in Geschichte* (3 vols). Leipzig.

Bastian, Adolf 1881. *Die Vorgeschichte der Ethnologie*. Berlin.

Bateson, Gregory 1972. *Steps to an Ecology of Mind*. New York: Balantine Books.

Baudrillard, Jean 1968. *The System of Objects*. Paris: Denoël-Gouthier. London: Verso, 2002.

Baudrillard, Jean 1970. *The Consumer Society*. London: Sage, 1998.

Baudrillard, Jean 1972. *For a Critique of the Political Economy of the Sign*. St Louis: Telos Press, 1981.

Baudrillard, Jean 1973. *The Mirror of Production*. St Louis: Telos Press, 1975.

Baudrillard, Jean 1976. *Symbolic Exchange and Death*. London: Sage, 1993.

Baudrillard, Jean 1978. *In the Shadow of the Silent Majorities*. New York: Semiotext(e), 1983.

Baudrillard, Jean 1979. *Seduction*. New York: St Martin's Press, 1990.

Baudrillard, Jean 1981. *Simulations*. New York: Semiotext(e), 1983.

Baudrillard, Jean 1983. *Fatal Strategies*. London: Pluto, 1999.

Bauman, Zygmunt 1989. *Modernity and the Holocaust*. Cambridge: Polity Press.

Bauman, Zygmunt 1992. *Intimations of Postmodernity*. London: Routledge.

Bauman, Zygmunt 1998. *Globalization*. Cambridge: Polity Press.

Bauman, Zygmunt 2000. *Liquid Modernity*. Cambridge: Polity Press.

Bauman, Zygmunt 2001. *The Individualized Society*. Cambridge: Polity Press.

Bauman, Zygmunt 2002. *Society under Siege*. Cambridge: Polity Press.

Beauvoir, Simone de 1949. *The Second Sex*. London: Jonathan Cape, 1953.

Beck, Ulrich 1986. *Risk Society: Towards a New Modernity*. London: Sage, 1992.

Beck, Ulrich 1988. *Ecological Politics in an Age of Risk*. Cambridge: Polity Press, 1995.

Beck, Ulrich 1993. *The Reinvention of Politics*. Cambridge: Polity Press, 1997.

Beck, Ulrich 1997. *What Is Globalization?* Cambridge: Polity Press, 2000.

Beck, Ulrich 1999. *World Risk Society*. Cambridge: Polity Press.

Beck, Ulrich and Beck-Gernsheim, Elizabeth 1995. *The Normal Chaos of Love*. Cambridge: Polity Press.

Becker, Gary S. 1976. *The Economic Approach to Human Behaviour*. Chicago: University of Chicago Press.

Becker, Gary S. 1981. *A Treatise on the Family*. Cambridge, Mass.: Harvard University Press.

Becker, Howard S. 1960. 'Notes on the Concept of Commitment' in Howard S. Becker, *Sociological Work*. Chicago: University of Chicago Press, 1970.

Becker, Howard S. 1963. *Outsiders: Studies in the Sociology of Deviance*. New York: Free Press.

Becker, Howard S., Greer, Blanche and Hughes, Everett Cherrington 1961. *Boys in White*. Chicogo: University of Chicago Press.

Beer, Stafford 1959. *Cybernetics and Management*. London: English Universities Press.

Beesley, Edward 1868. *The Social Future of the Working Classes*. London: Reeves.

Bell, Colin and Newby, Howard 1976. *Community Studies*. London: George Allen and Unwin.

Bell, Daniel 1957. 'The Breakup of Family Capitalism' in Daniel Bell, *The End of Ideology: The Exhaustion of Political Ideas in the Fifties*. New York: Free Press, 1961.

Bell, Daniel 1973. *The Coming of Post-Industrial Society*. New York: Basic Books.

Bell, Daniel 1976. *The Cultural Contradictions of Capitalism*. New York: Basic Books, 1976.

Bell, Michael Meyerfield 1998. *An Invitation to Environmental Sociology*. Thousand Oaks, Calif.: Pine Forge.

Bellamy, Richard 1987. *Modern Italian Social Theory*. Oxford: Basil Blackwell.

Bellini, Luigi 1934. *Saggi di una teoria generale della società*. Milan: Vita e Pensiero.

Bendix, Reinhard 1962. *Max Weber: An Intellectual Portrait*. New York: Anchor Books.

Bendix, Reinhard 1964. *Nation Building and Citizenship: Studies of Our Changing Social Order*. Berkeley: University of California Press.

Benedict, Ruth 1934. *Patterns of Culture*. London: Routledge, 1965.

Benjamin, Walter 1935. 'The Work of Art in the Age of Mechanical Reproduction' in Walter Benjamin, *Illuminations*. New York: Harcourt Brace Jovanovich, 1968.

Bentham, Jeremy 1776. 'A Fragment on Government' in Jeremy Bentham, *A Fragment on Government and an Introduction to the Principles of Morals and Legislation* (edited by Wilfrid Harrison). Oxford: Basil Blackwell, 1948.

Bentham, Jeremy 1789. 'Introduction to the Principles of Morals and Legislation' in Jeremy Bentham, *A Fragment on Government and an Introduction to the Principles of Morals and Legislation* (edited by Wilfrid Harrison). Oxford: Basil Blackwell, 1948.

Bentley, Arthur F. 1908. *The Process of Government: A Study of Social Pressure*. New Brunswick, NJ: Transaction Publishers.

Benton, Ted. 1993 *Natural Relations*. London: Verso.

Benton, Ted. 1999. 'Evolutionary Psychology and Social Science: A New Paradigm or Just the Same Old Reductionism'. *Advances in Human Ecology* 8: 65–98.

Berger, John 1972. *Ways of Seeing*. Harmondsworth: Penguin.

Berger, Peter L. 1969. *The Social Reality of Religion* [*The Sacred Canopy*]. London: Faber and Faber.

Berger, Peter L. and Luckmann, Thomas 1966. *The Social Construction of Reality*. Harmondsworth: Allen Lane, 1971.

Berger, Peter and Pullberg, Stanley 1966. 'Reification and the Sociological Critique of Consciousness'. *New Left Review* 35: 56–77.

Berkes, Niyazi (ed.) 1959. *Turkish Nationalism and Western Civilization: Selected Essays of Ziya Gökalp*. London: George Allen and Unwin.

Bernard, Louis L. 1925. 'A Classification of Environments'. *American Journal of Sociology* 31: 318–32.

Bernstein, Eduard 1899. *The Preconditions of Socialism* [*Evolutionary Socialism*]. Cambridge: Cambridge University Press, 1993.

Bertalanffy, Ludwig von 1950. 'An Outline of General Systems Theory'. *British Journal for the Philosophy of Science* 1: 139–64.

Bertalanffy, Ludwig von 1968. *General System Theory: Foundations, Development, Applications*. New York.

Bertalanffy, Ludwig von Hempel, Carl G., Bass, R.E., and Jonas, H. 1951. 'General System Theory: A New Approach to Unity of Science'. *Human Biology* 23: 302–61.

Besnard, Philippe 1983. *The Sociological Domain: The Durkheimians and the Founding of French Sociology*. Cambridge: Cambridge University Press.

Best, Steven and Kellner, Douglas 1991. *Postmodern Theory*. London: Macmillan.

Biggart, John, Dudley, Peter and King, Francis (eds) 1998 *Alexander Bogdanov and the Origins of Systems Thinking in Russia*. Aldershot: Ashgate.

Billington, James H. 1958. *Mikhailovsky and Russian Populism*. Oxford: Clarendon Press.

Binns, David 1978. *Beyond the Sociology of Conflict*. London: Macmillan.

Bion, Wilfred 1961. *Experiences in Groups*. London: Tavistock.

Bion, Wilfred 1963. *Elements of Psycho-Analysis*. London: Heinemann.

Blackburn, Robin O. 1998. *The Making of New World Slavery*. London: Verso.

Blackmore, Susan 1999. *The Meme Machine*. Oxford: Oxford University Press.

Blau, Peter M. 1964. *Exchange and Power in Social Life*. New York: John Wiley.

Bloch, Maurice 1931. *Les caractères originaux de l'histoire rurale française* (2 vols). Paris.

Bloch, Maurice 1938. *Feudal Society* (2 vols). London: Routledge and Kegan Paul, 1961.

Blood, Robert and Wolfe, Donald M. 1960. *Husbands and Wives*. New York: Free Press.

Blouet, Brian W. 1987. *Halford Mackinder: A Biography*. College Station: Texas A. and M. University Press.

Blouet, Brian W. 2001. *Geopolitics and Globalization in the Twentieth Century*. London: Reaktion Books.

Blumer, Herbert 1937. 'Social Psychology' in Emerson P. Schmidt (ed.) *Man and Society*. Englewood Cliffs, NJ: Prentice-Hall.

Blumer, Herbert 1962. 'Society as Symbolic Interaction' in Herbert Blumer, *Symbolic Interactionism*. Englewood Cliffs, NJ: Prentice-Hall, 1969.

Blumer, Herbert 1966. 'Sociological Implications of the Thought of George Herbert Mead' in Herbert Blumer, *Symbolic Interactionism*. Englewood Cliffs, NJ: Prentice-Hall, 1969.

Blumer, Herbert 1969. 'The Methodological Position of Symbolic Interactionism' in Herbert Blumer, *Symbolic Interactionism*. Englewood Cliffs, NJ: Prentice-Hall, 1969.

Boas, Franz 1911. *The Mind of Modern Man*. New York: Macmillan.

Boden, Deirdre and Zimmerman, Don H. (eds) 1990. *Talk and Social Structure: Studies in Ethnomethodology and Conversational Analysis*. Cambridge: Polity Press.

Bodin, Jean 1576. *Les six livres de la République*. Paris: Fayard, 1986.

Bogdanov, Aleksandr 1897. *A Short Course in Economics*. London: Communist Party of Great Britain, 1923.

Bogdanov, Aleksandr 1904–6. *Empiriomonism*. St Petersburg: Dorovatovskage i Charushnikova.

Bogdanov, Aleksandr 1905. *Red Star: The First Bolshevik Utopia*. Bloomington: Indiana University Press, 1984.

Bogdanov, Aleksandr 1913–22. 'Tektologia' in Peter Dudley (ed.) *Bogdanov's Tektology*. Hull: University of Hull, Centre for System Studies, 1996.

Böhm-Bawerk, Eugen von 1896. *Karl Marx and the Close of His System*, trans. 1898. New York: A.M. Kelley, 1966.

Boltanski, Luc 1993. *Distant Suffering: Morality, Media, and Politics*. Cambridge: Cambridge University Press, 1999.

Boltanski, Luc and Chiapello, Ève 1999. *Le nouvel esprit du capitalisme*. Paris: Gallimard.

Boltanski, Luc and Thévenot, Laurent 1991. *De la justification: Les économies de la grandeur*. Paris: Gallimard.

Bonald, Louis de 1796. 'La théorie du pouvoir politique et religieux' in Louis de Bonald, *Ouevres complètes,* Volume 1. Paris: Abbé Migne, 1859.

Bonald, Louis de 1826. *Sur les premiers objets des connaissances morales*. Paris: D'Adrien Le Clere.

Bonger, Willem 1905. *Criminality and Economic Conditions*. Boston: Little, Brown, 1916.

Bonger, Willem 1913. *Geloof en Misdaad*. Leiden.

Booth, Charles 1901–2. *Life and Labour of the People of London* (17 vols). London: Macmillan.

Bosanquet, Bernard 1897. *Psychology of the Moral Self*. London: Macmillan.

Bosanquet, Bernard 1899. *The Philosophical Theory of the State*. London: Macmillan.

Bosanquet, Bernard 1921. *The Meeting of Extremes in Contemporary Philosophy*. London: Macmillan.

Bosanquet, Helen 1898. *Rich and Poor*. London: Macmillan.

Bosanquet, Helen 1902. *Strength of the People*. London: Macmillan.

Bosanquet, Helen 1906. *The Family*. London: Macmillan.

Bottomore, Tom and Brym, Robert J. (eds) 1989. *The Capitalist Class*. Hemel Hempstead: Harvester Wheatsheaf.

Boucher, David (ed.) 1997 *The British Idealists*. Cambridge: Cambridge University Press.

Boucher, David and Vincent, Andrew 1993. *A Radical Hegelian: The Political and Social Philosophy of Henry Jones*. Cardiff: University of Wales Press.

Bouglé, Celestin 1899. *Les idées égalitaires*. Paris: F. Alcan.
Bouglé, Celestin 1904. *La démocratie devant la science*. Paris: F. Alcan.
Bouglé, Celestin 1908. *Essays on the Caste System*. Cambridge: Cambridge University Press, 1971.
Bouglé, Celestin 1922. *The Evolution of Values*. New York: Augustus M. Kelley, 1970.
Bourdieu, Pierre 1972. *Outline of a Theory of Practice*. Cambridge: Cambridge University Press, 1977.
Bourdieu, Pierre 1979. *Distinction: A Social Critique of the Judgment of Taste*. London: Routledge, 1984.
Bourdieu, Pierre 1989. *The State Nobility*. Cambridge: Polity Press, 1998.
Bourdieu, Pierre 1994. *Practical Reason*. Cambridge: Polity Press, 1998.
Bourdieu, Pierre 1998. *Masculine Domination*. Cambridge: Polity Press, 2002.
Bowlby, John 1965. *Child Care and the Growth of Love* (2nd edn). Harmondsworth: Penguin.
Bowlby, John 1969–80. *Attachment and Loss* (3 vols). London: Hogarth Press.
Bradley, Francis Herbert 1876. 'My Station and Its Duties' in Francis H. Bradley, *Ethical Studies*. New York: Bobbs-Merrill, 1951.
Bradley, Francis Herbert 1893. *Appearance and Reality*. London: Macmillan.
Brady, Robert A. 1943. *Business as a System of Power*. New York: Columbia University Press.
Braudel, Fernand 1949. *The Mediterranean and the Mediterranean World in the Age of Philip II*. London: Collins, 1972–3.
Braudel, Fernand 1967. *Capitalism and Material Life, 1400–1800*. London: Weidenfeld and Nicolson, 1973.
Braudel, Fernand 1979a. *The Perspective of the World*. London: Collins, 1984.
Braudel, Fernand 1979b. *The Structures of Everyday Life*. London: Collins, 1981.
Braudel, Fernand 1979c. *The Wheels of Commerce*. London: Collins, 1982.
Braudel, Fernand 1986–7. *The Identity of France*. London: Collins, 1988 and 1990.
Braverman, Harry 1974. *Labor and Monopoly Capitalism*. New York: Monthly Review Press.
Brentano, Franz 1874. *Psychology from an Empirical Standpoint*. London: Routledge and Kegan Paul, 1974.
Breuer, Josef and Freud, Sigmund 1895. *Studies in Hysteria*. Harmondsworth: Penguin, 1974.
Bridges, John 1866. *The Unity of Comte's Life and Doctrine*. London.
Brownmiller, Susan 1975. *Against Our Will*. Harmondsworth: Penguin, 1976.
Brubaker, Rogers 1984. *The Limits of Rationality*. London: Unwin.
Bruner, Jerome 1960. *The Process of Education*. Cambridge, Mass.: Harvard University Press.
Bruner, Jerome 1966. *Toward a Theory of Instruction*. Cambridge, Mass.: Belknap Press.
Bruner, Jerome 1991. *Acts of Meaning*. Cambridge, Mass.: Harvard University Press.
Bruner, Jerome, Goodnow, Jacqueline and Austin, George 1956. *A Study in Thinking*. New York: Wiley.
Brunhes, Jean 1910. *Human Geography*. Chicago: Rand McNally, 1920.
Buckle, H.T. 1857–61. *History of Civilization in England*, Volume 1. London: Watts and Co, 1930.
Buckley, Walter 1967. *Sociology and Modern Systems Theory*. Englewood Cliffs, NJ: Prentice-Hall.
Bukharin, Nikolai Ivanovich 1915. *Imperialism and World Economy*. London: Merlin Press, 1987.
Bukharin, Nikolai Ivanovich 1919. *The Economic Theory of the Leisure Class*. London: Martin Lawrence, 1927.
Bukharin, Nikolai Ivanovich 1920. 'The Economics of the Transition Period' in Nikolai Ivanovich Bukharin (ed.) *Nikolai I. Bukharin: The Politics and Economics of the Transition Period* (edited by Kenneth J. Tarbuck). London: Routledge and Kegan Paul, 1979.
Bukharin, Nikolai Ivanovich 1921. *Historical Materialism: A System of Sociology*. New York: International Publishers, 1925.
Burke, Edmund 1790. *Reflections on the Revolution in France*. Harmondsworth: Penguin, 1968.

Burke, Kenneth 1935. *Permanence and Change*. New York: New Republic.

Burkhardt, Jacob 1860. *The Civilisation of the Renaissance in Europe*. New York.

Burnham, James 1941. *The Managerial Revolution*. New York: John Day.

Burnham, James 1943. *The Machiavellians*. New York: John Day.

Bury, J.B. 1955. *The Idea of Progress: An Inquiry into Its Origin and Growth*. New York: Dover.

Byrne, David 1998. *Complexity Theory and the Social Sciences*. London: Routledge.

Cabanis, Pierre Jean Georges 1802. *Rapport du physique et du moral de l'homme*. Paris: J.-B. Baillière, 1844.

Caird, Edward 1885. *The Social Philosophy and Religion of Comte*. Glasgow: James Maclehose, 1893.

Calvet, Louis-Jean 1990. *Roland Barthes: A Biography*. Cambridge: Polity Press, 1996.

Camic, Charles 1983. *Experience and Enlightenment*. Chicago: University of Chicago Press.

Cannon, Walter Bradford 1932. *The Wisdom of the Body*. New York: W.W. Norton.

Carey, Henry C. 1858–9. *The Principles of Social Science* (3 vols). New York: Augustus Kelley, 1963.

Carey, Henry C. 1872. *The Unity of Law: As Exhibited in the Relation of Physical, Social, Mental, and Moral Science*. New York: Augustus M. Kelley, 1967.

Carlyle, Thomas 1837. *The French Revolution*. Oxford: Oxford University Press, 1989.

Carlyle, Thomas 1843. *Past and Present*. London: J.M. Dent, 1912.

Carrier, James G. 1994. *Gifts and Commodities: Exchange and Western Capitalism since 1700*. London: Routledge.

Cartwright, D. and Zander, A. (eds) 1953 *Group Dynamics*. London: Tavistock.

Carver, Terrell 1981. *Engels*. Oxford: Oxford University Press.

Carver, Thomas Nixon 1924. *The Economy of Human Energy*. New York: Macmillan.

Castells, Manuel 1972. *The Urban Question*. London: Edward Arnold, 1977.

Castells, Manuel 1978. *City, Class and Power*. London: Macmillan.

Castells, Manuel 1983. *The City and the Grassroots*. Berkeley: University of California Press.

Castells, Manuel 1996. *The Rise of the Network Society, Volume 1 of the Information Age: Economy, Society and Culture*. Oxford: Blackwell Publishers.

Castells, Manuel 1997. *The Power of Identity, Volume 2 of the Information Age: Economy, Society and Culture*. Oxford: Blackwell Publishers.

Castells, Manuel 1998. *End of Millenium, Volume 3 of the Information Age: Economy, Society and Culture*. Oxford: Blackwell Publishers.

Castells, Manuel 2000. 'Materials for an Exploratory Theory of the Network Society', *British Journal of Sociology* 51 (1): 5–24.

Certeau, Michel de 1974. *The Practice of Everyday Life*. Berkeley: University of California Press, 1984.

Chalupný, Emanuel 1916–22. *Sociologie* (5 vols). Prague: Melantrich.

Chamberlain, H.S. 1899. *Foundations of the Nineteenth Century*, 2 vols. Massachusetts: Elibron, 2003.

Chandler, Alfred D. 1963. *Strategy and Structure*. Cambridge, Mass.: Belknap Press.

Charon, Joel M. 1979. *Symbolic Interactionism*. Englewood Cliffs, NJ: Prentice-Hall.

Childe, V. Gordon 1936. *Man Makes Himself* (4th edn). London: Watts and Co., 1965.

Childe, V. Gordon 1941. *What Happened in History?* London: Book Club Associates, 1973.

Chodorow, Nancy 1978. *The Reproduction of Mothering: Psychoanalysis and the Sociology of Gender*. Berkeley: University of California Press.

Chomsky, Noam 1957. *Syntactic Structures*. The Hague: Mouton.

Cicourel, Aaron V. 1967. *The Social Organisation of Juvenile Justice*. New York: Wiley.

Cicourel, Aaron V. 1968. 'The Acquisition of Social Structure: Towards a Developmental Sociology of Language and Meaning' in Aaron V. Cicourel, *Cognitive Sociology*. Harmondsworth: Penguin, 1973.

Cicourel, Aaron V. 1970. 'Generative Semantics and the Structure of Social Interaction' in Aaron V. Cicourel, *Cognitive Sociology*. Harmondsworth: Penguin, 1973.

Cicourel, Aaron V. 1972. 'Interpretive Procedures and Normative Rules in the Negotiation of Status and Role' in Aaron V. Cicourel, *Cognitive Sociology*. Harmondsworth: Penguin, 1973.

Cicourel, Aaron V. and Kitsuse, John I. 1963. *The Educational Decision-Makers*. New York: Bobbs-Merrill.

Cixous, Hélène 1975. *The Newly Born Woman*. Manchester: Manchester University Press, 1987.

Clark, Colin 1940. *The Conditions of Economic Progress*. London: Macmillan.

Clark, Graham 1946. *From Savagery to Civilization*. London: Cobbett Press.

Clark, Terry N. 1969. *Gabriel Tarde: On Communication and Social Influence*. Chicago: University of Chicago Press.

Clark, Terry N. 1972. 'Education and the French University: The Institutionalization of Sociology' in Anthony Oberschall (ed.) *The Establishment of Empirical Sociology*. New York: Harper and Row, 1972.

Clark, Terry N. 1973. *Prophets and Patrons: The French University and the Emergence of the Social Sciences*. Cambridge, Mass.: Harvard University Press.

Codere, Helen (ed.) 1966 *Franz Boas: Kwakiutl Ethnography*. Chicago: University of Chicago Press.

Cohen, Gerry A. 1978. *Karl Marx's Theory of History*. Oxford: Oxford University Press.

Cole, George Douglas H. 1920. *Social Theory*. London: Methuen.

Coleman, James S. 1973. *The Mathematics of Collective Action*. London: Heinemann.

Coleman, James S. 1990. *Foundations of Social Theory*. Cambridge: Belknap Press.

Collingwood, Robin G. 1940. *Essay on Metaphysics*. Oxford: Oxford University Press.

Collins, F. Howard 1889. *An Epitome of the Synthetic Philosophy*. London: Williams and Norgate.

Collins, Randall 1994. *Four Sociological Traditions*. Oxford: Oxford University Press.

Colomy, Paul (ed.) 1990. *Neo-Functionalist Sociology*. Aldershot: Edward Elgar.

Commons, John R. 1899–1900. *A Sociological View of Sovereignty*. New York: Augustus M. Kelly, 1965.

Commons, John R. 1924. *The Legal Foundations of Capitalism*. New York: Macmillan.

Comte, Auguste 1830–42. *Cours de philosophie positive*. Paris: Société Positiviste, 1892–4.

Comte, Auguste 1844. *A Discourse on the Positive Spirit*. London: William Reeves, 1903.

Comte, Auguste 1848. *General View of Positivism*. London: Trübner and Co., 1865.

Comte, Auguste 1851–4. *System of Positive Polity* (6 vols). London: Longman's Green, 1875–7.

Comte, Auguste 1852. *Catechism of Positive Philosophy*. London: John Chapman, 1858.

Comte, Auguste 1855. *Appeal to Conservatives*. London: Trübner and Co., 1889.

Comte, Auguste 1856. *Subjective Synthesis*. London: Kegan Paul, Trench, Trübner, 1891.

Condorcet, Antoine Nicoles de 1794. *Sketch for a Historical Picture of the Progress of the Human Mind*. London: Weidenfeld and Nicolson, 1955.

Cook, Gary A. 1993. *George Herbert Mead: The Making of a Social Pragmatist*. Urbana: University of Illinois Press.

Cook, Karen S. 1977. 'Exchange and Power in Networks of Interorganizational Relations' in John Scott (ed.) *Power*, Volume 1. London: Routledge, 1994.

Cooley, Charles Horton 1902. *Human Nature and the Social Order*. New York: Scribner's.

Cooley, Charles Horton 1909. *Social Organization*. New York: Schocken.

Cooley, Charles Horton 1918. *Social Process*. New York: Charles Scribner's Sons.

Cooper, Anna Julia 1892. *A Voice from the South*. Xenia, Ohio: Aldine Printing House.

Coriat, Benjamin 1990. *L'atelier et le robot*. Paris: Christian Bourgeois Editor.

Coser, Lewis (ed.) 1992 *Maurice Halbwachs on Collective Memory*. Chicago: University of Chicago Press.

Coste, Adolphe 1899. *Les principes d'une sociologie objective*. Paris: F. Alcan.

Coste, Adolphe 1900. *L'expérience des peuples et les prévisions qu'elle autorise*. Paris: F. Alcan.

Coulter, Jeff 1979. *The Social Construction of Mind: Studies in Ethnomethodology and Linguistic Philosophy*. London: Macmillan.

Coulter, Jeff 1989. *Mind in Action*. Cambridge: Polity Press.

Cox, Oliver Cromwell 1948. *Caste, Class, and Race: A Study in Social Dynamics*. New York: Doubleday and Co.

Craib, Ian 1976. *Existentialism and Sociology*. Cambridge: Cambridge University Press.

Croce, Benedetto 1896–1900. *Historical Materialism and the Economics of Karl Marx*. London: Howard Latimer.

Croce, Benedetto 1907. *What Is Living and What Is Dead in the Philosophy of Hegel*. Lanham, MD: Universities Press of America, 1986.

Croce, Benedetto 1909. *Philosophy of the Practical: Economic and Ethic*. London: Macmillan, 1913.

Croce, Benedetto 1915. *Teoria e storia della storiografia*. Bari: G. Laterza.

Croce, Benedetto 1926. *Storia dell' erà barocca in Italia*. Bari: G. Laterza.

Croce, Benedetto 1932. *History of Europe in the Nineteenth Century*. London: George Allen and Unwin, 1965.

Culler, Jonathan 1983. *Barthes*. Glasgow: Fontana.

Cunliffe, Barry 2001. *Facing the Ocean: The Atlantic and Its Peoples, 8000 BC to AD 1500*. Oxford: Oxford University Press.

Curran, James 1977. 'Capitalism and the Control of the Press, 1800–1975' in James Curran, Michael Gurevitch and Jane Woolacott (eds) *Mass Communication and Society*. London: Edward Arnold.

Czarnowski, Stefan Zygmunt 1919. *La lutte des héros et ses conditions sociales*. Paris: Alcan.

Dahl, Robert 1961. *Who Governs?* New Haven: Yale University Press.

Dahl, Robert A. 1957. 'The Concept of Power' in John Scott (ed.) *Power*. London: Routledge, 1994.

Dahl, Robert A. 1971. *Polyarchy: Participation and Opposition*. New Haven: Yale University Press.

Dahrendorf, Ralf 1957. *Class and Class Conflict in an Industrial Society*. London: Routledge and Kegan Paul, 1959.

Dahrendorf, Ralf 1958. '*Homo Sociologicus*: On the History, Significance, and Limits of the Category of Social Role' in Ralf Dahrendorf, *Essays in the Theory of Society*. London: Routledge and Kegan Paul, 1968.

Daly, Mary 1978. *Gyn/Ecology: The Metaethics of Radical Feminism*. London: Women's Press.

Dandecker, Christopher 1990. *Surveillance, Power and Modernity*. Cambridge: Polity Press.

Danilevsky, Nikolai 1869. *Rossiyai Evropa*. Moscow: Kniga, 1991.

Darby, H. Clifford 1936. *An Historical Geography of England before 1800*. Cambridge: Cambridge University Press.

Darwin, Charles 1859. *On the Origin of Species*. Harmondsworth: Penguin, 1968.

Davy, Georges 1922. *La foi jurée*. Paris: F. Alcan.

Dawkins, Richard 1976. *The Selfish Gene*. Oxford: Oxford University Press.

Dealey, James Q. and Ward, Lester 1905. *Textbook of Sociology*. New York: Macmillan.

Deleuze, Gilles 1962. *Nietzsche and Philosophy*. New York: Columbia University Press, 1983.

Deleuze, Gilles 1969. *Difference and Repetition*. London: Athlone Press, 1994.

Deleuze, Gilles and Guattari, Félix 1972. *Anti-Oedipus: Capitalism and Schizophrenia*. New York: Viking, 1977.

Demolins, Edmond 1897. *Anglo Saxon Superiority: To What Is It Due?* New York: Charles Scribner's Sons, 1898.

Demolins, Edmond 1901–3. *Comment la route crée le type sociale* (2 vols). Paris: Firmin-Didot.

Den Otter, Sandra M. 1996. *British Idealism and Social Explanation*. Oxford: Clarendon Press.

Denzin, Norman K. 1992. *Symbolic Interactioism and Cultural Studies*. Oxford: Blackwell.

Derrida, Jacques 1967a. *Of Grammatology*. Baltimore: Johns Hopkins University Press, 1976.

Derrida, Jacques 1967b. *Writing and Difference*. London: Routledge, 1978.

Descartes, René 1637. *A Discourse on Method*. London: Dent, 1912.

Descartes, René 1641. *Meditations on First Philosophy*. London: Routledge, 1993.

Dewey, John 1922. *Human Nature and Conduct*. New York: The Modern Library, 1929.

d'Holbach, Paul [writing as M. Mirabaud] 1770. *Système social, ou principes naturelles de la morale et de la politique*. Paris: Fayard, 1994.

Dickens, Peter 1992. *Society and Nature: Towards a Green Social Theory*. Hemel Hempstead: Harvester-Wheatsheaf.

Dilthey, Wilhelm 1883. *Introduction to the Human Sciences*. Princeton: Princeton University Press, 1989.

Dilthey, Wilhelm 1910. *The Formation of the Human World in the Human Sciences*. Princeton: Princeton University Press, 2002.

Downs, Anthony 1957. *An Economic Theory of Democracy*. New York: Harper and Brothers.

Drucker, Peter 1951. *The New Society: The Anatomy of the Industrial Order*. London: Heinemann.

Du Bois, Cora 1944. *The People of Alor*. Minnesota: University of Minnesota Press.

Du Bois, William Edward Barghardt 1899. *The Philadelphia Negro*. Philadelphia: University of Pennsylvania Press, 1996.

Du Bois, William Edward Burghardt 1903. 'The Souls of Black Folk', in W.E.B. Du Bois, *Writings* (edited by Nathan I. Huggins). New York: Viking Press, 1986.

Dühring, Eugen 1873. *Kursus der National- und Sozialökonomie*. Leipzig: O.R. Reisland, 1925.

Dumont, Arsène 1890. *Dépopulation et civilisation*. Paris: Lecrosnier et Babé.

Durkheim, Émile 1893. *The Division of Labour in Society*. London: Macmillan, 1984.

Durkheim, Émile 1895. *The Rules of the Sociological Method*. London: Macmillan, 1982.

Durkheim, Émile 1895–6. *Socialism and Saint-Simon*. London: Routledge and Kegan Paul, 1959.

Durkheim, Émile 1897. *Suicide: A Study in Sociology*. London: Routledge and Kegan Paul, 1952.

Durkheim, Émile 1912a. *Elementary Forms of the Religious Life*. London: George Allen and Unwin, 1915.

Durkheim, Émile 1912b. *Moral Education*. New York: Free Press, 1961.

Durkheim, Émile 1913. *The Evolution of Educational Thought in France*. London: Routledge and Kegan Paul, 1977.

Durkheim, Émile 1917. *Professional Ethics and Civic Morals*. London: Routledge and Kegan Paul, 1957.

Durkheim, Émile and Mauss, Marcel 1903. *Primitive Classification*. London: Cohen and West, 1963.

Dworkin, Andrea 1981. *Pornography: Men Possessing Women*. London: Women's Press.

Easton, David 1953. *The Political System*. New York: Alfred A. Knopf.

Eco, Umberto 1976. *A Theory of Semiotics*. Bloomington: Indiana University Press.

Eco, Umberto 1984. *Semiotics and the Philosophy of Language*. London: Macmillan.

Eder, Klaus 1993. *The New Politics of Class: Social Movements and Cultural Dynamics in Advanced Societies*. London: Sage.

Eisenstadt, Shlomo N. 2001. 'The Challenge of Multiple Modernities' in Luigi Tomasi (ed.) *New Horizons in Sociological Theory and Research*. Farnborough: Ashgate, 2001.

Eisenstadt, Shmuel 1973. *Tradition, Change and Modernity*. New York: Free Press.

Eisenstadt, Shmuel 1978. *Revolution and the Transformation of Societies*. New York: Free Press.

Elias, Norbert 1969. *The Court Society*. Oxford: Basil Blackwell.

Elliot Smith, Grafton 1929. *The Ancient Egyptians and the Origins of Civilization*. Manchester: Manchester University Press.

Elliot Smith, Grafton 1932. *In the Beginning*. London: Watts and Co.

Ellwood, Charles 1917. *An Introduction to Social Psychology*. New York: Appleton.

Ellwood, Charles 1925. *The Psychology of Human Society*. New York: Appleton.

Ellwood, Charles 1927. *Cultural Evolution*. New York: The Century.

Elster, Jon 1983. *Sour Grapes*. Cambridge: Cambridge University Press.

Elster, Jon 1989. *The Cement of Society*. Cambridge: Cambridge University Press.

Elster, Jon 1999. *Alchemies of the Mind*. Cambridge: Cambridge University Press.

Emerson, Joan 1970. 'Behaviour in Private Places: Sustaining Definitions of Reality in Gynecological Examinations' in Hans-Peter Dreitzel (ed.) *Recent Sociology,* Number 2. New York: Macmillan.

Emerson, R.M. 1962. 'Power–Dependence Relations' in John Scott (ed.) *Power*, Volume 1. London: Routledge, 1994.

Endt, Piet 1931. *Sociologie*. Amsterdam: Nederlandsche Bibliotheek.

Engels, Friedrich 1876. *Anti-Duhring*. Moscow: Foreign Languages Publishing House, 1954.

Engels, Friedrich 1884. *The Origin of the Family, Private Property, and the State*. New York: International Publishers, 1942.

Engels, Friedrich 1886. *Dialectics of Nature*. Moscow: Progress Publishers, 1964.

Engels, Friedrich 1888. *Ludwig Feuerbach and the End of Classical German Philosophy*. Moscow: Foreign Languages Publishing House, 1949.

Erikson, Erik 1950. *Childhood and Society*. New York: W.W.Norton.

Erikson, Erik 1968. *Identity, Youth and Crisis*. New York: W.W. Norton.

Erikson, Robert and Goldthorpe, John H. 1992. *The Constant Flux: A Study of Class Mobility in Industrial Societies*. Oxford: Clarendon Press.

Espinas, Alfred 1877. *Des sociétés animals*. Paris: G. Baillière.

Espinas, Alfred 1897. *Les origines de la technologie*. Paris: F. Alcan.

Etzioni, Amatai 1968. *The Active Society*. New York.

Evans-Pritchard, Edward 1937. *Witchcraft, Oracles, and Magic among the Azande*. Oxford: Clarendon Press.

Evans-Pritchard, Edward 1940. *The Nuer*. Oxford: Oxford University Press.

Evans-Pritchard, Edward 1948. *Social Anthropology*. Oxford University Press.

Eve, Raymond, Hirsfall, Sara and Lee, Mary 1997. *Chaos, Complexity and Sociology*. London: Sage.

Fairbairn, W. Ronald D. 1952. *Psycho-Analytic Studies of the Personality*. London: Tavistock.

Fararo, Thomas J. 1988. *The Meaning of General Theoretical Sociology*. Cambridge: Cambridge University Press.

Fauconnet, Paul 1920. *La responsabilité*. Paris: F. Alcan.

Febvre, Lucien 1922. *A Geographical Introduction to History*. Westport, Conn.: Greenwood Press, 1974.

Fennema, Meindert 1982. *International Networks of Banks and Industry*. The Hague: Martinus Nijhof.

Fennema, Meindert and Carroll, William K. 2002. 'Is There a Transnational Business Community?'. *International Sociology* 17: 393–419.

Ferguson, Adam 1767. *An Essay on the History of Civil Society*. Edinburgh: Edinburgh University Press, 1966.

Ferguson, Adam 1783. *History of the Progress and Termination of the Roman Republic*. London: W. Strahan.

Fernández-Armesto, Felipé 2000. *Civilizations*. London: Macmillan.

Ferrari, Giuseppe 1851. *Filosofia della rivoluzione*. Milan: Marzorati, 1979.

Ferri, Enrico 1884. *Criminal Sociology*. Gainesville, Fla: Blue Unicorn Editions, 2001.

Ferri, Enrico 1901. *The Positive School of Criminology*. Pittsburgh: University of Pittsburgh Press, 1968.

Festinger, Leon 1957. *A Theory of Cognitive Dissonance*. Stanford: Stanford University Press.

Festinger, Leon, Riecken, Henry W. and Schachter, Stanley 1956. *When Prophecy Fails*. New York: Harper and Row.

Feuerbach, Ludwig 1841. *The Essence of Christianity*. New York: Harper and Row, 1957.

Feyerabend, Paul 1975. *Against Method*. London: New Left Books.

Finnbogasan, Guðmundur 1912. *Hugur og heimur*. Reykjavik: Bókaverslun Sigfúsar Eymundssonar.

Firestone, Shulamith 1970. *The Dialectic of Sex*. London: Jonathan Cape, 1971.

Firth, Raymond W. 1951. *Elements of Social Organization*. London: Watts.

Fisher, Irving 1919. *The Nature of Capital and Income*. New York: Macmillan.

Fisher, Irving 1926. *Mathematical Investigations into the Theory of Value and Prices*. New Haven: Yale University Press.

Fitzhugh, George 1854. 'Sociology for the South' in Harvey Wish (ed.) *Ante-Bellum*. New York: G.P. Putnam's Sons, 1960.

Fletcher, Ronald 1971. *The Making of Sociology* (2 vols). London: Thomas Nelson.

Fleure, Herbert John 1919. 'Human Regions'. *Scottish Geographical Magazine* 35: 94–105.

Fleure, Herbert John 1922. *The Peoples of Europe*. Oxford: Oxford University Press.

Fleure, Herbert John 1923. *The Races of England and Wales*. London: Benn Brothers.

Fleure, Herbert John 1926. *Wales and Her People*. Wrexham: Hughes and Son.

Fleure, Herbert John 1930–1. 'The Nordic Myth: A Critique of Current Racial Theories'. *Eugenics Review* 22: 117–21.

Forde, Daryll 1934. *Habitat, Economy, and Society*. London: Methuen, 1963.

Foucault, Michel 1961. *Madness and Civilization*. New York: Vintage Books, 1973.

Foucault, Michel 1963. *The Birth of the Clinic*. New York: Vintage Books, 1975.

Foucault, Michel 1966. *The Order of Things*. New York: Vintage Books, 1973.

Foucault, Michel 1971. *The Archaeology of Knowledge*. New York: Pantheon, 1972.

Foucault, Michel 1975. *Discipline and Punish*. London: Allen Lane, 1977.

Foucault, Michel 1975–6. *Society Must Be Defended*. Harmondsworth: Penguin, 2003.

Foucault, Michel 1976. *The History of Sexuality, Volume 1: An Introduction*. New York: Vintage Books, 1980.

Foucault, Michel 1984a. *The History of Sexuality, Volume 2: The Use of Pleasure*. New York: Vintage Books, 1986.

Foucault, Michel 1984b. *The History of Sexuality, Volume 3: The Care of the Self*. New York: Vintage Books, 1988.

Fouillée, Alfred 1880. *La science sociale contemporaine*. Paris: Hachette.

Fouillée, Alfred 1890. *L'evolutionisme des idées-forces*. Paris: F. Alcan.

Fouillée, Alfred 1893. *Le psychologie des idées-forces*. Paris: F. Alcan.

Fouillée, Alfred 1905. *Les éléments sociologiques de la morale*. Paris: F. Alcan.

Frank, Andre Gunder 1967. *Capitalism and Underdevelopment in Latin America*. New York: Monthly Review Press.

Frankenberg, Ronald 1967. *Communities in Britain*. Harmondsworth: Penguin.

Frazer, James 1887. *Totemism*. Edinburgh: Adam and Charles Black.

Frazer, James 1890. *The Golden Bough*. 2 vols. London: Macmillan.

Frazer, James 1910. *Totemism and Exogamy*. London: Macmillan, 1935.

Freeman, Derek 1984. *Margaret Mead and the Heretic*. Harmondsworth: Penguin, 1996.

Freidson, Eliot 1970a. *The Profession of Medicine*. New York: Dodd Mead.

Freidson, Eliot 1970b. *Professional Dominance*. Chicago: Aldine.

French, J.R.P. 1956. 'A Formal Theory of Social Power' in John Scott (ed.) *Power*, Volume 1. London: Routledge, 1994.

Freud, Anna 1936. *The Ego and the Mechanisms of Defence*. London: Hogarth Press, 1937.

Freud, Sigmund 1900. *The Interpretation of Dreams*. London: George Allen and Unwin, 1954.

Freud, Sigmund 1901. *The Psychopathology of Everyday Life*. Harmondsworth: Penguin, 1975.

Freud, Sigmund 1905. 'Three Essays on Sexuality' in Sigmund Freud, *On Sexuality*. Harmondsworth: Penguin, 1977.

Freud, Sigmund 1923. 'The Ego and the Id' in *Beyond the Pleasure Principle and Other Writings* (edited by Adam Phillips). Harmondsworth: Penguin, 2003.

Freyer, Hans 1922. *Theorie des Objektiven Geistes*. Darmstadt: Wiss. Buchges, 1973.

Freyer, Hans 1930. *Soziologie als Wirklichkeitswissenschaft*. Stuttgart: Teubner, 1964.

Freyer, Hans 1931. *Einleitung in die Soziologie*. Leipzig.

Friedan, Betty 1962. *The Feminine Mystique*. New York: Dell.

Fromm, Erich 1941. *The Fear of Freedom [Escape from Freedom]*. London: Routledge and Kegan Paul, 1942.

Fukuyama, Francis 1992. *The End of History and the Last Man*. Harmondsworth: Penguin.

Gadamer, Hans-Georg 1960. *Truth and Method*. London: Sheed and Ward, 1989.

Galton, Francis 1869. *Hereditary Genius*. Cleveland: Meridian, 1962.

Galton, Francis 1881. *Natural Inheritance*. London: Macmillan.

Garfinkel, Harold 1967. *Studies in Ethnomethodology*. Englewood Cliffs, NJ: Prentice-Hall.

Garfinkel, Harold 2002. *Ethnomethodology's Program: Working out Durkheim's Aphorism*. Lanham, Md: Rowman and Littlefield.

Garofalo, Raffaele 1891. *Criminology*. London: Heinemann, 1914.

Geddes, Patrick 1915. *Cities in Evolution*. London: Williams and Norgate, 1949.

Geiger, Theodor 1928. *Die Gestalten der Gesellung*. Karlsruhe: G. Braun.

Geiger, Theodor 1939. *Sociologi, grundrids og hovedproblemer*. Copenhagen.

Gellner, Ernest 1988. *Plough, Sword and Book*. London: Collins Harvill.

Gentile, Giòvanni 1943. *Genesis and Structure of Society*. Urbana: University of Illinois Press, 1960.

George, Henry 1879. *Progress and Poverty*. London: Hogarth Press, 1966.

Gerhardt, Uta 2002. *Talcott Parsons: An Intellectual Biography*. Cambridge: Cambridge University Press.

Gerretson, Frederik Carel 1911. *Prolegomena der Sociologie*. Haarlem: Tjeenk Willink.

Gershenkron, Alexander 1962. *Economic Backwardness in Historical Perspective*. Cambridge, Mass.: Belknap Press.

Gibbon, Edward 1776–81. *Decline and Fall of the Roman Empire*. New York: Modern Library, 1983.

Giddens, Anthony 1976. *New Rules of Sociological Method*. London: Hutchinson.

Giddens, Anthony 1979. *Central Problems in Social Theory*. London: Macmillan.

Giddens, Anthony 1981. *A Contemporary Critique of Historical Materialism, Volume 1: Power, Property and the State*. London: Macmillan.

Giddens, Anthony 1984. *The Constitution of Society*. Cambridge: Polity Press.

Giddens, Anthony 1985. *The Nation State and Violence, Volume 2 of a Contemporary Critique of Historical Materialism*. Cambridge: Polity Press.

Giddens, Anthony 1990. *The Consequences of Modernity*. Cambridge: Polity Press.

Giddens, Anthony 1991. *Modernity and Self-Identity*. Cambridge: Polity Press.

Giddings, Franklin Henry 1896. *Principles of Sociology*. New York: Johnson Reprint, 1970.

Giddings, Franklin Henry 1898. *Elements of Sociology*. New York: Macmillan.

Giddings, Franklin Henry 1922. *Studies in the Theory of Human Society*. New York: Macmillan.

Giddings, Franklin Henry 1924. *The Scientific Study of Human Society*. Chapel Hill: University of North Carolina Press.

Gilligan, Carol 1982. *In a Different Voice*. Cambridge, Mass: Harvard University Press.

Gilman, Charlotte Perkins 1898. *Women and Economics: A Study of the Economic Relations between Women and Men as a Factor in Social Evolution*. London: Prometheus Books, 1994.

Gilman, Charlotte Perkins 1911. *The Man-Made World, or Our Androcentric Culture*. New York: Humanity Books, 2001.

Giner de la Rios, Francisco 1899. 'Teoría de la persona social' in Francisco Giner de la Rios, *Obras completas,* Volumes 8 and 9. Madrid: La Lectura, 1923–4.

Gini, Corrado 1914. *L'ammontare e la composizione della ricchezza delle nazioni.* Turin: Fratelli Bocca.

Gini, Corrado 1921. *Problemi sociologici della guerra.* Bologna: Zanichelli.

Gini, Corrado 1930. *Nascita, evoluzione e morte delle nazioni.* Rome: Libreria del littorio.

Ginsberg, Maurice 1921. *The Psychology of Society.* London: Methuen.

Ginsberg, Maurice 1929. 'The Contribution of Professor Hobhouse to Sociology and Philosophy' in Maurice Ginsberg, *Essays in Sociology and Social Philosophy, Volume II: Reason and Unreason in Society.* London: William Heinemann, 1947.

Ginsberg, Maurice 1932. 'Emotion and Instinct' in Maurice Ginsberg, *Studies in Sociology.* London: Methuen, 1932.

Ginsberg, Maurice 1933. 'An Introduction to the Study of Social Institutions' in Maurice Ginsberg, *Essays in Sociology and Social Philosophy, Volume I: On the Diversity of Morals.* London: William Heinemann, 1956.

Gitlin, Todd 1991. *Inside Prime Time.* Berkeley: University of California Press.

Gobineau, Arthur de 1853. *The Moral and Intellectual Diversity of Races.* New York: Garland, 1984.

Goffman, Erving 1959. *The Presentation of Self in Everyday Life.* Harmondsworth: Penguin.

Goffman, Erving 1961a. *Asylums: Essays on the Social Situation of Mental Patients and Other Inmates.* New York: Doubleday.

Goffman, Erving 1961b. *Encounters.* Indianapolis: Bobbs-Merrill.

Goffman, Erving 1963a. *Behavior in Public Places.* New York: Free Press.

Goffman, Erving 1963b. *Stigma.* Englewood Cliffs, NJ: Prentice-Hall.

Goffman, Erving 1967. *Interaction Ritual: Essays on Face-to-Face Behavior.* New York: Doubleday.

Goffman, Erving 1971. *Relations in Public.* New York: Free Press.

Goffman, Erving 1983. 'The Interaction Order'. *American Sociological Review* 48: 1–17.

Gökalp, Ziya 1924. *Türk Medeniyet Tarihi.* Ankara: Kultur Bakanligi, 1976.

Goldblatt, David 1996. *Social Theory and the Environment.* Cambridge: Polity Press.

Goldthorpe, John H. 1998. 'Rational Action Theory for Sociology' in John H. Goldthorpe, *On Sociology.* Oxford: Oxford University Press, 2000.

Gorz, André 1964. *Strategy for Labour.* Boston: Beacon Press, 1968.

Gossen, Hermann 1853. *The Laws of Human Relations.* Cambridge, Mass.: MIT Press.

Gottfried, Paul 1990. *Carl Schmitt.* London: The Claridge Press.

Gould, Mark 1987. *Revolution in the Development of Capitalism.* Berkeley: University of California Press.

Gouldner, Alvin W. 1954a. *Patterns of Industrial Bureaucracy.* New York: Free Press.

Gouldner, Alvin W. 1954b. *Wildcat Strike.* New York: Harper and Row.

Gouldner, Alvin W. 1959. 'Reciprocity and Autonomy in Functional Theory' in Alvin W. Gouldner, *For Sociology.* Harmonsdworth: Penguin, 1973.

Gouldner, Alvin W. 1976. *The Dialectic of Ideology and Technology.* New York: Seabury Press.

Gouldner, Alvin W. 1979. *The Future of the Intellectuals and the Rise of the New Class.* New York: Seabury Press.

Gramsci, Antonio 1929–35. *The Prison Notebooks [Selections from].* London: Lawrence and Wishart, 1971.

Granet, Marcel 1922. *The Religion of the Chinese People.* Oxford: Basil Blackwell, 1975.

Granet, Marcel 1929. *Chinese Civilization.* New York: Barnes and Noble, 1951.

Grathoff, Richard (ed.) 1978. *The Theory of Social Action.* Bloomington: Indian University Press.

Greef, Guillaume de 1886–93 *Introduction á la sociologie* (3 vols). Brussels: G. Mayolez.

Greef, Guillaume de 1908. *La structure générale des sociétés* (3 vols). Brussels: Ferd. Larcier.

Green, Thomas H. 1879. *Lectures on the Principles of Poitical Obligation*. London: Longmans, Green, 1911.

Greer, Germaine 1970. *The Female Eunuch*. London: MacGibbon and Kee.

Griemas, Algirdus Julien 1966. *Structural Semantics*. Lincoln: University of Nebraska Press, 1983.

Griemas, Algirdus Julien 1976. *Semiotics and the Philosophy of Language*. Minneapolis: University of Minnesota Press, 1990.

Gross, Neal, Mason, Ward S., and McEachern, Alexander W. 1958. *Explorations in Role Analysis: Studies of the School Superintendency Role*. New York: John Wiley and Sons.

Gumplowicz, Ludwig 1875. *Rasse und Staat*. Vienna: Manz.

Gumplowicz, Ludwig 1883. *Der Rassenkampf*. Innsbruck: Wagner'sche Univ. Buchhandlung.

Gumplowicz, Ludwig 1905. *Outlines of Sociology* (2nd edn). New Brunswick: Transaction, 1980.

Guntrip, Harry 1961. *Personality Structure and Human Interaction*. London: Hogarth Press.

Gurvitch, Georges 1932. *L'ideé du droit social*. Paris: Libr. du Recueil Sirey.

Gurvitch, Georges 1942. *Sociology of Law*. New York.

Gurvitch, Georges 1964 *The Spectrum of Social Time*. Dordrecht: D. Reidel, 1964.

Habermas, Jürgen 1965. 'Knowledge and Interests' in Jürgen Habermas (ed.) *Knowledge and Human Interests*. London: Heinemann, 1971.

Habermas, Jürgen 1967. 'Labour and Interaction: Remarks on Hegel's Jena Philosophy of Mind' in Jürgen Habermas, *Theory and Practice*. London: Heinemann, 1974.

Habermas, Jürgen 1968. *Knowledge and Human Interests*. London: Heinemann, 1972.

Habermas, Jürgen 1968–9. *Towards a Rational Society*. London: Heinemann, 1971.

Habermas, Jürgen 1973. *Legitimation Crisis*. London: Heinemann, 1976.

Habermas, Jürgen 1981a. *The Theory of Communicative Action, Volume One: Reason and the Rationalization of Society*. London: Heinemann, 1984.

Habermas, Jürgen 1981b. *The Theory of Communicative Action, Volume Two: The Critique of Functionalist Reason*. London: Heinemann, 1987.

Habermas, Jürgen 1985. *The Philosophical Discourse of Modernity: Twelve Essays*. Cambridge, Mass.: MIT Press, 1987.

Haggett, Peter 1965. *Locational Analysis in Human Geography*. London: Edward Arnold.

Halbwachs, Maurice 1912. *La classe ouvrière et les niveaux de vie*. Paris: Alcan.

Halbwachs, Maurice 1925. *Les cadres sociaux de la mémoire*. Paris: Alcan.

Halbwachs, Maurice 1930. *The Causes of Suicide*. New York: Free Press, 1978.

Halbwachs, Maurice 1938a. *Population and Society: Introduction to Social Morphology*. Glencoe, Ill.: Free Press, 1960.

Halbwachs, Maurice 1938b. *The Psychology of Social Class*. London: William Heinemann, 1958.

Hall, John A. 1985. *Powers and Liberties*. Oxford: Basil Blackwell.

Hall, John A. and Ikenberry G. John 1989. *The State*. Buckingham: Open University Press.

Hall, Stuart 1977. 'The "Political" and the "Economic" in Marx's Theory of Classes' in Alan Hunt (ed.) *Class and Class Structure*. London: Lawrence and Wishart, 1977.

Hall, Stuart 1982. 'The Rediscovery of Ideology' in Michael Gurevitch, Tony Bennett, James Curran, and Jane Woolacott (eds) *Culture, Media and Society*. London: Methuen, 1982.

Halliday, Fred 1999. *Revolution and World Politics*. Basingstoke: Macmillan.

Haraway, Donna 1991. *Simians, Cyborgs, and Women*. London: Free Association Books.

Haret, Spirou 1910. *Mécanique sociale*. Bucharest: C. Göbl.

Harrison, Frederic 1862. *The Meaning of History*. London: Macmillan, 1894.

Harrison, Frederic 1877. *Order and Progress*. Brighton: Harvester Press, 1975.

Harrison, Frederic 1918. *On Society*. London: Macmillan.

Hartshorne, Richard 1939. *The Nature of Geography*. Lancaster, PA: Association of American Geographers.

Harvey, David 1973. *Social Justice and the City*. London: Edward Arnold.

Harvey, David 1982. *The Limits to Capital*. Chicago: University of Chicago Press.

Harvey, David 1985. *Consciousness and the Urban Experience*. Baltimore: Johns Hopkins University Press.

Harvey, David 1989. *The Condition of Postmodernity*. Oxford: Basil Blackwell.

Hassan, Ihab 1971. 'POSTmodernISM: A Paracritical Bibliography'. *New Literary History* Autumn. pp. 5–30.

Hauksson, Jóhann 2000. 'Mentality is Half of Perception: Guðmundur Finnbogason'. *Acta Sociologica* 43: 307–15.

Hayek, Friedrich von 1942. 'Scientism and the Study of Society, Part 1'. *Economica* 9: 267–91.

Hayek, Friedrich von 1945. 'The Use of Knowledge in Society', in Friedrich von Hayek, *Individualism and the Economic Order*. London: Routledge and Kegan Paul.

Hayek, Friedrich von 1962. 'Rules, Perception and Intelligibility' in Friedrich von Hayek, *Studies in Philosophy, Politics and Economics*. London: Routledge and Kegan Paul, 1967.

Hayek, Friedrich von 1965. 'Kinds of Rationality' in Friedrich von Hayek, *Studies in Philosophy, Politics and Economics*. London: Routledge and Kegan Paul, 1967.

Hayek, Friedrich von 1967. 'The Results of Human Action but Not of Human Design' in Friedrich von Hayek, *Studies in Philosophy, Politics and Economics*. London: Routledge and Kegan Paul, 1967.

Hearnshaw, L.S. 1964. *A Short History of British Psychology, 1840–1940*. London: Methuen.

Heath, Anthony 1976. *Rational Choice and Social Exchange*. Cambridge: Cambridge University Press.

Hegel, Georg W.F. 1807. *The Phenomenology of Spirit*. Oxford: Oxford University Press, 1977.

Hegel, Georg W.F. 1812–16. *Science of Logic*. London: George Allen and Unwin, 1929.

Hegel, Georg W.F. 1821. *Hegel's Philosophy of Right* [*Naturrecht Und Staatswissenschaft Im Grundrisse/Grundlinien Der Philosophie Des Rechts*]. London: Oxford University Press, 1952.

Hegel, Georg W.F. 1818–31. *Philosophy of History*. New York: P.F. Collier & Son 1902.

Heidegger, Martin 1927. *Being and Time*. Albany: State University of New York Press, 1996.

Heider, Fritz 1958. *The Psychology of Interpersonal Relations*. New York: Wiley.

Held, David 1987. *Models of Democracy*. Cambridge: Polity Press.

Held, David 1989. *Political Theory and the Modern State*. Cambridge: Polity Press.

Held, David 1995. *Democracy and the Global Order*. Cambridge: Polity Press.

Helm, Georg 1887. *Die Lehre von der Energie*. Leipzig: Felix.

Helvétius, Claude 1772. *A Treatise on Man*. New York: Columbia University Press, 1946.

Henderson, Lawrence J. 1935. *Pareto's General Sociology: A Physiologist's Interpretation*. Cambridge, Mass.: Harvard University Press.

Herbertson, Andrew John 1905. 'The Major Natural Regions'. *Geographical Journal* 25: 300–12.

Herbertson, Andrew John and Herbertson, F.D. 1920. *Man and His Work: An Introduction to Human Geography*. London: A. and C. Black.

Herder, Johann Gottfried von 1770. *On the Origin of Language*. Chicago: University of Chicago Press, 1986.

Herder, Johann Gottfried von 1784–91. 'Reflections on the Philosophy of the History of Man' in Adler, Hans and Menze, Ernst A. (eds.) *On World History*. New York: M.E. Sharpe, 1997.

Herf, Jeffrey 1984. *Reactionary Modernism: Technology, Culture, and Politics in Weimar and the Third Reich*. Cambridge: Cambridge University Press.

Heritage, John 1984. *Garfinkel and Ethnomethodology*. Cambridge: Polity Press.

Herrnstein, Richard J. and Murray, Charles 1994. *The Bell Curve: Intelligence and Class Structure in American Life*. New York: Free Press.

Hess, Moses 1841. *Die Europäische Triarchie*. Amsterdam: E.J. Bonset, 1971.

Hilferding, Rudolf 1910. *Finance Capital*. London: Routledge and Kegan Paul, 1981.

Hinckle, Roscoe 1994. *Developments in American Sociological Theory*. Albany: State University of New York Press.

Hitler, Adolf 1925. *Mein Kampf*. London: Pimlico, 1992.

Hjelmslev, Louis H. 1943. *Prolegomana to a Theory of Language*. Madison: University of Wisconsin Press, 1963.

Hobbes, Thomas 1651. *Leviathan*. Harmondsworth: Penguin, 1977.

Hobhouse, Leonard Trelawny 1896. *Theory of Knowledge: A Contribution to Some Problems of Logic and Metaphysics*. London: Methuen.

Hobhouse, Leonard Trelawny 1901. *Mind in Evolution*. London: Macmillan.

Hobhouse, Leonard Trelawny 1906. *Morals in Evolution*. London: Macmillan.

Hobhouse, Leonard Trelawny 1911. 'Liberalism' in Leonard Trelawny Hobhouse, *Liberalism and Other Writings*. Cambridge: Cambridge University Press, 1994.

Hobhouse, Leonard Trelawny 1913. *Development and Purpose: An Essay Towards a Philosophy of Evolution*. London: Macmillan.

Hobhouse, Leonard Trelawny 1918. *The Metaphysical Theory of the State*. London: George Allen and Unwin.

Hobhouse, Leonard Trelawny 1921. *The Rational Good*. London: George Allen and Unwin.

Hobhouse, Leonard Trelawny 1922. *The Elements of Social Justice*. London: George Allen and Unwin.

Hobhouse, Leonard Trelawny 1924. *Social Development: Its Nature and Conditions*. London: George Allen and Unwin, 1966.

Hobhouse, Leonard Trelawny 1966 *Sociology and Philosophy* (Ed. Morris Ginsberg). London: G. Bell.

Hobhouse, Leonard Trelawny, Wheeler, G.C., and Ginsberg, Maurice 1914. *The Material Culture and Social Institutions of the Simpler People*. London: Routledge and Kegan Paul, 1965.

Hobson, John Atkinson 1894. *The Evolution of Modern Capitalism*. London: George Allen and Unwin.

Hobson, John Atkinson 1902. *Imperialism: A Study*. London: George Allen and Unwin.

Hobson, John Atkinson 1914. *Work and Wealth: A Human Valuation*. London: Macmillan.

Hobson, John Atkinson 1931. 'The Work of L.T. Hobhouse' in John A. Hobson and Maurice Ginsberg (eds) *L.T. Hobhouse: His Life and Work*. London: George Allen and Unwin.

Hobson, John Atkinson and Ginsberg, Maurice (eds) 1931. *L.T. Hobhouse: His Life and Work*. London: George Allen and Unwin.

Hochschild, Arlie Russell 1979. 'Emotion Work, Feeling Rules and Social Structure'. *American Journal of Sociology* 84: 551–73.

Hochschild, Arlie Russell 1983. *The Managed Heart: Commercialization of Human Feeling*. Berkeley: University of California Press.

Hochstim, Paul 1966. *Alfred Vierkandt: A Sociological Critique*. New York: Exposition Press, 1966.

Homans, George Caspar 1950. *The Human Group*. London: Routledge and Kegan Paul, 1951.

Homans, George Caspar 1961. *Social Behaviour: Its Elementary Forms*. London: Routledge and Kegan Paul.

Homans, George Caspar. and Curtis, Charles P. 1934. *An Introduction to Pareto: His Sociology*. New York: Alfred A. Knopf.

Homans, George Caspar 1984. *Coming to My Senses*. New Brunswick, NJ: Transaction.

Horkheimer, Max 1947. *Eclipse of Reason*. London: Continuum, 1974.

Horkheimer, Max Fromm, Eric and Marcuse, Herbert 1936. *Studien über Autorität und Familie*. Lüneburg: zu Klampen, 1987.

Horney, Karen 1922–37. *Feminine Psychology*. New York: W.W. Norton, 1967.

Horney, Karen 1937. *The Neurotic Personality of Our Time*. New York: W.W. Norton.

Horney, Karen 1946. *Our Inner Conflict*. London: Routledge and Kegan Paul.

Hoskins, William G. 1955. *The Making of the English Landscape*. London: Hodder and Stoughton.

How, Alan 1998. '"That's Classic": A Gadamerian Defence of the Classic Text in Sociology'. *Sociological Review* 46: 828–48.

Howey, R.S. 1960. *The Rise of the Marginal Utility School, 1870–1889*. Lawrence: University of Kansas Press.

Hubert, Henri 1932a. *The Greatness and Decline of the Celts*. London: Constable, 1987.

Hubert, Henri 1932b. *The Rise of the Celts*. London: Constable, 1987.

Hughes, H. Stuart 1958. *Consciousness and Society: The Reorientation of European Social Thought, 1890–1930*. New York: Alfred Knopf.

Hughes, Henry 1854. *Treatise of Sociology: Theoretical and Practical*. New York: Negro Universities Press, 1968.

Humboldt, Wilhelm von 1795–7. 'Plan einer Vergleichenden Anthropologie' in Hans-Josef Wagner (ed.) *Wilhelm von Humboldt: Anthropologie und Theorie der Menschenkenntnis*. Darmstadt: Wissenschafliche Buchges, 2002.

Humboldt, Wilhelm von 1836. *On the Diversity of Human Language Construction and Its Influence on the Mental Development of the Human Species*. Cambridge: Cambridge University Press, 1999.

Hume, David 1739–40. *Treatise of Human Nature*. London and Glasgow: J.M. Dent, 1911 (Book One); Fontana, 1972 (Books Two and Three).

Hume, David 1751. 'Enquiry Concerning the Principles of Morality' in *Enquiries Concerning Human Understanding and Concerning the Principles of Morals* (edited by P.H. Nidditch). Oxford: Oxford University Press.

Hume, David 1754–62. *History of England*. Indianapolis: Liberty Classics, 1983.

Huntington, Ellsworth 1907. *The Pulse of Asia*. Boston: Houghton Mifflin.

Huntington, Ellsworth 1915. *Civilization and Climate*. New Haven: Yale University Press.

Huntington, Ellsworth and Cushing, S.W. 1920. *Principles of Human Geography*. New York: John Wiley.

Huntington, Samuel P. 1957. *The Soldier and the State*. Cambridge, Mass.: Harvard University Press.

Husserl, Edmund 1900–1. *Logical Investigations*. New York: Humanities Press, 1970.

Husserl, Edmund 1913. *Ideas: General Introduction to Pure Phenomenology*. London: George Allen and Unwin, 1931.

Imai, Ken'Ichi 1990. *Joho Nettowaku Shakai No Tenbo* [*Information Network Society: An Overview*]. Tokyo: Chikuma Shoba.

Ingham, Geoffrey K. 2004. *The Nature of Money*. Cambridge: Polity Press.

Ingham, Geoffrey K. 1984. *Capitalism Divided?* London: Macmillan.

Inglehart, Ronald 1990. *Culture Shift in Advanced Industrial Society*. Princeton: Princeton University Press.

Inglis, Fred 1982. *Radical Earnestness: English Social Theory, 1880–1900*. Oxford: Martin Robertson.

Irigary, Luce 1974. *Speculum of the Other Woman*. Ithaca, NY: Cornell University Press, 1985.

Irwin, Alan 2001. *Sociology and the Environment*. Cambridge: Polity Press.

Izoulet, Jean 1894. *La cité moderne et les métaphysique's de la sociologie*. Paris: F. Alcan.

Jacoby, Paul 1881. *Études sur la sélection dans ses rappports avec l'hérédité chez l'homme*. Paris: G. Baillière.

Jacques, Elliott 1955. *New Directions in Psychoanalysis*. London: Tavistock.

James, William 1890. *The Principles of Psychology*. New York: Dover Publications, 1950.

Jameson, Frederic 1984. 'Postmodernism, or the Cultural Logic of Late Capitalism' in Frederic Jameson (ed.) *Postmodernism, or the Cultural Logic of Late Capitalism*. London: Verso, 1991.

Jarvie, Ian C. 1972. *Concepts and Society*. London: Routledge and Kegan Paul.

Jaspers, Karl 1913. *General Psychopathology* (2 vols). Baltimore: Johns Hopkins University Press, 1997.

Jaspers, Karl 1919. *Psychologie der Weltanschauungen*. Zurich: Piper, 1988.

Jaspers, Karl 1932a. *On Max Weber*. New York: Paragon House, 1988.

Jaspers, Karl 1932b. *Philosophy* (3 vols). Chicago: University of Chicago Press, 1969–71.

Jencks, Charles 1977. *The Language of Post-Modern Architecture*. London: Academy Editions.

Jensen, Arthur 1972. *Genetics and Education*. London: Methuen.

Jevons, William Stanley 1871. *The Theory of Political Economy*. Harmondsworth: Penguin, 1970.

Joas, Hans 1980. *G.H. Mead*. Cambridge: Polity Press, 1985.

Jones, Ernest 1924. 'The Classification of Instincts'. *British Journal of Psychology* 14: 256–261.

Jones, Ernest 1936. 'Psycho-Analysis and the Instincts'. *British Journal of Psychology* 26: 273–288.

Jones, Ernest 1953–7. *Sigmund Freud: Life and Work*, (3 vols). London: Hogarth Press.

Jones, Henry 1883. 'The Social Organism' in David Boucher (ed.) *The British Idealists*. Cambridge: Cambridge University Press, 1997.

Jones, Henry 1910. *The Working Faith of the Social Reformer*. London: Macmillan.

Jones, Henry 1919. *The Principles of Citizenship*. London: Macmillan.

Jones, Steve 1993. *The Language of the Genes*. London: Flamingo.

Jung, Carl Gustav 1921. *Psychological Types*. London: Routledge and Kegan Paul, 1971.

Kahn, Herman and Wiener, Anthony J. 1967. *The Year 2000*. New York.

Kaldor, Mary 1982. *The Baroque Arsenal*. London: André Deutsch.

Kant, Immanuel 1781. *Critique of Pure Reason*. London: J.M. Dent, 1934. (A translation of the Second Edition of 1787.)

Kant, Immanuel 1784. 'Idea for a Universal History from a Cosmopolitan Point of View' in L.W. Beck (ed.) *Immanuel Kant on History*. Indianapolis: Bobbs-Merril, 1963.

Kant, Immanuel 1788. *Critique of Practical Reason*. Cambridge: Cambridge University Press, 1997.

Kardiner, Abram 1945. *The Psychological Frontiers of Society*. New York: Columbia University Press.

Kareev, Nikolai 1883–90. *Obshchii khod vsemirnoi istorii* [*Basic Questions of the Philosophy of History*] (3 vols). St Petersburg: Brokgauz-Efron, 1903.

Kareev, Nikolai 1918. *Osnovy russkoi sotsiologii* Basics of Russian Sociology. St Petersburg: Izd-vo Ivana Limbakha, 1996.

Karsten, Rafael 1905. *The Origin of Worship*. Wasa: F.W. Unggren.

Katznelson, Ira 1981. *City Trenches*. New York: Pantheon Books.

Kauffman, Stuart 1993. *The Origins of Order*. Oxford: Oxford University Press.

Kauffman, Stuart 1995. *At Home in the Universe*. Oxford: Oxford University Press.

Kaufmann, Felix 1936. *The Methodology of the Social Sciences*. New York: Oxford University Press, 1944.

Kautsky, John H. 1994. *Karl Kautsky: Marxist, Revolution and Democracy*. New Brusnwick, NJ: Transaction.

Kautsky, Karl 1887. *The Economic Doctrines of Karl Marx*. London, A&C Black 1925.

Kautsky, Karl 1899. *The Agrarian Question* (2 vols). London: Zwan Publications, 1988.

Kautsky, Karl 1918. *The Dictatorship of the Proletariat*. Ann Arbor: University of Michigan Press, 1964.

Kautsky, Karl 1927. *The Materialist Conception of History*. New Haven: Yale University Press, 1988.

Keller, Albert Galloway 1915. *Societal Evolution*. New York: Macmillan.

Keller, Albert Galloway 1923. *Starting Points in Social Science*. New York: Ginn and Co.

Kennedy, Paul 1987. *The Rise and Fall of the Great Powers, 1500–2000*. London: Fontana Press, 1989.

Kerr, Clerk, Dunlop, John T., Harbison, Frederick, and Myers, C.A. 1960. *Industrialism and Industrial Man*. Cambridge, Mass.: Harvard University Press.

Kettler, David, Meja, Volcker, and Stehr, Nico 1984. *Karl Mannheim*. Chichester: Ellis Horwood.

Keynes, John Maynard 1936. *General Theory of Employment, Interest and Money*. London: Macmillan.

Khaldun, Ibn 1377. *The Muqaddimah: An Introduction to History*. Princeton: Princeton University Press, 1967.
Kidd, Benjamin 1894. *Social Evolution*. London: Macmillan.
Kidd, Benjamin 1903. *Principles of Western Civilization*. London: Macmillan.
Kidd, Benmjamin 1918. *The Science of Power*. London: Methuen.
Kistiakovsky, Bogdan 1899. *Gesellschaft und Einzelwesen: Eine methodologische Studie*. Berlin.
Kistiakovsky, Bogdan 1916. *Sotsialnyje nauki i pravo*. [*Social Sciences and Law*]. Moscow: M. and C. Sabashnikovy.
Klein, Melanie 1932. *The Psychoanalysis of Children*. London: Hogarth Press.
Klein, Melanie 1957. *Envy and Gratitude: A Study of Unconscious Sources*. London: Tavistock.
Klein, Viola 1946. *The Feminine Character*. London: Routledge and Kegan Paul.
Knies, Karl 1853. *Die Politische Ökonomie vom Geschichtlichen Stundpunkte*. Osnabrück: Zeller, 1883.
Kohlberg, Lawrence 1969. 'Stage and Sequence', in David A.Goslin (ed.) *Handbook of Socialization Research*. Boston: Houghton-Mifflin.
Kohlberg, Lawrence 1971 'From Is to Ought' in Lawrence, Kohlberg, *Essays on Moral Development,* Volume 1. New York: Harper and Row, 1981.
Köhler, Wolfgang 1917. *The Mentality of Apes*. London: Routledge and Kegan Paul, 1924.
Kohut, Heinz 1971. *The Analysis of the Self*. New York: International Universities Press.
Kohut, Heinz 1978. *The Search for the Self*. New York: International Universities Press.
Kolakowski, Leszak 1978. *Main Currents in Marxism* (3 vols). Oxford: Oxford University Press.
Kovalevsky, Maksim 1891. *Modern Customs and Ancient Laws in Russia*. McMaster University: http://socserv2.socsci.mcmaster.ca/~econ/ugcm/3ll3/kovalevsky/index.html.
Kovalevsky, Maksim 1905. Sovremennyje Sotsiologi [Contemporary Sociologists]. St Petersburg. *Contemporary Sociologists*. (2 vols).
Kovalevsky, Maksim 1910. Sotsiologija [Sociology], St Petersburg.
Kristeva, Julia 1969. *Séméiotiké*. Paris: Seuil.
Kristeva, Julia 1974. *Revolution in Poetic Language*. New York: Columbia University Press, 1984.
Kristeva, Julia 1980. *Powers of Horror: An Essay on Abjection*. New York: Columbia University Press, 1982.
Kristeva, Julia 1983. *Tales of Love*. New York: Columbia University Press, 1989.
Kristeva, Julia 1987. *Black Sun*. New York: Columbia University Press, 1989.
Kroeber, Alfred 1917. 'The Superorganic'. *American Anthropologist* 19: 163–213.
Kroeber, Alfred 1923. *Anthropology*. New York: Harcourt Brace.
Kroeber, Alfred 1944. *Configurations of Cultural Growth*. Berkeley: University of California Press.
Krzywicki, Ludwig 1914. *Ustroje spolecz'no-gospodarcze w okresie dzikosci i barbarzynstwa* [*Social Structures of Savagery and Barbarism*]. Warsaw: Kasa im Mianowskiego.
Krzywicki, Ludwig 1934. *Primitive Society and Its Vital Statistics*. London: Macmillan (First Polish publication, 1937).
Kuhn, Thomas S. 1962. *The Structure of Scientific Revolutions*. Chicago: University of Chicago Press.
Kumar, Krishan 1978. *Prophecy and Progress*. Harmondsworth: Penguin.
Kuper, Adam 1996. *Anthropology and Anthropologists* (3rd edn). London: Routledge.
Labriola, Antonio 1896. *Essays on the Materialist Conception of History*. Chicago: Chas. H. Kerr, 1908.
Labriola, Antonio 1898. *Socialism and Philosophy*. Chicago: Charles H. Herr, 1907.
Lacan, Jacques 2001. *Ecrits*. London: Routledge, 1966a.
Lacan, Jacques 1966b. *The Language of the Self*. Baltimore: Johns Hopkins University Press, 1968.
Laing, Adrian 1994. *R.D. Laing: A Biography*. London: Peter Owen.

Laing, Ronald D. 1959. *The Divided Self*. London: Tavistock.

Laing, Ronald D. 1961. *Self and Others*. London: Tavistock.

Laing, Ronald D. 1969. *The Politics of the Family*. Harmondsworth: Penguin.

Laing, Ronald D. and Esterson, Aaron V. 1964. *Sanity, Madness, and the Family*. Harmondsworth: Penguin.

Landtman, Gunnar 1909. *The Origin of the Inequality of the Social Classes*. London: Routledge and Kegan Paul, 1938.

Lane, Ann J. 1990. *To Herland and Beyond: The Life and Work of Charlotte Perkins Gilman*. Charlottesville: University of Virginia Press.

Lash, Scott and Urry, John 1987. *The End of Organized Capitalism*. Cambridge: Polity Press.

Lash, Scott and Urry, John 1994. *Economies of Signs and Space*. London: Sage.

Latour, Bruno 1991. *We Have Never Been Modern*. Cambridge, Mass.: Harvard University Press, 1993.

Latour, Bruno 1999. *Pandora's Hope*. Cambridge, Mass.: Harvard University Press.

Latour, Bruno and Woolgar, Steve 1979. *Laboratory Life*. London: Sage.

Lavrov, Pytor 1868. *Historical Letters*. Berkeley: University of California Press, 1967.

Lazarus, Moritz 1855–7. *Das Leben der Seele*. Berlin.

Le Bon, Gustave 1884. *The World of Islamic Civilization*. New York: Tudor, 1994.

Le Bon, Gustave 1887. *The World of Ancient India*. New York: Tudor, 1994.

Le Bon, Gustave 1895a. *The Crowd*. London: Ernest Benn, 1896.

Le Bon, Gustave 1895b. *The Psychology of Peoples*. New York: Macmillan, 1898.

Le Bon, Gustave 1912. *The Psychology of Revolution*. London: T.F. Unwin, 1913.

Le Play, Frédéric 1855. 'Les ouvriers européens' in Carle C. Zimmerman, and Merle E. Frampton (eds) *Family and Society* (condensed translation.) New York: D. van Nostrand, 1935.

Le Roy Ladurie, Emmanuel 1965. *The Peasants of Languedoc*. Champaign: University of Illinois Press, 1974.

Leach, Edmund 1954. *Political Systems of Highland Burma*. London: Athlone Press.

Lefebvre, Henri 1939. *Dialectical Materialism*. London: Jonathan Cape, 1968.

Lefebvre, Henri 1947. *Critique of Everyday Life,* Volume 1. London: Verso, 1991.

Lefebvre, Henri 1961. *Critique of Everyday Life,* Volume 2. London: Verso, 2002.

Lefebvre, Henri 1968a. *Everyday Life in the Modern World*. Harmondsworth: Penguin, 1971.

Lefebvre, Henri 1968b. 'The Right to the City' in Henri Lefebure, *Writings on Cities* (edited by Eleonore Kofman and Elizabeth Lebas). Oxford: Blackwell, 1996.

Lefebvre, Henri 1971. *La révolution urbaine*. Paris: Gallimard.

Lefebvre, Henri 1972. *La pensée marxiste et la ville*. Paris: Casterman.

Lefebvre, Henri 1974. *The Production of Space*. Oxford: Basil Blackwell, 1991.

Lefebvre, Henri 1981. *Critique of Everyday Life,* Volume 3. London: Verso, 2003.

Lefebvre, Henri 1992. *Rhythmanalysis: Space, Time, and Everyday Life*. London: Continuum, 2004.

Leiter, Kenneth 1980. *Primer on Ethnomethodology*. Oxford: Oxford University Press.

Lemert, Edwin (ed.) 1967 *Human Deviance, Social Problems and Social Control*. Englewood Cliffs, NJ: Prentice-Hall.

Lenin, Vladimir Ilyich 1899. *The Development of Capitalism in Russia*. Moscow: Progress Publishers, 1967.

Lenin, Vladimir Ilyich 1902. *What Is to Be Done?* Harmondsworth: Penguin, 1988.

Lenin, Vladimir Ilyich 1909. *Materialism and Empirio-Criticism*. Peking: Foreign Languages Publishing House, 1976.

Lenin, Vladimir Ilyich 1917. *Imperialism: The Highest Stage of Capitalism*. Moscow: Progress Publishers, 1966.

Letourneau, Charles 1880. *Sociology, Based upon Ethnography*. London: Chapman and Hall, 1893.

Letourneau, Charles 1888. *The Evolution of Marriage and the Family*. London: Walter Scott, 1891.

Letourneau, Charles 1889. *Property: Its Origin and Developoment*. London: Walter Scott, 1892.

Levasseur, Émile 1859–67. *Historie des classes ouvrieres en France* (2 vols). Paris: Guillaumin.

Levasseur, Émile 1889–92. *La population française* (3 vols). Paris: Arthur Rousseau.

Levinas, Emmanuel 1930. *The Theory of Intuition in Husserl's Phenomenology*. Evanston, Ill.: North Western University Press, 1973.

Lévi-Strauss, Claude 1945. 'Structural Analysis in Linguistics and Anthropology' in Claude Lévi-Strauss, *Structural Anthropology*, Volume 1. London: Allen Lane The Penguin Press, 1968.

Lévi-Strauss, Claude 1949a. *The Elementary Structures of Kinship*. Boston: Beacon Press, 1969.

Lévi-Strauss, Claude 1949b. 'Introduction: History and Anthropology' in ClaudeLévi-Strauss, *Structural Anthropology*, Volume 1. London: Allen Lane The Penguin Press, 1968.

Lévi-Strauss, Claude 1953. 'Social Structure' in Claude Lévi-Strauss, *Structural Anthropology*, Volume 1. London: Allen Lane The Penguin Press, 1968.

Lévi-Strauss, Claude 1958. *Structural Anthropology*, Volume 1. London: Allen Lane The Penguin Press, 1968.

Lévi-Strauss, Claude 1962a. *The Savage Mind*. Chicago: University of Chicage Press, 1966.

Lévi-Strauss, Claude 1962b. *Totemism*. London: Merlin Press.

Lévi-Strauss, Claude 1964. *The Raw and the Cooked* [*Mythologiques, Volume 1*]. London: Cape, 1969.

Lévi-Strauss, Claude 1967. *From Honey to Ashes* [*Mythologiques, Volume 2*]. London: Cape, 1973.

Lévi-Strauss, Claude 1968. *The Origin of Table Manners* [*Mythologiques, Volume 3*]. London: Cape, 1978.

Lévi-Strauss, Claude 1971. *The Naked Man* [*Mythologiques, Volume 4*]. London: Cape, 1981.

Lévy-Bruhl, Lucien 1900. *La morale et la science des moeuers*. Paris: Presses Universitaires de France, 1971.

Lévy-Bruhl, Lucien 1910. *How Natives Think*. London: George Allen and Unwin, 1926.

Lévy-Bruhl, Lucien 1921. *Primitive Mentality*. Boston: Beacon Press, 1966.

Lewes, George 1853. *Comte's Philosophy of the Positive Sciences*. London: George Bell and Sons, 1878.

Lewin, Kurt 1936a. *A Dynamic Theory of Personality*. New York: McGraw Hill.

Lewin, Kurt 1936b. *Principles of Topological Psychology*. New York: Harper and Row.

Lilienfeld, Pavel Feodorovich 1873–81. *Gedanken über die Sozialwissenschaft der Zukunft* (5 vols). Mitau: E. Behre's verlag.

Lilienfeld, Pavel Feodorovich 1898. *Zur Verteidigung der Organischen Methode in der Soziologie*. Berlin: G. Reimer.

Linton, Ralph. 1945. *The Cultural Background of Personality*. London: Routledge and Kegan Paul, 1946.

Lippert, Julius 1884. *Die Geschichte der Familie*. Stuttgart: Enke.

Lippert, Julius 1886. *The Evolution of Culture*. New York: Macmillan, 1931.

List, Friedrich 1841. *The National System of Political Economy*. London: Longman's Green, 1904.

Littré, Émile [Paul-Maximilien-Émile] 1863. *Auguste Comte et la philosophie positive*. Paris: Librairie Hachette.

Littré, Émile [Paul-Maximilien-Émile] 1876. *Fragments de philosophie positive et de sociologie contemporaine*. Paris: Bureau de la Philosophie Positive.

Locke, John 1689. *Two Treatises on Government*. London: Allen and Unwin, 1987.

Locke, John 1690. *Essay Concerning Human Understanding*. Harmondsworth: Penguin, 1998.

Lockwood, David 1956. 'Some Remarks on the Social System'. *British Journal of Sociology* 7: 134–46.

Lockwood, David 1964. 'Social Integration and System Integration' in George Zollschan and Walter Hirsch (eds) *System, Change and Conflict*. Boston: Houghton Mifflin.

Lockwood, David 1996. 'Civic Integration and Class Formation'. *British Journal of Sociology* 47: 531–50.

Lombroso, Cesare 1875. *Criminal Man*. London: G.P. Putnam's Sons, 1911. (A partial translation by his daughter.)

Lombroso, Cesare 1899. *Crime: Its Causes and Remedies*. Montclair, NJ: Patterson Smith, 1968.

Lombroso, Cesare, Ferri, Enrico, Garafalo, Raffael, and Fioretti, Giulio 1886. *Polemica in difésa della scuola criminale positiva*. Bologna: Zanichelli.

Lorenz, Konrad 1963. *On Aggression*. New York: Harcourt Brace.

Loria, Achille 1886. *The Economic Foundations of Society*. London: S. Sonnenschein, 1899.

Loria, Achille 1901. *Sociologia*. Verona.

Loria, Achille 1921. *Aspetti sociali ed economica della guerra mondiale*. Milan: Treves.

Lowie, Robert 1917. *Culture and Ethnology*. New York: D.C. McMurtrie.

Lowie, Robert 1920. *Primitive Society*. New York: Boni and Liveright.

Lowie, Robert 1927. *The Origin of the State*. New York: Harcourt Brace.

Löwith, Karl 1932. *Max Weber and Karl Marx*. London: George Allen and Unwin, 1982.

Lubbock, John 1865. *Prehistoric Times*. London: Williams and Norgate.

Lubbock, John 1870. *The Origin of Civilization and the Primitive Condition of Man*. Chicago: University of Chicago Press, 1978.

Luhmann, Niklas 1965. *A Sociological Theory of Law*. London: Routledge and Kegan Paul, 1985.

Luhmann, Niklas 1968/1975. *Trust and Power*. New York: Wiley, 1979.

Luhmann, Niklas 1982. *The Differentiation of Society*. New York: Columbia University Press.

Luhmann, Niklas 1984. *Social Systems*. Stanford: Stanford University Press, 1995.

Luhmann, Niklas 1986. *Love as Passion*. Palo Alto, Calif.: Stanford University Press, 1998.

Luhmann, Niklas 1991. *Risk*. Berlin: W. de Gruyter, 1993.

Luhmann, Niklas 1996. *The Reality of the Mass Media*. Cambridge: Polity Press, 2000.

Luhmann, Niklas 1997. *Der Gesellschaft der Gesellschaft*. Frankfurt: Suhrkamp.

Luhmann, Niklas and Habermas, Jürgen 1971. *System Theorie oder Sozial Technologie*. Frankfurt: Suhrkamp.

Lukács, Gyorgy. 1910. *The Soul and the Forms*. London: Merlin, 1974.

Lukács, Gyorgy. 1914–15. *The Theory of the Novel*. London: Merlin, 1971.

Lukács, Gyorgy 1923. *History and Class Consciousness*. London: Merlin Press, 1971.

Lukes, Steven 1973. *Émile Durkheim: His Life and Work*. Harmondsworth: Allen Lane The Penguin Press.

Lukes, Steven 1974. *Power: A Radical View*. London: Macmillan.

Lundberg, George 1939. *Foundations of Sociology*. New York: Macmillan.

Luria, Aleksandr Romanovich *Cognitive Development: Its Cultural and Social Foundations*. Cambridge, Mass.: Harvard University Press, 1976.

Lurie, Alison 1967. *Imaginary Friends*. London: Heinemann.

Luxemburg, Rosa 1906. *The Mass Strike, the Political Party and the Trade Unions*. New York: Harper and Row, 1971.

Luxemburg, Rosa 1913. *The Accumulation of Capital*. London: Routledge and Kegan Paul, 1951.

Lyotard, Jean-François 1979. *The Postmodern Condition*. Manchester: Manchester University Press, 1984.

Macaulay, Thomas Babington 1849–61. *History of England* (5 vols). London: Longmans, 1898.

McBriar, Angus M. 1987. *An Edwardian Mixed-Doubles: The Bosanquets versus the Webbs*. Oxford: Oxford University Press.

McCarthy, Thomas 1978. *The Critical Theory of Jürgen Habermas*. London: Hutchinson.

McDougall, William 1905. *Physiological Psychology*. London: Dent.

McDougall, William 1908. *An Introduction to Social Psychology*. London: Methuen, 1923.

McDougall, William 1919. 'Theories of Action' in William McDougall, *An Introduction to Social Psychology* (20th edn). London: Methuen, 1926.

McDougall, William 1920. *The Group Mind*. Cambridge: Cambridge University Press, 1939.

McDougall, William 1923. *An Outline of Psychology*. London: Methuen.

McDougall, William 1936. *Psychoanalysis and Social Psychology*. London: Methuen.

Macfarlane, Alan 1978. *The Origins of English Individualism*. Oxford: Basil Blackwell.

Machiavelli, Niccolò 1505. *The Prince*. Oxford: Oxford University Press, 1984.

MacIntyre, Alasdair 1967. *A Short History of Ethics*. London: Routledge and Kegan Paul.

MacIver, Robert 1917. *Community: A Sociological Study*. London: Macmillan, 1924.

MacIver, Robert 1921. *Elements of Social Science*. London: Methuen.

MacIver, Robert 1937. *Society*. New York: Rinehart.

MacIver, Robert 1942. *Social Causation*. New York: Harper and Row, 1964.

Mackenzie, John S. 1895. *An Introduction to Social Philosophy*. Glasgow: James Maclehose.

Mackenzie, John S. 1918. *Outline of Social Philosophy*. London: George Allen and Unwin, 1963.

Mackinder, Halford 1902. *Britain and the British Seas*. Oxford: Clarendon Press.

Mackinder, Halford 1904. 'The Geographical Pivot of History'. *Geographical Journal* 23: 421–37.

Mackinder, Halford 1919. *Democratic Ideals and Reality*. Harmondsworth: Penguin, 1944.

McLellan, David 1973. *Karl Marx: His Life and Thought*. London: Macmillan.

Macnaghten, Philip and Urry, John 1998. *Contested Nature*. London: Sage.

McNeill, John R. and McNeill, William H. 2003. *The Human Web*. New York: W.W. Norton.

McNeill, William H. 1963. *The Rise of the West*. Chicago: Chicago University Press.

McNeill, William H. 1967. *A World History*. Oxford University Press, 1979.

McNeill, William H. 1976. *Plagues and People*. Oxford: Basil Blackwell.

McNeill, William H. 1982. *The Pursuit of Power: Technology, Armed Force and Society since AD 1000*. Oxford: Basil Blackwell.

McNeill, William H. 1989. *Arnold J. Toynbee: A Life*. New York: Oxford University Press.

McNeill, William H. 1996. *A History of the Human Community* (5th edn) (Originally 1963). Englewood Cliffs, NS: Prentice-Hall.

Macpherson, Crawford B. 1962. *The Political Theory of Possessive Individualism*. Oxford: Clarendon Press.

Maine, Henry 1861. *Ancient Law*. London: George Routledge and Son, no date.

Maines, David R. 2001. *The Faultline of Consciousness*. New York: Aldine de Gruyter.

Maistre, Joseph de 1796. *Considerations on France*. Cambridge: Cambridge University Press, 1994.

Maistre, Joseph de 1810. *On God and Society: Essay on the Generative Principles of Political Constitutions*. Chicago: H. Regnery, 1959.

Malinowski, Bronislaw 1922. *Argonauts of the Western Pacific*. London: George Routledge.

Malinowski, Bronislaw 1926. *Crime and Custom in Savage Society*. London: George Routledge.

Malinowski, Bronislaw 1929. *The Sexual Life of Savages*. London: George Routledge.

Malinowski, Bronislaw 1935. *Coral Gardens and Their Magic*. London: George Routledge.

Malinowski, Bronislaw 1939. 'The Functional Theory' in Bronislaw Malinowski, *A Scientific Theory of Culture and Other Essays*. Chapel Hill: University of North Carolina Press, 1944.

Malinowski, Bronislaw 1941. 'A Scientific Theory of Culture' in Bronislaw Malinowski, *A Scientific Theory of Culture and Other Essays*. Chapel Hill: University of North Carolina Press, 1944.

Mallet, Serge 1963. *The New Working Class*. Nottingham: Bertrand Russell Peace Foundation for Spokesman Books, 1975.

Malthus, Thomas Robert 1798. *Essay on the Principles of Population*. Harmondsworth: Penguin, 1970.

Malthus, Thomas R. 1820. *Principles of Political Economy*. Cambridge: Cambridge University Press, 1989.

Mandel, Ernest 1972. *Late Capitalism*. London: New Left Books, 1975.

Mann, Michael 1985. 'War and Social Theory: Into Battle with Classes, Nations and States' in Michael Mann, *States, War, and Capitalism*. Oxford: Basil Blackwell, 1988.

Mann, Michael 1986. *The Sources of Social Power, Volume 1: A History of Power from the Beginning to AD 1760*. Cambridge: Cambridge University Press.

Mann, Michael 1987. 'Ruling Class Strategies and Citizenship'. *Sociology* 21: 339–354.

Mann, Michael 1993. *The Sources of Social Power, Volume 2: The Rise of Classes and Nation States, 1760–1914*. Cambridge: Cambridge University Press.

Mann, Michael 2004. *Fascists*. Cambridge: Cambridge University Press.

Mannheim, Karl 1924. 'Historicism' in Karl Mannheim (ed.) *Essays on the Sociology of Knowledge*. London: Routledge and Kegan Paul, 1952.

Mannheim, Karl 1925a. 'The Problem of a Sociology of Knowledge' in Karl Mannheim, *Essays on the Sociology of Knowledge*. London: Routledge and Kegan Paul, 1952.

Mannheim, Karl 1925b. *Conservatism: A Contribution to the Sociology of Knowledge*. London: Routledge and Kegan Paul, 1986.

Mannheim, Karl 1929. 'Ideology and Utopia' in Karl Mannheim, *Ideology and Utopia, Chapters 2–4*. London: Routledge and Kegan Paul, 1936.

Mannheim, Karl 1931. 'The Problem of the Sociology of Knowledge' in Karl Mannheim, *Ideology and Utopia, Chapter 5*. London: Routledge and Kegan Paul, 1936.

Mannheim, Karl 1942. 'The Crisis in Valuation' in Karl Mannheim, *Diagnosis of Our Times*. London: Routledge and Kegan Paul, 1943.

Mannheim, Karl 1947. *Freedom, Power and Democratic Planning*. London: Routledge and Kegan Paul, 1951.

Manning, Philip 1992. *Erving Goffman and Modern Sociology*. Cambridge: Polity Press.

Marcuse, Herbert 1941. *Reason and Revolution* (2nd edn). New York: Humanities Press, 1954.

Marcuse, Herbert 1964. *One Dimensional Man*. London: Routledge and Kegan Paul.

Marshall, Alfred 1890. *Principles of Economics*. London: Macmillan.

Marshall, Thomas H. 1949. 'Citizenship and Social Class' in Thomas H. Marshall, *Sociology at the Crossroads*. London: Heinemann, 1963.

Martell, Luke 1994. *Ecology and Society: An Introduction*. Cambridge: Polity Press.

Martindale, Don 1961. *The Nature and Types of Sociological Theory*. London: Routledge and Kegan Paul.

Martineau, Harriet 1837. *Society in America*. New York: Doubleday, 1962. (Abridged edition edited by S.M. Lipset.)

Martineau, Harriet 1838. *How to Observe Manners and Morals*. London: Charles Knight.

Martineau, Harriet 1848. *Eastern Life, Present and Past*. London: Edward Moxon.

Martineau, Harriet 1853. *Comte's Positive Philosophy* (3 vols). London: George Bell, 1896.

Martins, Herminio 1993. *Knowledge as Passion*. London: I.B. Tauris.

Marwick, Arthur 1977. *War and Social Change in the Twentieth Century*. London: Macmillan.

Marx, Karl 1844. *Economic and Philosophical Manuscripts*. London: Lawrence and Wishart, 1959.

Marx, Karl 1847. *Poverty of Philosophy*. Chicago: C.H. Kerr, 1910.

Marx, Karl 1858. *Grundrisse*. Harmondsworth: Penguin, 1973.

Marx, Karl 1859. *Contribution to the Critique of Political Economy*. London: Lawrence and Wishart.

Marx, Karl 1862–63. *Theories of Surplus Value*. London: Lawrence and Wishart, 1969–72.

Marx, Karl 1864–65. *Capital, Volume 3*. Harmondsworth: Penguin, 1981.

Marx, Karl 1865–78. *Capital, Volume 2*. Harmondsworth: Penguin, 1978.

Marx, Karl 1867. *Capital, Volume 1*. Harmondsworth: Penguin, 1976.

Marx, Karl and Engels, Friedrich 1845. *The Holy Family*. London: Lawrence and Wishart, 1956.

Marx, Karl and Engels, Friedrich 1848. *The Communist Manifesto*. Harmondsworth: Penguin, 1967.

Maryanski, Alexandra and Turner, Jonathan H. 1992. *The Social Cage*. Palo Alto, Calif.: Stanford University Press.

Masaryk, Thomas Garrique 1881. *Suicide and the Meaning of Civilization*. Chicago: University of Chicago Press, 1970.

Masaryk, Thomas Garrique 1912. *The Spirit of Russia* (3 vols). London: George Allen and Unwin, 1919.

Matza, David 1964. *Delinquency and Drift*. New York: John Wiley and Sons.

Mauss, Marcel 1902. *A General Theory of Magic*. London: Routledge and Kegan Paul, 1972.

Mauss, Marcel 1925. *The Gift*. London: Routledge and Kegan Paul, 1966.

Mauss, Marcel 1934. 'Techniques of the Body'. *Economy and Society* 2: 70–87.

Maxwell, James Clerk 1865. *A Dynamical Theory of the Electromagnetic Field*. Edinburgh: Scottish Academic Press, 1982.

Maxwell, James Clerk 1877. *Matter and Motion*. London: Routledge, 1996.

Mayhew, Leon 1997. *The New Public*. Cambridge: Cambridge University Press.

McCarthy, Thomas 1978 *The Critical Theory of Jürgen Habermas*. London: Hutchinson.

Mead, George Herbert 1909. 'Social Psychology as a Counterpart to Physiological Psychology' in George Herbert Mead, *Selected Writings* (edited by Andrew J. Reck), Chicago: University of Chicago Press, 1964.

Mead, George Herbert 1910. *Essays in Social Psychology*. New Brunswick, NJ: Transaction Publishers, 2001.

Mead, George Herbert 1927. *Mind, Self and Society from the Standpoint of Social Behaviorism*. Chicago: University of Chicago Press, 1934.

Mead, Margaret 1928. *Coming of Age in Samoa: A Study of Adolescence and Sex in Primitive Societies*. Harmondsworth: Penguin, 1943.

Mead, Margaret 1930. *Growing up in New Guinea: A Study of Adolescence and Sex in Primitive Societies*. Harmondsworth: Penguin, 1942.

Mead, Margaret 1935. *Sex and Temperament in Three Primitive Societies*. London: Routledge and Kegan Paul, 1977.

Mead, Margaret 1950. *Male and Female*. London: Gollancz.

Mehring, Franz 1893. *On Historical Materialism*. London: New Park Publications, 1975.

Meillet, Antoine 1903. *Introduction a l'étude comparative des langues indo-européenes*. Paris.

Meillet, Antoine 1921–36. *Linguistique historique et linguistique générale* (2 vols). Paris.

Menger, Carl 1871. *Grundsätze der Volkwirtschaftslehre*. Aalen: Scientia Verlag, 1968.

Menger, Carl 1883. *Investigations into the Methods of the Social Sciences*. New York: New York University Press, 1985.

Merton, Robert K. 1938. *Science, Technology and Society in Seventeenth-Century England*. New York: Harper and Row, 1970.

Merton, Robert K. 1957. 'The Role Set: Problems in Sociological Theory'. *British Journal of Sociology* 8: 106–20.

Meszaros, Istuan 1970. *Marx's Concept of Alienation*. London: Merlin Press.

Meyer, John W., Boli, J., Thomas, G.M. and Ramirez, F.O. 1997. 'World Society and the Nation State'. *American Journal of Sociology* 103, 144–181.

Middlemas, Keith 1979. *Politics in an Industrial Society*. London: André Deutsch.

Miege, Bernard 1989. *The Capitalization of Cultural Production*. New York: International General.

Mikhailovskii, Nikolai 1870. *Qu'est-ce que le progrès?* Paris, 1897.

Milgram, Stanley 1974. *Obedience to Authority*. London: Pinter and St Martin's Press, 1997.

Miliband, Ralph 1969. *The State in Capitalist Society*. London: Weidenfeld and Nicolson.

Miliband, Ralph 1982. *Capitalist Democracy in Britain*. Oxford: Oxford University Press.

Miliband, Ralph 1983. *Class Power and State Power*. London: Verso.

Miliband, Ralph 1989. *Divided Societies*. Oxford: Oxford University Press.

Mill, James 1821. *Elements of Political Economy*. New York: G. Olms, 1971.

Mill, James 1829. *Analysis of the Phenomenon of the Human Mind*. London: Continuum, 2001.

Mill, John Stuart 1848. *Principles of Political Economy*. Harmondsworth: Penguin, 1970.

Mill, John Stuart 1865. *Auguste Comte and Positivism*. Bristol: Thoemmes Press, 1993.

Mill, John Stuart 1869. *On Socialism*. New York: Prometheus Books, 1976.

Millar, John 1779. *The Origin of the Distinction of Ranks*. London: J. Murray.

Millett, Kate 1970. *Sexual Politics*. New York: Doubleday.

Mills, C. Wright 1940. 'Situated Actions and Vocabularies of Motive' in C. Wright Mills, *Power, Politics, and People*. New York: Oxford University Press, 1963.

Mills, C. Wright 1951. *White Collar*. New York: Oxford University Press.

Mills, C. Wright 1953. *Character and Social Structure*. New York: Oxford University Press.

Mills, C. Wright 1956. *The Power Elite*. New York: Oxford University Press.

Milne, Alan J.M. 1962. *The Social Philosophy of English Idealism*. London: George Allen and Unwin.

Mirabeau, Honoré de 1772. *Essai sur le despotisme*. Paris: Brissot-Thivars, 1821.

Mirowski, Philip 1989. *More Heat Than Light*. Cambridge: Cambridge University Press.

Mises, Ludwig von 1922. *Socialism*. Indianapolis: Liberty Fund, 1981.

Mises, Ludwig von 1949. *Human Action*. New Haven: Yale University Press.

Mitchell, Juliett 1974. *Psychoanalysis and Feminism*. Harmondsworth: Penguin.

Moi, Toril (ed.) 1986. *The Kristeva Reader*. New York: Columbia University Press.

Montesquieu, Baron de 1721. *Persian Letters*. Harmondsworth: Penguin Books, 1973.

Montesquieu, Baron de 1734. *Reflections on the Causes of the Rise and Fall of the Roman Empire*. Edinburgh: A. Donaldson, 1775.

Montesquieu, Baron de 1748. *The Spirit of Laws*. Cambridge: Cambridge University Press, 1989.

Moore, Barrington 1958. *Political Power and Social Theory*. Cambridge, Mass.: Harvard University Press.

Moore, Barrington 1966. *The Social Origins of Dictatorship and Democracy*. Harmondsworth: Pelican.

Moreno, J.L. 1934. *Who Shall Survive?* New York: Beacon Press.

Moret, Alexandre and Davy, Georges 1924. *From Tribe to Empire*. London: Kegan Paul, Trench, Trubner & Co.,1926.

Morgan, Lewis Henry 1877. *Ancient Society*. Chicago: Charles H. Kerr.

Morley, David 1980. *The Nationwide Audience: Structure and Decoding*. London: BFI.

Morrill, Richard 1970. *The Spatial Organisation of Society*. Belmont, Calif.: Wadsworth.

Morrill, Richard, Gaile, Gary L., and Thrall, Grant 1988. *Spatial Diffusion*. Beverly Hills: Sage.

Morris, Charles W. (ed.) 1938. *The Philosophy of the Act*. Chicago: University of Chicago Press.

Morris, Lydia 2002. *Managing Migration: Civic Stratification and Migrants' Rights*. London: Routledge.

Morselli, Emilio 1879. *Suicide: An Essay on Comparative Moral Statistics*. London: Kegan Paul, Trench, Trubner, 1899.

Morselli, Emilio 1898. *Elementi di sociologia generale*. Milan: Hoepli.

Mosca, Gaetano 1896. 'Elementi di scienza politica, Volume One' in Gaetano Mosca *The Ruling Class, Chapters 1–11*. New York: McGraw Hill, 1939.

Mosca, Gaetano 1923. 'Elementi di scienza politica, Volume Two' in Gaetano Mosca *The Ruling Class, Chapters 12–17*. New York: McGraw Hill, 1939.

Mozeti , Gerald 1992. 'Outsiders and True Believers: Austrian Sociologists Respond to Fascism' in Stephen P. Turner and Dirk Käsler (eds) *Sociology Responds to Fascism*. London: Routledge, 1992.

Mueller, Franz (ed.) 1941 *Sociology, by Leopold von Wiese*. New York: Oskar Piest.

Mukerjee, Radhakamal 1926. *Regional Sociology*. New York: Century.

Müller-Lyer, Franz 1908. *The History of Social Development* [*Phasen der Kultur und Richtungslinien des Fortschritts*]. London: George Allen and Unwin, 1920.

Müller-Lyer, Franz 1912. *The Family*. London: George Allen and Unwin, 1931.

Müller-Lyer, Franz 1913. *The Evolution of Modern Marriage* [*Phasen der Liebe*]. London: George Allen and Unwin, 1930.

Mumford, Lewis 1934. *Technics and Civilization*. New York: Harcourt Brace.
Mumford, Lewis 1938. *The Culture of Cities*. New York: Harcourt Brace.
Mumford, Lewis 1944. *The Condition of Man*. New York: Harcourt Brace.
Murdock, Graham and Golding, Peter 1978. 'The Structure, Ownership and Control of the Press, 1914–76' in George Boyce, James Curran, and Pauline Wingate (eds) *Newspaper History*. London: Constable.
Myrdal, Gunnar 1944. *An American Dilemma*. New York: Harper.
Neumann, Franz 1942. *Behemoth: The Structure and Practice of National Socialism*. New York: Octagon Books, 1963.
Newman, W. Russell 1991. *The Future of the Mass Audience*. New York: Cambridge University Press.
Newton, Isaac 1687. *Mathematical Principles of Natural Philosophy*. London: Dawsons, 1969.
Niceforo, Alfredo 1910. *Antropologia delle classi povere*. Milan: Vallardi.
Nicolis, Gregoire and Prigione, Ilya 1977. *Self-Organisation in Nonequilibrium Systems*. New York: John Wiley.
Nicolis, Gregoire and Prigogine, Ilya 1989. *Exploring Complexity: An Introduction*. New York: W.H. Freeman.
Nisbet, Robert A. 1966. *The Sociological Tradition*. New York: Basic Books.
Novicow, Yacov 1894. *Les luttes entre sociétés humaines et leurs phases successives*. Paris: F. Alcan.
Novicow, Yacov 1897. *Conscience et volonté sociales*. Paris: V. Giard et E. Brière.
Novicow, Yacov 1898. 'Théorie organique des sociétés'. *Annales del'Institut de sociologie*, 4, 169–96 and 5, 71–223.
Novicow, Yacov 1912. 'The Mechanism and Limits of Human Association'. *American Journal of Sociology* 23 (3), 1917: 289–349.
O'Brien, Mary 1981. *The Politics of Reproduction*. London: Routledge.
O'Brien, Mary 1989. *Reproducing the World*. Boulder, Colo.: Westview Press.
O'Connor, James 1973. *The Fiscal Crisis of the State*. New York: St Martins Press.
Odum, Howard F. 1971. *Environment, Power, and Society*. New York: Wiley-Interscience.
Odum, Howard F. 1983. *Systems Ecology: An Introduction*. New York: John Wiley.
Odum, Howard F. and Odum, Elizabeth C. 1976. *Energy Basis for Man and Nature*. New York: McGraw-Hill.
Odum, Howard Washington and Moore, Harry Estil 1938. *American Regionalism*. New York: H. Holt and Co.
Offe, Claus 1970. *Industry and Inequality*. London: Edward Arnold, 1976.
Offe, Claus 1985. *Disorganized Capitalism: Contemporary Transformations of Work and Politics*. Cambridge: Polity Press.
Offe, Claus and Wiesenthal, Helmut 1980. 'Two Logics of Collective Action: Theoretical Notes on Social Class and Organizational Forms'. *Political Power and Social Theory* 1: 67–115.
Ogilvie, Alan G. (ed.) 1928 *Great Britain: Essays in Regional Geography*. Cambridge: Cambridge University Press.
Oppenheimer, Franz 1914. *The State*. Montreal: Black Rose Books, 1975.
Oppenheimer, Franz 1922. *System der Soziologie*. Jena: G. Fischer.
Orbach, Susie 1978. *Fat is a Feminist Issue*. London: Arrow, 1988.
Orbach, Susie 1986. *Hunger Strike*. New York: W.W. Norton.
Ortega y Gasset, José 1929. *The Revolt of the Masses*. New York: Norton, 1957.
Ostwald, Wilhelm 1909. *Energetische Grundlagen der Kulturwissenschaften*. Leipzig: Duncker.
Ostwald, Wilhelm 1912. *Der Energetische Imperativ*. Leipzig: Akademische Verlagsgesellschaft.
Ostwald, Wilhelm 1914. *Auguste Comte, der Mann und seine Werk*. Leipzig: Unesma.
Pareto, Vilfredo 1896–7. *Course d'economie politique*.
Pareto, Vilfredo 1916. *A Treatise on General Sociology*. New York: Dover, 1963.

Park, Robert E. 1921. *Introduction to the Science of Sociology*. Chicago: University of Chicago Press.

Park, Robert E. and Burgess, Ernest W. (eds) 1925. *The City*. Chicago: University of Chicago Press, 1967.

Parsons, Talcott 1937. *The Structure of Social Action*. New York: McGraw-Hill.

Parsons, Talcott 1942. 'Age and Sex in the Social Structure of the United States' in Talcott Parsons (ed.) *Essays in Sociological Theory*. New York: Free Press, 1954.

Parsons, Talcott 1945. 'The Present Position and Prospects of Systematic Theory in Sociology' in Talcott Parsons (ed.) *Essays in Sociological Theory* (rev. edn). New York: Free Press, 1954.

Parsons, Talcott 1951. *The Social System*. New York: Free Press.

Parsons, Talcott (ed.) 1954. *Essays in Sociological Theory* (rev. edn). New York: Free Press.

Parsons, Talcott 1960a. 'The Mass Media and the Structure of American Society' in Talcott Parsons (ed.) *Politics and Social Structure*. New York: Free Press, 1969.

Parsons, Talcott 1960b. 'Pattern Variables Revisited: A Response to Robert Dubin' *American Sociological Review*, 25: 467–83.

Parsons, Talcott 1961. 'An Outline of the Social System' in Talcott Parsons, Edward Shils, Kaspar D. Naegele, and Jesse R. Pitts (eds) *Theories of Society, Volume 1*. New York: Free Press.

Parsons, Talcott 1963. 'On the Concept of Political Power'. *Proceedings of the American Philosophical Society* 107: 232–62.

Parsons, Talcott 1966. *Societies: Evolutionary and Comparative Perspectives*. Englewood Cliffs, NJ: Prentice-Hall.

Parsons, Talcott 1968. 'Social Systems' in Talcott Parsons (ed.) *Social Systems and the Evolution of Action Theory*. New York: Free Press, 1977.

Parsons, Talcott 1970. 'Some Problems of General Theory' in Talcott Parsons (ed.) *Social Systems and the Evolution of Action Theory*. New York: Free Press.

Parsons, Talcott 1970. 'On Building Social Systems Theory' in Talcott Parsons (ed.) *Social Systems and the Evolution of Action Theory*. New York: Free Press, 1977.

Parsons, Talcott 1971. *The System of Modern Societies*. Englewood Cliffs, NJ: Prentice-Hall.

Parsons, Talcott 1975. 'The Present Status of Structural-Functional Theory in Sociology' in Talcott Parsons (ed.) *Social Systems and the Evolution of Action Theory*. New York: Free Press, 1977.

Parsons, Talcott and Bales, Robert F. 1956. *Family, Socialization and Interaction Process*. London: Routledge and Kegan Paul.

Parsons, Talcott, Bales, Robert F., and Shils, Edward A. 1953. *Working Papers in the Theory of Action*. New York: Free Press.

Parsons, Talcott and Smelser, Neil J. 1956. *Economy and Society*. New York: Free Press.

Pateman, Carole 1988. *The Sexual Contract*. Stanford: Stanford University Press.

Pearson, Karl 1909. *The Groundwork of Eugenics*. London: Dulaou.

Peel, John D.Y. 1971. *Herbert Spencer: The Evolution of a Sociologist*. London: Heinemann.

Perry, William J. 1923. *The Origin of Magic and Religion*. London: Methuen.

Perry, William J. 1924. *The Growth of Civilization*. Harmondsworth: Penguin, 1937.

Petrazycki, Leon 1908–10. *Law and Morality*. Cambridge, Mass.: Harvard University Press, 1955.

Piaget, Jean 1924. *Judgment and Reasoning in the Child*. London: Routledge and Kegan Paul, 1928.

Piaget, Jean 1936. *The Origins of Intelligence in the Child*. London: Routledge and Kegan Paul, 1953.

Piaget, Jean 1954. *Construction of Reality in the Child*. London: Routledge and Kegan Paul.

Piaget, Jean 1975. *Equilibration of Cognitive Structures*. Chicago: University of Chicago Press.

Piaget, Jean and Inhelder, Barbel 1958. *Growth of Logical Thinking*. London: Routledge and Kegan Paul.

Pigou, Alfred Cecil 1912. *Wealth and Welfare*. London: Macmillan.

Pinker, Steve 1994. *The Language Instinct*. London: Allen Lane.

Pinker, Steve 2002. *The Blank Slate*. Harmondsworth: Allen Lane.

Piore, Michael J. and Sabel, Charles F. 1984. *The Second Industrial Divide*. New York: Basic Books.

Pipping, Knut 1982. 'The First Finnish Sociologist'. *Acta Sociologica* 25: 347–57.

Plekhanov, Georgy 1895. 'On the Development of the Monist Conception of History' in Andrew Rothstein (ed.) *G.V. Plekhanov: In Defence of Marxism*. London: Lawrence and Wishart, 1947.

Plekhanov, Georgy 1908. *Materialismus Militans: Reply to Mr Bogdanov*. Moscow: Progress Publishers, 1973.

Plekhanov, Georgy 1912–13. *Art and Social Life*. London: Lawrence and Wishart, no date.

Plummer, Ken 1995. *Telling Sexual Stories*. London: Routledge.

Poggi, Gianfranco 1978. *The Development of the Modern State*. London: Hutchinson.

Poggi, Gianfranco 1993. *Money and the Modern Mind: George Simmel's Philosophy of Money*. Berkeley: University of California Press.

Popper, Karl R. 1945. *The Open Society and Its Enemies*. London: Routledge and Kegan Paul.

Popper, Karl R. 1957. *The Poverty of Historicism*. London: Routledge and Kegan Paul.

Popper, Karl R. 1967. 'Epistemology without a Knowing Subject' in Karl R. Popper (ed.) *Objective Knowledge*. Oxford: Oxford University Press, 1972.

Popper, Karl R. 1968. 'On the Theory of the Objective Mind' in Karl R. Popper *Objective Knowledge*. Oxford: Oxford University Press, 1972.

Posada, Adolfo 1903. *Sociología contemporánea*. Barcelona: Sucesores de Manuel Soler.

Posada, Adolfo 1908. *Principios de sociología* (2 vols). Madrid: D. Jorro.

Powers, Charles H. 1987. *Vilfredo Pareto*. Beverley Hills: Sage Publications.

Pusey, Michael 1987. *Jürgen Habermas*. London: Tavistock.

Pusey, Michael 1987. *Jurgen Habermas*. London: Tavistock.

Puttfarken, Thomas 2000. *The Discovery of Pictorial Composition*. New Haven: Yale University Press.

Quadagno, Jill S. 1984. 'Welfare Capitalism and the Social Security Act of 1935' *American Sociological Review*, 49: 632–47.

Quesnay, François 1758. *Tableau Économique*. London: Macmillan, 1972.

Quetelet, Lambert Adolphe Jacques 1835. *Treatise of Man and the Development of His Faculties*. New York: Burt Franklin, 1968.

Quetelet, Lambert Adolphe Jacques 1848. *Du système sociale et des lois qui le régissent*. Paris: Guillaumin.

Radcliffe-Brown, Alfred Reginald 1922. *The Andaman Islanders*. New York: Free Press, 1964.

Radcliffe-Brown, Alfred Reginald 1935. 'On the Concept of Function in Social Science' in Alfred Reginald Radcliffe-Brown *Structure and Function in Primitive Society*. London: Cohen and West, 1952.

Radcliffe-Brown, Alfred Reginald 1937. *A Natural Science of Society*. Glencoe, Ill.: Free Press, 1957.

Ratzel, Friedrich 1882–91. *Anthropogeographie: Die geographische Verbreitung des Menschen*. Darmstadt: Wissenschaftliche Buchgesellschaft.

Ratzel, Friedrich 1887–8. *History of Mankind*. London: Macmillan, 1896.

Ratzel, Friedrich 1897. *Politische Geographie*. Munich: R. Oldenbourg.

Ratzenhofer, Gustav 1893. *Wesen und Zweck der Politik*. Leipzig: F.A. Brockhaus.

Ratzenhofer, Gustav 1898. *Die Soziologische Erkenntnis*. Leipzig: F.A. Brockhaus.

Ratzenhofer, Gustav 1907. *Soziologie: Positive Lehre von den Menschlichen Wechselbeziehungen*. Leipzig: F.A. Brockhaus.

Reck, Andrew J. (ed.) 1964 *Selected Writings: George Herbert Mead*. Chicago: University of Chicago Press.

Reclus, Élie 1885. *Primitive Folk: Studies in Comparative Ethnology*. London: Walter Scott, 1891.

Reclus, Elisée 1867–8. *The Earth: A Descriptive History of the Life of the Globe*. New York: Harper and Brothers, 1872.

Reclus, Elisée 1876–94. *The Earth and Its Inhabitants*, (19 vols). London: H. Virtue & Co. 1878–94.

Reclus, Elisée 1905–8. *L'homme et la terre*. Paris: Librairie Universelle.

Reich, Wilhelm 1933a. *Character Analysis*. New York: Farrar, Strauss, and Giroux, 1972.

Reich, Wilhelm 1933b. *The Mass Psychology of Fascism*. Harmondsworth: Penguin, 1975.

Reich, Wilhelm 1942. *The Function of the Orgasm*. London: Panther Books, 1968.

Reisman, D. and others 1953. *The Lonely Crowd*. New Haven: Yale University Press.

Rex, John A. 1961. *Key Problems of Sociological Theory*. London: Routledge and Kegan Paul.

Rex, John A. 1970. *Race Relations in Sociological Theory*. London: Weidenfeld and Nicolson.

Rex, John A. 1981. *Social Conflict*. Harlow: Longman.

Rex, John A. and Moore, Robert 1969. *Race, Community and Conflict: A Study of Sparkbrook* (corrected edn). London: Oxford University Press.

Rex, John A. and Tomlinson, Sally 1979. *Colonial Immigrants in Great Britain: A Class Analysis*. London: Routledge and Kegan Paul.

Ricardo, David 1817. *Principles of Political Economy and Taxation*. London: J.M. Dent, 1911.

Rich, Adrienne 1980. 'Compulsory Heterosexuality and Lesbian Existence'. *Signs* 5: 631–60.

Ridley, Matt 1999. *Genome*. London: HarperCollins.

Riesman, David 1950. *The Lonely Crowd* (abridged edn). New Haven: Yale University Press, 1961.

Ritchie, D.G. 1895. *Natural Rights*. London: Allen and Unwin, 1924.

Ritter, Karl 1817–59. *Die Erdekunde in Verhältnis zur Natur und zur Geschichte des Menschen* (19 vols). Berlin.

Rivers, William H.R. 1914. *Kinship and Social Organization*. London: Athlone Press, 1968.

Rivers, William H.R. 1920. *Instinct and the Unconscious*. Cambridge: Cambridge University Press.

Rivers, William H.R. 1924. *Social Organization*. London: Dawsons of Pall Mall, 1968.

Rizzi, Bruno 1939. *The Bureaucratisation of the World*. London: Tavistock, 1985.

Roberts, Brian K. 1982. *Village Plans*. Aylesbury: Shire.

Roberts, Brian K. 1987. *The Making of the English Village*. London: Longman.

Robertson, Roland 1992. *Globalization: Social Theory and Global Culture*. London: Sage.

Roberty, Evgeniy de Valentinovich 1881. *La sociologie*. Paris: Germer-Baillière.

Roberty, Evgeniy de Valentinovich 1904. *Nouveau programme de sociologie*. Paris: F. Alcan.

Roberty, Evgeniy de Valentinovich 1908. *Sociologie de l'action*. Paris: F. Alcan.

Roemer, John 1988. *Free to Lose*. London: Radius.

Rorty, Richard 1980. *Philosophy and the Mirror of Nature*. Princeton: Princeton University Press.

Roscher, Wilhelm 1854. *Principles of Political Economy* (2 vols). New York: H. Holt, 1878.

Ross, Dorothy 1991. *The Origins of American Social Science*. Cambridge: Cambridge University Press.

Ross, Edward 1901. *Social Control*. New York: Macmillan.

Ross, Edward 1908. *Social Psychology*. New York: Macmillan.

Ross, Edward 1921. *Principles of Sociology*. New York: The Century Co.

Rostow, Walter Whitman 1960. *The Stages of Economic Growth*. Cambridge: Cambridge University Press.

Roszack, Theodore 1969. *The Making of a Counter Culture*. New York: Doubleday.

Rousseau, Jean-Jacques 1755. *A Discourse on Inequality*. Harmondsworth: Penguin, 1984.

Rousseau, Jean-Jacques 1762. *The Social Contract*. Harmondsworth: Penguin.

Rousiers, Paul de 1895. *Le question ouvrière en angleterre*. Paris: Firmin-Didot.

Rowntree, Seebohm 1901. *Poverty: A Study of Town Life*. London: Macmillan.

Rubin, Gayle 1975. 'The Traffic in Women: Notes on the "Political Economy" of Sex' in Rayna Reiter (ed.) *Toward an Anthropology of Women*. New York: Monthly Review Press.

Rumney, Jay 1937. *Herbert Spencer's Sociology*. New York: Atherton Press, 1965.

Russett, Cynthia E. 1966. *The Concept of Equilibrium in American Social Thought*. New Haven: Yale University Press.

Sacks, Harvey 1965–72. *Lectures on Conversation*. Oxford: Basil Blackwell, 1992.

Saint-Simon, Henri de 1813. 'Essay on the Science of Man' in Henri de Saint-Simon, *Social Organization, the Science of Man* (edited by Felix Markham). New York: Harper and Row, 1964.

Saint-Simon, Henri de 1825. 'On Social Organization' in Henri de Saint-Simon, *Social Organization, the Science of Man* (edited by Felix Markham). New York: Harper and Row, 1964.

Sapir, Edward 1921. *Language*. New York: Harcourt, Brace.

Sartre, Jean-Paul 1943. *Being and Nothingness*. London: Routledge, 2003.

Sartre, Jean-Paul 1944. *In Camera*. Harmondsworth: Penguin, 1946.

Sassen, Saskia 1991. *The Global City: New York, London, Tokyo*. Princeton: Princeton University Press.

Sauer, Carl 1925. 'The Morphology of Landscape'. *University of California Publications in Geography* 2: 19–53.

Sauer, Carl 1941. 'Foreword to Historical Geography'. *Annals, Association of American Geographers* 31: 1–24.

Saussure, Ferdinand de 1916. *Course in General Linguistics*. New York: McGraw-Hill, 1966.

Savorgnan, Franco 1918. *La guerra e la populazione*. Bologna: Zanichelli.

Savorgnan, Franco 1924. *Demografia di guerra e altri saggi*. Bologna: Zanichelli.

Savorgnan, Franco 1936. *Corso di demografia*. Pisa: Nistri-Lischi.

Say, Jean-Baptiste 1803. *A Treatise on Political Economy*. New Brunswick, NJ: Transaction, 2001.

Scarfe, Norman 1972. *The Making of the English Landscape: The Suffolk Landscape*. London: Hodder and Stoughton.

Schäffle, Albert 1875–80. *Bau und Leben des Sozialen Körpen* (4 vols). Tübingen: Laupp, 1906.

Schäffle, Albert 1903. *Abriss der Soziologie* (posthumously edited by K. Bücher) Tubingon: J.C.B. Mohr, 1906.

Schallmayer, Wilhelm 1891. *Über die drohende Körperliche Entartung der Kulturmenschheit*. Berlin: Newied.

Schallmayer, Wilhelm 1903. *Vererbung und auslese im Lebenslauf der Völker*. Jena: G. Fischer.

Scheff, Thomas J. 1990. *Microsociology: Discourse, Emotion and Social Structure*. Chicago: University of Chicago Press.

Scheler, Max 1926. *Problems of a Sociology of Knowledge*. London: Routledge and Kegan Paul, 1980.

Schelling, Friedrich 1797. *Ideas for a Philosophy of Nature*. Cambridge: Cambridge University Press, 1988.

Schlesinger, Philip 1978. *Putting 'Reality' Together*. London: Methuen.

Schmitt, Carl 1932. *The Concept of the Political*. Piscataway, NJ Rutgers University Press, 1976.

Schmoller, Gustav 1918. *Die Soziale Frage*. Munich: Duncker and Humblot.

Schreiner, Olive 1899. 'The Woman Question' in Carol Barash (ed.) *An Olive Schreiner Reader*. London: Pandora Press, 1987.

Schreiner, Olive 1911. *Women and Labour*. London: Unwin.

Schütz, Alfred 1924–7. *Life Forms and Meaning Structure*. London: Routledge and Kegan Paul, 1972.

Schütz, Alfred 1932. *The Phenomenology of the Social World*. London: Heinemann Educational Books, 1972.

Schütz, Alfred 1947–59. *Reflections on the Problem of Relevance*. New Haven: Yale University Press, 1970.

Schütz, Alfred 1962–6. *Collected Papers*, (3 vols). The Hague: Martinus Nijhof.

Schütz, Alfred and Luckmann, Thomas 1973. *Structures of the Life-World,* Volume 1. Evanston, Ill: Northwestern University Press, 1974.

Schütz, Alfred and Luckmann, Thomas 1983. *Structures of the Life-World,* Volume 2. Evanston, Ill: Northwestern University Press, 1989.

Schwendinger, Herman and Schwendinger, Julia 1974. *The Sociologists of the Chair*. New York: Basic Books.

Scott, John 1996. *Stratification and Power: Structures of Class, Status and Command*. Cambridge: Polity Press.

Scott, John 1997. *Corporate Business and Capitalist Classes*. Oxford: Oxford University Press.

Scott, John 1998. 'Relationism, Cubism, and Reality: Beyond Relativism' in Tim May and Malcolm Williams (eds) *Knowing the Social World*. Buckingham: Open University Press.

Scott, John 2000. *Social Network Analysis*. London: Sage.

Scott, John 2001. *Power*. Cambridge: Polity Press.

Semple, Ellen Churchill 1903. *American History and Its Geographic Conditions*. Boston: Houghton Mifflin.

Semple, Ellen Churchill 1911. *Influences of Geographic Environment: On the Basis of Ratzel's System of Anthropo-Geography*. London: Constable, 1933.

Sennett, Richard 1978. *The Fall of Public Man*. New York: Vintage Books.

Shapin, Stephen 1994. *The Social History of Truth*. Chicago: University of Chicago Press.

Shaw, George Bernard (ed.) 1889. *Fabian Essays in Socialism*. London: Fabian Socirty.

Shaw, George Bernard 1928. *The Intelligent Woman's Guide to Socialism and Capitalism*. London: Constable and Co.

Shelley, Mary 1818. *Frankenstein*. Harmondsworth: Penguin, 1994.

Shields, Rob 1999. *Lefebvre, Love, and Struggle: Spatial Dialectics*. London: Routledge.

Sidgwick, Henry 1883. *Principles of Political Economy*. London: Macmillan.

Sighele, Scipio 1891. *La folla delinquente*. Venice: Marsilio, 1985.

Sighele, Scipio 1903. *L'intelligenza della folla*. Toxino: F. Lli Bocca.

Simiand, Françoise 1932. *Le salaire, L'evolution sociale et la monnaie*. Paris: F. Alcan.

Simmel, Georg 1890. *Uber sociale Differenzierung*. Leipzig: Duncker und Humblot.

Simmel, Georg 1892. *The Problems of the Philosophy of History*. New York: Free Press, 1977.

Simmel, Georg 1900. *The Philosophy of Money*. London: Routledge and Kegan Paul, 1978.

Simmel, Georg 1903. 'The Metropolis and Mental Life' in Kurt H. Wolf (ed.) *The Sociology of Georg Simmel*. New York: Free Press.

Simmel, Georg 1908. *Soziologie: Untersuchungen über die Formen der Vergesselshaftung*. Berlin: Duncker und Humblot, 1968.

Sims, Newell Leroy 1924. *Society and Its Surplus: A Study in Soicial Evolution*. New York: D. Appleton and Co.

Skocpol, Theda 1979. *States and Social Revolutions*. Cambridge: Cambridge University Press.

Skocpol, Theda 1980. 'Political Responses to Capitalist Crisis: Neo-Marxist Theories of the State and the Case of the New Deal' *Politics and Society* 10: 155–201.

Skocpol, Theda 1992. *Protecting Soldiers and Mothers*. Cambridge, Mass,: The Belknap Press of the Harvard University Press.

Skocpol, Theda and Finegold, Kenneth 1982. 'State Capacity and Economic Intervention in the Early New Deal' *Political Science Quarterly* 97: 255–78.

Slobdin, Richard 1978. *W.H.R. Rivers*. Stroud: Sutton Publishing, 1997.

Small, Albion Woodbury 1905. *General Sociology*. Chicago: University of Chicago Press.

Small, Albion Woodbury 1910. *The Meaning of Social Science*. Chicago: Chicago University Press.

Small, Albion Woodbury 1924. *Origins of Sociology*. Chicago: University of Chicago Press.

Small, Albion Woodbury and Vincent, George 1894. *Introduction to the Study of Society*. New York: American Book Co.

Smith, Adam 1759. *The Theory of Moral Sentiments*. Oxford: Oxford University Press, 1976.

Smith, Adam 1766. *The Wealth of Nations*. London: J.M. Dent, 1910.

Smith, Dennis 1988. *The Chicago School: A Liberal Critique of Capitalism*. London: Macmillan.

Smith, Greg 1999. *Erving Goffman and Social Organization*. London: Routledge.

Smith, Neil 1984. *Uneven Development*. Oxford: Blackwell.

Snow, Charles P. 1959. *The Two Cultures and the Scientific Revolution*. Cambridge: Cambridge University Press.

Soja, Edward W. 1989. *Postmodern Geographies: The Reassertion of Space in Critical Social Theory*. London: Verso.

Solvay, Ernest 1904. *L'energétique consideré comme principe d'orientation rationelle pour la sociologie*. Brussels: Misch et Thron.

Solvay, Ernest 1910. *Questions d'énergétiques sociales*.

Sombart, Werner 1902. *Der Modernen Capitalismus*. Berlin: Duncker und Humblot.

Sombart, Werner 1906. *Why Is There No Socialism in the United States?* London: Macmillan, 1976.

Sombart, Werner 1908. *Socialism and the Social Movement*. London: J.M. Dent, 1909.

Sombart, Werner 1911. *The Jews and Modern Capitalism*. London: T. Fisher Unwin, 1913.

Sombart, Werner 1913a. *Luxury and Capitalism*. Ann Arbor: University of Michigan Press, 1967.

Sombart, Werner 1913b. *The Quintessence of Capitalism* [*Der Bourgeois*]. New York: E.P. Dutton and Co., 1915.

Somervell, David C. 1946. *Arnold J. Toynbee: A Study of History* (abridgement of Volumes 1–6). Oxford: Oxford University Press.

Sorel, Georges 1906. *Reflections on Violence*. New York: Peter Smith, 1915.

Sorokin, Pitirim 1925. *The Sociology of Revolution*. Philadelphia: Lippincott.

Sorokin, Pitirim 1927. *Social Mobility*. New York: Free Press, 1959.

Sorokin, Pitirim 1928. *Contemporary Sociological Theories*. New York: Harper and Row.

Sorokin, Pitirim 1937–41. *Social and Cultural Dynamics* (4 vols). London: G. Allen and Unwin.

Sorokin, Pitirim 1941. *The Crisis of Our Age*. New York: E.P. Dutton.

Sorokin, Pitirim 1942. *Man and Society in Calamity*. New York: E.P. Dutton.

Soysal, Yasemin 1994. *Limits of Citizenship: Migrants and Postnational Membership in Europe*. Chicago: University of Chicago Press.

Spann, Othmar 1923. *Gesellschaftslehre*. Leipzig: Quelle und Meyer (original, shorter edition 1914).

Spann, Othmar 1928. *Gesellschaftsphilosophie: Mit Einem Anhang über die Philosophischen Voraussetzungen der Wirtschaftswissenschaften*. Munich: R. Oldenbourg.

Spaventa, Silvio 1909. *La politica della destra*. Bari: G. Laterza.

Spencer, Baldwin and Gillen, F.J. 1899. *The Native Tribes of Central Australia*. Boston: Elibron, 2003.

Spencer, Herbert 1850. *Social Statics*. New York: D. Appleton, 1897.

Spencer, Herbert 1862. *First Principles* (2 vols). London: Williams and Norgate, 1910.

Spencer, Herbert 1864–7. *Principles of Biology* (2 vols). London: Williams and Norgate.

Spencer, Herbert 1870–2. *The Principles of Psychology* (2 vols). London: Longman, Brown, Green, and Longmans.

Spencer, Herbert 1873. *The Study of Sociology*. London: Kegan Paul, Trench and Co., 1889.

Spencer, Herbert 1873–93. *Principles of Sociology* (3 vols). London: Williams and Norgate.

Spencer, Herbert 1879–93. *Principles of Ethics* (2 vols). London: Williams and Norgate, 1892.

Spencer, Herbert 1904. *An Autobiography* (2 vols). London: Williams and Norgate.

Spender, Dale 1980. *Man Made Language*. London: Routledge.

Spengler, Oswald 1918–22. *The Decline of the West*. New York: Alfred A. Knopf, 1932.

Sprott, W.J.H. 1937. *General Psychology*. London: Longmans.

Spykman, Nicholas J. 1925. *The Sociology of Georg Simmel*. Chicago: University of Chicago Press.

Stacey, Margaret 1969. 'The Myth of Community Studies'. *British Journal of Sociology* 20: 34–47.

Stäel, Germaine de 1801. *De la littérature considérée dans ces rapports avec les institutions sociales*. Paris: Maradan, 1818.

Stamp, L. Dudley and Beaver, Stanley H. 1933. *British Isles*. London: Longman.

Starcke, Carl Nikolai 1889. *The Primitive Family in Its Origin and Development*. New York: D. Appleton and Co, 1889 (originally in Denmark).

Stark, David and Bruszt, Laszlo 1998. *Postsocialist Pathways: Transforming Politics and Property in East Central Europe*. New York: Cambridge University Press.

Steane, J.M. 1974. *The Making of the English Landscape: The Northamptonshire Landscape*. London: Hodder and Stoughton.

Steffen, Gustaf 1910. *Sosiologi: En allmän samhällslära* [Sociology: A General Theory of Society] Stockholm: Geber.

Stein, Lorenz von 1850. *History of the Social Movement in France from 1789 to Our Day*. Totowa, NJ: Bedminster Press, 1964 (a translation of the 3rd edn of 1856).

Stein, Lorenz von 1856. *Gesellschaftslehre, System der Staatswissenschaft* Volume 2. Stuttgart: Cotta.

Steinmetz, Rudolf 1892. *Ethnologische Studien zur Ersten Entwicklung der Strafe*. Leiden: Van Doesburgh.

Steinmetz, Rudolf 1899. *Der Krieg als Soziologisches Problem*. New York: Arno Press, 1975.

Steinmetz, Rudolf 1900. *Wat is Sociologie?*. Leiden: Van Doesburgh.

Steinthal, Heymann 1851. *Der Ursprung der Sprache*. Hildesheim: Olms, 1974.

Stocking, George W. (ed.) 1996 *Volksgeist as Method and Ethic: Essays on Boasian Ethnography and the German Anthropological Tradition*. Madison: University of Wisconsin Press.

Stokes, Kenneth Michael 1995. *Paradigms Lost: A Cultural and Systems Theoretical Critique of Political Economy*. New York: M.E. Sharpe.

Strauss, Anselm L. 1959. *Mirrors and Masks: The Search for Identity*. London: Martin Robertson, 1977.

Strauss, Anselm 1978. *Negotiations*. San Fransico: Jossey Bass.

Strauss, Anselm 1993. *Continual Permutations of Action*. New York: Aldine, de Gruyter.

Strauss, Anselm, Schatzman, Leonard, Ehrlich, Danuta, Bucher, Rue, and Sabshin, Melvin. 1963. 'The Hospital and Its Negotiated Order' in Eliot Friedson (ed.) *The Hospital in Modern Society*. New York: Free Press, 1963.

Stuckenberg, John H.W. 1880. *Christian Sociology*. New York: I.K. Funk and Co.

Stuckenberg, John H.W. 1898. *Introduction to the Study of Sociology*. New York: A.C. Armstrong and Son.

Stuckenberg, John H.W. 1903. *Sociology: The Science of Human Society*. New York: G. Putnam's Sons.

Sullivan, Harry Stack 1939. *Conceptions of Modern Psychiatry*. New York: W.W. Norton, 1947.

Sumner, William Graham 1883. *What Social Classes Owe to Each Other*. New York: Arno Press, 1972.

Sumner, William Graham 1906. *Folkways*. Boston: Ginn and Co.

Sumner, William Graham and Keller, Albert Galloway 1927–8. *The Science of Society* (4 vols). New Haven: Yale University Press.

Sutherland, Edwin 1939. *Principles of Criminology*. Chicago: J.B. Lippincott.

Swartz, David 1997. *Culture and Domination: The Social Theory of Pierre Bourdieu*. Chicago: University of Chicago Press.

Szelenyi, Ivan and Conrad, George 1978. *The Intellectuals on the Road to Class Power*. New York: Harcourt Brace and Jovanovich, 1979.

Szelenyi, Ivan, Eyal, Gil, and Townsley, Eleanor 1998. *Making Capitalism without Capitalists*. London: Verso.

Takata Yasuma 1922. *Principles of Sociology*. Tokyo: University of Tokyo Press, 1989.

Takata Yasuma 1925. *Kaikyu Oyobi Dai San Shikan* [*Social Class and the Third View of History*]. Tokyo: Kaizosha.

Takata Yasuma 1926. *Shakai Kankei No Kenkyu* [*A Study of Social Relations*]. Tokyo: Iwanami.

Takata Yasuma 1940. 'Seiryoku Ron [On Power]' in Takata Yasuma (ed.) *Power Theory of Economics*. London: Macmillan, 1995.

Tarde, Gabriel 1890. *The Laws of Imitation*. New York: H. Holt and Co., 1903.

Tarde, Gabriel 1895. *La logique sociale*. Paris: F. Alcan.

Tarde, Gabriel 1897. *L'opposition universelle*. Paris: F. Alcan.

Tarde, Gabriel 1898. *Social Laws*. New York: Macmillan, 1899.

Tarde, Gabriel 1901. *L'opinion et la foule*. Paris: Presses Universitaires de France, 1989.

Tawney, Richard Henry 1921. *The Acquisitive Society*. Brighton: Wheatsheaf, 1982.

Tawney, Richard Henry 1926. *Religion and the Rise of Capitalism*. London: John Murray.

Tawney, Richard Henry 1931. *Equality*. London: George Allen and Unwin.

Taylor, C.C. 1973. *The Making of the English Landscape: The Cambridgeshire Landscape*. London: Hodder and Stoughton.

Thom, René 1972. *Structural Stability and Morphogenesis*. New York: Addison Wesley, 1975.

Thomas, Franklin 1925. *The Environmental Basis of Society*. New York: Johnson Reprint, 1965.

Thomas, William I. and Znaniecki, Florian 1918–19. *The Polish Peasant in Europe and America*. New York: Dover Publishing, 1958.

Thompson, John B. 1990. *Ideology and Modern Culture*. Cambridge: Polity Press.

Thornhill, Randy and Palmer, Craig T. 2000. *A Natural History of Rape: Biological Bases of Sexual Coercion*. Cambridge, Mass.: MIT Press.

Thurnwald, Richard 1931–5. *Die Menschliche Gesellschaft in Ihren Ethnosoziologischen Grundlagen* (5 vols), Berlin: W. de Gruyter.

Tillett, Alfred W. 1939. *Herbert Spencer Betrayed*. London: P.S. King.

Tilly, Charles 1978. *From Mobilization to Revolution*. Reading, Mass.: Addison-Wesley.

Tocqueville, Alexis de 1835–40. *Democracy in America* (2 vols). London: Collins, 1969.

Tocqueville, Alexis de 1856. *The Old Regime and the French Revolution*. London: Collins, 1969.

Tourville, Henri de 1904. *The Growth of Modern Nations*. London: Edward Arnold, 1907.

Tomalin, Claire 1974. *The Life and Death of Mary Wollstonecraft*. Harmondsworth: Penguin, 1985.

Tönnies, Ferdinand 1889. *Community and Association*. London: Routledge and Kegan Paul, 1955 (based on the 1912 edn).

Tönnies, Ferdinand 1909. *Custom*. New York: Free Press, 1961.

Tönnies, Ferdinand 1931a. 'Einführung in die Soziologie [extracts from]' Ferdinand Toennies, *On Sociology: Pure, Applied, and Empirical* (edited by W.J. Cahnman and R. Heberle). Chicago: University of Chicago Press, 1971.

Tönnies, Ferdinand 1931b. 'Estates and Classes' in John Scott (ed.) *Class*. London: Routledge, 1996.

Tooby, John and Cosmides, Leda 1992. 'The Psychological Foundations of Culture' in J.H. Barkow, L. Cosmides and J. Tooby (eds) *The Adapted Mind: Evolutionary Psychology and the Generation of Culture*. Oxford: Oxford University Press, 1992.

Toulmin, Stephen 1990. *Cosmopolis*. New York: Free Press.

Toulmin, Stephen 2001. *Return to Reason*. Cambridge, Mass.: Harvard University Press.

Touraine, Alain 1955. *L'évolution du travail ouvrier aux usines Renault*. Paris: CNRS.

Touraine, Alain 1965. *Sociologie de l'action*. Paris.

Touraine, Alain 1966. *La conscience ouvrière*. Paris: Éditions du Seuil.

Touraine, Alain 1969. *The Post-Industrial Society – Tomorrow's Social History: Classes, Conflicts and Culture in the Programmed Society*. New York: Random House, 1971.

Touraine, Alain 1973. *The Self-Production of Society*. Chicago: University of Chicago Press.

Touraine, Alain 1978. *The Voice and the Eye: An Analysis of Social Movements*. Cambridge: Cambridge University Press, 1981.

Touraine, Alain 1984. *The Return of the Actor*. Minneapolis: University of Minnesota Press.

Touraine, Alain 1992. *Critique of Modernity*. Oxford: Basil Blackwell, 1995.

Touraine, Alain, Wieviotka, Michel, and Dubet, François 1984. *Le mouvement ouvrier*. Paris: Fayard.

Toynbee, Arnold J. 1881–2. *Lectures on the Industrial Revolution of the Eighteenth Century in England*. London, 1884.

Toynbee, Arnold J. 1934–9. *A Study of History,* Volumes 1–6. London: Oxford University Press.

Tracey, Michael 1977. *The Production of Political Television*. London: Routledge and Kegan Paul.

Troeltsch, Ernst 1906. *Protestantism and Progress*. London: Matthews and Norgate, 1912.

Troeltsch, Ernst 1912. *The Social Teaching of the Christian Churches*. London: George Allen and Unwin, 1931.

Troeltsch, Ernst 1922. *Der Historismus und Seine Probleme*. Tübingen: J.C.B. Mohr.

Troeltsch, Ernst 1924. *Der Historismus und Seine Überwindung*. Aalen: Scientia Verlag, 1966.

Trotsky, Leon 1904. *Our Political Task*. London: New Park Publications, 1971.

Trotter, Wilfred 1908. 'Herd Instinct and Civilized Psychology' in Wilfred Trotter, *Instinct of the Herd in Peace and War* (1917 edn). London: Ernest Benn, 1947.

Trotter, Wilfred 1909. 'The Psychology of Herd Instinct', in Wilfred Trotter, *Instinct of the Herd in Peace and War*, (1917 edn). London: Ernest Benn, 1947.

Trotter, Wilfred 1915. 'Speculations upon the Human Mind' in Wilfred Trotter, *Instinct of the Herd in Peace and War* (1917 edn). London: Ernest Benn, 1947.

Tugan-Baranovsky, Mikhail 1905. *Modern Socialism in Its Historical Development*. London: Sonnenschein, 1910.

Turgot, Anne Robert 1750. 'Plan de deux discourses sur l'histoire universelle' in Anne Robert Turgot, *Oeuvres de Turgot*. Paris: Guillaumin, 1844.

Turnbull, Colin 1961. *The Forest People*. London: Pan, 1979.

Turnbull, Colin 1973. *The Mountain People*. London: Cape.

Turnbull, Colin 1976. *Man in Africa*. Harmondsworth: Penguin.

Turner, Frederick Jackson 1893. 'The Significance of the Frontier in American History' in Frederick Jackson Turner, *The Frontier in American History*. New York: Holt, Rinehart and Winston, 1962 (originally 1920).

Turner, Frederick Jackson 1896. 'The Problem of the West' in Frederick Jackson Turner, *The Frontier in American History*. New York: Holt, Rinehart and Winston, 1962 (originally 1920).

Turner, Stephen P. 1994. *The Social Theory of Practices: Tradition, Tacit Knowledge and Presuppositions*. Cambridge: Polity Press.

Tylor, Edward 1871. *Primitive Culture* (2 vols). London: John Murray, 1920.

Tylor, Edward 1881. *Anthropology*. New York: Appleton, 1897.

UNESCO 1969. *Four Statements on the Race Question*. Paris: UNESCO.

Unstead, John F. 1935. *A Systematic Regional Geography, Volume 1: The British Isles*. London: University of London Press.

Urry, John 1990. *The Tourist Gaze*. London: Sage.

Urry, John 1995. *Consuming Places*. London: Routledge.

Urry, John 2000. *Sociology beyond Societies: Mobilities for the Twenty-First Century*. London: Routledge.

Urry, John 2003. *Global Complexity*. Cambridge: Polity Press.

Urwick, Edward Johns 1908. *Luxury and Waste of Life*. London: J.M. Dent.

Urwick, Edward Johns 1912. *A Philosophy of Social Progress*. London: Methuen.

Urwick, Edward Johns 1927. *The Social Good*. London: Methuen.

Useem, Michael 1984. *The Inner Circle*. New York: Oxford University Press.

Vaccaro, Michelangelo 1886. *La lotta per l'esisteriza e i suoi effetti nel'umanitá*. Turin: Fratella Bocca.

Vacher de la Pouge, Georges 1896. *Social Selections*. London, 1896.

Vacher de la Pouge, Georges 1909. *Système et faits sociaux: Race et milieu sociale*. Paris: M. Rivière.

Vaihinger, Hans 1911. *The Philosophy of As If*. London: Routledge and Kegan Paul, 1935.

Vallaux, Camille 1908. *Géographie sociale: La mer*. Paris: O. Doin.

Vallaux, Camille 1911. *Géographie sociale: Le sol et l'état*. Paris: O. Doin.

Vallaux, Camille 1925. *Les sciences géographique*. Paris: Armand Colin.

Vanni, Icilio 1888. *Prime linee di un programma critico di sociologia*. Perugia: Tipografia di V. Santucci.

Veblen, Thorstein 1899. *The Theory of the Leisure Class: An Economic Study of Institutions*. New York: Macmillan.

Veblen, Thorsten 1904. *The Theory of Business Enterprise*. New York: Scribner, 1915.

Veblen, Thorstein 1911. *The Vested Interests*. London: George Allen and Unwin, 1924.

Veblen, Thorstein 1915. *Imperial Germany and the Industrial Revolution*. London: Secker and Warburg, 1939.

Veblen, Thorstein 1918. *The Higher Learning in America*. New York: Sagamore Press, 1965.

Veblen, Thorsten 1919. *The Industrial System and the Captains of Industry*. New York: Oriole Chapbooks.

Veblen, Thorstein 1923. *Absentee Ownership and Business Enterprise in Recent Times*. London: George Allen and Unwin, 1924.

Venable, Vernon 1946. *Human Nature: The Marxian View*. London: Dennis Dobson.

Venturino, Agustin 1927–8. *Sociologia primitiva Chileindiana*. Barcelona: Editorial Cervantes.

Venturino, Agustin 1931. *Sociologia general Americana*. Barcelona: Editorial Cervantes.

Vico, Giambattista 1725. *New Science*. Harmondsworth: Penguin, 1999.

Vidal de la Blache, Paul 1908. *La France: Tableau géographique*. Paris: Hachette.

Vidal de la Blache, Paul 1922. *Principles of Human Geography*. New York: H. Holt and Co., 1926.

Vierkandt, Alfred 1896. *Naturvölker und Kulturvölker*.Leipzig: Duncker und Humblot.

Vierkandt, Alfred 1908. *Die Stetigkeit im Kulturwandel*. Leipzig: Duncker und Humblot.

Vierkandt, Alfred 1923. *Gesellshaftslehre*. Stuttgart: F. Enke.

Vignes, Joseph Bernard Maurice 1897. *La sciènce sociale d'après les principes de Le Play* (2 vols). Paris: V. Giard et E. Brière.

Vincent, Andrew and Plant, Raymond 1984. *Philosophy, Politics and Citizenship*. Oxford: Basil Blackwell.

Vinogradoff, Paul 1892. *Villeinage in England*. Oxford: Clarendon Press.

Vinogradoff, Paul 1905. *The Growth of the Manor*. London: Sonnenschein.

Vinogradoff, Paul 1908. *English Society in the Eleventh Century*. Oxford: Oxford University Press.

Virilio, Paul 1977. *Speed and Politics: An Essay on Dramology*. New York: Semiotext(e), 1986.

Visser, Herman Lodewijk Alexandre 1911. *de Psyche Der Menigte*. Haarlem: H.D. Tjeenk Willink & Zoon.

Visser, Herman Lodewijk Alexandre 1916. *De collectief psyche in recht en staat*. Haarlem: H.D. Tjeenk Willink & Zoon.

Voet, Rian 1998. *Feminism and Citizenship*. London: Sage.

Vogler, Carolyn 1998. 'Money in the Household'. *Sociological Review* 46: 687–713.

Volgraf, Karl 1864. *Erster Versuch einer Wissenschaftlichen Begründung der Allgemeinen Ethnologie*.

Voltaire [François Marie Arovet] 1745. 'Essay on Manners and the Spirit of Nations', in *The Portable Voltaire*. Harmondsworth: Penguin, 1977.

Vygotsky, Lev 1930–4. *Mind in Society*. Cambridge, Mass: Harvard University Press, 1978.

Vygotsky, Lev 1934. *Thought and Language*. Cambridge, Mass.: MIT Press, 1986.

Wallas, Graham 1908. *Human Nature in Politics*. London: Constable, 1948.

Wallas, Graham 1914. *The Great Society*. London: Macmillan.

Wallerstein, Immanuel 1974. *The Modern World System I: Capitalist Agriculture and the Origins of the European World-Economy in the Sixteenth Century*. New York: Academic Press.

Wallerstein, Immanuel 1980. *The Modern World System II: Mercantilism and the Consolidation of the European World-Economy, 1600–1750*. New York: Academic Press.

Wallerstein, Immanuel 1989. *The Modern World System III: The Second Era of Great Expansion of the Capitalist World-Economy, 1730–1840s*. New York: Academic Press.

Walras, Léon 1874. *Elements of Pure Economics*. London: George Allen and Unwin, 1965.

Ward, Lester 1883. *Dynamic Sociology*. New York: D. Appleton, 1913.

Ward, Lester 1893. *The Psychic Factors of Civilization*. Boston: Ginn and Co.

Ward, Lester 1897. *Outlines of Sociology*. New York: Macmillan, 1913.

Ward, Lester 1903. *Pure Sociology*. New York: Macmillan, 1914.

Ward, Lester 1906. *Applied Sociology*. New York: Ginn and Co.

Watson, John B. 1919. *Psychology from the Standpoint of a Behaviorist*. London: Frances Pinter, 1983.

Waxweiler, Émile Pierre Clément 1906. *Esquisse d'une sociologie*. Brussels: Misch et Thron.

Webb, R.K. 1960. *Harriet Martineau: A Radical Victorian*. New York: Columbia University Press.

Webb, Sydney and Webb, Beatrice 1923. *The Decay of Capitalist Civilization*. London: George Allen and Unwin.

Weber, Alfred 1909. *Theory of the Location of Industries*. Chicago: University of Chicago Press, 1929.

Weber, Alfred 1920–1. *Fundamentals of Culture-Sociology: Social Process, Civilization Process and Cultural Movement*. New York: Columbia University Press, 1939.

Weber, Alfred 1935. *Kulturgeschichte als Kultursoziologie*. Leiden: Sijthoff.

Weber, Alfred 1946. *Farewell to European History: Or the Conquest of Nihilism*. London: Kegan Paul, 1947.

Weber, Marianne 1926. *Max Weber: A Biography*. New York: Wiley, 1975.

Weber, Max 1892. 'Die Verhältnisse der Landarbeiter im Ostelbischen Deutschland'. *Schriften des Vereins für Socialpolitik*, Band 55.

Weber, Max 1894a. *The History of Commercial Partnerships in the Middle Ages*. Lanham: Ravman and Littlefield, 2003.

Weber, Max 1894b. 'Stock and Commodity Exchanges'. *Theory and Society* 29, 2000: 305–38.

Weber, Max 1895. 'The Nation State and Economic Policy' in Peter Lassman and Ronald Speirs (eds) *Weber: Political Writings*. Cambridge: Cambridge University Press.

Weber, Max 1896a. 'Commerce on the Stock and Commodity Exchanges'. *Theory and Society* 29, 2000: 339–71.

Weber, Max 1896b. 'The Social Causes of the Decline of Ancient Civilizations' in Max Weber (ed.) *The Agrarian Sociology of Ancient Civilizations*. London: New Left Books, 1976.

Weber, Max 1904. '"Objectivity" in Social Science and Social Policy' in Max Weber, *The Methodology of the Social Sciences*. New York: Free Press, 1949.

Weber, Max 1904–5. 'The Protestant Ethic and the Spirit of Capitalism' in *The Protestant Ethic and the 'Spirit' of Capitalism, and Other Writings* (edited by Peter Baehr and Gordon C. Wells) Harmondsworth: Penguin, 2002.

Weber, Max 1909. 'Agrarian Relations in Antiquity' in Max Weber, *The Agrarian Sociology of Ancient Civilizations* (as Chapters 1 and 2). London: New Left Books, 1976.

Weber, Max 1911. *The Rational and Social Foundations of Music*. Carbondale: Southern Illinois University Press, 1958.

Weber, Max 1914. 'The Economy and the Arena of Normative and De Facto Powers' in *Economy and Society* (edited by Guenther Roth and Claus Wittich). New York: Bedminster Press, 1968.

Weber, Max 1915a. *The Religion of China*. New York: Macmillan, 1951.

Weber, Max 1915b. 'Religious Rejections of the World and Their Directions [the 'Intermediate Reflections']' in Hans Gerth and C. Wright Mills (eds) *From Max Weber*. New York: Oxford University Press, 1946.

Weber, Max 1916. *The Religion of India*. New York: Macmillan, 1958.

Weber, Max 1917. *Ancient Judaism*. New York: Macmillan, 1952.

Weber, Max 1919–20. *General Economic History*. New York: Greenberg, 1927.

Weber, Max 1920a. 'Conceptual Exposition' in *Economy and Society* (edited by Guentier Roth and Clauswittich). New York: Bedminster Press, 1968.

Weber, Max 1920b. '"Prefatory Remarks" to Collected Essays in the Sociology of Religion' in *The Protestant Ethic and the Spirit of Capitalism* (edited by Stephen Kalberg) Oxford: Blackwell, 2002.

Weber, Max 1920c. 'The Protestant Ethic and the Spirit of Capitalism' in *The Protestant Ethic and the Spirit of Capitalism* (edited by Stephen Kalberg). Oxford: Blackwell, 2002.

Webster, Richard 1995. *Why Freud Was Wrong*. London: Fontana.

Westermarck, Edvard 1891. *The History of Human Marriage*. London: Macmillan.

Westermarck, Edvard 1906. *Origin and Development of Moral Ideas*. London: Macmillan.

Westermarck, Edvard 1926. *A Short History of Marriage*. London: Macmillan.

Westermarck, Edvard 1932. *Ethical Relativity*. London: Routledge, 2000.

Whitehead, Alfred North 1926. *Science and the Modern World*. Harmondsworth: Penguin 1938.

Whorf, Benjamin Lee 1956. *Language, Thought and Reality*. Cambridge, Mass.: MIT Press.

Wiener, Norbert 1948. *Cybernetics: Or, Control and Communication in the Animal and the Machine*. New York: Wiley.

Wiener, Norbert 1950. *The Human Use of Human Beings*. Boston: Houghton Mifflin.

Wiese-Becker 1932. *Systematic Sociology, on the Basis of the Beziehungslehre and Gebildelehre of Leopold von Wiese, Adapted and Amplified by Howard P. Becker*. New York: Wiley.

Wiese, Leopold von 1924–9. *Allgemeine Soziologie* (2 vols). Munich: Duncker und Humblot.

Wilkens, Claudius 1881. *Samfundslegemets grundlove: Et grundrids af sociologien* [The Social Organism: A Grounding in Sociology]. Copenhagen.

Wilkins, Leslie T. 1964. *Social Deviance: Social Policy, Action and Research*. London: Tavistock.

Williams, Eric 1944. *Capitalism and Slavery*. London: André Deutsch, 1964.

Williams, Raymond 1961. *The Long Revolution*. Harmondsworth: Penguin, 1965.

Williams, Raymond 1977. *Marxism and Literature*. Oxford: Oxford University Press.

Williams, Raymond 1981. *Culture*. Glasgow: Collins.

Wilson, Bryan R. (ed.) 1970. *Rationality*. Oxford: Basil Blackwell.

Wilson, Edward O. 1975. *Sociobiology: The New Synthesis*. Cambridge, Mass.: Belknap Press.

Wilson, T.P. 1970. 'Normative and Interpretive Paradigms in Sociology' in Jack Douglas (ed.) *Understanding Everyday Life*. Chicago: Aldine Press, 1970.

Winch, Peter 1958. *The Idea of a Social Science*. London: Routledge and Kegan Paul.

Winnicott, Donald W. 1964. *The Child, the Family and the Outside World*. Harmondsworth: Penguin.

Winnicott, Donald W. 1965a. *The Family and Individual Development*. London: Tavistock.

Winnicott, Donald W. 1965b. *The Motivational Process and the Facilitating Environment*. London: Hogarth Press.

Winston, Brian 1998. *Media, Technology and Society, a History: From the Telegraph to the Internet*. London: Routledge.

Wirth, L. 1938. 'Urbanism as a Way of Life'. *American Journal of Sociology* 44: 1–24.

Wittgenstein, Ludwig 1953. *Philosophical Investigations*. Oxford: Blackwell.

Wolf, Naomi 1991. *The Beauty Myth: How Images of Beauty Are Used against Women*. New York: William Morrow.

Wolfe, Donald M. 1959. 'Power and Authority in the Family' in Dorwin Cartwright (ed.) *Studies in Social Power*. Ann Arbor: University of Michigan Press.

Wolff, Kurt H. 1950. *The Sociology of Georg Simmel*. New York: Free Press.

Wollstonecraft, Mary 1792. *A Vindication of the Rights of Woman*. Harmondsworth: Penguin, 1975.

Woolfolk, Alan and Imber, Jonathan B. (eds) 1994 *Constructive Sociological Theory: Thomas G. Masaryk*. New Brunswick, NJ: Transaction Publishers.

Worms, René 1896. *Organisme et société*. Paris: V. Giard et E. Brière.

Worms, René 1910. *Les principes biologique de l'évolution sociale*. Paris: V. Giard et E. Brière.

Worms, René 1921. *La sociologie*. Paris: M. Giard.

Wrong, Denis 1961. 'The Oversocialized Concept of Man in Modern Sociology'. *American Sociological Review* 26: 183–93.

Wundt, Wilhelm 1912. *Elements of Folk Psychology*. London: George Allen and Unwin, 1916.

Yearley, Steve 1991. *The Green Case: A Sociology of Environmental Issues*. London: HarperCollins.

Young, Jock 1971. *The Drugtakers*. London: McGibbon and Kee.

Young, Michael W. 2004. *Malinowski: Odyssey of an Anthropologist, 1884–1920*. New Haven: Yale University Press.

Zimmerman, Don H. and Wieder, D.L. 1970. 'Ethnomethodology and the Problem of Order: Comment on Denzin' in Jack Douglas (ed.) *Understanding Everyday Life*. London: Routledge and Kegan Paul, 1971.

Znaniecki, Florian 1919. *Cultural Reality*. Chicago: University of Chicago Press.

Znaniecki, Florian 1925. *The Laws of Social Psychology*. Chicago: University of Chicago Press.

Znaniecki, Florian 1936. *Social Actions*. New York: Farrar and Reinhart.

Index